Japanese Religion

Unity and Diversity

Fourth Edition

H. BYRON EARHART
Professor Emeritus
Western Michigan University

THOMSON

WADSWORTH

Australia • Canada • Mexico • Singapore • Spain
United Kingdom • United States

THOMSON

™

WADSWORTH

Publisher: Holly J. Allen
Religion Editor: Steve Wainwright
Assistant Editors: Lee McCracken, Anna Lustig
Editorial Assistant: Melanie Cheng
Marketing Manager: Worth Hawes
Marketing Assistant: Kristi Bostock
Advertising Project Manager: Bryan Vann
Print/Media Buyer: Jessica Reed

Composition Buyer: Ben Schroeter
Permissions Editor: Joohee Lee
Production Service: Pre-Press Company, Inc.
Copy Editor: Denise Cook-Clampert
Cover Designer: Annabelle Ison
Cover Image: Glen Allison/Photodisc
Compositor: Pre-Press Company, Inc.
Cover and Text Printer: Webcom, Limited

Printed in Canada
1 2 3 4 5 6 7 07 06 05 04 03

For more information about our products,
contact us at:
Thomson Learning Academic Resource Center
1-800-423-0563
For permission to use material from this text,
contact us by:
Phone: 1-800-730-2214
Fax: 1-800-730-2215
Web: http://www.thomsonrights.com

Library of Congress Control Number: 2003108359
ISBN 0-534-17694-1

Wadsworth/Thomson Learning
10 Davis Drive
Belmont, CA 94002-3098
USA

Asia
Thomson Learning
5 Shenton Way #01-01
UIC Building
Singapore 068808

Australia/New Zealand
Thomson Learning
102 Dodds Street
Southbank, Victoria 3006
Australia

Canada
Nelson
1120 Birchmount Road
Toronto, Ontario M1K 5G4
Canada

Europe/Middle East/Africa
Thomson Learning
High Holborn House
50/51 Bedford Row
London WC1R 4LR
United Kingdom

Latin America
Thomson Learning
Seneca, 53
Colonia Polanco
11560 Mexico D.F.
Mexico

Spain/Portugal
Paraninfo
Calle/Magallanes, 25
28015 Madrid, Spain

Contents

CONTENTS

SHINTO 161

The Political and Religious Significance of the Meiji
Restoration 162

The Attempt to Restore Shinto as the Only Japanese Religion 163

The Establishment of Nonreligious Shrine Shinto 167

Japan as a Nation-State—Nationalism in World Perspective 168

Shrine Shinto as an Expression of Nationalism and Militarism 172

16 RELIGIOUS CURRENTS FROM 1868 TO 1945 180

Buddhism: The Quest for Renewal, Especially Within Buddhist
Scholarship 181

Christianity: Strength and Weakness Since 1868 184

The New Religions: New Variations from Old Traditions 187

The Fortunes of Religion 1868-1945: From Freedom of
Religion to State Orthodoxy 189

17 TWO NEW RELIGIONS: TENRIKYO AND SOKA
GAKKAI 195

The Many New Religions: Differences and Similarities 196

Tenrikyo: A Living *Kami* and a Joyous Life 197

Soka Gakkai: Faith in the *Lotus Sutra* and a Happy Life 200

The Significance of the New Religions: Old Wine in
New Bottles 204

18 RELIGION IN POSTWAR JAPAN 206

Shinto: Disestablishment and Popular Disfavor 207

Buddhism: The Continuing Quest for Renewal 208

Christianity: The Problems of Denominationalism 209

The Postwar Boom of New Religions 210

19 RELIGIOUS LIFE IN CONTEMPORARY JAPAN 214

Are the Japanese Religious? 214

Persistent Themes in Contemporary Japanese Religion 217

Approaches to Religious Change 219

Transformations of Religious Life in Contemporary Japan 222

20 CONCLUSION: THE CHALLENGE FOR JAPANESE
RELIGION 230

Study Questions 239
Annotated Bibliography on Japanese Religion 253
Index 289

Preface

First experiences are always memorable. I remember many years ago my initial glimpse of Shinto and Japanese religion in a college class on world religions. One thing that fascinated me was the amazing variety of *kami* and how closely they were linked to the forces of nature. At the time Japan and its religious traditions were just a small part of the wealth of information in an undergraduate course. Not until some years later in graduate school did I take steps to learn Japanese and study Japanese religion more closely. I was fortunate enough to be able to continue my studies in Japan, and actually visit Shinto shrines, Buddhist temples, and New Religions headquarters.

For me, Japanese religion has been a life commitment, researching, teaching, and writing about a subject that is just as interesting to me today as it was decades ago. Those of you picking up this book will come to it with different backgrounds and experiences. Many will be entering Japanese religion for the very first time; some will have the benefit of previous reading about the subject; others will have their curiosity piqued by travel to Japan and visits to its religious sites. Only a few will share my decision to make Japanese religion a lifetime project. Whatever your starting point, I hope your armchair tour through Japanese religious history is as interesting for you as it has been for me.

Perhaps the best preface to this book is to start at its beginning point, which was not Japan, but Los Angeles in 1965. My family and I had returned from three years of dissertation research in Japan on a Fulbright grant. We disembarked from a Japanese immigration ship (headed for South America) in Los Angeles, having accepted the invitation of my graduate school colleague,

Fred Streng (then teaching at the University of Southern California) to stay with him and his family for a few days. He and his family provided a warm and pleasant reentry into America.

At the end of our stay Fred sprang a surprise: he wanted me to write an introductory text on Japanese religion for a series on world religions he had proposed. As diplomatically as possible I told my friend and host that I would have to decline, because "Japanese religion" is such a vast subject with such a lengthy history, that it would be impossible for me to complete such a book. I had just spent three years researching the mountain religion of Shugendo, but that was just a tiny part of the larger picture of Japanese religion. Fred would not withdraw his invitation; I countered with a request to give me time—years—to work on it. Fred was disappointed, but still did not concede, insisting that after I began teaching I would change my mind.

His prediction came true, because when I looked for texts for classroom use, the treatments of Japanese religion were altogether too short and sketchy. During my initial year of teaching I began writing this book as an attempt to fill the gap of an introductory text on the Japanese religious heritage. Fred Streng passed away several years ago, but once more I offer him my thanks for his encouragement to undertake this work.

This text is conceived and written as an introduction to Japanese religion, a primer for readers interested in Japanese studies or religious studies. No knowledge of Japanese history, Japanese religion, or the Japanese language is required for understanding the material.[1] I hope the work will also be of use to advanced students and teachers who are acquainted with one area of Japanese history and culture and are looking for a comprehensive interpretation of religion in Japan. Whereas general readers may use the book as a stepping stone through the Annotated Bibliography to a deeper understanding of Japanese religion, advanced students and teachers may utilize it as a unified context in which they can integrate their specialized readings.

The basic format of the previous editions has been preserved—an interpretation of persistent themes through three historical periods and the changing patterns of the various religious traditions. The features of the previous editions have also been retained: a map to help place Japan and some of its religious sites geographically; a historical chart for locating significant events on a time line; a set of study questions for guiding readers through sections of each chapter (correlated to the companion sourcebook, *Religion in the Japanese Experience,* second edition); and photographs from my field work emphasizing the dynamics of religious life. A new feature of this edition is a computer tutorial that has proven helpful to my own students to check reading comprehension; it can serve as a bridge to class discussion, and the questions on the tutorial can be used for exam purposes. The tutorial is available online at http://wadsworth.com/religion.

---

1. All markings for long vowels have been omitted; no publications in Japanese are cited. Reference to Japanese names in the text follows the Japanese convention of giving the family name first.

The photographs deserve a special word to account for their selection. Whereas the "picture postcard" presents an important record of famous shrines and temples, scenic landscapes, and illustrious artwork (such as statues), this genre does not show much of the activities and experiences of Japanese religion. This kind of photograph is not included here—after all, professional cameramen and art books provide much better pictures, and they are readily available in coffee table works. Included here are amateur shots of religion in action from my own field work, the stuff of Japanese religious life, to illustrate how Japanese religion "looks," lending concreteness to the generalities of the text. All the photos except one (courtesy of Robert J. Smith) are mine.

Although much of the book preserves the outline of the previous editions, the contents have been expanded and revised significantly. One of the remarkable advances in the study of Japanese religion since I was a graduate student has been the large number of specialists who have taken up this field, each with his or her own concentration. Indeed, these scholars, in addition to publishing many monographs on aspects of Japanese religion, have formed two scholarly groups for advancing the understanding of this field. Such developments have several immediate consequences for the present work: first, within the limited space available, many of the recent publications on Japanese religion have been included in the Annotated Bibliography (at the expense of removing many earlier works); second, the text incorporates much of the information and insights of these recent works, to provide a more complete and accurate picture, and at least touch on some major theoretical issues; and third, recent scholarship has helped provide greater coverage of the role of women in Japanese religion, and an extended treatment of the inter-relationship between religion, nationalism, and militarism. Readers who wish to explore the documentation and scholarly discussion behind generalizations in the text may consult the notes.

In addition to those who helped in the writing of the earlier editions, I would like to thank the following reviewers who made helpful suggestions: John Keenan of Middlebury College and Vasudha Narayanan of the University of Florida. Thanks also go to those who made suggestions on style and content for the fourth edition, especially Charles Hallisey, former series editor, and Peter Adams, Steve Wainwright, and Lee McCracken of the editorial team at Wadsworth Publishing Company; copy editor Denise Cook-Clampert; Bob Caceres of Pre-Press Company; and my son David who read and helped improve Part Three.

For the fourth time, it is a pleasure to dedicate this work to our Japanese friends and to the continued friendship between Japan and other countries.

H. Byron Earhart is professor emeritus of Comparative Religion at Western Michigan University, where he continues to teach an online course on Japanese religion through Distance Education using this book. For information on the course send an email to de-info@wmich.edu.

Table of Japanese Religious History, with Chronological Periods and Corresponding Cultural Features

For a more complete account, see "A Chronological Table of Religious Affairs in Japan," in Religious Studies in Japan, ed. Japanese Association for Religious Studies (Tokyo: Maruzen, 1959), pp. 467–77.

I. FORMATIVE PERIOD

Chronology in Japanese Historical Periods	Economic, Social, and Political Features	Religious Events and Characteristics
Jomon Yayoi Kofun — Prehistoric and Protohistoric (to sixth century C.E.)	Hunting and gathering culture gives way to rice agriculture and more sedentary, small village organization; increasing centralization around leading families.	Indigenous Japanese tradition: agricultural festivals, reverence for the dead, divine descent of the imperial line, family as the religious unit.
Taika Reform (645–710)	Influx of Chinese culture marks Japan's first contact with a literate and highly organized culture; the first centralized government, patterned after Chinese models (such as legal codes).	Importation of foreign traditions: Buddhism, Confucianism, Taoism; Shinto emerges from the indigenous traditions; earliest interaction of these traditions.
Nara (710–94)	First permanent capital; elaborate life at the imperial court and among the nobility, widely separated from the common farmer; first Japanese writings, including dynastic chronicles and *Manyoshu.*	Six philosophical schools of Buddhism; system of provincial temples with Todai-ji at Nara as the central cathedral; further interaction of the native tradition with Buddhism and Taoism

II. PERIOD OF DEVELOPMENT AND ELABORATION

Heian (794–1185)	Capital moved to Kyoto; highly developed aesthetic life among court and nobility; *Tale of Genji*, the world's first novel; increasing importance of feudal estates and the warrior class.	Buddhist sects of Shingon and Tendai founded; Buddhism becomes more closely related to Japanese culture and begins to penetrate the countryside; Shinto becomes more highly organized; *Engishiki* compiled 927.

Kamakura (1185–1333)	Military dictator controls political power (emperor is secluded at Kyoto); real seat of government moves to Kamakura; attention shifts from the effeminate nobleman to the powerful warrior; Mongol invasions of 1274 and 1281; rise of the merchant class; growing sense of uncertainty with increased civil strife.	Buddhist sects of Pure Land, Nichiren, and Zen founded; Buddhism enters the life of the common people and spreads thoroughout the land; development of eclectic medieval Shinto; thorough blending of these traditions.
Muromachi (1333–1568) and Momoyama (1568–1600)	Great civil strife; expansion and development of agricultural lands and techniques; growth of towns and markets; blending of the warriors' and noblemen's cultures; greater unification of the country under the military ruler; subjugation of religious headquarters to political authority; first major contact with the West.	Kitabatake writes in support of the imperial line's supremacy (1339); crystallization of sect and denominational lines; Saint Francis Xavier and introduction of Christianity (sixteenth century).

III. PERIOD OF FORMALISM AND RENEWAL

Tokugawa (1600–1867)	Widespread peace and stability under supreme control of the military dictator; expulsion of Christianity, and "closed door" policy limiting foreign access to Japan; dominance of merchant class; cities grow in size and importance; rise of popular arts such as woodblock prints and novels.	Christianity proscribed; Buddhism made a branch of the state; Neo-Confucianism made the rationale of the state; Shinto overshadowed by Buddhism but developing rationale for separation from Buddhism; first appearance of the New Religions; secularism expressed in popular arts.
Meiji (1868–1912) Taisho (1912–26) Showa (1926–89) } Modern (1846–1945)	Transition from feudal to modern period; military dictator steps down while emperor is formally made head of state; feudal state is abolished and modern nation-state established with centralized authority at Tokyo; remarkable educational and industrial achievements; three major wars: Sino-Japanese (1894–95), Russo-Japanese (1904–05), World War II (1937–45).	Buddhism disestablished; Shinto established as state religion; ban on Christianity lifted; Catholicism reintroduced and Protestantism introduced for the first time; all traditions become nationalistic; more New Religions appear.
Postwar (since 1945) and Heisei (1989–)	Allied Occupation (1945–52) marks Japan's first major defeat and occupation of her territory; prewar nationalism and militaristic control give way to greater liberty and tendency toward "democracy" and internationalism; remarkable rebuilding of Japan's cities and industrial facilities; Japan emerges as a major economic and political force in Asia.	Shinto disestablished; complete religious freedom; general demoralization and disorganization among the older religions, with gradual recovery and reorganization; New Religions the most conspicuous religious activity; religious indifference and secularism widespread.

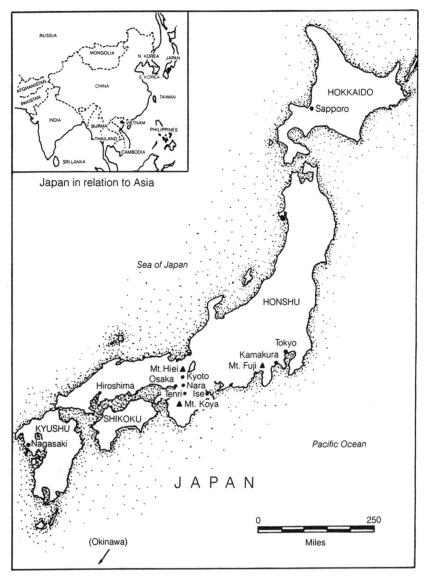

Japan in relation to Asia

For more detailed maps showing the distribution and concentration of various religions in Japan, see Joseph M. Kitagawa, "Shinto" and "Mahayana Buddhism (Japan)," in Historical Atlas of the Religions of the World, ed. Ismai'il Ragi al Faruqui and David E. Sopher (New York: Macmillan, 1974), pp. 127–32, 195–99.

1

❦

Introduction

From prehistoric times to the present, religion has played an important role in the life of the Japanese people. Archaeological evidence documents religious activities dating back more than two millennia; in recent centuries many so-called New Religions have arisen in Japan and have become active in other lands such as the United States and South America. Yet, there has never been a single institution called "Japanese Religion" with its own scriptures, priests, buildings, and rituals, and most people do not "belong" to one Japanese religious organization the way modern Americans and Europeans say they "belong" to a church. (In other words, Japanese religion is not a single monolithic ecclesiastical body such as Roman Catholicism.) The religious heritage of the Japanese includes a number of individual traditions—some native to Japan and some imported, some highly organized and some not formally institutionalized. Through time, various influences interacted to form a distinctive religious system, and it is in this sense that we refer to "Japanese religion."

The term "Japanese religion" is not the title of a specific religious organization, but rather a general abstraction we can conveniently use to refer to the total Japanese religious heritage—its beliefs, practices, and institutions in Japan. Looking at Japanese religion in this way also has benefits for understanding religion outside Japan. First, it shows us the limitations of looking at religion and religious life as mutually exclusive churches or religious institutions (even in America and Europe). And second, recognizing the fact that "Japanese religion" is a general abstraction helps us realize that a single term used to represent any complex tradition with a long history—be that tradition Christianity or Islam, Hinduism or Buddhism, Taoism or Confucianism—is also necessarily a general abstraction.[1] Our pilgrimage through Japanese religion should not only help us better understand the Japanese tradition, but also throw light on the complex character of other cultures and religions.

FIVE RELIGIOUS STRANDS

Japanese religion is a variegated tapestry created by the interweaving of at least five major strands: Shinto, Buddhism, Taoism, Confucianism, and folk religion. Christianity, which entered Japan in the sixteenth century, may be considered a sixth strand, but because it did not contribute to the formation of traditional Japanese religion, it will be treated later, at the point of its appearance in Japanese history (in Chapter 12).

Shinto today is a formal religion of myths, rituals, shrines, and priests. It emerged from the beliefs and practices of prehistoric Japan, but in close contact with the religious influences of China and Korea. Central to Shinto is the notion of Japan as the land of the *kami* (gods or spirits), who both embody the national tradition and inhabit the natural surroundings of every locale. ("Shinto" means "the way of the *kami*.") The presence of Shinto shrines in small villages and even on the roofs of city department stores is living testimony to the pervasiveness of Shinto in Japan.

Three strands of the Japanese religious tradition—Buddhism, Taoism, and Confucianism—are importations from Korea and China. Buddhism, the most prominent of the three, was founded in India by the Buddha (Prince Gautama, April 8, 565 [or 563] to February 15, 486 B.C.E.)[2] in the sixth century B.C.E.[3] The formal message of Buddhism known by most Westerners is the existential philosophy or way of life expressed in the traditional account of the founder's life. From this viewpoint the Buddha, dissatisfied with the prevailing religious system in India, practiced meditation until he arrived at a realization (or enlightenment) of the true nature of human life. He taught freedom from suffering by avoiding the desire that causes suffering and thereby achieving a peaceful existence. This philosophy of life became the basis for a monastic community that developed commentaries and ritual practice, and provided religious services for lay followers. Before Buddhism arrived in Japan, it traveled to China and Korea and underwent considerable transformation into a philosophically, ritually, and institutionally complex religious tradition. At this time Buddhism was received by the Japanese as part of Chinese civilization. Initially, Japanese Buddhists continued Indian and Chinese practices, but they later developed distinctively Japanese forms of practice, thought, and organization.

Taoism and Confucianism arose in China. Taoism developed out of the ancient Chinese reverence for nature and notions of the orderly but ever-changing rhythm of the cosmos. Philosophical expressions of Taoism are found in writings such as the *Tao Te Ching*. The beliefs and practices of Taoism have much in common with Chinese religious customs associated with cosmological notions, the almanac, and divination. Although Taoism never existed in Japan as a formal religion, elements of Taoism (together with aspects of Chinese religion) were accepted there, and heavily influenced Buddhism and Shinto as well as popular religion.

Confucianism is the Chinese tradition set in motion in the sixth century B.C.E. by the teachings of Confucius (K'ung Ch'iu or Kong Qiu, 551–479 B.C.E.) and thereafter institutionalized by the Chinese state and accepted in other parts of Asia. Confucius, who grew up in a time of great social and political turmoil, insisted on a return to virtue and benevolence. After his death, his teachings became the basis for education and government, serving as the wider rationale for the hierarchical social and political relationships within an agricultural economy. The formal tradition of Confucian teachings and institutions—known in the West as "Confucianism"—provided a comprehensive system for ordering governmental and social harmony, placing great emphasis on family stability and filial piety (obedience of children to parents).[4] Various aspects of Confucian teachings have been prominent in Japan. At times the state directly supported Confucian teachings and institutions, but the indirect influence of Confucianism through family upbringing and education was equally if not more important than direct government support; both directly and indirectly Confucianism provided notions of social and political identity.

"Folk religion" generally refers to beliefs and practices that have been handed down and have existed outside organized traditions. Some folk practices, such as rituals associated with hunting and rice agriculture, may date back to prehistoric times. Some more recent aspects of folk religion are actually the popular adaptation of formal traditions and might be termed "popular religion." Whether called folk religion or popular religion, these beliefs and practices are woven into the fabric of people's everyday life in areas such as personal experience, home, work, and annual celebrations.

UNITY AND DIVERSITY

The saying "the whole is greater than the sum of its parts" is quite appropriate to the study of Japanese religion. We must view it as a unified whole or complex tapestry because the individual strands did not exist in isolation, neither in the course of history nor in the dynamics of religious life, but the "whole" of Japanese religion did continue through time. Throughout Japanese history each "part" or strand was influenced by one or more of the others. Shinto, for example, arose out of ancient Japanese religious practices (such as rituals related to the growing of rice); but it was organized more systematically in reaction to the introduction of highly organized Buddhism, and it assimilated some aspects of Buddhism, Taoism, and Confucianism. We will trace this process of mutual influence in later accounts of each religious strand. The important thing to remember here is that any one strand such as Shinto is not just Shinto pure and simple: it is a combination of several influences.

Even more important, people experienced Japanese religion as a unified worldview rather than as separate alternatives or individual traditions. A distinctive feature of Japanese religious history is that individuals usually have not belonged exclusively to one religious tradition but instead have consciously affiliated themselves with, or unconsciously participated in, several traditions. In the West, people have commonly claimed to be (or are conveniently labeled) Protestant or Catholic or Jewish, usually as "members" of particular religious institutions. In Japan, it has been customary for a person (usually a family) to participate in both Shinto festivals and Buddhist memorial services, to practice Confucian ethics, to observe Chinese customs, *and* to follow beliefs of Taoism and folk religion. In general, it is better to characterize Japanese religion as "both/and" instead of "either/or." If we could have asked the traditional Japanese person, "Are you Shinto or Buddhist or Confucian or Taoist?" an appropriate response could have been a simple "yes," meaning that the person was Shinto and Buddhist and Confucian and Taoist. There would be no contradiction in this answer, for the person would have participated in the various traditions at different moments of his or her life. Japanese women and men usually have found religious fulfillment not in one tradition by itself but in the total sacred power embodied in a number of traditions.[5]

How can we make sense of the coexistence of so many religious traditions? It is best to approach them much as the Japanese people have experienced them. In the Japanese religious heritage there is both unity and diversity. Even within the context of a single tradition, a diversity of attitudes may be found. For example, both Buddhism and Shinto include a wide range of religious expression, from the most widely held beliefs to the most abstract philosophy. In earlier ages an illiterate peasant might practice popular forms of Shinto worship and popular Buddhist devotion, while a scholar combined the abstract theories of Shinto and Buddhism. Within a religious tradition there are several levels of religiosity, and an individual finds his or her own experience of unity by participating at a particular level in several different traditions. An average person would pick up the popular threads of the Buddhist and Shinto strands to weave a popular worldview; an intellectual would select the theoretical threads of the same strands to develop a more sophisticated worldview. The unity is in the worldview of the individual, and each person has a particular version of the common worldview. When seen from the perspective of individual worldviews, there are as many Japanese religions as there are Japanese people: the unity called "Japanese religion" (in the singular) is what they share in common. (The same can be said of any religious tradition: there are as many Christianities or Buddhisms as individual Christians or Buddhists; the general terms "Christianity" and "Buddhism" refer to the respective shared commonality.)

Japanese religion can be seen as a balance of unity and diversity, but it is too complex a subject to be explained by the simple metaphor of threads and strands. An important aspect of this unity and diversity is the tension between national unity and local traditions. From ancient times, myths and rituals have been deliberately brought together to express national unity under the imperial line; yet the people of every area liked to pride themselves on their unique local rites and usages. This diversity, however, has usually strengthened rather than threatened the overall national unity. The great importance of local custom for Shinto shrines makes the shrines all the more highly esteemed in the eyes of the nearby people as concrete symbols of their involvement in the long Japanese tradition. Local customs tend to enhance rather than diminish national traditions such as reverence for the emperor. Therefore, as we encounter features of diversity and elements of tension in Japanese religion, we should not assume that they necessarily represent contradictions. Rather than outright contradictions, they may be seen as expressions of the variety and tension within a larger pattern of unity.

One of the easiest ways to trace the interaction of unity and diversity is to follow the interweaving of the various strands throughout the course of history, and this book takes such a historical approach. As any culture (or religion as part of a culture) moves through time, it maintains an ongoing identity and continuity while constantly undergoing change. "History," as the sequence of human events, flows through time as an endless process with no obvious compartments or labels, and follows no written script.[6] Nevertheless, historical study of a total culture (or the religious dimension of a culture) enables us to distinguish dominant aspects of continuity and change. For convenience in study and ease of comprehension, in this book Japanese religious history is discussed in terms of three major periods, each one marked by significant change. (Elements of continuity, or "persistent themes," in Japanese religion will be discussed in Chapter 2.)

The three major periods—discussed respectively in Parts I, II, and III—emphasize the discontinuity in religious institutions. The first period (from prehistoric times to the ninth century C.E.) sets the stage for the formation of Japanese religion. In this initial period, the most important religious traditions all make their appearance. In the second period (between the ninth and the seventeenth centuries), these traditions develop and organize independently and interact with each other. The third period (from the seventeenth century to the present) witnesses the tendency toward formalism, which in turn stimulates renewal. (For a concise overview of the history of Japanese religion, see the "Table of Japanese Religious History," pp. x–xi.) This brings us to the present, where we must wait for the next act in the unending drama of Japanese religion. For religious history does not end with the third period; it will continue and be transformed by future events.

NOTES

1. Such historical terms and generalizations carry their own ambiguities; for the ambiguity of the term "Japanese religion," see Neil McMullin, "Historical and Historiographical Issues in the Study of Pre-Modern Japanese Religions," *Japanese Journal of Religious Studies,* vol. 16, no. 1 (1989), pp. 3–40, especially pp. 24–25.

2. The Buddha's birth and death are recognized by different dates from country to country.

3. Dates in this book will be given according to the Common Era (C.E.) or as Before Common Era (B.C.E.) instead of A.D. and B.C.

4. For a critical treatment of Confucianism, commenting on both its historical significance and its relevance for the present in China and world history, see Wm. Theodore de Bary, *The Trouble with Confucianism* (Cambridge: Harvard University, 1991).

5. The point emphasized here is that Japanese people have usually found religious fulfillment within a number of traditions, rather than in affiliation to a single organization. Tension and conflict appear within any social group, a theme developed in *Conflict in Modern Japanese History: The Neglected Tradition,* eds. Tetsuo Najita and J. Victor Koschmann (Princeton: Princeton University, 1982). See also Ian Reader and George J. Tanabe, eds., *Conflict and Religion in Japan,* vol. 21, no. 2–3, of *Japanese Journal of Religious Studies* (June–Sept. 1994).

6. Richard K. Payne has pointed out the dangers of reifying history in "organic" patterns, because "there was no script . . ." to history. See his preface to *Re-Visioning "Kamakura" Buddhism,* ed. Richard K. Payne (Honolulu: University of Hawai'i, 1998), pp. 13–14. Three major historical periods are used in this book as a means of seeing patterns within the continuity and discontinuity of Japanese religion, and enabling the student to enter the concreteness of Japanese religious history.

2

🌿

Persistent Themes in Japanese Religious History

The unity of Japanese religion is evidenced by a nexus of persistent themes that are present in most historical periods and cut across most of the religious strands. One may be dominant in a particular period or more prominent in a single religious strand, but generally they all blend together in the formation of the traditional person's worldview. The recurrence of six themes indicates the unity of Japanese religion: (1) the closeness of human beings, gods, and nature; (2) the religious character of the family; (3) the significance of purification, rituals, and amulets; (4) the prominence of local festivals and individual cults; (5) the pervasiveness of religion in everyday life; and (6) the intimate bond between religion and the nation.

THE CLOSENESS OF HUMAN BEINGS, GODS, AND NATURE

In contrast with the formal teaching of monotheistic religions such as Judaism, Islam, and Christianity, Japanese religion emphasizes neither one sovereign God nor a sharp distinction between the many gods and human beings. In Japan, mortals and gods alike share in the beauty of nature. The tendency of Jewish and Christian theology is to think of a hierarchy with God first, human beings second, and nature a poor third. In the worldview of Japanese religion, these three realms are on more nearly equal terms: the aim is for humans, gods, and nature to form a triangle of harmonious interrelationships. Agriculture and fishing, for example, are closely related to the rituals and festivals of Shinto shrines and Buddhist temples. Zen Buddhism, in particular, together with Shinto, expresses a love of nature akin to the Taoist sentiments of living in harmony with nature. The ideal of harmony among humans, the gods, and nature is a cornerstone of Japanese religion.[1]

In this context, "gods" can be understood as either the *kami* of Shinto or the Buddhas and *bodhisattvas* (Buddhist divinities) of Buddhism. (Because there is no exact English equivalent for the word *kami,* it will be used throughout the text without translation.) The important thing to remember is that *kami* is much more inclusive than the English word "god." The notion of *kami* is elusive because of the great number of *kami* and their various forms. Early Japanese writings relate that many *kami* participated in the creation of the world and in a mythological age of specialized divinities (not too different from the mythological world believed in by the ancient Greeks and Romans). In addition to the *kami* of mythology, natural objects, animals, and even human beings have been identified as *kami,* in ancient times as well as today. In fact, according to one of the greatest Shinto scholars, Motoori Norinaga (1730–1801),

> Generally speaking, [the word] "*kami*" denotes, in the first place, the deities of heaven and earth that appear in the ancient texts and also the spirits enshrined in the shrines; furthermore, among all kinds of beings—including not only human beings but also such objects as birds, beasts, trees, grass, seas, mountains, and so forth—any being whatsoever which possesses some eminent quality out of the ordinary, and is awe-inspiring, is called *kami*.[2]

If they were considered powerful enough, "evil and mysterious things" also rated as *kami,* because the primary consideration was the power to inspire and not "goodness or meritorious deeds." The identity of *kami* is so elastic that perhaps the best general term for understanding *kami* is the notion of the sacred.[3]

Humans are closely related to both *kami* and Buddhas. In fact, men and women can even rise to the status of a *kami* or Buddha. The emperor was considered to be a living *kami* because he was a direct descendant of the *kami*. Other human beings can attain divinity, also. For example, the military ruler (*shogun*) Tokugawa Ieyasu (1542–1616) was venerated as divine or semidivine even during his lifetime, and was enshrined as a major object of worship when he died. The founders of Buddhist sects, too, have been revered as semidivine or divine, and during the last two centuries many founders of New Religions have been viewed as powerful, living *kami*.

THE RELIGIOUS CHARACTER OF THE FAMILY

A second theme of Japanese religious history is the crucial religious function of the family, which is said to include both living and dead members. The dead are so important that the label of ancestor worship has been applied to Japanese religion. Family unity and continuity are essential for carrying out the

Clothing and eyeglasses of family dead are placed on statues of Jizo on Mount Asama, near the Ise Shrines. The custom is to bring objects of clothing, toys, glasses, and even false teeth as a partial means of enshrining spirits of family dead. (New Year's week, 1980)

Paper-thin strips of wood are placed in these racks on Mount Asama, near the Ise Shrines. The strips represent the spirits of the dead and contain the deceased's Buddhist posthumous name, granted by a Buddhist priest during the funeral ceremony. The faithful may "purify" the spirits of the dead by pouring water over the wooden strips. (New Year's week, 1980)

important rituals honoring the spirits of family ancestors. Even beyond the family itself as a living unity, the dead—their burial or cremation—and periodic memorials have great religious significance.[4] The deceased can rise to the status of "gods." A departed family member is referred to euphemistically as

Lighting a candle for the dead is a custom practiced in many traditions. In Japan, the candles are often enclosed in a glass case, as they are here on Mount Asama near the Ise Shrines. (New Year's week, 1980)

Rain does not cancel a trip to visit the ancestors on Mount Asama, near the Ise Shrines. The visitors are flanked on the left by large wooden, memorial stupa (distinctive of Mount Asama) and on the right by the more customary stone memorials. (New Year's week, 1980)

a Buddha (*hotoke*), and the tacit understanding is that after a fixed number of periodic memorials a dead person joins the company of ancestors as a kind of *kami*. Some shrines are dedicated to the spirits of famous men, such as the great ruler Tokugawa Ieyasu. At present, the religious function of most Buddhist priests and temples is to perform masses and memorials for family ancestors.

The family is important not only for revering ancestors but also for providing cohesion for religious activities. In Japan the family unit has usually consisted of more than one set of parents and their children. The Japanese family has often been an extended family of three or more generations and some relatives; sometimes workers who were not biologically related to the family members were part of the group. From ancient times, the head of the family line served as a priest, and prominent families combined political and religious leadership in their family heads. The home was formerly the center of religious devotion. Traditionally, every home featured a miniature shrine (sometimes called a "god-shelf," or *kamidana*) for daily prayers. There was also a Buddhist altar (*butsudan*) for daily offerings to family ancestors in general and periodic memorials for specific ancestors. *Kamidana* are still found in some homes, especially in rural areas, and are retained in such places as small shops and even in oceangoing ships. *Butsudan* are found in many homes, even in some modern apartments where *kamidana* are often missing. These family altars indicate the central religious function of the home. Various semireligious seasonal activities (notably at New Year's) also take place in the home.[5]

Because the family was such an important social and religious institution, it is not surprising that as Shinto and Buddhism became highly organized, their priesthoods eventually developed along hereditary lines. Japanese social as well as religious organization emphasizes a hierarchical ordering based on respect for elders. Even modern businesses and the New Religions are organized in terms of loyalty and belonging that have been compared to the model of the Japanese family.[6] During the past century of industrialization and urbanization, the Japanese family has experienced many changes, and yet the notion of family remains an important social and religious ideal.

THE SIGNIFICANCE OF PURIFICATION, SPECIFIC RITUALS, AND AMULETS

A third persistent theme in Japanese religious history is the significance of purification, specific rituals, and amulets. These elements often represent borrowings from Indian and Chinese traditions, but they have become thoroughly integrated into the Japanese religious scene. Purification is present in all religious traditions, but is especially prominent in Japan. In front of every Shinto shrine, water is provided for washing the hands and rinsing the mouth before approaching the shrine. The insistence on purification—both physical and spiritual—is basic to Japanese religion. Formerly, many prohibitions and purifications were connected with matters such as death and menstruation. The emphasis on purity carries over into contemporary customs such as the practice of soaking in a hot bath and the provision of a damp face cloth for guests. Purification rituals using salt, water, and fire—all considered to be purifying agents—abound in Buddhist, Shinto, and folk traditions. The danger of impurity and the ideal of a pure state is central to the Japanese religious ethos.[7]

The performance of specific rituals is much more important than the acceptance of comprehensive creedal statements (such as those found in Christianity).[8] A host of rituals takes care of every conceivable human and spiritual need. Many rituals are connected with agriculture and fishing in order to relate humans, gods, and nature in a beneficial manner. Some rituals meet personal crises such as sickness. In traditional Japan, religion served the needs of the people not with a uniform, weekly, service, but with a large number of particular rituals tailored for the individual and the occasion, from blessing a fishing fleet to rites for transplanting rice, from the purification and blessing of a building site to the exorcism of a possessed person.

Amulets (also called charms or talismans) are found within the popular practice of many traditions, with varying attitudes of formal sanction, reluctant tolerance, or outright rejection. Although a minority in Japan objects to the use of amulets, Japan is one culture (in some ways similar to Thailand) where amulets are both formally sanctioned and widespread in popular practice. Talismans or amulets distributed by Shinto shrines and Buddhist temples include a number that provide blessings or protection such as blessing of the home, warding off fire, or preventing or curing sickness. These amulets may be paper, wood, cloth, metal, or even plastic. In modern times, one of the most popular amulets is for "traffic safety"—protection against car accidents.

The "charm" of religious power can be conveyed not only through physical form, but also in verbal or recited form. Buddhist scriptures (in Chinese translation) are recited by priests as blessings; phrases from the scriptures are memorized and recited by laypeople not so much from intellectual assent to their doctrinal content, as out of respect for their power and ability to provide immediate benefit to the reciter. Taoistic charms and formulas have influenced both Shinto and Buddhism, but Buddhism is the major source of popular prayers and magical formulas.[9]

THE PROMINENCE OF LOCAL
FESTIVALS AND INDIVIDUAL CULTS

A fourth theme of Japanese religious history is the prominence of local festivals and individual cults.[10] Unlike Christian churches, Buddhist temples and Shinto shrines are not the sites of weekly services, but this does not diminish their importance. Because periodic festivals usually are the expression of the whole village or section of a large city, they are unifying forces that link individual homes in a common religious expression based on a shared worldview. Social and economic activities of small villages often have centered on the Shinto shrine. The local festival with its carnival atmosphere is typical of Japanese religiosity: this is the place and time when most Japanese come into contact with the sacred power of *kami* and Buddhas.[11] In this light we can understand why the celebration of Christmas has become a popular "festival" in modern Japan, even though Christianity as an organized religion has not prospered there.

Performing the "hundredfold" (ohyakudo) repentance by walking back and forth one hundred times while silently repenting. Usually the path is marked by stone pillars at each end, and even during cold weather the walk is performed barefoot. (At the "sacred land" [goreichi] of the New Religion called Gedatsu-kai, Kitamoto, 1979)

An example of the interrelationship of religious practices: At the left is the stone pillar marking one end of the "hundredfold" repentance path. At the right is a stone basin where visitors are rinsing hands and mouth with water. In the background (behind several trees) is a sacred archway or torii; behind the torii and at the left is seen the outline of a Shinto shrine. Visitors to such religious headquarters are free to perform religious practices at one or more (or all) of these sites. (At the "sacred land" [goreichi] of the New Religion called Gedatsu-kai, Kitamoto, New Year's Day, 1980)

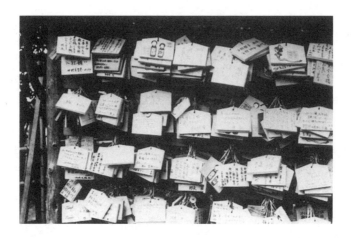

Votive pictures (ema) *bought at a Shinto shrine are inscribed with the person's petition and hung on a special rack near the shrine. (Kyoto, 1979)*

Individual cults for Shinto and Buddhist deities, though not organized on a national scale, play an important role in religious devotion. The *bodhisattvas* of Buddhism, especially popular *bodhisattvas* such as Jizo and Kannon, have claimed probably the largest following. Statues of these *bodhisattvas* are found in the villages or along the roadside as well as in temples, and they receive the worship and prayers of all those who look to them for spiritual help. Usually priests play little or no role in these devotional cults. Ordinarily a small group of people will form a voluntary association (called *ko*), which meets regularly in the members' homes for services dedicated to one *bodhisattva,* and individuals or the entire association may go on pilgrimage to one site or a series of sites sacred to the *bodhisattvas* (or other object of worship). Various *kami* (including gods of Indian and Chinese origin) are revered by groups of fishermen or other tradespeople. Often the existence of a flourishing cult of this kind at a shrine or temple accounts for most of its visitors and financial income. An individual need not join a specific group to say prayers at home or visit a nearby or distant holy site to pay respects and make offerings to a particular *bodhisattva* or *kami*—one that has provided blessing or protection to the person.[12]

THE PERVASIVENESS OF
RELIGION IN EVERYDAY LIFE

A fifth theme in Japanese religious history is the pervasiveness of religion in everyday life. The Japanese identification with gods and nature, the importance of the family, the significance of specific rituals and amulets, the prominence of individual cults—all bring religion into natural and close relationship to everyday life. For example, although there is no regular weekly attendance at Shinto shrines and Buddhist temples, people visit shrines and temples at regular stages or extraordinary occasions in an individual's life. Traditionally, about a month after birth a young infant was carried to the local Shinto shrine and presented to the guardian deity. In case of sickness or special need, one usually went to the shrine or temple that granted an appropriate blessing. Likewise, in recent times the traditional wedding often takes place in a Shinto shrine, and the funeral mass is performed (like the subsequent memorial celebrations) in a Buddhist temple.

Through both formal and informal means, religion has been specifically related to economic activities. Some temples and shrines, for example, are oriented to the fishing communities in which they are found; priests of these institutions pray for large catches, safety on the sea, and repose for the drowned. Some saints are formally considered the patron figures of certain crafts. In an informal sense, many folk practices are inseparable from the various stages of rice cultivation.[13]

Even human sexuality and reproduction are perceived and expressed in religious terms. For example, conjugal harmony of married couples and fertility for rice fields are requested from wayside deities (*dosojin*), which are represented by stones on which are carved explicitly sexual symbols or the figures of a man and woman embracing. Religion even pervades the Japanese sense of humor. For example, the great Zen saint of China, Bodhidharma (who sat in meditation until his legs fell off) is remembered in Japan as the legless doll called Daruma, who, as many times as he falls, always rights himself.[14]

Fortune papers (mikuji) *are hung on a special rack over small statues of Jizo near a Buddhist temple. (Kyoto, 1979)*

THE INTIMATE BOND BETWEEN
RELIGION AND THE NATION

The sixth theme of Japanese religious history is the close relationship between religion and the Japanese nation—a bond that has existed practically from the birth of the identity of the Japanese people. One of the central mythical tales of ancient Japan relates that the emperor, as descendant of the Sun Goddess, is the sacred leader of the Japanese islands (which were created by the gods or *kami*). In effect the emperor was the symbolic head of ritual and government. Although he seldom ruled the government directly, the rituals he performed were for the benefit of the entire country.

This ancient connection between religion and nation is at the heart of Shinto; yet Buddhism also expressed this theme. Buddhists helped unify and support the government, and the state patronized Buddhism. Buddhist priests prayed for the safety of the imperial family and read special scriptures for the peace and prosperity of the state. Imperial families donated private homes for use as temples, and the state eventually built provincial temples in every province so that Buddhist prayers and scriptures for the state could be read in every area of the country.

Taoism and Confucianism, too, were used in early Japan to support the emperor and the state. The government's Bureau of Divination (Onmyoryo, the bureau of *yin-yang*) ensured that the state and the ruler conformed to the "way" of the universe; this bureau, patterned after Chinese practices, shared many features with Taoism. Confucian ethical notions were incorporated in the view of emperors as embodying Confucian virtues of social harmony and benevolence.

Between 1868 and 1945, the intimate bond between religion and the nation was used by the state to support nationalism and militarism. Many people, both Japanese and Westerners, feel that this particular policy was a distortion of the Japanese tradition. In Chapters 17 through 19 of this book we will see how the problem of the relationship of state and religion is being debated in Japan. However this question is resolved, the close tie between religion and the nation at large is an indelible feature of Japanese history.[15]

THE TRADITIONAL WORLDVIEW

These six themes give us some idea of the dynamics of religious life in Japan. Traditionally people did not belong exclusively to one organized religion but drew upon various traditions as they participated in religious activities. A person wishing to express reverence for nature was not likely to stop and distinguish between the Shinto notion of *kami* dwelling in natural objects, Zen Buddhist ideas of oneness with nature, and Taoist concepts of conforming to the way of nature. It was more important to venerate the sacred forces of nature than to identify and separate the historical influences upon the Japanese view of nature. Similarly, there has not been a clear-cut distinction between separate themes. Veneration of *kami* in nature and respect for Japan as a divine nation (land of the *kami*), for example, usually have been seen as closely related.

The six themes express the general view of the world held by most traditional Japanese people. A Japanese person acquires these perceptions of the world by seeing memorials held for ancestors in the home, participating in shrine festivals, and taking part in rituals for the transplanting of rice. More often than not, such a worldview is held unconsciously. Although parts of it may be written down in formal doctrine, the entire worldview is more a matter of personal memory than a written handbook. The worldview is shaped as a person gradually develops a sense of identity by participating in cultural life. As we trace the historical formation of Japanese religion, we should keep in mind that this shared worldview has given continuity to religious life. We will focus on this shared worldview, remembering that, as in any religious tradition, there are as many individual variations or expressions of the worldview as there are individuals who hold it.

NOTES

1. As in any culture, the Japanese view of nature is highly idealized, and in actual practice Japanese people have acted to control and exploit nature in ways that contradict the ideal of harmony with nature. For a volume of essays emphasizing the ambivalence and diversity in Japanese views of nature, see Pamela J. Asquith and Arne Kalland, eds., *Japanese Images of Nature: Cultural Perspectives* (Surrey: Curzon, 1997), especially "Japanese Perceptions of Nature: Ideals and Illusions," pp. 1–35.

2. Quoted in Shigeru Matsumoto, *Motoori Norinaga (1730–1801)* (Cambridge: Harvard University, 1970), p. 84.

3. Mircea Eliade has elaborated the notion of the sacred as a general feature of all religion, but dominant within cosmic religions. See his *The Sacred and the Profane: The Nature of Religion,* trans. Willard R. Trask (New York: Harcourt Brace Jovanovich, 1959).

4. See Elizabeth Kenney and Edmund T. Gilday, eds., *Mortuary Rites in Japan,* vol. 27, no. 3–4 of *Japanese Journal of Religious Studies* (Fall 2000).

5. In a comparison of the "worlds" of Japanese and Americans, Gordon Mathews notes that "the distinct institutional presence of religion is often greater in American lives than in Japanese lives," and "the most common form of religious observance in Japan is in the home." See Gordon Mathews, *What Makes Life Worth Living? How Japanese and Americans Make Sense of Their Worlds* (Berkeley: University of California, 1996), p. 229.

6. The family is important in all religious traditions, so the Japanese family is not unique in this regard. The point here is that family (and home) are much more prominent in Japanese religion than in contemporary America and Europe. Both Japanese and foreign scholars have discussed at length the complex subject of the interaction between self and society in Japan—see, for example, Chie Nakane, *Japanese Society* (Berkeley: University of California, 1970); Robert J. Smith, *Japanese Society: Tradition, Self, and the Social Order* (Cambridge: Cambridge University, 1983); Dorrine K. Kondo, *Crafting Selves: Power, Gender, and Discourses of Identity in a Japanese Workplace* (Chicago: University of Chicago, 1990), especially Chapters 4 and 5; Nancy R. Rosenberger, ed., *Japanese Sense of Self* (Cambridge: Cambridge University, 1992); Jane M. Bachnik and Charles J. Quinn, Jr., eds., *Situated Meaning: Inside and Outside in Japanese Self, Society, and Language* (Princeton: Princeton

University, 1994). For ancestors, see Robert J. Smith, *Ancestor Worship in Contemporary Japan* (Stanford: Stanford University, 1974). For a comparison of self and society within Japanese and American culture, see Mathews, *What Makes Life Worth Living?* Bito Masahide writes that "Between the fourteenth and sixteenth centuries, . . . one social phenomenon that is central to the development of religion and thought . . . " is "the establishment of the *ie* (house or lineage) as the basic unit of social organization among both the *bushi* (warrior class) and the rest of the population." See his "Thought and Religion: 1550–1770," in *Early Modern Japan,* vol. 4 of *The Cambridge History of Japan,* ed. John Whitney Hall (Cambridge: Cambridge University, 1991), pp. 373–424; see p. 373. For an extended treatment of "traditional" family religion, see Michael Jeremy and M. E. Robinson, *Ceremony and Symbolism in the Japanese Home* (Manchester: Manchester University, 1989).

7. For two works emphasizing the importance of purification in Japanese religion, see Geoffrey Bownas, *Japanese Rainmaking and Other Folk Practices* (London: Allen & Unwin, 1963), and Emiko Namihira, "Hare, Ke and Kegare: The Structure of Japanese Folk Belief" (Ph.D. diss., University of Texas at Austin, 1977). For a briefer treatment, see Emiko Namihira, "Pollution in the Folk Belief System," *Current Anthropology,* vol. 28, no. 4 (Aug.–Oct. 1987), pp. S65–S72.

8. "Japanese religion . . . stresses action rather than analytic thought or understanding"; "ritual . . . pervades Japanese life . . . more so than does religious doctrine." Herbert E. Plutschow, *Chaos and Cosmos: Ritual in Early and Medieval Japanese Literature* (Leiden: E. J. Brill, 1990), p. ix. The priority of ritual over doctrine is also noted by McMullin, "Historical and Histiographical Issues," pp. 10–12, and Scott Schnell, *The Rousing Drum: Ritual Practice in a Japanese Community* (Honolulu: University of Hawai'i, 1999).

9. For an article on amulets, see Ian Reader, "Actions, Amulets and the Expression of Meaning," in his *Religion in Contemporary Japan* (Honolulu: University of Hawaii, 1991), pp. 168–93; for a treatment of magic and rituals in medieval Japan, see Jolanta Tubielewicz, *Superstitions, Magic, and Mantric Practices in the Heian Period* (Warszawa: Wydawa VW, ZGWN, 1980).

10. The term "cult" has assumed negative meaning in modern times, such as "Satanic cult." Here we use "cult" in the neutral sense of devotion to or worship of a particular saint or deity—such as the cult of Mary or the cult of Shiva—by people who are not necessarily members of one large organization.

11. Among a number of books focusing on Shinto festival, *matsuri,* three are *Matsuri: Festival and Rite in Japanese Life,* trans. Norman Havens (Tokyo: Institute for Japanese Culture and Classics, Kokugakuin University, 1988); Michael Ashkenazi, *Matsuri: Festivals of a Japanese Town* (Honolulu: University of Hawai'i, 1993); and Herbert E. Plutschow, *Matsuri: The Festivals of Japan* (Surrey: Japan Library, 1996). For a "taste" of festivals, see Keiichi Yanagawa, "The Sensation of Festivals," in *Matsuri: Festival and Rite in Japanese Life;* this article is excerpted in my *Religion in the Japanese Experience,* 2d ed. (Belmont, CA: Wadsworth Publishing Co., 1996), pp. 212–17. For a handy popular treatment see Hiroshi Miyazaki, *Illustrated Festivals of Japan,* trans. John Howard Loftus (Tokyo: Japan Travel Bureau, 1985).

12. For two treatments of the Kasuga cult, see Allan G. Grapard, *The Protocol of the Gods: A Study of the Kasuga Cult in Japanese History* (Berkeley: University of California, 1992) and Royall Tyler, *The Miracles of the Kasuga Deity* (New York: Columbia University, 1990); for a treatment of a more specifically Buddhist cult, see Janet R. Goodwin, *Alms and Vagabonds: Buddhist Temples and Popular Pilgrimage in Medieval Japan* (Honolulu: University of Hawaii, 1994). For the cult of Inari, see Karen Smeyers, *The Fox and the Jewel: Shared and Private Meanings in Contemporary Japanese Inari Worship* (Honolulu: University of Hawai'i, 1999).

13. In traditional Japan specific occupations/activities such as fishing and agriculture were sanctified by specific rituals; Grapard has shown that Zen utilized no ritual in advocating the "view that the entire realm of human activity is the site for realization of Buddhahood," and that for the Shinto-Confucian writer Hayashi Razan the divine was an internal

experience: "'The divine is located within the heart-mind of human beings.'" See Allan Grapard, "Flying Mountains and Walkers of Emptiness: Toward a Definition of Sacred Space in Japanese Religions," *History of Religions,* vol. 20, no. 3 (Feb. 1982), pp. 195–221, especially p. 221.

14. For a study describing the interrelationship of folk customs and folk religion in theater and the arts, see Jane Marie Law, *Puppets of Nostalgia: The Life, Death, and Rebirth of the Japanese Awaji Ningyo Tradition* (Princeton: Princeton University, 1997). For a work treating the theme of sexuality and religion, see Michael Czaja, *Gods of Myth and Stone: Phallicism in Japanese Folk Religion* (New York: Weatherhill, 1974). For a work on Buddhist folk art, see H. Neill McFarland, *Daruma: The Founder of Japanese Art and Popular Culture* (Tokyo: Kodansha, 1987).

15. For a discussion of the "commingling of 'political' and 'religious' symbols" in Japan, see McMullin, "Historical and Histiographical Issues," pp. 12–19. For a notion of Japan as a "sacred nation," which was "much more than nationalism or ultranationalism" see Grapard, "Flying Mountains and Walkers of Emptiness," pp. 214–18.

PART I

❦

The Formation of Japanese Religion

The formative period of Japanese religion extends from prehistory to the ninth century C.E. During this stage, the major traditions that were to form and influence Japanese religion first appeared or entered Japan: the prehistoric heritage, Shinto, Buddhism, Confucianism, Taoism, and folk religion. The prehistoric heritage is the most difficult to grasp because it is the cumulative result of many centuries of local cultures, which gradually became centralized and unified. Shinto is the successor to these ancient beliefs and practices. Buddhism, a foreign religion, arose in India, was transformed in China, and then was transmitted to Japan. China was the birthplace for Confucianism and Taoism, both entering Japan at about the same time as Buddhism. Folk religion arose from the prehistoric heritage and borrowed from the organized religions, enriching the religious life of the common people. Each tradition made a considerable contribution to the initial process of the shaping of Japanese religion, creating the general outlines of this tradition. Because a religious heritage is a living process, it is ever changing and never reaches a final form.

The fact that the first period is labeled "formative" does not mean that the formation of Japanese religion was complete by the ninth century. Rather, in this period the major traditions appeared and the general outlines of Japanese religion took shape. Changes that occurred in subsequent periods took this foundation as their point of departure, as we will see in Parts II and III.

3

❦

The Prehistoric Heritage

O ur story begins with the earliest form of Japanese religion, the prehistoric heritage. The beginning of religion in Japan, like all other aspects
of her ancient culture, is complex and not well known. For example,
we cannot determine the exact relationship of the Japanese people of historic
times (from about 500 C.E.) to the peoples of prior ages; nor can we identify
precisely the relationship of the Japanese language to other languages. What we
know as "Japan" today certainly was the recipient of ethnic, linguistic, and
cultural influence from at least several other areas; scholars have gathered
information and developed a number of theories to account for the emergence of the people and culture of Japan.

Japanese language and culture show affinities to the language and culture
of areas both north and south of Japan, but scholars disagree on the relative
importance of these two areas. Some have favored a southern hypothesis, seeing the primary source of the Japanese tradition in the Pacific regions south
of Japan. Others have preferred a northern hypothesis, seeing the main contribution to Japanese culture enter from the Asian continent by way of the
Korean peninsula. Future research will continue to weigh and balance these
hypotheses. We will look first at the origins of the Japanese people and their
culture, and then arrive at some generalizations about the initial stage of
Japanese religion.[1]

THE BEGINNINGS OF JAPANESE CULTURE

From the longer perspective of prehistory and archaeology, human beings seem to be a relatively recent arrival to Japan, especially compared to the neighboring Asian continent. Some of the world's oldest human remains and oldest evidence for religion (religious burial), hundreds of thousands of years old, have been excavated in China. By contrast, from the archaeological evidence in Japan, it appears that humans and religious activity are later developments. Artifacts in Japan can be dated to about a half million years ago, yet the oldest clearly identifiable human remains are from about 30,000 B.C.E. Geologists and archaeologists are still evaluating the prehistoric evidence in Japan, hampered by the fact that changes in climate and water levels may have inundated and destroyed the earliest sites. Although what can be summarized about the prehistoric age is limited and vague, it is important to keep it in mind for two reasons: first, this gives us the best clue to the initial foundation of Japanese culture and religion; second, it reminds us how complicated the question of "origins" and "indigenous culture" is.[2]

During the Ice Age (Pleistocene period)[3] a land mass extended from the Asian continent to what is now Japan, and certainly there was movement of peoples and cultures throughout this entire area. After the Ice Age when higher water levels separated the Asian continent from the Japanese islands, movement of peoples was more limited until larger ships were built and sailors could traverse the open sea, bringing people from various regions. The Old Stone Age, or Paleolithic period, was before the appearance of ceramics but marked by stone tools, and bridged the Ice Age down to about 10,000 B.C.E. Remains from this time are too limited to draw clear conclusions about lifestyle and culture.

The New Stone Age, or Neolithic period, is dated from about 10,000 B.C.E. to 300 B.C.E. and is distinguished by the development of pottery and polished stone tools. In Japan the Neolithic period is known as the Jomon period, "*jomon*" referring to the "cord pattern" pottery distinctive of this culture. During early Jomon times the basic economic activity was hunting and gathering (including shellfish and other fishing); there was some plant cultivation but not the later form of wet-rice agriculture (in paddy fields). Much of the evidence for this time comes from the large shell mounds along the coast, the locations for dumping shells and fish bones, and also for burying the dead. We know much more about Jomon culture and people because of the association of human remains with cultural artifacts. They were concerned with fertility, as evidenced by stone phalli and female figurines with enlarged breasts and stomachs. Another spiritual dimension seems to have been shamanism, as indicated by the finds of drums usually involved in shamanism. In addition, burial practices demonstrate consideration for the dead and an afterlife.[4]

Small villages existed even in Jomon times, but not until the Yayoi period of about 300 B.C.E. to 300 C.E., marking the transition from hunting and gathering cultures to rice cultivators, was there the permanent larger village pattern characteristic of Japan until early modern times. (The term "Yayoi" comes from the name of a site in present-day Tokyo where the first evidence of this culture was found.) With the introduction of wet-rice agriculture as the main economic activity, and the influx of technology from China and Korea, came the use of bronze (mainly for ritual and status objects) and iron (mainly for tools). These economic and technological achievements were the basis for significant social developments: gradually the concentrations of a larger population came to be organized in political units led by regional chieftains. Religious life during the Yayoi also seems to have become more communal in character, with archeological evidence of religious festivals. (The stone fertility figures of Jomon times were no longer utilized.) Divination was practiced by applying heat to deer bones. Burial became more elaborate in mounds, and there is considerable evidence of burying objects with the dead. The pattern of village life and agricultural religious activities of the Yayoi period shows greater continuity with later Japan than anything that preceded the Yayoi.

Following the Yayoi period is the Kofun, or Tomb period—"*kofun*" being the general name for tomb mounds built from about the fourth to eighth centuries C.E. (the approximate dates for the Kofun period). These elaborate tomb mounds (the largest occupies eighty acres) are ample testimony to the tremendous economic and social development as well as political unification that took place in Kofun times, based on the agricultural and technological advances of the Yayoi. The tomb mounds themselves appear to be an outgrowth of previous burial practices in conjunction with continental patterns of social organization and tomb burial.

Such expansive tombs, obviously, were only for the ruling class, and reflect a much higher degree of stratification of society and greater distance between the rulers and the ruled, as well as a diversity of specialized occupations. "The Kofun period (ca 300–710) was a time of continued transition during which Japan changed from a land of small polities to a unified state with a strong central government and a vital civilization."[5] The tomb mounds varied considerably over several centuries and a wide area (appearing first in the Kyoto-Nara area, and later in northeastern Honshu), but generally this period gives clear evidence of the recognition of an imperial line ruling a more unified people. Indeed, as more of the elite society came to build tombs, imperial proscriptions on the size and extent of the tombs apparently were intended to curb expenses and the drain on the economy. At the same time, following the introduction of Buddhism, the elite families who formerly would have constructed tomb mounds began to have Buddhist temples built, and at this time the practice of mound-building stopped. Outside Japan, these tomb mounds may be best known for the clay sculptures known as *haniwa,* which were used to decorate the surface of the mounds. These *haniwa,* unglazed hollow sculptures of human figures, horses, and other objects, are prized aesthetically today for their simplicity and natural texture.

This overview of prehistory from the distant Ice Age through the Kofun period[6] sketches the beginnings of the people and culture that came to be known as Japanese; however, this was not the only people and tradition to be found in these islands. The people who considered themselves "Japanese," as they pushed east and north, encountered native groups who eventually became known by the common name of Ainu.

A difficult question of early history is the relationship of the Ainu and their culture to the Japanese. The Ainu groups, who once occupied much of Honshu, the main Japanese island, were gradually driven east and north by the advancing Japanese and now survive in small numbers in Hokkaido. Racially the Ainu have been considered Caucasoid (related especially to the people of Siberia) and have much body hair; this places them in sharp contrast to the Japanese, who have been considered Mongoloid (related to the people of continental Asia) and have little body hair. In physical appearance the Japanese generally are distinguished by the fold of skin at the corner of the eye, which Westerners have seen as a "slant eye." Economic life also presents a contrast: from about 300 B.C.E. the Japanese came to depend heavily on rice agriculture; the Ainu traditionally lived by hunting, fishing, and gathering.

At one time Western scholars thought the Ainu were forerunners of the later Japanese, and they tried to find the origin of Japanese language, culture, and religion among the Ainu. Now scholars tend to view the Ainu more as an isolated pocket of Caucasoid people in northeast Asia, for they are linked with prehistoric northern Asia and Europe not only racially, but also by their most important traditional ritual, the bear sacrifice. Nevertheless, there was a great deal of interaction between the Ainu and the Japanese. Especially in northern Honshu and Hokkaido, place names are borrowed from the Ainu, and some places formerly sacred to the Ainu have been taken over by the Japanese. One of the controversial factors relating the religions of the two peoples is the similarity in their names for "divinity"–*kami* in Japanese and *kamui* in Ainu language. Unfortunately, the passing of two millennia since their first interaction prevents us from identifying the nature and extent of the influence of the Ainu on Japanese religion.

The southernmost of the Japanese islands (the Ryukyu Archipelago, including Okinawa) present yet another comparison-contrast with the present-day Japanese. Although the Ainu are quite distinct from the Japanese, the people of Okinawa (today Okinawa Prefecture) are much more closely related to the contemporary Japanese ethnically, linguistically, and religiously. Probably the culture of Okinawa represents a continuation of earlier Jomon life, possibly mixed with Melanesian influence. In traditional Okinawan religion the worship of spirits of nature, shamanism, and a chief priestess were prominent; Japanese folklorists have studied Okinawan customs for parallels and possible forebears of Japanese tradition.[7]

This overview of Japanese prehistory shows us that, from the beginning, Japanese religion represented a combination of diverse elements. Indeed, the geographical location of the Japanese islands is a clue to the formation of Japanese religion. These islands have been in a good position to receive periodic transmissions from several directions. Especially the recurring influence from the Asian continent has played a crucial role. However, until more recent times there was no constant contact with the mainland. The span of ocean between Japan and Asia was short enough to allow occasional voyages, but the difficulty of the trip severely limited their frequency. Consequently, every Asian element that entered Japan was left to ferment in a rather isolated setting. This geographical condition is an important factor in the development of a distinctively Japanese religion, a blend of different components from divergent sources.

THE EVIDENCE AND MEANING OF THE EARLIEST RELIGION IN JAPAN

To understand the prehistoric contribution to Japanese religion, we have to synthesize the archaeological evidence that precedes written records. If the earliest archaeological finds are excluded, the bulk of this evidence falls into the two prehistoric periods described earlier, the Jomon and the Yayoi, followed by the transitional or protohistoric Kofun period (also described earlier), which shades into early history. Lines of continuity between the Jomon and later culture are difficult to define with precision. But in the Yayoi period four developments laid the foundation for later religious history: (1) full-scale wet-rice agriculture; (2) use of bronze and iron; (3) active exchange (including migration) from China and Korea; and (4) the beginnings of social stratification and political unification.[8]

These developments contain traces of the earliest known religion in Japan, the fertile soil in which later religion grows and evolves. Due to the fragmentary character of the evidence it is impossible to reconstruct the whole pattern of religion in these early periods, but certain features are prominent and have persisted. Although one must recognize the great diversity for different regions and different periods, there were many religious expressions concerned with the dead and afterlife, fertility, and sacred objects. Mythology, rituals, and religious organization can be inferred only by ethnological comparison.

THE RELIGIOUS SIGNIFICANCE OF BURIAL AND THE DEAD

From the earliest records of human life, people have performed religious rites for the dead, because they recognize the symbolic passage from earthly life to a spiritual existence. The early Japanese were no exception, for they practiced several types of burial. The first evidence of intentional burials is the simple burial of bodies in a flexed position or covered with red ochre and stones. During the Yayoi period, the dead were interred in jars, a custom apparently originating in Korea. Later the jars were covered with stone slabs (dolmen burial). This seems to have been the forerunner of *kofun*, the previously described large tombs. Often these tombs are characterized by a huge mound covering a stone chamber, all of which is surrounded by a moat. Boat-shaped coffins of wood and stone in the tombs may have been for the voyage of the soul to the next world. In general, there was an increasing emphasis on the ritual disposal of the dead: all these practices probably indicate spiritual passage to an afterlife. The transition to agriculture in Yayoi times apparently led to a higher valuation of interment, or burial in the earth; the erection of tombs probably was the result of influence from the Asian continent.

How can we interpret all these concerns for the dead and afterlife? The initial Western scholarship on Japanese religion was led astray in asking whether the origin of Japanese religion was ancestor worship or nature worship, as if the question could be answered in an either-or fashion. Whether ancestor worship was indigenous to Japan or was imported from China also fueled controversy. There is no simple explanation to account for the beginning of religion in Japan, however, because we can identify no single point of origin. The evidence suggests that from prehistoric times the Japanese people have always observed rites for the dead, but these rites have assumed various forms, not only in prehistoric but also in historic times. Much of the archaeological evidence for understanding ancient Japanese religion is found in burials, especially in the elaborate tomb burials of the Kofun period: in both prehistoric and protohistoric times ritual treatment of the dead was associated with interment, although with some variations.[9] In later periods the religious significance of the dead is expressed more directly in Buddhist funeral and memorial services, often in the form of cremation and memorial masses.

THE RELIGIOUS
SIGNIFICANCE OF FERTILITY

From Jomon times on, archaeological evidence points to a connection between religion and fertility. Large stone clubs suggest a phallic symbol; small clay figurines are probably symbols of female fertility and protection. (The fertility and sacred power of women, especially their ability to communicate with the other world, is a theme echoed in the careers of female shamans, and in recent centuries, by female founders of New Religions.) During the Yayoi period, the burial of metal spears and bells (indicating the entry of continental metal-working techniques) may also have been linked to the notion of fertility. With the introduction of rice cultivation in Yayoi times, we begin to see an increased emphasis on fertility, which colors the agricultural and religious life of all later Japanese history. Annual rituals linked religious ceremonies to the growing and harvesting of rice.

Archaeology has turned up many sacred objects of prehistoric Japan, such as the phallic stone clubs and clay figurines already mentioned. Three sacred objects are particularly noteworthy because of their importance in historic times: the *magatama* (comma-shaped jewels), swords, and mirrors. In later times a set of these three objects became the sacred regalia of the emperor.[10] Their exact religious significance is unknown, but their similarity to materials from the Asian continent and their connection with the rising imperial tradition highlight two important trends: an increasing continental influence and a growing consolidation of religion around one lineage and one political center.

THE RELIGIOUS
SIGNIFICANCE OF DIVINE DESCENT

From about the first to the eighth century C.E., we cross the border from pre-history to early history. In order to describe this period we must rely upon ethnological comparisons and written records, both Chinese and Japanese. For example, the earliest surviving records about Japan are Chinese accounts suggesting both female rulers and female shamans, and the oldest Japanese chronicles also include ruling queens who performed the religious function of mediating divine oracles.[11] These ancient accounts of women in Japan indicate that formally and institutionally they had a more powerful role politically (as rulers) and religiously (as oracular priestesses) than they had in later times. After the introduction of Chinese patterns of culture and government and the traditions of Confucianism and Buddhism in early history, men came to dominate both political and religious leadership. Probably each family had a *kami* (god or spirit), with rituals performed by the family's male head. Nevertheless, women have been perceived as possessing special sacred power and have served informally as intermediaries with extraordinary access to the spiritual realm.[12]

In the light of the "northern" and "southern" hypotheses, several inferences have been made about the pantheon and religious organization in prehistoric Japan in terms of a dual character—both "horizontal" and "vertical." For example, the southern contribution may have included a horizontal cosmology with the conception that the gods come from afar or across the sea, just as the dead go to this distant land. The northern contribution may have featured a vertical cosmology in which the gods are thought to descend from heaven and the dead to ascend to heaven. Actually a number of religious elements have been drawn together from different areas and periods, so that it is difficult to correlate all these variables. One of the crucial questions is whether the emerging imperial line (which mythologically traces its divine descent from the sun) evolved from the existing Japanese family system or was founded by families migrating from the Asian continent. Very old stone circles found in Japan may indicate some kind of solar cult (possibly linked to the mythology of the descent of the imperial line). At any rate, in late Kofun times, a greater sense of political and religious unity appeared. The people came to have political loyalty and religious respect for the major family, the budding imperial family, as descendants of the Sun Goddess.

At the end of the prehistoric period, early Japanese religion already contained many of the themes that would pervade later history, but they were not yet organized into set forms. The imperial line was emerging with a nucleus of mythology and agricultural rituals, all of which would be perpetuated mainly within the framework of Shinto. Up to this point, neither Shinto nor any other clearly defined religion was recognizable. Although Shinto later became the main receptacle for the earlier traditions, none of them was transmitted as an isolated element, without receiving the influence of Buddhism and Chinese religion. Most of these elements found their way into one or more of the organized religions, while some continued to exist in folk religion outside any organized religion. Although prehistoric Japanese religion was quite diverse in localized forms and lacked large-scale formal organization, it contained themes and practices that were the foundation for later religious developments.

NOTES

1. For a more complete treatment of prehistoric Japanese religion, see Joseph M. Kitagawa, "Prehistoric Background of Japanese Religion," *History of Religions*, vol. 2 (Winter 1963), pp. 292–328.

2. Scholars disagree considerably over the archaeological evidence as well as the periodization of prehistoric Japan; much of the summary and periodization in this chapter is based on the uniform chronology of *Kodansha Encyclopedia of Japan*, especially "History of Japan, Prehistory," by Peter Bleed, vol. 3 (Tokyo, 1983), pp. 158–60, and related articles. This encyclopedia is a convenient reference with many succinct articles on "paleolithic culture," "Jomon culture," "Yayoi culture," as well as articles on "Japanese people, origin of," "Japanese language," and so on. For a more thorough presentation that sifts through a vast amount of archaeological evidence and discusses various notions of the periods, dating, and theories about prehistoric Japanese culture, see Keiji Imamura, *Prehistoric Japan: New Perspectives on Insular East Asia* (Honolulu: University of Hawai'i, 1996). For a critical view of the way archaeology has been practiced and how archaeological evidence has been interpreted, see Koji Mizoguchi, *An Archaeological History of Japan 30,000 B.C. to A.D. 700* (Philadelphia: University of Pennsylvania, 2002). Mizoguchi is skeptical of attempts to locate an essential continuity of contemporary Japanese with the prehistoric inhabitants of Japan: "If we define the identity of the Japanese as something transcendental to which the people who inhabit the archipelago refer when they try to confirm who they are, it will be shown that there was and is no such thing as the identity of the Japanese" (p. xii).

3. We use the standard "periods" or "ages" for prehistoric times, which most readers are likely to encounter in treatments of other early cultures; Imamura in *Prehistoric Japan* discusses at length the arguments about whether these standard ages should be applied to Japan or whether the conditions and formation of prehistoric Japanese culture were "unique." See especially p. 9 of Imamura. Mizoguchi in *An Archaeological History of Japan* argues against "a unique Japanese identity" (p. 2) and the way "archaeological evidence has consistently been mobilized for the self-identification of the Japanese" (p. 5).

4. For more information on prehistoric culture such as burial, see J. E. Kidder, Jr., *Japan Before Buddhism,* rev. ed. (London: Thames and Hudson, 1966).

5. Bleed, "History of Japan, Early and Middle Kofun Period," p. 160.

6. For a comparison-contrast of Jomon, Yayoi, and Kofun times, see Mizoguchi, *An Archaeological History of Japan,* pp. 29–48, especially the graphic characterization of each period on p. 30.

7. See William P. Lebra, *Okinawan Religion: Belief, Ritual, and Social Structure* (Honolulu: University of Hawaii, 1966). For a detailed study, see Cornelius Ouwehand, *Hateruma: Socio-Religious Aspects of a South-Ryukyuan Island Culture* (Leiden: E. J. Brill, 1985).

8. Imamura, *Prehistoric Religion,* p. 127. For the full significance of rice in Japanese culture and religion, see Emiko Ohnuki-Tierney, *Rice as Self: Japanese Identities Through Time* (Princeton: Princeton University, 1993). "Thus, the symbolism of rice is bifurcated: on the one hand, 'rice as *our* food' and, on the other hand, 'rice paddies as *our* land,' each reinforcing the other" (p. 4).

9. For the significance of "double burial rites" in ancient Japan, see Gary L. Ebersole, *Ritual Poetry and the Politics of Death in Early Japan* (Princeton: Princeton University, 1989).

10. For a discussion of "the Japanese regalia, as examples of the primary symbols of early kingly office [that] tend to partake of a magical character," see D. C. Holtom, *The Japanese Enthronement Ceremonies: With an Account of the Imperial Regalia,* 2d ed. (Tokyo: Sophia University, 1972).

11. See Joan R. Piggott, *The Emergence of Japanese Kingship* (Stanford: Stanford University, 1997), especially Ch. 1, "Himiko, Paramount of *Wa,*" for treatment of Queen Himiko, "a theurgic ruler who 'enchanted the people'" (p. 15). This book discusses the formation of the state in early Japan.

12. For an overview of the significance of women and their changing roles in Shinto, see Haruko Okano, "Summary: Woman and the Shinto Religion," *Die Stellung der Frau im Shinto* (Wiesbaden: Otto Harrassowitz, 1976), pp. 206–13.

4

❧

Early Shinto

S hinto is Japan's own contribution to the history of religion: Shinto is the only major religion to originate on Japanese soil. With the exception of some shrines in Japan's colonial territories prior to 1945, and some shrines outside Japan serving people of Japanese descent today, Shinto has been found only in Japan and has been practiced only by Japanese people. Shinto arose out of the prehistoric practices of the Japanese islands and tended to preserve these practices in modified forms. To a great extent, the religious life within Shinto represents a continuity with ancient customs and therefore has enjoyed a long association with the Japanese nation.

However, Shinto is not simply the "indigenous" religion of Japan; as we have seen, even the prehistoric background is too complex to be labeled simply an "indigenous" tradition.[1] Also, a historical tracing of Shinto demonstrates that its organization and much of its content owe a great deal to Chinese and Buddhist influences. The blending of prehistoric Japanese and later foreign religious elements into one great national tradition is the enduring contribution of Shinto. The word "Shinto" covers a complex tradition, from its early and loosely organized shape to its modern and highly organized institution, with tension between "native" and "foreign" elements as well as between national and local concerns, and including a wide variety of beliefs and practices.

Shinto forms the next subject for discussion because, historically viewed, it is the main channel through which many of the earliest Japanese religious forms were handed down and preserved. In discussing Shinto at this point, however, we must realize that we are making a chronological jump past the stimulus provided by the entrance of Buddhism. The time span and complex character of Shinto's emergence can be appreciated just by looking at the origins of the word "Shinto."

For many centuries the religious traditions and practices within the Japanese islands were loosely organized around family lines, with no central organization, without even a common name. Gradually the imperial family and its traditions came to be considered supreme over all other families, but still no name was given to the larger or smaller traditions. Not until Buddhism and advanced Chinese culture formally entered Japan (about the middle of the sixth century C.E.) was there any need to distinguish the traditional practices from any contrasting cult. Then, apparently because Buddhism called itself the "way of the Buddha" (*Butsudo*), the traditional religion set itself apart by the counterpart term "Shinto," meaning "way of the *kami*." The two Chinese characters forming the word "Shinto" originated in an earlier Chinese term pronounced *shentao*, but in Japanese "Shinto" is traditionally understood in the Japanese expression *kami no michi* ("way of the *kami*"). The significance of these words is to indicate the "way of the Japanese divinities," even though Shinto as an organized religion was influenced by the "foreign" religious traditions of Buddhism, Confucianism, and Taoism.[2]

MYTHOLOGICAL MATERIALS
AND THE ORIGINS OF SHINTO

A major difficulty in comprehending the formation of Shinto is that as soon as we pass from prehistory into history, Chinese cultural influence is already evident. In fact, foreign influence is most conspicuous in the written documents because the Japanese had no written language prior to the influx of the Chinese script. Among the first written records in Japan are the *Kojiki* and *Nihon Shoki* (the latter is also known in the West as the *Nihongi*), chronicles compiled on court order and completed in 712 and 720 C.E., respectively. These early Japanese documents, mixtures of cosmology, mythology, and chronicles, contain the earliest recorded forms of Shinto. Thus, there is good reason to begin an investigation of Shinto's formation with these two writings.

In some Western publications the *Kojiki* and *Nihongi* have been viewed as the watershed of myth from which later Japanese religion (particularly Shinto) is derived, but this general notion is misleading. In the first place, these scriptures reflect both political and religious motives for unifying Japan. They were compiled by the court elite and did not necessarily mirror the faith of the country at large. In the second place, there is no such thing as a "foundational myth" in Japanese religion. For the Japanese there is neither one sacred myth nor one set of sacred scriptures considered as authoritative for all people. Within a prehistoric or tribal people a common myth typically defines the worldview or the emergence of reality. In so-called higher cultures, such as

India, sacred scriptures like the *Vedas* blend with indigenous motifs to provide the religious base on which later scriptures, commentaries, epics, and even popular dramas are based. In contrast, in Japan no common myth or body of religious scripture pervades the whole religious scene. Even apart from the question of foreign influence, the *Kojiki* and *Nihongi* were never that popular and important in the religious thought and practice of the people.

These reservations concerning the *Kojiki* and *Nihongi* have been made not to minimize their importance for Japanese religious history, but rather to set them in the proper perspective so that we may see more clearly their complex character and their relevance for comprehending the formation of Shinto. For example, the opening passage of the *Nihongi* is a creation story that is not Japanese but is borrowed from a Chinese account of creation (in terms of the Chinese bipolarity of *yin* and *yang,* or female and male). It appears that the Japanese writers sought prestige for their own traditions by prefacing them with a Chinese form of cosmology. (Throughout most of Japanese history there has been reverence or at least respect for the cultural tradition of China, to a much greater degree than Europeans glorify their cultural roots in the Greco-Roman tradition; on the other hand, in some periods such as the Tokugawa there was a reaction to excessive praise for Chinese culture, with exaggerated preference for Japanese culture and religion as unique and superior.) From this point—the beginning of recorded history in Japan—all things Chinese tended to have an exalted status in Japanese eyes. Even the notion of possessing a history or dynastic chronology and recording it in written form seems to have been borrowed from China. These ancient Japanese books begin with a Chinese tale, and Chinese elements are sprinkled throughout.

The Chinese cosmological episode sets the stage for introducing the unorganized Japanese traditions. The Chinese contribution is the notion that the cosmos emerged out of "a chaotic mass like an egg," which then separated into heaven (male) and earth (female). This notion serves as a general explanation for the origin of the world and all the divinities. The first two chapters of *Kojiki* and *Nihongi,* entitled "The Age of the Gods," give a patchwork picture of tales concerning the generations of gods and the founding of the Japanese islands. In this mythical period, seven generations of divinities, or *kami,* culminated in the marriage of Izanagi (a male *kami*) and Izanami (a female *kami*). They brought about the appearance of the Japanese islands by thrusting the "jewel-spear of Heaven" from the bridge of heaven into the briny waters below. Then they descended to the land that had appeared, and they produced other *kami* as well as other features of the universe.

One major theme of the mythology is the descent of the so-called Sun Goddess Amaterasu from this couple: from Amaterasu comes the imperial line of Japan. This is only one of a number of themes or cycles that have been blended together into a combination of mythology and chronology. In general the other themes have been subordinated to the tradition of an imperial line descended from the Sun Goddess Amaterasu. One purpose of "The Age of the Gods" is to justify the divine origin of the emperors and empresses whose reigns are recorded in the remainder of the book. In fact, these chronologies were written on command of the imperial court. According to one account, a person who had memorized all the ancient stories and genealogies recited them for transcribers (who wrote them down by using Chinese characters). Nevertheless, the records in both their intention and their content favor the stories surrounding the imperial line.

We noted earlier that in ancient Japan there were many large lineages (*uji,* or extended families) independent of each other in their religious and political leadership. Probably the imperial line derives from a lineage that became dominant over other extended families and subsequently unified the country both politically and religiously. To unify the religion in pre-Buddhist times apparently meant to orient all the competing traditions around the tradition of the ruling line. After the entrance of Buddhism and advanced Chinese culture, this composite tradition was enhanced with Chinese elements for prestige and was written down.

The *Kojiki* and *Nihongi* illustrate two important aspects of early Japanese religion: first, the divine (or semidivine) descent of Japan and her people, and, second, the proliferation of *kami* intimately related to the land and people. For example, even in these early records we can recognize the characteristic Japanese love of nature as a combination of religious and aesthetic emotion. These themes are not limited to the *Kojiki* and *Nihongi;* rather, they seem to have persisted in the life of the people from prehistoric times onward.[3]

Other early Japanese writings are helpful for understanding the religious context out of which Shinto was formed. The seventh/eighth-century *Manyoshu* is the first anthology of Japanese poetry, blending lyric and religious themes.[4] The ninth-century *Kogoshui* is a valuable document recording a rivalry between several priestly families. Even as early as the seventh and eighth centuries C.E., there were distinct theological and ritual factions. "Shinto" is the name applied to the religious tradition that attempted to unify and perpetuate these themes, beliefs, and practices; the development of this tradition as a more highly organized institution came much later.

In this light, it is much easier to understand how, traditionally speaking, the Japanese could not divorce themselves from Shinto. Even though Shinto did not exist as a comprehensive ecclesiastical body until recent times, it has defined much of the character of the Japanese cultural and religious heritage. On both the local and national planes Shinto hallows the homeland and the Japanese people, as well as the nexus of the religious, political, and natural order. Given this situation, we can understand why Shinto scholars emphasize that Shinto is a natural expression of Japanese life—rather than the product of a definite set of doctrines or the result of a conscious conversion or the act of becoming a "member" of a particular institution. Also, we can realize why there has been a close association of religious devotion, patriotism, and reverential respect for the emperor. Indeed, archaeological evidence documents the fact that the imperial regalia (sword, mirror, and jewel) were sacred from prehistoric times.

THE ORGANIZATION OF SHINTO:
PRIESTS AND RITUALS IN SHRINES

We have seen that the religio-political combination was present even in the lineages or extended families of early Japan. The government of eighth-century Japan continued this tendency by establishing a powerful department of religion as part of the state's administration. Sir George Sansom has given a succinct description of the department of religion:

> It was concerned with the performance of the great religious ceremonies (such as the rites of enthronement and national purification, and the festivals of the first-fruits and harvest thanksgiving), the upkeep of shrines, the discipline of shrine wardens, and the recording and observance of oracles and divinations. It presided over the worship of the national divinities, and had nothing to do with Buddhism.[5]

In Japan, as in many early civilizations, religion and the priesthood served as two complementary arms of the government: the emperor (as the divine ruler) was responsible for the ritual as well as the administrative propriety of the realm. In many ancient traditions, the perpetuation of the ritual order was seen as necessary for maintaining the whole cosmic order. Therefore, it is important to note the contents of this ritual.

From Yayoi times to the present, Japanese religion has been linked with every phase of growing rice. Although the planting of rice occasions a festival, this and other phases are overshadowed by the climax of the rice harvest, at which time the new rice is offered up to the *kami* as thanksgiving. The enthronement ceremony for a new emperor was patterned after the annual thanksgiving harvest ceremony. Even today rice is an important offering both in Shinto shrines and also in the small Shinto altar in homes. Other important annual ceremonies are the public purifications that take place at the midpoint and end of the year.

The ritual prayers (*norito*) for the public ceremonies are recorded in codes called the *Engishiki*.[6] The *Engishiki*, or Codes of the Engi Era, were not written down until 927 C.E., but they contain much earlier materials. In particular the *norito* prayers or liturgies presented in Shinto ceremonies, recorded in the *Engishiki*, are valuable for understanding early Shinto. The priest who reads the *norito* serves as an intermediary between humans and the *kami*. After undergoing a period of preliminary purification, the priest "calls down" the *kami* at the beginning of the ceremony and "sends them away" at the close of the ceremony. Sometimes this is acted out by opening and closing the doors to the inner sanctum (*shinden*, or "*kami* hall") housing the sacred object (*shintai*, or "*kami* body"), which symbolizes the presence of the enshrined *kami*.[7]

In recent times Shinto institutions and rites have been dominated by male priests, while women known as *miko* are assistants or general labor. In ancient times, women played a much more important role both in government and in Shinto: unmarried princesses served as priestesses at the Ise and Kamo shrines.

The sacred archway (torii) *before a local Shinto shrine. (Kawarayu, 1979)*

These priestesses maintained their virginity and purity in order to preside over the main rituals of these shrines.[8]

The rites and celebrations of Shinto center around shrines (*jinja*), which are still found in the smallest villages as well as in the largest cities. (In English usage the word "shrine" is the general term for the Shinto building—*jinja* or *miya;* the word "temple" is the general term for the Buddhist building—*tera* or *-ji.*) Usually one passes through a sacred arch (*torii*), which helps define the sacred precincts of the shrine. Devout believers purify themselves by pouring water on their hands and rinsing their mouths. The present shrine buildings reveal Buddhist and Chinese architectural influence, but some are still constructed according to the ancient models. These shrines are built on poles above the ground and have a thatched roof: they can be seen today at Ise, one of the Shinto strongholds that consciously attempted to reject Buddhist influence. (At Ise, the Sun Goddess, Amaterasu, is enshrined.) This ancient shrine architecture seems to have affinities with architecture to the south of Japan. As Shinto scholars like to point out, its natural beauty is accentuated by the use of wood and thatch left bare of decorations.

One theory concerning ancient Japanese religion is that originally there were no shrine buildings; rather, a shrine was simply a sacred precinct set apart in a certain area or around a sacred object such as a tree or stone. Sacred precincts often were the sites where the ancestral spirits dwelled. This is a valuable insight for linking ancestor worship with Japanese notions of *kami* and festivals. Only later did the twofold Shinto architecture appear, with a worship hall (*haiden*) in front and a smaller *kami* hall in back. The worship hall is where the priests (and sometimes the people) direct prayers toward the *kami* hall, which contains the presence of the enshrined *kami* symbolized by a

On May 5, the boys' festival, paper or cloth streamers of carp are flown from tall bamboo poles next to the home. Usually there is one carp for each young son in the family. (Sendai, 1963)

sacred object such as a mirror or sword. Shinto ritual involves elaborate offerings of food—rice, vegetables, salt, fruit, and fish—which at the conclusion of the ceremony may be consumed by priests and laypeople as an act of communion with the *kami*. As Shinto became more highly organized in medieval times, local shrines were considered to enshrine specific *kami* named in the *Kojiki*.

Religious activities at the Shinto shrine centered around the rhythm of the religious year and an individual's lifespan. The earlier Japanese religious tradition seems to have observed the seasonal order of the year, with spring festivals and fall festivals to mark the planting and harvesting of rice. Even today, spring and fall festivals are still important celebrations in most city shrines. Of great importance, too, have been the purification ceremonies at midyear and New Year's, to wash away the physical and spiritual "pollutions" or "defilements" of the previous half-year.[9]

Five traditional festivals (also revealing Chinese influence) have come to be celebrated throughout Japan: (1) first day of the first month, New Year's festival; (2) third day of the third month, the girls' festival (or dolls' festival); (3) fifth day of the fifth month, boys' festival; (4) seventh day of the seventh month, star festival; and (5) ninth day of the ninth month, chrysanthemum festival. Although this formal system of five festivals is a complex mixture of Chinese and Japanese elements, the festivals have become an integral part of Japanese home and village life.[10]

Religious activities at the shrine also revolved around the events in an individual's life. Traditionally, the newborn child was dedicated at a shrine on his or her first trip out of the house. At other specific ages a child visited the shrines again. Usually special youth groups helped carry out the processions of festivals. In more recent times it has become the custom to be married in a shrine. Also, a visit to a shrine has always been appropriate in any time of crisis. For example, a soldier going off to war would pray for safekeeping at his local (guardian) shrine where he had been carried as a baby. All such visits brought individuals into contact with the *kami,* the sacred power that sustains human life.

DISTINCTIVE
CHARACTERISTICS OF SHINTO

The preceding discussion of the history and nature of Shinto shows how native and foreign elements were blended together into one great national tradition. At the same time, the discussion shows that Shinto cannot be viewed simply as the indigenous religion of Japan by contrasting all other traditions as foreign. Misconceptions have arisen partly because earlier Western scholars tried too hard to compartmentalize Shinto and Buddhism into separate religions. Also, the emphatically national character of Shinto was exaggerated by Western scholars who studied Shinto during its nationalistic phase from about 1867 to 1945, and this image of Shinto has persisted in the West. Shinto is best understood within the broader historical context of Japanese religion.

Because Shinto has such a long history and has interacted so much with other traditions, it is difficult to sharply distinguish Shinto from all other Japanese traditions. Muraoka Tsunetsugu, a Japanese scholar widely respected for his critical interpretations of Shinto history, claims that there are three distinctive characteristics of Shinto. First, there is Shinto's emphasis on the identity of the Japanese nation with the imperial family and the descent of this family from ancestral *kami.* Second, Shinto practices a "realistic" affirmation of life and values in this world, accepting life and death, good and evil, as inevitable parts of the world we live in. Third, Shinto features a reverence for the "bright" and "pure" in all matter and thought, attempting to overcome physical pollution with rites of exorcism and bad thoughts with a "pure and bright heart." In Muraoka's interpretation of Shinto and its distinctive features, the first characteristic is political, the second is philosophical, and the third is ethical. The three are interrelated and interact to form the "intellectual strain" that defines Shinto throughout Japanese history.[11] This interpretation is valuable because it locates *distinctive* characteristics of Shinto without claiming that they are the *unique* property of Shinto. As we have seen in the chapters on persistent themes and prehistoric developments, and as we will see later, these hallmarks of Shinto play a large role in Japanese religious history.

A brief summary of the formative period of Shinto will help us focus on the most significant developments. Of greatest importance is the fact that shortly after Buddhism's appearance from China, Shinto appeared as a loosely organized tradition and assumed its basic shape. Shinto did not create completely new forms, but organized the preexisting heritage into a distinctive tradition. This tradition included a mythology, pantheon, priesthood, liturgies, and shrines. Recorded in the *Engishiki,* a tenth-century official writing, is a system of over six thousand shrines named in connection with annual offerings from the court. Shinto fashioned this tradition in reaction to, and partly in imitation of, Buddhist and Chinese importations. Throughout Japanese history, Shinto has manifested a tension between the intention of preserving Japanese traditions and the process of adopting foreign traditions. Next we will discuss the imported traditions; in Part II we will return to the problem of how Shinto adopted these imported traditions; in Part III we will view Shinto as a modern, highly organized religion.

NOTES

1. The term "indigenous" has been used to refer to the synthesis of Japanese culture that existed prior to extensive Korean and Chinese influence from the early centuries of the Common Era. This usage of "indigenous" is helpful for contrasting the earliest Japanese culture with the influence of later continental civilization, so long as we remember that even the prehistoric Japanese culture itself was a combination of diverse strands.

2. Toshio Kuroda has emphasized that the term "Shinto" as the name of a separate religious institution is a relatively modern development. See Kuroda, "Shinto in the History of Japanese Religion," trans. Suzanne Gay and James C. Dobbins, *Journal of Japanese Studies,* vol. 7, no. 1 (1981), pp. 1–21; reprinted in *Religion and Society in Modern Japan: Selected Readings,* ed. Mark R. Mullins et al. (Berkeley, CA: Asian Humanities Press, 1993), pp. 7–30. Kuroda's views, and the distinction between Shinto as a specific institutional organization and as a broad cultural influence, will be discussed in Chapter 11. Kuroda and some other scholars have seen Taoist influence in the Chinese precedents of *shentao* for the term Shinto and *tianhuang* for the term *tenno* (emperor in Japanese); see the discussion of these issues in Mark Teeuwen, "Shinto and Taoism in Early Japan," in *Shinto in History: Ways of the Kami,* eds. John Breen and Mark Teeuwen (Surrey: Curzon, 2000), pp. 13–31.

3. *Nihongi: Chronicles of Japan from the Earliest Times to A.D. 697,* trans. W. G. Aston, *Transactions of the Japan Society,* supp. 1, vol. 2 (London: Kegan, Paul, Trench, Trübner, 1896; subsequently reprinted separately), p. 106; Donald L. Philippi, trans. *Kojiki* (Tokyo: University of Tokyo, 1968). For comments on the *Kojiki* and *Nihongi* by the eighteenth-century scholar Motoori Norinaga, see Chapter 14. For an excerpt of the *Kojiki,* see my *Religion in the Japanese Experience,* 2d ed., pp. 13–19.

4. See *The Manyoshu,* trans. Japan Society for the Promotion of Scientific Research (Tokyo: Iwanami Shoten, 1940; reprinted, New York: Columbia University, 1965). For an excerpt, see my *Religion in the Japanese Experience,* 2d ed., pp. 170–72.

5. Sir George Sansom, *A History of Japan,* vol. 1 (Stanford: Stanford University, 1958), p. 68. For a detailed treatment of the department of religion established in 702 C.E., see Sir George Sansom, "Early Japanese Law and Administration," *Transactions of the Asiatic Society of Japan,* Second Series, vol. 9 (1932), pp. 67–109; vol. 11 (1935), pp. 117–49.

6. See Donald L. Philippi, trans., *Norito: A New Translation of the Ancient Japanese Ritual Prayers* (Tokyo: Institute for Japanese Culture and Classics, Kokugakuin University, 1959); for an excerpt see my *Religion in the Japanese Experience,* 2d ed., pp. 196–200. Also see Felicia Gressitt Bock, trans., *Engi-Shiki: Procedures of the Engi Era, Books I–V* (Tokyo: Sophia University, 1970) and *Engi-Shiki: Procedures of the Engi Era, Books VI–X* (Tokyo: Sophia University, 1972).

7. For a historical overview of the Shinto priesthood, see Tatsuo Hagiwara, "The Position of the Shinto Priesthood: Historical Changes and Development," in *Studies in Japanese Folklore,* ed. Richard Dorson (Bloomington, IN: Indiana University, 1963; reprinted, New York: Arno Press, 1980), pp. 221–36. For "internal diversity" within the Shinto priesthood, especially in early Meiji, see Helen Hardacre, "The Shinto Priesthood in Early Meiji Japan: Preliminary Inquiries," *History of Religions,* vol. 27, no. 3 (Feb. 1988), pp. 294–320.

8. See Robert S. Ellwood, "The Saigu: Princess and Priestess," *History of Religions,* vol. 7 (Aug. 1967), pp. 35–60; he notes the ideal of intensive purification, exclusion of Buddhist and non-Shinto traditions, the "taboo" of forbidden words, and avoidance of defilement. However, in actual practice, even as a "High Priestess," such women could participate in Buddhism; such was the case with Senshi, who "wrote 'Buddhist poems,' and through them expressed something of her Buddhist faith, while she was at the same time High Priestess of the Kamo Shrines (*Saiin*)." The interaction and tension between Shinto and Buddhism is seen in Edward Kamens, *The Buddhist Poetry of the Great Kamo Priestess Daisaiin and Hosshin Wakashu* (Ann Arbor: University of Michigan, 1990); see especially pp. 5–8. Ebersole, *Ritual Poetry and the Politics of Death in Early Japan,* p. 269, notes that "The process by which female loci of religio-political power were abolished . . . needs to be explored." It is noteworthy that although men came to dominate formal positions of power in religion, especially priesthoods, women continued to play important religious roles in home and village. D. P. Martinez has discussed the "muted group model" of women's religious experience in general and has proposed a new model for viewing women and religion in Japan that does not accept the argument of "some feminists . . . that there was a decrease in women's status as the more male-dominated Buddhist ideology was accepted in Japan." See D. P. Martinez, "Women and Ritual," in Jan van Bremen and D. P. Martinez, eds., *Ceremony and Ritual in Japan: Religious Practices in an Industrialized Society* (London: Routledge, 1995), pp. 83–200, especially pp. 185–86.

9. For references to Shinto festivals, see note 11 in Chapter 2.

10. A colorful description of these five festivals is found in U. A. Casal, *The Five Sacred Festivals of Ancient Japan: Their Symbolism & Historical Development* (Tokyo and Rutland, VT: Sophia University and Charles E. Tuttle, 1967).

11. See Tsunetsugu Muraoka, "Characteristic Features of Japanese Shinto: Japan's Uniqueness in Oriental Thought," in his *Studies in Shinto Thought,* trans. Delmer M. Brown and James T. Araki (Tokyo: Ministry of Education, 1964), pp. 1–50.

5

❧

Early Japanese
Buddhism: Indian
Influence with
Chinese Coloration

Buddhism, like any major religious tradition, is a complex subject that can
be viewed from many angles. To take just two examples, it can be seen as
an Indian export that entered and dominated other Asian cultures and
religions, or as a local religious development that radically transformed the
entering Indian import. It can be described as an elite monastic and priestly
heritage with its lengthy scriptures and abstract teachings, or as a popular
movement with various "folk" beliefs and devotional practices. In fact, the
various religious, philosophical, and institutional phenomena that can be
grouped under the category of "Buddhism" are so diverse that it is hard to include all of them, and it is difficult to find a single category large enough to
hold all of them. Where we begin, and what we focus on, largely determines
what we mean by Buddhism. In this book we will start with India and move
quickly to Japan, emphasizing the interaction of Buddhism with the Japanese
religious world.

Buddhism arose in India, but by the time it reached Japanese shores, it had
already been transformed within India as well as in the passage across the Asian
continent. Buddhism has a long, rich heritage worthy of its own description
and interpretation; here we can treat only the place of Buddhism in Japanese
religious history. On the one hand, Buddhism made a tremendous contribution to the religious scene in Japan; on the other hand, Buddhism was transformed by its synthesis with the Japanese tradition. The twofold result is that as
Japan became a Buddhist nation, Buddhism became a Japanese religion. In the
initial or formative period, the Buddhist impact upon Japanese culture and

religion was more prominent. In the second or developmental period, the Japanese transformation of Buddhism became more conspicuous.

Within Buddhist history two major divisions evolved along the lines of geography, doctrine, and practice. In southern Asia, in countries such as Sri Lanka (Ceylon) and Burma (Myanmar), the tradition of monastic Buddhism continued, which emphasized strict adherence to monastic rules or discipline, preservation of the scriptures attributed to the Buddha, and doctrines that made the spiritual goal of enlightenment a long and difficult road for laypeople. This division is often called Southern Buddhism or Theravada (School of the Elders or Monks). To the north of India and spreading across China to Japan, the form of Buddhism that placed less importance on monastic discipline continued. Instead, this form emphasized the later scriptures (such as the *Lotus Sutra*), aspiration to the status of a Buddha, and rebirth in a heavenly paradise. Especially because this Northern Buddhism insisted on the "easy" path of enlightenment for all people, it called itself Mahayana (the Large or Great Way) and looked down on Southern Buddhism as Hinayana (the Small or Inferior Way). Although there are many similarities between these two divisions of Buddhism, and although the traditions of Southern Buddhism were brought to China and Japan, it was the Mahayana form that made the decisive impact in the Far East in general and Japan in particular.

THE INTRODUCTION OF
BUDDHISM AS A FOREIGN RELIGION

Buddhism formally entered Japan by way of Korea in the middle of the sixth century; the official entry is dated at 552 C.E. or 538 C.E., but some Buddhist influence from China and Korea was present earlier. The *Nihongi* records the first Japanese reference to Buddhism, when one of the Korean kings sent tribute to the Japanese emperor, including an image of Buddha and Chinese translations of Buddhist scriptures. The Korean king praised Buddhism as the religion of distant India whose doctrine surpassed even the understanding of the Chinese and whose value was without limit.

Just as women were preeminent in ancient Japan as divine or oracular rulers, they were also pioneers in the earliest Japanese Buddhist tradition. A woman was the "the first ordained Buddhist in Japan" in 584, and shortly thereafter was joined by two other women to "become the first Japanese to go abroad to study [Buddhism] in Paekche in the Korean Peninsula." After the three received full ordination in 590, they returned to Japan and resided in a Buddhist temple called an *amadera,* a temple headed by a woman.[1]

Because Buddhism was the first foreign religion to enter Japan, it provoked a conflict with the preexisting Shinto tradition. Shinto's encounter with the more highly organized Buddhism actually stimulated the preexisting tradition to adopt the name "Shinto" and to become more formally organized. However, the interaction between Shinto and Buddhism was not carried on in terms of abstract doctrine or philosophical principles. Instead, the immediate concern was the more practical religious question of whether the nobility should worship the statue of Buddha, and if they did, would this offend the *kami*. Korean immigrants to Japan (who had long practiced Buddhism) favored the adoption of Buddha-worship, whereas some leading Japanese families maintained a firm opposition.

The worship of Buddha underwent several temporary reversals, as in the case when a pestilence was attributed to the wrath of the national gods because the people were worshiping foreign deities. Eventually, though, Buddhism was accepted as one of the religions of the realm and was elevated from the status of a private cult practiced in elite families to a state religion with responsibility for the welfare of the country. Buddhism's success as a religious influence on the state is partly due to the fact that the state was in the initial stages of formation and partly due to the power of Buddhism's formal organization and teaching, as well as the great appeal of its art, ritual, and magic. As a matter of fact, Buddhist magical formulas were brought to Japan together with formal scriptures, and the Buddha was even worshiped in the same manner as a *kami*. Already in the early period Buddhism was practiced in a religious pattern similar to Shinto, with its appeal to divine powers for immediate human needs. Shinto had its shrines, *kami, * ritual prayers (*norito*), and priests. Buddhism likewise had its temples, Buddhas or Buddhist divinities, scriptures and rites, and priests. Buddhism had its own way of bringing people to religious fulfillment or sacred power, conceived in Buddhist terms.

BUDDHISM'S IMPACT ON
THE COURT AND THE STATE

The story of early Buddhism in Japan is marked by the unsteady but gradual acceptance of Buddhism by prominent families, the imperial court, and the state; Buddhism was not disseminated to and accepted by the common people until some centuries later. Subsequent diplomatic missions from Korea brought more Buddhist images and scriptures, but most important was the arrival of Buddhist priests. At this time the Japanese were just learning to manage the Chinese writing system, so it took a specially trained Buddhist priest to read and expound the Chinese translations of Buddhist scriptures. Also, the Buddhist priests began to serve the religious needs of the court and state.

In the private sphere, Buddhism came to be appropriated for every imaginable occasion, one of the most important being the Buddhist memorial service. Already by the first years of the eighth century, a Buddhist priest and an empress set the Japanese precedent for Buddhist funerals by arranging to have their bodies cremated. Memorial services were performed for the spirits of Buddhist priests, the imperial family, and the aristocracy, establishing the pattern for Buddhism as the major provider of memorial services for all social classes in later times. Eventually, Buddhism developed a comprehensive ritual system for the dead; Buddhist priests recited scriptures for the repose of souls, accepted ashes of the dead for safekeeping in their temples, and performed memorial services at regular intervals. Wooden memorial tablets (*ihai*) were enshrined in the family Buddhist altar (*butsudan*), and often cemeteries with memorial gravestones grew up around Buddhist temples. But even in its earlier and more aristocratic phase, Buddhism's appeal was much broader than funeral and memorial services—for example, members of the court had scriptures read for such purposes as relieving sickness and easing childbirth.

While Buddhism was being accepted by the court in the private sphere, it was being appropriated by the state in the public sphere. We can say that Buddhism played a major role in shaping the Japanese state, so great was its influence. The contrast between the acceptance of Buddhism in China and in Japan is worth noting. When Buddhism came to China, Chinese culture possessed such a rich heritage of literature, philosophy, religion, and centralized government that Buddhism had to fight an uphill battle to be accepted. By contrast, when Buddhism arrived on Japanese shores, Japan had no literature and philosophy to speak of, and her religion and government were only loosely formed. It is no wonder, then, that Buddhism and Chinese culture exerted such a great influence on Japanese culture and religion. The budding Japanese attempts to unify and centralize the country were greatly aided by the stimulus and even some of the models of highly organized Chinese culture. Buddhist priests in early Japan possessed two highly valued treasures: first, the religious tradition of Indian Buddhism in the garb of Chinese culture, which included the models for a well-ordered kingdom; second, the many technical skills associated with Buddhism, such as carpentry and architecture. For centuries to come, priests played a major role in the importation and implementation of Chinese models of government. A number of Buddhist priests, who went from Japan to China on court order, combined commercial, religious, and governmental functions.

Not only Buddhist priests, but also the emperors themselves were responsible for the importance of this religion in state affairs. Of the sixth-century emperor Yomei, it is said that he "believed in the Law of the Buddha and reverenced the Way of the Gods" (Shinto).[2] (Plurality of religions is the rule rather than the exception in Japanese history.) Prince Shotoku (573–621), second son of Emperor Yomei, is traditionally honored as the founder of Japanese Buddhism. He ordered the construction at Nara of a large temple complex, Horyu-ji, housing many fine examples of Buddhist art. According to his traditional image, Prince Shotoku saw in Buddhism both a profound philosophy of life and a sound foundation for the state. Tradition also credits him with writing several commentaries on difficult Buddhist scriptures; furthermore, he is remembered for declaring Buddhism to be one of the pillars of the state (together with Confucianism) in the famous set of principles—a "Constitution" of seventeen articles[3]—attributed to him. This was a landmark recognition of Buddhism's profound message and the formal precedent of Buddhism as the rationale for the state.

We need to remember that during this formative period the Japanese tried to use Chinese models to organize Japanese society. Buddhism was one element in this program of organization and was an active force in determining how the organizing activity took place. For example, as early as 624 C.E., Empress Suiko regulated the Buddhist priesthood, establishing the supervision of monks and nuns. The Taiho Code of 702 included several sections dealing with religious administration, including the organization of the Shinto bureau and the Bureau of Divination.[4] A special section of the code dealt with the regulation of monks and nuns.[5] Buddhism had flourished so much that the state had to step in to curb excesses and maintain religious uniformity. Nevertheless, if the state tended to control Buddhism, Buddhism in turn tended to unify and support the state.

BUDDHISM AS A STATE RELIGION

During the Nara period (710–84, named after the capital city of Nara), Buddhism became a state religion, for all practical purposes. Emperor Shomu (reigned 724–49), one of the most devout emperors, contributed greatly to Buddhism's national status. The greatest symbol of the unifying power of Buddhism was a magnificent cathedral built at Nara in 728 on the order of Emperor Shomu. This was the famous temple called Todai-ji (Todai Temple), still a popular tourist attraction due to the huge wooden structure and large Buddha statue enshrined there. In the Nara period there were six formal schools of Buddhism, and technically Todai-ji was the headquarters of one of them—the Kegon school. In actuality, this central cathedral within the capital served to protect the emperor and the realm, and it unified Buddhism throughout the provinces.

In 741 Emperor Shomu ordered two "provincial temples" (*kokubunji*) to be built in every province: a monastery for monks and a nunnery for nuns. A primary function of the monks and nuns was to recite Buddhist scriptures, thereby bringing divine protection and blessings to the whole countryside. In Buddhism the copying and reciting of scriptures—even thumbing through scriptures or chanting short phrases—has been considered a means to accumulate merit or magical power. The special feature in this case is that the nation at large was to be the recipient of these benefits.

The building of provincial temples and the central cathedral of Todai-ji, and the religious practices in these institutions, exemplify how Buddhism interacted with Japanese culture and religion: The national prestige of Buddhism grew, while Buddhism began to unify the country and spread among the people. The main temple controlling the provincial temples was Todai-ji, which not only served as a geographical and administrative center, but also as a religious focus for the nation as a whole. A large statue of the Sun Buddha Birushana (Vairocana in Sanskrit) was erected within Todai-ji. The funds for the statue are said to have been raised by popular subscription; thus, the country was united symbolically by the common spiritual task of erecting this statue. Just as Buddhism provided a main national temple and provincial temples to recite scriptures and prayers for the benefit of the state and its people, individuals contributed to the establishment of Buddhism as a kind of national religion.

One might say that the Japanese people were able to find a greater sense of religious and national unity in Buddhism than in the less highly organized Shinto, for in the Nara period the people were not directly related to the emperor, who lived and performed both his governmental duties and his ritual activities in seclusion from the people. Shinto rituals involving the imperial family, though national in significance, allowed little possibility for any sense of participation by the common people. Buddhism had been engaged in a process of mutual influence with Shinto from the time it arrived in Japan (as seen in the previously mentioned controversy over whether to worship the Buddha as a foreign *kami*); from this historical point on, the interrelationship between Buddhism and Shinto becomes more complex, but Buddhism tends to dominate the scene.

Most scholars feel that by the Nara period Buddhism as an organized religion had overshadowed Shinto, and some scholars view Buddhism as the major religion of early and medieval Japan, considering Shinto as an independent religion that developed during recent centuries.[6] However we interpret Shinto, in earlier times Shinto tended to borrow on the glory of Buddhism. The close ties between the two traditions is illustrated by two interesting developments at Todai-ji. Worship of the large Buddhist statue there was facilitated by invoking the presence of a divinity called Hachiman, who became a protective or tutelary deity of Todai-ji. Hachiman's origins are unclear, but as a *kami* Hachiman came to be seen as the deified spirit of Emperor Ojin. Hachiman, as the protecting spirit for the erection of Todai-ji's large Buddhist statue, was also called "*bosatsu.*" "*Bosatsu*" is the Japanese version of the Buddhist term "*bodhisattva*" (in Sanskrit), which here means a Buddhist divinity. The word "*bodhisattva*" is literally "enlightenment-being," and it can even refer to a living person or "saint" who has attained a high level of spiritual insight. Hachiman enjoyed a rich history in later Japan, with many thousands of shrines, but always incorporated both Shinto and Buddhist features.[7] Hachiman is a good example of the blurring of boundaries between Shinto and Buddhism.

Additionally, we may note that Birushana, the large statue in Todai-ji, was a form of the so-called Sun Buddha (Dainichi in Japanese, Vairocana in Sanskrit). According to one tradition, messengers had to be sent to Ise to gain the approval of the Sun Goddess Amaterasu of Shinto for the erection of this statue. The answer of the oracle seemed to indicate that the Sun Buddha was identical to the Sun Goddess. The tradition of this oracle may not date back to the eighth century, but in later times the two were closely associated, just as so many Buddhist divinities and Shinto *kami* came to be considered counterparts. Several centuries later, throughout Japan we find popular conceptions that blend together a local spirit or *kami,* a specific *kami* of the Shinto pantheon, and a Buddhist divinity—into one and the same object of worship. The close relationship of Hachiman and Amaterasu to Todai-ji shows how thoroughly Buddhism and Shinto became intertwined.

Our overall impression of Buddhism up through the Nara period is that it had become firmly entrenched in the hearts of the nobility and the bureaucracy of the state. In contrast, the popular acceptance of Buddhism was not nearly so widespread. The attempt to propagate Buddhism to the masses was carried out by only a few devoted priests, especially Gyogi (668–749), who not only preached to the people, but also promoted Buddhism through charitable projects such as founding hospitals. He was granted the posthumous title of *bosatsu (bodhisattva),* in this case equivalent to "saint."

The inclusion of "The Law Concerning Monks and Nuns" in the Taiho Code of 702 was an admission that Buddhist monks and nuns were becoming more numerous and that the common people were beginning to accept Buddhism. It also reflected the state's effort to control the activities of clerics trying to spread Buddhism. We might say that Buddhism already was considered a state religion of Japan and later, with increasing popularity, became a national religion. Buddhism tended to dominate the whole religious scene but paralleled Shinto rather than actually superseding it.

THE SIX PHILOSOPHICAL
SCHOOLS OF NARA BUDDHISM

The general picture of Nara Buddhism suggests a religion of the aristocracy and monks, largely confined to the court and monasteries. During this period numerous sumptuous temples were founded, many of which can still be seen at Nara. Although these wooden structures were frequently damaged by fires, they have been accurately rebuilt and house some of the oldest treasures of Japan, including items from ancient China and beyond. In their flourishing period these temples were overflowing with scholar-monks who frequently catered to the religious needs of the court and state but were also committed to scholarship on Buddhist scriptures and doctrines. "As centers of propagation among the masses they were not successful," because the government saw their purpose as being "to conduct rites and services for the protection of the nation, the Imperial family and aristocracy and to promote culture and study."[8]

In the Nara period the state recognized six divisions within Buddhism. These were "study groups established at the great temples at Nara"[9] rather than full-fledged religious sects. These six schools transmitted the philosophical heritage of Indian Buddhism in the vessels of Chinese translations; there was no original Japanese contribution at this point. Although these schools are of great importance for tracing Buddhist philosophy from India to Japan, they are of lesser consequence for understanding the practice of Japanese religion. Therefore, we will touch on them but briefly, in order to illustrate the diversity of the religious heritage in Japan. The six philosophical schools and their traditional dates of entry into Japan are Jojitsu (625), Sanron (625), Hosso (654), Kusha (658), Kegon (736), and Ritsu (738). Each school focused on one or more of the classic Buddhist scriptures (in Chinese translation), expounding and defining the viewpoint of its distinctive scripture.[10]

The Kusha school was a continuation of the Sarvastivada (literally, "all exists") school of Buddhism. The Jojitsu school, taking its name from the Satyasiddhi school, "The Establishment of Truth," attempted to go beyond the

Kusha (or Sarvastivadin) view of the Four Noble Truths with emphasis on the doctrine of "emptiness," a notion that was central to Sanron. The Sanron school (which we will discuss in some detail) continued one of the most glorious philosophical streams of Buddhism, including the Madhyamika philosophy of Nagarjuna (circa 150 C.E.). The Hosso school perpetuated the "consciousness-only" philosophy (Vijnanavada, or Yogacara), which played a great role in Chinese Buddhism. The Kegon school (Avatamsaka, "philosophy of totality") has been of great intellectual influence on Japanese Buddhism, as its affiliation with Todai-ji might suggest. The Ritsu school concerned itself with Buddhism's monastic discipline. ("Discipline" is *vinaya* in Sanskrit, *ritsu* in Japanese.) The Ritsu school was important for establishing the rules and actual altars for ordination (one of which was established in front of the great Buddha at Todai-ji), but in general the priests of Japanese Buddhism have not conformed to all the Indian prescriptions of discipline.

These philosophical schools were not mutually exclusive in Japan even in the beginning; monks often studied the doctrines of several of them. A number of the famous old temples, especially those at Nara, are still counted as belonging to several of the six schools, but for the most part the schools live on today as indirect intellectual influences within the later sects of Japanese Buddhism. The schools, although never popular in scope, represent philosophical resources for Japanese Buddhism and much Japanese thought.

Buddhist philosophy was highly developed in India, and Chinese Buddhists further refined this tradition before passing it on to Japan, where once again some of the best minds were attracted to the subtlety and complexity of Buddhist teachings. Although the majority of Buddhists in any country are more involved in devotional practices and ritual activities, there has always been a small group of priests (usually monks) and more intellectually inclined believers who have appreciated the grandeur of Buddhist philosophy. Indeed, the features of Buddhist thought that attracted great minds several thousand years ago are the same features that make it appealing today for many Asian and Western people: Buddhist philosophy possesses a comprehensive worldview combining a profound understanding of the complexity of human existence with a detailed interpretation of the nature of the universe. Such philosophical systems are too complex and elaborate to be summed up quickly, but a brief look at one of the foremost Buddhist schools of philosophy, Sanron, will give some indication of the character and depth of these systems.

THE SANRON SCHOOL

The Sanron school took its name from the Chinese school San-lun ("three treatises"), which in turn was a Chinese elaboration of the Indian school of thought Madhyamika associated with the Indian Buddhist named Nagarjuna. The Buddha is credited with discovering the truth of an enlightenment that goes beyond human suffering, but later Buddhists sought a more complete interpretation of the nature of human existence and enlightenment (*nirvana*).

There is almost no begging for religious purposes in Japan. This young Buddhist priest, apparently as part of his religious training, recites a Buddhist scripture and accepts donations at the gate of the famous Asakusa Kannon temple in Tokyo. (1979)

On the question of the nature of human existence, there were two contrary tendencies: one was to view human existence as having material reality (a materialistic argument); the other was to view human existence not as material reality but as a kind of reflection of an ideal (an idealistic argument). The Sanron school (following Indian and Chinese arguments) boldly rejected both materialistic and idealistic arguments, and denied all four arguments about life and all phenomena: (1) Their character is (permanent) existence. (2) Their character is nonexistence. (3) Their character is a combination of existence and nonexistence. (4) Their character is neither existence nor nonexistence. Sanron rejected all known arguments about life and phenomena based on human reason. Sanron scholars argued that it is much better to rely on the truth of enlightenment that goes beyond mere human reasoning.

At first reading, Sanron's argument may appear to be a play on words. That this argument is quite serious, however, is shown by its treatment of another key problem in Buddhism—the nature of enlightenment (*nirvana*). From the earliest days of Buddhism, there was difficulty in communicating the nature of *nirvana,* which seemed to be so "absolute," in contrast to the impermanence of human life. There were some positive analogies for describing *nirvana,* such as bliss and security, but many descriptions were negative, such as destruction of desire or "to be extinguished" (as fire is extinguished or "goes out"). Even in the lifetime of the Buddha, as well as in modern times, some critics of Buddhism have called the notion of *nirvana* "nihilistic," for not only was *nirvana* expressed in negative terms, but the goal of *nirvana* was judged to be an "escapist" withdrawal from everyday life to an inexpressible state. Buddhist philosophers were caught on the horns of a dilemma: If they taught that the conventional expressions of life and phenomena in this world were ultimately true, they would be denying the basic Buddhist truth of enlightenment. If they taught that conventional life experiences were simply illusions, then they would be implying a nihilistic destruction of phenomena when *nirvana* was attained.

Sanron arrived at a solution for the dilemma similar to the solution for the problem of explaining worldly phenomena and human existence. Sanron rejected the view of *nirvana* as simultaneously a form of absolute reality (that is, absolute form or being) and a form of nihilism (that is, a negative kind of nonexistence). Sanron maintained this position by stating that any attempt to grasp *nirvana* as a positive or negative "thing" was a limited viewpoint and must be rejected, because both *nirvana* and conventional phenomena are "empty" of any self-substantiating quality. This means that the only positive statement that can be made about *nirvana* is that it is "empty" of all attributes; because *nirvana* is devoid of particular attributes, it is characterized as "emptiness."

One of this brilliant philosophy's major conclusions is that, when viewed from the realization of *nirvana* (enlightenment), both *nirvana* and human life (and related phenomena) in this world are "empty." This enabled Sanron to avoid the one-sided mistakes of materialism and idealism for the questions of both existence and *nirvana*. This is a radical development of the notion that the truth of enlightenment goes beyond any attempt at human reasoning. One of the remarkable features of the argument is its unflinching honesty in denying the absoluteness of any proposition about reality, including its own.

These theoretical issues are similar to the questions of the nature of human existence and the nature of the universe that have interested philosophers in all traditions, not only in ancient times but today as well. Because there was no highly developed Japanese philosophical system when these Buddhist schools entered Japan, it is not surprising that they were quickly accepted and continued to attract great minds. Later, as Buddhism assimilated Japanese culture and developed along Japanese lines, these abstract arguments were linked to native notions such as the reverence for nature.

In any country, the abstract and philosophical expressions of religion appeal only to the intellectual elite. In early Japan, too, the complex subtleties of Buddhist teachings such as Sanron spoke only to an educated minority (very few people were able to read). But the genius of Buddhism and other religious traditions is the ability to offer to varied audiences both profound interpretations about the nature of life and the universe, and practical beliefs and rituals for daily living.

THE DECLINE OF NARA BUDDHISM

If Nara Buddhism became famous for its profound philosophy and glorious temples, it became infamous for its increasing decadence and corruption. Japan is no exception to the rule that money and power tend to corrupt. The Nara temples grew in prestige and wealth by attracting bequests from the nobility and favoritism from the state. In turn, the prestige and wealth of the temples attracted politically ambitious men to the priesthood. In a short time the temples had become so wealthy and their priests so powerful that their interference in the politics of the capital could not be tolerated. This condition seems to have been a factor in a decision to move the capital from Nara to Kyoto in the transitional period from 784 to 794. (Before the Nara period, it was the normal custom to move the capital at the death of every emperor, apparently on the belief that the emperor's death defiled the capital.) This move helped free the court from the intrigues of the Nara temples, which were left behind in the former capital; the move also marked the beginning of a religious renewal by the Nara schools and the new Buddhist sects of Tendai and Shingon, which we will discuss in Chapter 9.

NOTES

1. Paula Kane Robinson Arai, *Women Living Zen: Japanese Soto Buddhist Nuns* (New York: Oxford, 1999), pp. 32–33, 170. A book on a similar topic, announced as this work goes to press, is Barbara Ruch, ed., *Engendering Faith: Women and Buddhism in Premodern Japan* (Ann Arbor: University of Michigan).

2. *Nihongi,* p. 106.

3. See *Nihongi,* pp. 128–33, for the text of this "Constitution." An excerpt of this work is included in my *Religion in the Japanese Experience,* 2d ed., pp. 235–36. For a brief treatment of Shotoku accompanying translated documents that record his life and achievements, see William E. Deal, "Hagiography and History: The Image of Prince Shotoku," in *Religions of Japan in Practice,* ed. George J. Tanabe, Jr. (Princeton: Princeton University, 1999), pp. 316–33. For the changing image of Shotoku, especially in association with the invented tradition of *wa* (harmony) and collectivism in changing historical circumstances, see Ito Kimio, "The Invention of *Wa* and the Transformation of the Image of Prince Shotoku in Modern Japan," in *Mirror of Modernity: Invented Traditions of Modern Japan,* ed. Stephen Vlastos (Berkeley: University of California, 1998), pp. 37–47.

4. The Bureau of Divination, Onmyoryo, is the Japanese version of the Chinese bureau of *yin* and *yang.*

5. See Sansom, "Early Japanese Law and Administration," *Transactions of the Asiatic Society of Japan,* Second Series, vol. 11 (1935), pp. 127–34, for a translation of "The Law Concerning Monks and Nuns."

6. This is the view of Toshio Kuroda, who in an influential and controversial article writes that "before modern times Shinto did not exist as an independent religion." See Kuroda, "Shinto in the History of Japanese Religion," p. 9.

7. For a closer look at Hachiman see Christine Guth, *Hachiman Imagery and Its Development* (Cambridge: Harvard University, 1985), and Ross Bender, "The Hachiman Cult and the Dokyo Incident," *Monumenta Nipponica,* vol. 34, no. 2 (Summer 1979), pp. 125–53, especially pp. 127–38.

8. Daigan and Alicia Matsunaga, *Foundation of Japanese Buddhism,* vol. 1 (Los Angeles: Buddhist Books International, 1974–1976), pp. 27–28.

9. Ryuichi Abe, *The Weaving of Mantra: Kukai and the Construction of Esoteric Buddhist Discourse* (New York: Columbia University, 1999), p 36.

10. For a detailed description of each of the six schools and their teachings, see Matsunaga, *Foundations of Japanese Buddhism,* vol. 1.

6

ಟಿ

Confucianism
and Taoism:
Chinese Importations

Confucianism and Taoism developed in China from a common background of ancient Chinese thought and practice and therefore share
many features, although each emphasizes different aspects of the same
heritage. Both traditions are based on early Chinese cosmological notions,
such as the "way" (*tao* or *dao*[1]) of the universe: the world or cosmos has its own
"way," or inherent order, and humans should conform to that way. Viewed as
systems of thought or philosophy, the main difference between the two
traditions is that Confucianism emphasizes the "way" of social action and
political order, advocating human responsibility in developing personal virtue,
practicing ancestral rites, and preserving social order; Taoism stresses the "way"
of mystical practice and natural order, favoring "nonaction" in meditation and
the performance of practical rituals such as divination. Such philosophical distinctions were not the basis for separating people into opposing camps of
thought, however, because most Chinese framed their worldview out of a
blend of Taoist and Confucian (as well as Buddhist and folk) elements. Also,
we must remember that Confucianism and Taoism included individual and
group religious practices as well as intellectual thought, and Chinese laypeople
usually did not belong exclusively to one organized religion, but instead observed beliefs and practices from several traditions.

Partly because their role in Japanese culture was as intellectual and spiritual
influences rather than as organized religions, there are no formal dates for the
entry of Confucianism and Taoism into Japan; they arrived from China (and
Korea) along with Buddhism by the fifth or sixth century C.E. together with a

host of other components of Chinese culture. The careers of these two traditions in Japan demonstrate both the significant influence of Chinese culture and religion upon Japan and the tendency for Japanese culture to modify and reshape whatever it accepted.

In the context of Japan, the "*ism*" in Confucia*nism* and Tao*ism* does not identify an institutional organization of religion (as is the case for such terms as Juda*ism,* Hindu*ism,* and Buddh*ism* in other cultures), but indicates a pattern of cultural influence—a way of thinking and acting. Nevertheless, the Taoist and Confucian traditions made important contributions both to the life of the people and to the organized religions of Shinto and Buddhism. Confucian influence played an explicit role in the religious and ethical foundation of the government and shaped general conceptions of social relations. Taoist influence in Japan did not constitute a distinct body of material, but was associated with the complex set of beliefs and customs received from China, sometimes in the guise of Buddhist practices, sometimes in the form of the government bureau controlling the calendar and techniques of divination. Eventually these general Chinese features and specific Taoist elements became integrated into "Japanese" beliefs and customs.

CONFUCIANISM: EXPLICIT CHINESE INFLUENCE ON STATE AND SOCIETY

It is not surprising that Confucianism had a great impact in early Japan. The early Japanese viewed Confucianism as the guiding light of the entering Chinese culture, which they held in high esteem. "Confucius" is the Latinized form of the name of the Chinese thinker K'ung Ch'iu (Kong Qiu, 551–479 B.C.E) who built upon earlier Chinese thought to develop his own teaching, centered in personal virtue and social reform. "Confucianism" is the general term used to describe the system of thought, educational institutions, and ritual practices developed in China over the centuries by later followers and the government.[2] The Confucianism that was transmitted to Japan was the rationale and practices of China's centralized state and its bureaucracy.

The initial role of Confucianism in Japan was to provide a model for organizing the fledgling state. The great Japanese leader Prince Shotoku (573–621 C.E.) is credited with recognizing the true principles of Confucianism in the "Constitution" of seventeen articles attributed to him. Buddhist influence is found in this document, but its main rationale is Confucian political and ethical thought. Indeed, the opening statement of the first clause reads: "Harmony is to be valued," a direct borrowing from the *Analects* (the collection of Confucius's teachings).[3] In short, Confucianism helped provide a moral basis for the state, encouraging government officials to work in harmony for the good of the central government. The Japanese, seeking an effective means to unify their country around a centralized authority, found a powerful rationale in the Confucian notion of social harmony: the ruler rules justly; the ministers administer honestly; and, most important, the country and its people are united in obedience and loyalty to the emperor. The Constitution attributed to Shotoku, as well as other adaptations of Chinese bureaucracies and codes, supported the Japanese emperor as a true Son of Heaven—the Chinese notion of a heavenly ordained ruler. This idea reinforced the native Japanese notion of the divine character of the Japanese emperor (by virtue of his descent from the Sun Goddess Amaterasu).

When Confucianism entered Japan as an ideology (set of ideas) and formal institutions, it was more than a thousand years removed from the actual person Confucius, and it had developed into a political philosophy dominating much of Chinese culture and society, especially intellectual elites and the ruling class. At this time Japanese leaders welcomed Confucian institutions as part of their general intentions of adopting Chinese models of government, thought, and religion (primarily Buddhism) in order to unify the people within a centralized state.

The first formal attempt to organize the Japanese state along Chinese lines is seen in the Taika ("Great Change") era of 645 to 710. Confucianism came to permeate the structure of the government and official codes (such as the Taiho Code of 701). This code included measures for a "university" and provincial schools along Chinese lines; "A major function of these official institutions of learning was identified as the twice-annual observance of the *sekiten* [worship] rite of Confucius."[4] State rites for Confucius were held in Japan for the first time in 701; subsequently the rites were not performed regularly, but were practiced during times when the state was most receptive to Chinese influence. Nevertheless, the Japanese not only adopted, but also adapted, this Confucian rite.[5] For example, in the Japanese observance of these state rituals, after the performance of rites honoring Confucius, a "palace exposition" was held in the imperial palace. Similar practices were found in China, but if the two ceremonies are compared, "the ritual deference accorded the Japanese emperor . . . significantly exceeds that accorded the Chinese emperor," and the Japanese setting for the ceremony "seems intended symbolically to reinforce the transcendence of the Japanese emperor over his Confucian scholars."[6]

This highlights a major difference in the notions of political leadership in the two countries. In China, the rationale was that Heaven appointed the ruler by bestowing a "heavenly mandate"; this also meant that Heaven could withdraw the mandate from a corrupt dynasty in order to give it to a new dynasty. In Japan, the notion of the emperor was grounded in the sacred mythology of divine descent, which established the imperial line as a permanent institution—and denied the possibility of a new dynasty. In effect, Japan borrowed Confucian ideology to lend moral support to a divinely ordained, hereditary Japanese institution: Confucianism added to but did not fundamentally alter the nature of the imperial line. (A sharp contrast is presented by neighboring Korea, where the adoption of Confucianism was more influential, and more central, in shaping its premodern society.)

One of the major purposes of the Chinese pattern of a "university" and provincial schools was the training of officials for government service, and for a short time in Japan the Confucian model of civil service examinations was adopted, but it soon became more of a formality than a measure of talent and merit. Government positions and leadership in early Japan depended more on aristocratic birth than on academic achievement. But, the significance of Confucianism in Japanese history goes far beyond formal, official institutions and practices. Although Confucianism did not constitute a separate religion, it became a vital part of the Japanese heritage.[7] Confucianism came to be instilled in the minds of the learned class by means of an educational system based on study of the Chinese classics, and it made a valuable contribution in encouraging scholarship.

In early Japan, Confucian notions also played a crucial role in the fostering of social attitudes and the reinforcement of social institutions. Confucian thought supported a hierarchically arranged class society and compliance to this order. The "harmony" that the Confucian rationale praised was peaceful cooperation between benevolent rulers and obedient people. According to the Confucian model, just as Earth is subordinate to Heaven, so the ruled are subordinate to the ruler: there is a cosmic order that sets the pattern for the social order. Increasingly, Confucian ideals provided the main ethical model for social action, which was interpreted as prescribing loyalty to specific social groups.

One of the most important Confucian social virtues adopted in Japan was filial piety, which linked the development of human virtue with rites honoring family ancestors. In this case, too, a borrowed ethical model was used to reinforce and expand preexisting Japanese notions and practices related to the family. Since prehistoric times, the Japanese had revered the dead, and they came to accept the Confucian notion of filial piety, both to idealize and actualize the custom. (At the same time, they used Buddhist memorial rites to sanctify the practice.) Extended families or lineages had been important before the arrival of Confucianism, but eventually most social groups tended to internalize the rationale of filial piety and loyalty. The families of common people drew much of their strength and identity from the fact that they participated as economic units in activities such as farming, but gradually they came to *understand* their identity through Confucian notions. Later, in medieval times, the warrior came to see his relationship to his lord as a combination of duty and privilege defined by absolute loyalty.[8] When Confucianism reentered Japanese history as Neo-Confucianism about the sixteenth century, it became more directly related to government policy, and its notions of self-cultivation became a more personal philosophy of life.[9] (This development will be discussed in Chapter 14.)

From early history to recent times, one can see reminders of this hierarchical authority used as a rationale for political policies and economic practices. Both Prince Shotoku's "Constitution" of the seventh century and Emperor Meiji's Constitution of the late nineteenth century were handed down on the initiative of the ruler. In Anglo-Saxon history, there are important precedents of the people *demanding* their rights from the monarch, the most famous example recorded in the thirteenth century Magna Carta. In Japan, there have been some periods of peasant uprisings and protests, but usually the people have waited for the imperial rescript or the military ruler's command.[10] Especially during the modernization and military campaigns of the past century, there was an explicit identity of a man's filial piety to his father, his absolute loyalty to the emperor, and his supreme sacrifice for his country. The government has taken the initiative in telling the people what they must do, and the people usually have complied.[11] Some scholars have noted that there was a tendency to emphasize loyalty even more than filial piety in the adaptation of Confucian ideas to Japanese society. Confucianism was not responsible for the creation of these social attitudes and institutions; rather, such facts demonstrate how well suited Confucian thought was to conditions in Japan and how easily it could legitimate existing patterns (and even justify new government policy).

By the Tokugawa and Meiji periods, beginning in the seventeenth century and extending into the twentieth, the notion of filial piety became synonymous with being a good child and a good Japanese citizen. Confucian ideas became closely tied to the process of growing up, maintaining a strong family, and becoming a member of society. In this manner Confucian ideals gradually have been woven into the fabric of Japanese society as models of filial piety and loyalty that tend to be taken for granted rather than being consciously linked to Chinese tradition and Confucianism.

TAOISM: IMPLICIT CHINESE
INFLUENCE ON BELIEFS AND RITUALS

Taoism entered Japan about the same time as Confucianism, within the wave of Chinese culture that swept over the capital and nobility, and gradually filtered down to the common people. In China, Taoism's complex philosophical and religious character, and its close relationship to other aspects of court ritual and popular practice, have made it difficult to define as a distinct tradition. Not only in China, but also in early Japan and even in the modern West, "Taoism" has proven to be an elusive subject—its importance is recognized, but it has been hard to identify its central character and separate it from other aspects of Chinese thought and culture.

Scholars in ancient China, classifying Chinese literature and thought, dealt with the problem of treating Taoism and related movements by creating two categories, the philosophical school of the *tao* (*Tao-chia* or *Daojia*) and the religion of the *tao* (*Tao-chiao* or *Daojiao*). Philosophical Taoism *(Tao-chia)* was treated as the mystical and speculative writings of two seminal works: the *Tao Te Ching (Daodejing,* written by the legendary Lao Tsu or Laozi, whose name is also given as the title of this work) and *Chuang Tzu (Zhuangzi,* the work known by the name of its author). By contrast, Religious Taoism has been seen as the religious groups organized for the worship of deities (including the *tao* itself and the deified Lao Tsu) and the performance of various rituals.

However, as is often the case with both ancient and modern scholarly distinctions, these two terms were not really neutral and value-free. The way the terms were framed (especially the way they have been used in modern times), Philosophical Taoism is the "true" or "pure" or "original" Taoism, and Religious Taoism is looked down upon as what Philosophical Taoism had degenerated into— corrupt movements and superstitious practices.[12]

If we move abruptly from ancient China to contemporary times, we find the identity of Taoism still not resolved, and perhaps even more complex. At least three views of Taoism vie with one another today. First is the ancient Chinese distinction between the "philosophical texts" of the *tao* and the "religious teachings" of the *tao,* a view held by some Chinese, Japanese, and Western scholars, although this viewpoint is being questioned and reexamined.[13] Second is the Western popular view of Taoism, which is interested only in the philosophical texts of the *Tao Te Ching* and *Chuang Tzu,* seeing them as an Eastern answer to the Western existential quest. In this context, the word "Tao" (somewhat like the Buddhist term "Zen") has become synonymous with existential truth and self-realization.[14] Third is the view of a recent generation of scholars who have advanced the study of Taoism as a religious tradition in its own right. These scholars have rejected ancient Chinese and some modern Western views of Taoism that favor philosophical thought over religious practice, and they have described and interpreted beliefs and practices of Taoism's movements and organizations. In doing so they have attempted to trace both the historical relationship of Taoism to the general Chinese heritage and also the beliefs and practices shared by Taoism and Chinese culture, while insisting on the identity of Taoism (or "Taoist religion") as a distinct tradition (with its own clergy, scriptures, gods, and so on) in order "to distinguish it from popular religion."[15] These scholars, still vigorously arguing over the exact dating and definition of Taoism in China, have helped us see how important Taoism—in all its religious diversity—was in China, and also how much it contributed to Japanese culture and religion.

This recent generation of scholars has presented various interpretations of Taoism in China, and it is to be expected that there are also various alternatives for viewing Taoism within Japanese religion. In spite of that, there is consensus on two major points. First, "The presence of Taoism in Japanese culture has as such never been a question."[16] Second, "The Taoist religion was never officially introduced and never established any clerical organisation in Japan."[17] In other words, Taoism, which never existed in Japan as a separate, organized religion, nevertheless has exerted a significant influence upon Japanese life and thought through the presence of Taoist elements. Between the consensus on these two certainties are the more troublesome questions of how to define and understand Taoism, and how to treat the "Taoist elements" that found their way to Japan.

Resolving the major issues of the identification, dating, and definition of Taoism as a distinct Chinese tradition will have to be handled by the specialists on Taoism. For our purposes here—the study of Japanese religion—two points are important. First—looking just at Japan—although Taoist specialists have their own interests in separating the Taoist religion from court observances and popular practices in China (and in Japan), for our purpose of understanding Japanese religion it is best to see all these Chinese importations in their close interrelationships. The course of history in early Japan reveals a process of free borrowing and mixing of numerous items of continental culture: the dominant tendency was to accept Taoist and other Chinese beliefs and practices (and also Buddhist usages) as part of the general influence from China, and then to incorporate them into the thought and practice of Japanese religion. Second—from a comparative perspective—it is interesting to note that the role of Taoism presents a sharp contrast in the cultures of Korea and Japan. Korea, possibly due to its close geographical connection to China, not only received a much stronger influence from Confucianism, but also a much more conspicuous contribution from Taoist religion. "Taoist religion" as such never existed in Japan, but in Korea there was a long tradition of ordained Taoists, Taoist monasteries, and also Taoist formal rituals and scriptures.[18]

"Taoist elements" entered Japan together with court traditions, general Chinese culture, Buddhism, and even Chinese folk religion, and must be seen as an aspect of the overall Chinese contribution to Japanese culture. Taoist elements colored almost every dimension of the Japanese government and life in general. In addition to the "philosophy" of the *Tao Te Ching* and *Chuang Tzu,* Taoist elements were closely related to cosmology and other teachings (such as *yin* and *yang*[19]) and were associated with divination (*I Ching* or *Yijing*), the calendar, astronomy, astrology, geomancy *(feng shui),* and even medicine (especially as techniques for longevity and immortality). Recent scholarship has suggested sorting Taoism and Taoist elements into three types: "first a part of Chinese traditional thinking in general" (such as *yin-yang* thought and *I Ching* divination), which is not Taoism as such; second, the ideas "including the ancient Taoist philosophy" of the *Tao Te Ching* and *Chuang Tzu,* and associated notions of immortality and longevity, which can be called "'proto-Taoist'"; and "Third, Taoism is an organized religion that developed in the Chinese middle ages," such as the Koshin cult.[20] Because these aspects of Taoism and Taoist elements are too diverse to treat here, we select for purposes of illustration one example of Taoist elements as Chinese traditional thinking—the Onmyoryo—and briefly mention the influence of Taoism in the form of the Koshin cult.

In Japan, the most conspicuous institutional role of Taoist elements as Chinese traditional thinking is found in the Japanese government's seventh-century adoption of a Bureau of Divination, the Onmyoryo, patterned after procedures at the Chinese imperial court.[21] Its responsibility was to regulate divination, astrology, and the calendar for the court. The Japanese bureau differed from its Chinese prototypes, because in early China, "the religious functions of diviners and such were separate from the secular operations of observing the skies, the weather, . . . and making the calendar"; by contrast, "The Yin-yang Bureau [Onmyoryo] of Japan combined under it the observation of the heavens, the recording and interpreting of heavenly movements, signs, and portents, the use of yin-yang techniques of divination, . . . geomancy . . ., calendar calculation, and timekeeping."[22]

To understand the Onmyoryo and its great significance we have to recognize the complex of Chinese thought on which it was based. A clue to this thought is found in the name of the bureau, Onmyoryo. The word "*onmyo*" is the Japanese pronunciation for the Chinese term "*yin-yang*," so this institution is literally the "*yin-yang* bureau" *(ryo)*. The bureau's specialists had comparable titles: *onmyohakase* (yin-yang "doctors") and *onmyoshi* (yin-yang "practitioners"). This pair of key philosophical terms, important in the earliest Chinese notions of an organic universe, and later shared by both Confucianism and Taoism (and also Buddhism) refers to two complementary categories. All particular phenomena within the universe can be either *yin* or *yang,* and their presence and arrangement can be in balance or out of balance. *Yin* is the passive, feminine; it is associated with darkness, cold, and even numbers. *Yang* is the active, masculine; it is associated with brightness, heat, and odd numbers.

In ancient China, *yin-yang* was one of a larger set of cosmological theories that were used to account for everything that exists and occurs within the universe. The notion of *yin-yang* polarity became inseparably linked to another cosmological theory, the five "elements" or phases, before both were transmitted to Japan (along with other Chinese culture).[23] In this manner of "categorical" thinking, the interaction of *yin* and *yang* produces matter, which consists of five phases—wood, fire, earth, metal, and water. These phases always act in relationship to each other (and even transform from one phase to another). These and other categories were linked to form a unified cosmology. The forces of *yin* and *yang* and the five phases interact not only in space, but also in time. In short, this way of thinking presupposes a living universe made up of opposing or complementary forces. Ideally these forces can be harmonized. If they get out of balance, the result is disharmony and catastrophe. (The popular practice of siting or arranging buildings, especially homes, according to these principles—*feng-shui* in Chinese—is usually known in English as "geomancy," divination about the earth or the world.)

Early Chinese notions of the cosmos are more complex than can be treated here, but there is no need to trace all the philosophical details because the Japanese of early times "were not so interested in the philosophical and theoretical aspects" of this teaching, but rather "eagerly adopted the study of heavenly patterns and phenomena, the observation of weather and portents, techniques of geomancy, and various methods of divination in order to protect the lives and ensure the prospects of royalty and nobility."[24] What attracted the Japanese to these notions was not so much their abstract theories such as *yin* and *yang,* as the practical benefits of the methods of divination and exorcism based on the notions.

In early Japan, the role of the Bureau of Divination was to make sure the order of government and society conformed to the cosmic order, paying particular attention to natural events that could be read as omens or portents by *yin-yang* "doctors" or "practitioners." Therefore it was only natural for the Bureau of Divination to regulate the calendar so that human time would correspond to cosmic time. The bureau itself, like some of the other eighth-century attempts to adopt Chinese governmental models, was not long-lived. But just as Confucianism made a lasting social and educational contribution without continuing formal institutions and practices (such as the civil service exams and the spring and fall state rites for Confucius), so Taoist elements left an indelible imprint on Japanese culture without maintaining the institution of the Bureau of Divination.

This bureau and its "doctors" and "practitioners" disappeared, but they gave way to popular "masters" of *yin-yang* who spread the worldview and customs of this Chinese cosmology beyond the court to the common people, such that they became inseparable from and indispensable to spiritual life. This way of thinking and its practice came to be known as *onmyodo* (literally the "*yin-yang* way"), "the collective Japanese name for various methods of divination, originally based on the Chinese theories of *yin* and *yang*, ... the 'five elements'..., and the influence thereof in the natural and human spheres."[25] Even in its early stages, "Japanese *onmyodo* was distinguished from its Chinese models by the extent to which it incorporated other arts of divination, natural science, and what were probably native forms of magic."[26] Some of these forms of divination (such as the use of the *I Ching*[27]) apparently were practiced even before the formation of the Bureau of Divination, and after its demise, they were continued within some schools of Shinto and by Buddhist priests and popular practitioners. These beliefs and customs are pervasive in Japanese culture from ancient times right down to the present.

The best example of such enduring influence is the calendar. The introduction of the Chinese calendar, was of great importance to Japanese religious history, for it seems that earlier the Japanese had only a seasonal calendar. The Chinese calendar, adopted and modified in folk religion and Shinto (and previously incorporated in Chinese Buddhism), carried with it a host of cosmological theories and beliefs.[28] Although the official Bureau of Divination had a relatively short history, its legacy blended with a treasure trove of Chinese astrological beliefs and divination practices, and eventually became embedded in the life and customs of the common people. Even today, this calendar and its associated beliefs regulate the time and rhythm of much of everyday experience and popular mentality, and people have long forgotten about any Chinese origins.

These beliefs and practices are such an integral part of common knowledge, that many Japanese people today take this "folk wisdom" for granted. For example, the traditional calendar or almanac is usually consulted to avoid an unlucky day and to pick a lucky day for events such as marriages and funerals. Almanacs are sold in large volume around New Year's and are used as handy reference works in many homes. Aspects of geomancy, especially the belief in the northeast as an unlucky direction, still persist. Additionally, the influence of the *I Ching* remains, either through direct consultation of the text or indirectly in the beliefs and customs associated with it. Although some Japanese ridicule such "superstitions," and only a few people are aware of their Chinese or "Taoist" origins, these beliefs and practices are generally followed as time-honored customs not to be lightly ignored.[29]

Fortune-telling of all kinds is popular in Japan. This woman has set up her portable stand in front of a closed bank (whose sign is above her head). On her tablecloth are printed examples of her means of telling fortunes: a Chinese hexagram (two sets of three black lines), plus an ear lobe and a hand. (Tokyo, 1979)

From the Heian period (794–1185) onward, many Chinese beliefs and practices directly or indirectly related to Taoism became a major force in daily life. During this period, Taoist elements influenced Shinto and Buddhism in the shape of formulas, charms, and cosmological theories.[30] Eventually various divinities of Taoism became accepted within both Shinto and Buddhism, almost losing their Taoist identity. Many of the most typical Japanese beliefs about lucky days and lucky directions came from this complex of Chinese thought and Taoist elements. In medieval novels such as the *Tale of Genji,* the movements of the characters ever and again are determined by the stars and the "unlucky directions." Taoist festivals, legends, and cults became woven into the fabric of Japanese life. Taoist immortals of Chinese origin (*hsien* or *xian* in Chinese, *sen* or *sennin* in Japanese) were thought to dwell in the Japanese mountains.

Perhaps the most explicit example of Taoism's influence as an organized religion is seen in the Japanese Koshin cult, an adaptation of the beliefs and celebrations in some Taoist groups in China. In ancient China, especially within Taoist understanding, and as observed by several Taoist religious organizations, there was a particular time of the calendrical cycle marked as the occasion when three worms within the body ascended to inform a celestial deity of the person's sins: to avoid this misfortune and prolong life, people stayed up all night, refrained from sexual relations, and performed rituals. In Japan this day, and a corresponding deity, are called Koshin. Although no Taoist religious organizations were transmitted to Japan, the custom of staying awake on Koshin nights was first observed by the court and aristocracy, and eventually by common people. This cult is typical of Japanese village associations organized to worship specific divinities at regular intervals.[31] Of course, not many people were aware of the Chinese or Taoist origin of this celebration or completely understood the intricacies of the cosmic system associated with it. Nevertheless, Koshin beliefs and celebrations greatly affected their lives.

CONFUCIANISM AND TAOISM
AS JAPANESE TRADITIONS

These two Chinese importations—Confucianism (later Neo-Confucianism) and Taoism—became transformed into Japanese notions and practices. The role of Confucianism is more easily recognized, because it has functioned more explicitly as an official philosophy of the learned class and the state. By contrast, the influence of Taoism and Taoist elements was indirect or implicit and more difficult to recognize (and to separate from general Chinese cultural influence), but can be seen even today in such areas as popular beliefs, divination, and fortune-telling.

As we leave these two Chinese traditions, we may best remember them as both complementary and competing movements. For example, the use of the *I Ching* is a good reminder of how fluid the boundaries are between these two traditions. In China the *I Ching* was claimed as a classic by both Confucian and Taoist schools, and even Buddhists consulted it. In Japan the *I Ching* was accepted as a Chinese classic rather than as the text of a specific religion. In seventh-century Japan, as we have seen, the state was formally organized along Chinese lines, with explicit Confucian influence, and possibly indirect Taoist influence. The moral authority of a Confucian-styled ruler was reinforced with notions of cosmic legitimacy by the Bureau of Divination, which was based on cosmological notions similar to those in the *I Ching;* this ensured that the emperor and government acted in accordance with workings of the cosmos (timing actions to avoid unlucky times and coincide with lucky times). In ancient Japan there was no distinct boundary between Confucian and Taoist traditions in the working of the state. Similarly, in later Japan there has been no black and white distinction in the minds of the people who may use Confucian notions to order social relations and may resort to Chinese beliefs and Taoist practices to regulate their activities. Understanding the contribution of Confucianism and Taoism to Japanese culture helps us appreciate that the role of religion goes far beyond the boundaries of organized religion.

NOTES

1. The character for *tao* or *dao* ("road" or "way") has the Japanese pronunciation of *michi,* or *do* or *to* (as in *butsudo* and Shinto).

2. The terms "Confucianism" and "Confucian" are so broad that they must be applied with care; see Nathan Sivin, "On the Word 'Taoist' as a Source of Perplexity: With Special Reference to the Relations of Science and Religion in Traditional China," *History of Religions,* vol. 17 (1978), pp. 303–31; see pp. 316–17.

3. An excerpt from this Constitution is included my *Religion in the Japanese Experience,* 2d ed., pp. 235–36. Out of the many translations of the *Analects,* one considered a classic is Arthur Waley, trans., *The Analects of Confucius* (London: Allen & Unwin, 1938; reprint ed., New York: Random House, 1966). For translated excerpts and introductions to Confucius and the Confucian tradition, see *Sources of Chinese Tradition,* compiled by Wm. Theodore de Bary and Irene Bloom, 2d ed. (New York: Columbia University, 1999), Chapters 3 and 6. A general treatment of Confucianism as a religious tradition is Rodney Taylor, *The Religious Dimensions of Confucianism* (Albany, NY: State University of New York, 1990). For a critical treatment of the way Westerners have perceived Confucius and interpreted Confucianism, see Lionel M. Jensen, *Manufacturing Confucianism: Chinese Traditions & Universal Culture* (Durham, NC: Duke University, 1997).

4. I. J. McMullen, "The Worship of Confucius in Ancient Japan," in *Religion in Japan: Arrows to Heaven and Earth,* by P. F. Kornicki and I. J. McMullen (Cambridge: Cambridge University, 1996), pp. 39–77. This article surveys both the development of "state Confucianism" and the state rites for Confucius in China (*shidian* in Chinese, *sekiten* in Japanese) and the adoption (and modification) of these rites in early Japan.

5. For a translation of the ritual details of clothing, offerings, and other requirements for the *sekiten,* see Felicia G. Bock, trans. and annotator, *Classical Learning and Taoist Practices in Early Japan: With a Translation of Books XVI and XX of the Engi-Shiki* (Tucson: Center for Asian Studies, Arizona State University, 1985), Occasional Paper No. 17, pp. 49–76.

6. McMullen, "The Worship of Confucius in Ancient Japan," p. 61.

7. For a succinct treatment of Confucianism and its role in Japan, see James McMullen, "Confucianism," *Kodansha Encyclopedia of Japan,* vol. 1, pp. 352–58. For a more complete treatment, especially of the modern period, see Warren W. Smith, Jr., *Confucianism in Modern Japan: A Study of Conservatism in Japanese Intellectual History,* 2d ed. (Tokyo: Hokuseido, 1973).

8. For literary examples of filial piety and loyalty, see Mae J. Smethurst, *Dramatic Representations of Filial Piety: Five Noh in Translation* (Ithaca, NY: Cornell University, 1998).

9. A long-running debate has considered the question of whether Neo-Confucianism can be called "religion." Usually the English term "religion" calls to mind organized religious institutions such as the Catholic church or Protestant denominations. For a discussion of "the Religious Dimensions of Neo-Confucianism," which shifts the question from "religion" as institutions and dogma to "being religious" as "self-transformation and self-transcendence," see Mary Evelyn Tucker, *Moral and Spiritual Cultivation in Japanese Self-Cultivation: The Life and Thought of Kaibara Ekken, 1630–1740[1714]* (Albany, NY: State University of New York, 1989), pp. 6–10, and the citation of other works discussing Confucianism as religion, pp. 362–63.

10. In Japanese society, as in any society, conflict is inevitable; see Najita and Koschmann, eds., *Conflict in Modern Japanese History,* and Reader and Tanabe, eds., *Conflict and Religion in Japan.*

11. In the economic sphere, in modern times large companies have used the traditional idea of loyalty to promote loyalty to senior employees and to the company itself, as a way of organizing and running their businesses. Actual practices, such as lifetime employment, are recent innovations, but they may make use of a much older rationale. See Thomas P. Rohlen, *For Harmony and Strength: Japanese White-Collar Organization in Anthropological Perspective* (Berkeley: University of California, 1979), especially pp. 58–61. An excerpt from this work is included in my *Religion in the Japanese Experience,* 2d ed., pp. 298–304.

12. Anna Seidel attributes the rather late development of Taoist studies in the West, and the disparaging attitudes towards Taoism, as due to the "ideological blind spot" created especially by Christian missionaries to China who were instructed by their Confucian teachers to take a highly "Confucian" and overly rational view of Chinese society. These missionaries "described to their European audience a Chinese civilisation that resembled more the Confucian ideal of an agnostic and well-regulated society than the reality of

Chinese life." See Anna K. Seidel, "Chronicle of Taoist Studies in the West 1950–1990," *Cahiers d'Extreme-Asie,* vol. 5 (1989–1990), pp. 223–47. Jensen, in his *Manufacturing Confucianism* has also pointed to the way Jesuit missionaries to China helped shape the Chinese Confucian scholars' views of a "rational" and "ethical" Confucianism.

13. The first edition of *Sources of Chinese Tradition,* ed. by Wm. Theodore de Bary et al. (New York: Columbia University, 1960), treats Taoism by including only translations of the *Tao Te Ching* and *Chuang Tzu,* and excludes religious aspects of Taoism on the grounds that "the Taoist school itself became more and more a cult of popular religion, . . . absorbing all sorts of popular superstitions and demon lore, until it became an object of ridicule among educated Chinese" (paperback ed., vol. 1, p. 49). The second edition of *Sources of Chinese Tradition,* ed. Wm. Theodore de Bary and Irene Bloom (New York: Columbia University, 1999, vol. 1) features a chapter on Taoist religion (Chapter 14, "Daoist Religion") in addition to Chapter 5, "The Way of Laozi and Zhuangzi." For recent evaluations of these two categories of Taoism, see Nathan Sivin, "On the Word 'Taoist' as a Source of Perplexity"; and Russell Kirkland, "Person and Culture in the Taoist Tradition," *Journal of Chinese Religion,* no. 20 (Fall 1992), pp. 77–90, especially p. 79.

14. Here we do not intend to criticize those Westerners who have accepted Taoism (of any form, philosophical or religious), but merely to indicate that the Western popular view of Taoism (which has produced a huge number of "translations" and interpretations of works such as the *Tao Te Ching*) is in part a development out of the distinction between "pure" Philosophical Taoism and "superstitious" Religious Taoism. For an overview of the Western acceptance and adaptation of Taoism, see John James Clarke, *The Tao of the West: Western Transformations of Taoist Thought* (London: Routledge, 2000).

15. For a convenient, detailed overview see Anna Seidel, "Chronicle of Taoist Studies in the West 1950–1990"; she calls the distinction between *tao-chia* and *tao-chiao* "incompatible with historical reality" (p. 328). In general, modern studies on Taoism have been sharply divided by two kinds of scholars with different interests, and the materials and approaches each set of scholars used to study Taoism. Those scholars, primarily Sinologists, who are interested in the "civilization" of elites and who have focused on philological and textual studies of the writings before the Han dynasty (202 B.C.E.–220 C.E.), have tended to favor a "pure" philosophical Taoism and disparage what they see as the corrupt and superstitious development of religious Taoism. On the other hand, those scholars, especially specialists in Taoism, who are interested in popular culture as well as elite "civilization," and who have focused on the vast Taoist canon from post-Han times, and have also adopted a more anthropological view of accepting religious practices in their actual living circumstances, have rejected as false the view of an original or "pure" philosophical Taoism. These specialists in Taoist studies, by accepting the practices of living Taoism, have advanced the understanding and appreciation of Taoism as a religious tradition in its own right.

16. Livia Kohn, "Taoism in Japan: Positions and Evaluations," *Cahiers d'Extreme-Asie,* vol. 8 (1995), pp. 389–412; see p 390. This is the most comprehensive treatment of the subject to date.

17. Seidel, "Chronicle of Taoist Studies," p. 301.

18. Korea, as we have seen, was more heavily influenced by the Confucian and Taoist traditions which it passed on to Japan. Korea also played a key role in introducing Buddhism to Japan, but in this third case, Korea's contribution, reinforced by direct transmission of Buddhism from China, resulted in lasting institutions: Buddhism became the major organized religion in Japan.

19. The notion of *yin* and *yang,* and also *feng shui,* will be discussed later in connection with the Bureau of Divination (Onmyoryo).

20. Kohn, "Taoism in Japan," pp 390, 393. An excerpt describing the Koshin cult is found in my *Religion in the Japanese Experience,* 2d ed., pp. 120–25.

21. This bureau's name is also written as Ommyoryo, or On'yoryo. For a translation of the original Japanese legislation defining this bureau, see Sir George Sansom, "Early Japanese Law and Administration," *Transactions of the Asiatic Society of Japan,* Second Series, vol. 9 (1932), p. 81.

22. Bock, *Classical Learning and Taoist Practices in Early Japan,* pp 9–10. Bock, a specialist in early Shinto, uses the term "Taoist practices" for the Onmyoryo and other beliefs and practices borrowed from China. Two specialists in Taoism prefer to call these practices "Chinese traditions cultivated at every Chinese court," and "generic parts of the Chinese worldview" rather than Taoism. See Seidel, "Chronicle of Taoist Studies," p. 301; and Kohn, "Taoism in Japan," p. 391. Whatever they are called, there is no disagreement that such practices made a major contribution to Japanese life and religion.

23. For a convenient overview of these two notions of *yin-yang* and the five phases *(wu-hsing),* see John S. Major, "Yin-yang wu-hsing," *Encyclopedia of Religion,* vol. 15, pp. 515–16.

24. Bock, *Classical Learning and Taoist Practices,* p. 10.

25. Edward Kamens, "Onmyodo," *Encyclopedia of Religion,* vol. 11, pp. 76–79; see p. 76.

26. Ibid., p. 77.

27. This work has become popular in the West, especially in counter-culture and New Age circles; for an English translation, see Richard Wilhelm and Cary F. Baynes, trans., *The I Ching or Book of Changes* (Princeton: Princeton University, 1967).

28. For a general picture of the Japanese calendar, see articles in the *Kodansha Encyclopedia of Japan:* "Calendar, Dates, Time," vol. 1, pp. 229–32, by Herschel Webb; "Jikkan Junishi," vol. 4, pp. 55–57, by Tomio Fujita; and "Ommyodo," vol. 6, p. 103, by Minoru Sonoda.

29. For an overview of Japanese fortune-telling, divination, and the horoscope, see Thomas Crump, *The Japanese Numbers Game: The Use and Understanding of Numbers in Modern Japan* (London: Routledge, 1992), pp. 76–95. For a brief overview of current divination practices and the results of a survey of 300 clients at a "divination hall," see Kentaro Suzuki, "Divination in Contemporary Japan: A General Overview and an Analysis of Survey Results," *Japanese Journal of Religious Studies,* vol. 22, no. 3–4 (Fall 1995), pp. 249–66.

30. One example of such Taoist influence is the Taoist "spell" called *kuji* ("nine characters"); its origin in China and its transmission to Japan and use by various religious groups is detailed in David Waterhouse, "Notes on the *Kuji,*" in *Religion in Japan: Arrows to Heaven and Earth,* ed. P. F. Kornicki and I. J. McMullen (Cambridge: Cambridge University, 1996), pp. 1–38.

31. For a description of the Koshin cult, see my *Religion in the Japanese Experience,* 2d ed., pp. 120–25.

7

❧

Folk Religion: Religiosity Outside Organized Religion

Every literate culture has what can be called a "little tradition" as well as a "great tradition." The great tradition within a culture such as Japan's is the written tradition formally recorded and consciously used by major institutions such as the state and organized religion. The little tradition is the unwritten sets of customs transmitted orally within contexts such as family, village, and occupation.[1] Organized religion (Shinto, Buddhism, Taoism, and Confucianism) is conspicuous because of its writings, priests, liturgies, shrines, and temples. In Japan, however, much religion is practiced outside formal institutions. Because of its informal character, folk religion does not lend itself to simple identification and historical tracing; nevertheless, this little tradition is an important part of religious experience, particularly in the premodern period. We look at folk religion and the little tradition not to set it apart as an isolated unit, but to make sure we do not neglect an important part of the Japanese worldview.[2]

ASPECTS OF JAPANESE FOLK RELIGION

In Japan there are at least three aspects of folk religious practices: (1) native, or indigenous, folk religion, (2) popular religion, and (3) local customs. Native, or indigenous, folk religion is the sum of all the unorganized beliefs and practices of ancient Japanese religion. These elements often became overlaid with the structures of organized religion, but they existed prior to the importation or formation of organized traditions. One might say that indigenous folk religion "filtered up" into Shinto and Buddhism. An example of indigenous folk religion is the rituals associated with the growing of rice, especially rice-transplanting celebrations, which existed from Yayoi times and were never fully incorporated into organized religion.

Popular religion consists of unofficial expressions of organized religion among laypeople. In this sense, popular religion can be found within any organized religion in any culture (whether it is Christianity in North America, or Buddhism in Japan). Although a religion like Buddhism has its own doctrinal, ritual, and ecclesiastical orthodoxy, it undergoes considerable reformulation as it is accepted and practiced by the masses. From a scholarly or ecclesiastical viewpoint, popular Buddhism may diverge from orthodox formulas, but the aim of popular religion is to provide direct access to spiritual resources in the language and style of the people, not to preserve the orthodox forms of elite culture. Popular religion generally can be described as the result of organized religion filtering down to the people. An example of popular religion is the neighborhood club (*ko*) that meets once a month to venerate a divinity, often a Buddhist divinity. Such a group and its activities may borrow elements from Buddhism, but they are expressed and handed down by ordinary men and women in their own homes, and are maintained without the direct utilization of the priests, writings, and temples of organized Buddhism.

Local customs are distinctive regional and communal practices that usually combine features of time-honored folk religion and popular religion. From ancient times, religious practices were heavily influenced by the dominant legends, customs, and activities of the surrounding region. Even Shinto and Buddhism lack the centralized uniformity found in Roman Catholicism and Protestant denominations, allowing Shinto in particular to develop distinctive local practices. This aspect of folk religion contributes much local color to Japanese religion. An example of such a local usage is the preservation of a mythical tale or legend associated with only one region (such as the visit of a specific *kami* to an area in ancient times). The tale may be memorialized in a local shrine or temple and often is dramatized in an annual village festival. Sometimes the occasion for a local custom is a universal religious event, such as the "Buddhist" festival of the dead, *bon,* but there are local variations on the manner of celebration, such as special village gatherings and specially prepared foods.

Ancient folk religion, popular religion, and local customs cannot be sharply separated from one another, for they form the living fabric of the everyday practice of religion in traditional Japan. For example, folk tales can be found in each as a kind of informal, unwritten "scripture" that unifies and preserves religion. It would also be difficult to separate the aspects of folk religion from organized religion, because they mutually influence each other to such a great degree. In fact, folk religion is so important that one scholar has emphasized that "in Japan the little tradition is the great tradition."[3] In premodern times, folk religion was the main channel of expression for religious beliefs and practices, especially in the countryside and in farm villages.

In more recent times folk religious beliefs and activities have become severely abbreviated because of economic and social changes. The expansion of cities and commerce in the late medieval period and the increasing dominance of an urban-industrial way of life after 1868 greatly disturbed conditions in rural villages. These changes drew people from the countryside to the city and generally shifted attention from the agricultural lifestyle of traditional Japan to the economic activities of the cities. Thus our description of folk religion here refers generally to traditional patterns prominent until the late nineteenth century, and still found in some instances today.

However, the loss of older cultural forms—for example, so-called "traditional" folk tales and festivals—has not resulted in a vacuum. Actually, as traditional folk crafts and arts (as well as folk performances and celebrations) have been about to slip into extinction, they have been revived by private groups and governmental bodies attempting to preserve what they perceive as traditional Japan. Museums all across Japan, including some commercial ventures, claim to bring the modern nontraditional Japanese in touch with what today they view as traditional Japan. In any country, the memory and reconstruction of the past (such as the tourist attraction of reconstructed "colonial" Williamsburg, Virginia, in the United States) usually invokes an idealized version of what contemporary people would like to think once existed. Part of the Japanese agenda in preserving the traditional is to reshape the Japanese identity by constructing a uniquely Japanese folk heritage. Whatever the motives of this "retraditionalizing," the Japanese people have certainly exhibited a widespread interest in such folk customs; these customs are featured regularly in the mass media, especially in television documentaries, and are often broadcast live from remote sites.[4]

Although part of the new folk tradition is revival of the older and "unique" (or distinctive) Japanese tradition, perhaps the most remarkable contemporary innovation in the popular arena is the new mythology of the mass media, which rapidly is becoming an international or cosmopolitan tradition. Probably the most widely read material in Japan today is comic books, with "niche" comics for every age and gender, from young teen girls to middle-aged businessmen. Some of the more fantastic stories have found their way into animated cartoons and video games, a lucrative export market. From the now classic monster Godzilla to the heroes and villains of video games, these Japanese creations have become part of the late night, Saturday morning, and leisure time fantasy world of an international mythology. Japanese inventiveness and innovation can be seen even in Tokyo Disneyland, which is as much a product of native Japanese culture as it is the intrusion of a foreign culture.[5] These modern developments are good reminders that tradition is never a static element that may disappear, but rather is an active process inevitably altered as it is received and transmitted. In fact, the literal meaning of the word "tradition" is "that which is handed down," or transmitted. The main difference in contemporary Japanese mythology is that it is being transmitted to a global audience while it is being handed down to the next generation of Japanese.

FOLK RELIGION IN FAMILY, VILLAGE, AND OCCUPATION

Just as there is no single religion called "Japanese religion," so there has never been a simple entity called "Japanese folk religion." Rather, folk religion exists informally in family, village, and occupation. Each setting, in its own way, participates in the little tradition and serves to transmit it to the next generation, both by word of mouth and by direct example.

The family is an important religious institution for both organized and folk practices. The traditional home is a center of Buddhist worship by virtue of the presence of the *butsudan* (Buddhist altar for the ancestors); it is also a center of Shinto worship through the presence of the *kamidana* ("god-shelf," or Shinto altar).[6] But the family and home do not gain their religious significance merely by borrowing from organized religion; rather, they have a religious character that stands apart from organized religion. In the words of one scholar, "Certain types of psychological security found in a relationship to a personal God in the West are found only in relation to the actual family in Japan."[7] Traditional Japanese identified membership in the family with a sense of belonging in the world. The family as a religious institution has at least three levels: (1) the ancestors, semidivine figures who are memorialized and grant blessings; (2) the living, who perform memorial rites and receive blessings; and (3) the unborn, who are the link between the ancestors and the living, and the future. Although the religious importance of the family was never fully spelled out by organized religion, it was communicated and perpetuated in the loose set of beliefs and customs known as folk religion.

A New Year's decoration in the center of the grill of a Tokyo taxi. After a week or so, the decorations are removed. (New Year's week, 1980)

Religious activities centering in the home had their own rhythmic unity. Traditionally most families practiced memorial rites for the family dead, especially on the monthly and annual anniversaries of the death of immediate family ancestors. Daily offerings of food might be placed in front of the *butsudan* or the *kamidana*. In addition, there were important annual celebrations at the home, such as New Year's. Without any priestly help, the family consecrated the house for New Year's. Family members placed a pine branch on the gate or erected a pine tree in the yard. In the entryway a special New Year's decoration of cooked rice was customary. In the countryside there were distinctive New Year's foods, such as specially prepared New Year's soup and pounded glutinous rice. In olden times it was the custom to purify the house at the end of the year by a thorough cleaning, including the use of salt and sacred water; in many locales the fire in the hearth was extinguished and a new fire was obtained from a nearby temple or shrine. The celebration of New Year's is only one example of the family's informal religious heritage.

The village is a larger setting in which folk religion is expressed and handed down. People living in a village or sometimes in a larger region share a special myth or legend that has been preserved and passed down and is celebrated by one or more groups, often in connection with distinctive customs. One legend may serve as an illustration of this aspect of folk religion. In one locale of northern Japan there is a legend that in ancient times the people were bothered by a poisonous insect. Eventually, the insect was driven away by the performance of a ritual in which a mock insect made of straw was burned. According to one version, an imperial prince first began the ritual; in another version, the ritual was revealed to the daughter of a Shinto priest. (In folk religion there is not always one "true" version, as there tends to be in a written scripture.) Every year the ritual is performed again; but before the mock insect is burned, sections of straw rope around the mock insect are thrown among the youth of the village, who try to grab a piece. The pieces of rope are said to represent the "bones" of the insect. They are taken home by the youths, who hang them under the eaves of their houses. Not only is the ritual said to drive away insects, but the rope sections are believed to prevent fires in the homes where they are displayed.

This is but one example of many local beliefs and practices that endure and touch people's lives with little help from organized religion. Almost every village in every district makes claim to some more or less distinctive legend and its celebration. The legend may connect a mythological figure to the locale and an annual festival, or it may have to do with the economic life of the region. Often special crafts and distinctive foods are associated with such legends.[8]

Folk beliefs and practices were also closely tied to occupations. Fishermen with small wooden boats had special rites to drive out the spirit of the trees from a newly built boat, at the same time invoking a spirit of the sea. A small altar was often placed by the mast of the boat, and offerings were made at the altar. The spirit of the sea helped protect against drowning and gave large catches, but was offended by the presence of women and Buddhist priests, who usually were not allowed aboard the boats. Traditional lumbermen had their own rites for pacifying the spirit of a tree they cut down, and they observed various taboos within their mountain lodges. Certain words offended the tree spirits, and while they were in the mountains the lumbermen had to use a special "mountain language" when referring to the tabooed terms.

A widespread folk tradition among rice farmers was the notion that the *kami* of the rice field alternated with the *kami* of a nearby hill or mountain. Each spring the mountain *kami* descended the mountain and became the rice-field *kami* for the duration of the growing season; in the fall they ascended in the smoke of the rice straw to become once more the mountain *kami*. A number of regions have special celebrations in spring and fall to mark the movement of the *kami*. Rice farmers in other regions believe that the rice-field *kami* resides in the family home during the winter. Most folk beliefs related to occupations have been strongest in the old traditional forms of work and have tended to weaken or die out as work has become organized as mass production in large factories. Even in the midst of contemporary factories and corporations, however, some folk elements survive and are adapted to these apparently secular settings.[9]

THE INDIVIDUAL AND FOLK RELIGION

The individual learned the "little tradition" informally, absorbing it in his or her family life and village activities, and even during work. People might participate in folk religion within all three of these contexts; yet there were other ways in which folk religion spoke directly to them in the course of their lives. One example was the notion of *yakudoshi,* unlucky or dangerous years of age for a person; these beliefs are part of the heritage of Onmyodo, although most people are unaware of this historical background. These unlucky years were ages 25 and 42 for men, and ages 19 and 33 for women. One had to be very careful during these critical years, and it was a very bad omen if during one's unlucky year an acquaintance of the same age became sick or died. To offset the ominous character of the critical age, a person was supposed to be diligent in attending festivals and in using protective amulets. The reverse of *yakudoshi* is *toshi iwai,* or years of celebration: attaining one's sixty-first and seventieth year of age was considered lucky and was an occasion for celebration. These beliefs and practices are still followed by many people today.

Not only did folk religion supply beliefs and practices for ordinary individuals, but also it provided specialists who ministered to their religious needs. The most conspicuous of these specialists was the traditional shaman (or medium), usually a blind woman who had undergone extensive training with another shaman and was able to enter a trancelike state and speak with the dead. In some periods shamans were brought under indirect control of organized religion, but most of the time they lived in ordinary homes within villages, carrying out their role of medium upon the request of another individual. Such shamans are still found in Japan today.[10]

The person making the request may be concerned about the well-being of a deceased relative, so he or she visits the shaman with the customary payment for her to act as medium with the dead. The shaman presents an offering to her guardian spirit, recites the liturgy and formulas she learned in her training, and enters into a kind of trance, so that the voice of the dead can speak through her mouth. The conversation between the grieving person and the dead relative is rather formal—how the dead relative is faring in the other world, what offerings might make the spirit of the dead happy. Nevertheless, this religious service, performed outside organized religion, speaks directly to the relationship between the living and dead, one of the most important aspects in all of Japanese religion. The significance of folk religion is demonstrated by this ability to work within the everyday ordinary contexts of daily life and minister directly to the basic religious needs of the people.

The shaman is an important religious practitioner, with prehistoric precedents (and contemporary parallels in Okinawa), but there are other popular religious practitioners who operate outside organized religion. For example, fortunes and fortune-telling span both organized and unorganized activities. A person may inquire about his or her "fortune" at a Shinto shrine or a Buddhist temple: usually, by shaking numbered sticks out of a cylinder and reading a fortune paper corresponding to the number of the stick, or by purchasing a fortune paper (*omikuji*) from a coin vending machine found at most temples and shrines. Or, a person may consult any of the freelance fortune-tellers who set up small stalls on crowded urban sidewalks, usually at night; these

A blind shaman (itako) is communicating with the dead. The shaman is the woman holding the rosary of black beads. The woman who has requested the shaman's services is to her right, holding a handkerchief to her face and stifling her tears as she hears a message from her dead relative. This is an annual festival of late summer near Mount Osore, and most of the people who come are women of the area. The young woman in the background holding a microphone is a student of linguistics from a Tokyo university recording the distinctive dialect used by these shamans. (Mount Osore, 1963)

fortune-tellers use one or more of a variety of techniques for determining a fortune, most of them based on Chinese models. (See illustration, p. 61.) In addition to fortune-tellers, there are other popular practitioners who are similar to shamans or who engage in religious healing.

Folk religion has been treated separately here to highlight its features. In the lives of Japanese people, however, folk religion has blended imperceptibly with organized religion. Just as folk religion often borrowed from organized religion, it was also the case that many popular and folk practices occurred within the general context and even inside the buildings of Shinto and Buddhism. As we will see in the next chapter, this interaction is characteristic of Japanese religion as a whole.

NOTES

1. See Robert Redfield, *Peasant Society and Cultures* (Chicago: University of Chicago, 1956), p. 70. For an application of Redfield's notions of little tradition and great tradition to an example of Japanese religious history, see Ichiro Hori, *Folk Religion in Japan: Continuity and Change,* ed. Joseph M. Kitagawa and Alan L. Miller (Chicago: University of Chicago, 1968), pp. 49–81; an excerpt from Hori's work is included in my *Religion in the Japanese Experience,* 2d ed., pp. 221–25. A recent volume of essays on folk religion is Hitoshi Miyake, *Shugendo: Essays on the Structure of Japanese Folk Religion,* ed. H. Byron Earhart (Ann Arbor: University of Michigan, 2001).

2. There has been criticism of the set of notions of little tradition and great tradition (originally developed by the anthropologist Robert Redfield), and of terms such as "folk religion" and "popular religion," on the grounds that there is no distinct separation between elite/organized religions and folk/informal religiosity. This point is well taken, and we focus on the folk tradition here not to artificially separate it from the larger worldview, but to more clearly recognize the oral, folk, and informal religious heritage in order to make sure it is part of the total religious picture.

3. Winston Davis, *Toward Modernity: Developmental Typology of Popular Religious Affiliations in Japan* (Ithaca, NY: Cornell China-Japan Program, 1977), p. 6.

4. Some scholars have criticized the folklore studies pioneered by authors such as Kunio Yanagita for using folk materials to construct or invent a unified or "unique" Japanese identity that never actually existed. See H. D. Harootunian, "Disciplinizing Native Knowledge and Producing Place: Yanagita Kunio, Origuchi Shinobu, Takata Yasuma," pp. 99–127 in *Culture and Identity: Japanese Intellectuals During the Interwar Years,* ed. J. Thomas Rimer (Princeton: Princeton University, 1990). Such studies remind us that scholarship—and all writing—carries an agenda either open or hidden. Just as the Grimm brothers had their agenda of recording (or "creating") the German spirit in their collection of German folk tales, so, too, have Yanagita and other folklorists advanced their own agenda of describing (or "creating") the picture of a unified Japanese spirit. Our concern in this book is not to promote the ideology (the set of ideas) of Japanese folklorists, but to focus on the beliefs, customs, and practices they collected for our reflection. Part of our own agenda here (insofar as we can recognize our own motives) is to acknowledge the importance of folk and popular elements in Japanese religion, in order to balance the treatment of elite expressions of religion. Or, to return to the language of Redfield, we want to include the "little tradition" as well as the "great tradition." Keeping in mind the potential misunderstandings, we retain the use of the term "folk religion" until a better term is devised to account for these phenomena (or set of facts) found within Japanese religion. For a sample of different

viewpoints on Yanagita and the use of the category "folk," see J. Victor Koschmann et al., eds., *International Perspectives on Yanagita Kunio and Japanese Folklore Studies* (Ithaca, NY: China-Japan Program, 1985).

5. Aviad E. Raz, *Riding the Black Ship: Japan and Tokyo Disneyland* (Cambridge: Harvard University, 1999). In the same way that American children assimilate as "American" characters the Japanese cartoons on Saturday morning, so do the Japanese children who visit Tokyo Disneyland perceive Mickey Mouse as a "Japanese" character. See Raz, p. 160.

6. For religious practices in a "traditional" family and village—from *butsudan* and *kamidana* to marriage and New Year's—see Jeremy and Robinson, *Ceremony and Symbolism in the Japanese Home.*

7. George De Vos, quoted in David W. Plath, "Where the Family of God Is the Family: The Role of the Dead in Japanese Households," *American Anthropologist,* vol. 46, no. 2 (April 1964), p. 307.

8. A whole class of literature, *engi* (or *jisha engi*), includes the legends about the founding of a shrine or temple. These stories, often miraculous tales, are vital connections between the sacred historical past and contemporary religious practice, also serving as links between institutional organization and popular devotion. These *engi,* or legends, are often summarized on sign boards or distributed as printed pamphlets at shrines and temples. See Ian Reader, "Sites and Sights: Temples and Shrines as Centres of Power and Entertainment," in his *Religion in Contemporary Japan* (Honolulu: University of Hawaii, 1991), pp. 134–67, especially pp. 141–49.

9. For religious values and ancestral rites in the white collar setting of a modern bank, see Rohlen, *For Harmony and Strength;* for the spiritual values of artisans and machines in the blue collar setting of a plastics factory and in the food industry, see Dorinne Kondo, *Crafting Selves.* These works are excerpted in my *Religion in the Japanese Experience,* 2d ed., pp. 298–304 and pp. 305–7. For a visual example of folk religion, see my video, "Fuji: Sacred Mountain of Japan," available from the University of Hawai'i.

10. For a description of Japanese shamans, see Carmen Blacker, *The Catalpa Bow: A Study of Shamanistic Practices in Japan* (London: Allen & Unwin, 1963). An excerpt from this work is included in my *Religion in the Japanese Experience,* 2d ed., pp. 129–35.

8

୧৶

Interaction in
the Formation of
Japanese Religion

We have now seen the major traditions—Shinto, Buddhism, Confucianism, Taoism, and folk religion—that contributed to Japanese religious history. After the Nara period, new currents of the older traditions entered Japan, but there were no new major traditions (with the exception of the late arrival of Christianity). By the eighth century, all the dominant forces in the drama of Japanese religious history had made their first appearance, and the stage was set for the formation of a genuinely Japanese religion. Even at this early point, we can see the future course of development. A general consideration of these five traditions will show their interaction in a common religious milieu.

THE INTERACTION OF
RELIGIOUS TRADITIONS

A statement attributed to Prince Shotoku has been used to view the relationship of Shinto, Confucianism, and Buddhism:

> A saying ascribed to Prince Shotoku, the founder of Japanese civilization, compares the three religious and moral systems found in Japan to the root, the stem and branches, and the flowers and fruits of a tree. Shinto is the root embedded in the soil of the people's character and national traditions; Confucianism is seen in the stem and branches of legal institutions, ethical codes, and educational

systems; Buddhism made the flowers of religious sentiment bloom and gave the fruits of spiritual life. These three systems were moulded and combined by the circumstances of the times and by the genius of the people into a composite whole of the nation's spiritual and moral life.[1]

This traditional view of Japanese religion may not have been expressed by Shotoku, but it is quite perceptive.[2] We might add two other traditions to the metaphor without radically changing it—ancient folk religion dating back to prehistoric times and Taoism. We might say that the earliest (or indigenous) tradition is the native soil in which the roots grew, supporting the tree. Similarly, we might say that Taoism is imperceptibly mixed in the sap of the tree, being absorbed into the triad of Buddhism, Confucianism, and Shinto, and even seeping into the surrounding soil. This metaphor, in its expanded version, gives a useful overall picture of the interrelatedness of Japanese religion. (Even popular religion and the New Religions, although not fully developed in this early period, fit well into the same metaphor. Popular religion may be seen as the "leafing out" of the tree into full foliage, whereas the New Religions can be viewed as the new sprouts that emerge after the tree has temporarily died back.)

THE FORMATION OF A DISTINCTIVE JAPANESE RELIGIOUS TRADITION

These traditions mutually contributed to the formation of a distinctive Japanese religious heritage, especially in areas such as ancestor worship, the religious character of the family, and the tie between religion and the nation. Already in prehistoric times there was elaborate veneration of the dead, probably the departed of particular extended families. Shinto was soon relieved of funeral rites by Buddhism, but even today several important Shinto shrines still venerate the spirits of national heroes. Buddhism greatly emphasized veneration of the dead by means of regular memorial rites, just as Confucianism provided the ethical rationale of filial piety. The Chinese calendar or almanac (including Chinese customs and "Taoist elements") contributed notions of lucky and unlucky times for funerals. Therefore, whether we retain the older term "ancestor worship" or adopt a new term such as "veneration of the dead," this typical expression of Japanese religion must be seen as the outgrowth of most of the formative traditions.

A second area, closely related to ancestor worship, is the religious continuity of the family, living and dead. Many important shrines and temples in early Japan were the private sanctuaries of separate clans. Affiliation with Shinto shrines was usually determined either by blood relationship or by geographical boundaries. Families later became linked to a specific Buddhist temple through regular memorials to family ancestors. Confucian teaching generally stressed social harmony and lines of obedience in the family and country at large. Thus all of the formative traditions reinforced the social solidarity of the Japanese people.

A third area these traditions shared was the close link between nation and religion, which has characterized most of Japanese history. The earliest religious tradition only weakly supported a centrally unified religion and state, partly because the families combined a political and religious leader in their own family heads or chiefs. Shinto advocates sought to raise the status of the emperor by appeal to the mythological account of his divine descent from the Sun Goddess, and the role of the emperor was supported by both Buddhist and Confucian ideals (and indirectly by the Bureau of Divination and by Taoist influence). Buddhism practically became a state religion protecting the ruler and his realm, while Confucianism supplied the notion of a Son of Heaven with a divine mandate. Chinese cosmology and Taoist elements, represented by the Bureau of Divination, promised the proper foundation of nation and society on the basis of cosmic harmony.

Several other areas of Japanese religion that reveal the influence of the five traditions can be summed up more briefly. These areas are pluralism of religions and religious beliefs, emphasis on ritual and magical[3] procedures, and religious sentiment in a love of nature. Pluralism has always been a conspicuous feature of Japanese religion. There have been incidents of antagonism between the religious traditions, but they are the exception rather than the rule. Usually it has not been the case that any one religious tradition thought of itself as the true religion to the exclusion of other (false) religions. (The Jodo Shin sect and Nichiren sect of Buddhism are important exceptions to this general rule.) One tradition presupposed the existence of the other traditions and either consciously or unconsciously borrowed from them. In this kind of atmosphere the people could participate simultaneously in most or all of the traditions. The common people might not be aware of an indigenous tradition or of Taoism, and might not give second thought to the formal teachings of Confucianism, but they followed beliefs and practices originating in these sources. And even when they could see some differences between Buddhism and Shinto, they usually accepted the two traditions as similar or complementary. It was only natural that the Buddha was first seen by the Japanese people as a foreign *kami*. Later, as Buddhism became more Japanized, Buddhist divinities were worshiped with the same fervor that was directed toward the native *kami*.

The use of rituals, rather than formal affirmation of a creedal statement, is central to Japanese religiosity. This is seen in the prominence of rituals, magical formulas, and amulets in each religious tradition. Initially Buddhism was rejected because it was seen as malevolent, causing offense to the *kami* and resulting in pestilence; later it was accepted because its ritual and magical practices were seen as benevolent and equal to or surpassing those of Shinto. The embodiment of ritual and magical formulas in amulets is one of the most conspicuous features of religious practices in recent times.[4] Most of the larger Buddhist temples, Shinto shrines, and New Religions display and sell amulets—some of which contain Taoist phrases. Another example of ritual process rather than creedal commitment is reliance on shamanistic possession in trance, which has been practiced in the native tradition, Shinto, Buddhism, and also New Religions.

Love of nature is a distinctive feature of the Japanese spirit and is reflected in most artistic and religious expressions, although it is difficult to define. The earliest image of Japan in the eighth-century poetry anthology *Manyoshu,* and also in the early Shinto rituals, shows a refined appreciation of the religious and creative resources in the natural world. For the sake of contrast we might say that in the Western tradition the tendency has been to define God and human beings apart from nature; in Japan, *kami* and humans are defined in relation to nature or as parts of nature. The Japanese appreciation of nature is found within the earliest religious tradition and in Shinto, and is reinforced by the other traditions. The aim of Taoism was to be in harmony with nature, and Confucianism drew on this natural harmony for its insistence on social harmony. Buddhism's openness to the natural world later was developed in a return to nature by the Zen sect, which had received Taoist influence in China.

This brief survey of the cooperation among the five formative traditions is not an exhaustive analysis of Japanese religion but does provide a basis for understanding its nature and development in the subsequent centuries. These basic elements continued to interact with each other while developing specific religious organizations and while contributing to the wider religious situation. The appearance of new religious currents, particularly Buddhist importations, was of great importance in determining the way in which these elements interacted.

NOTES

1. Masaharu Anesaki, *History of Japanese Religion* (London: Kegan Paul, Trench, Trübner, 1930; reprint ed., Rutland, VT: Charles E. Tuttle, 1963), p. 8.

2. See Ryusaku Tsunoda et al., *Sources of Japanese Tradition* (New York: Columbia University, 1958), paperback ed., vol. 1, p. 265, where this passage is traced to the writings of Yoshida Kanetomo (1435–1511) and a different interpretation is given; Yoshida's purpose for writing is to demonstrate the primacy of Shinto over Buddhism and Confucianism: "Thus all foreign doctrines are offshoots of Shinto." We borrow the metaphor to illustrate the close interrelationship of Japanese religious traditions, not to determine primacy or hierarchical ranking.

3. The word "magic" calls for an explanation. "Magic," a much-maligned term, often is unfairly contrasted with "religion": religion is viewed as spiritual, otherworldly, focused on altruism and salvation, whereas "magic" is seen as physical, this-worldly, and concerned with manipulation of ritual for personal benefit. A closer look at the actual practice of the members of the world's religions, rather than the stated ideals of some of its leaders, shows that all the major traditions use the power of religion to ritually diminish the poverty (material, bodily, or spiritual) of human life and enhance the richness (material, bodily, or spiritual) of existence. In other words, religion and magic (or whatever we call these two interrelated aspects of spiritual life) are most often two sides of the same coin. What distinguishes Japanese religion is not that it is magical (for this is inherent in most religion) and

other religious traditions are not magical, but that the Japanese tradition is more openly and obviously magical than some other traditions claim to be (especially in contemporary Western traditions). One of the benefits of studying Japanese religion is to use it as a lens to see comparable features, such as magic and folk religion, in one's own heritage. In this book we are necessarily more concerned with the history and dynamics of Japanese religion, and cannot stop to explore all matters of definition and theory related to religion, even though they are inevitably intertwined in the description and interpretation of things Japanese. The best general reference for such larger issues—not only "magic," but also "ritual," "purification," and other religious topics—is *The Encyclopedia of Religion,* ed. Mircea Eliade (New York: Collier Macmillan, 1987), 16 vols. (A new edition is planned.) For "Magic," see vol. 9, pp. 81–89, and the more detailed articles that follow. For one interesting book on magic in the West, see Keith V. Thomas, *Religion and the Decline of Magic* (London: Oxford University, 1971). For magic in Japan, see Tubielewicz, *Superstitions, Magic, and Mantric Practices in the Heian Period.*

4. For a general treatment of the use of Japanese amulets as a ritual process, see my "Mechanisms and Process in Japanese Amulets," *Nihon shukyo e no shikaku* (Osaka: Toho Shuppan, 1994), pp. 611–20.

PART II

〰

The Development
and Elaboration of
Japanese Religion

P art I began the story of Japanese religion with the prehistoric heritage, the emergence of Shinto, and the importation of the Buddhist, Taoist, and Confucian traditions. The appearance of these religious strands was closely related to political and social developments, such as the creation of a unified nation and a centralized state, and culminated in the political and religious developments at Nara, the capital at the end of the eighth century. By this time the contours of Japanese religion were taking shape.

As we enter Part II, we must keep in mind these formative elements and their initial pattern, yet we must also be ready to see new aspects of these elements (particularly new importations of Buddhism) and changes within them. These elements had not assumed a final shape by the ninth century; rather, they continued to evolve through the seventeenth century in ways that further inform the religious worldview of the Japanese people.

As in Part I, the religious developments described in Part II are related to social and political developments. For example, the founders of Tendai and Shingon Buddhism went to China to bring back new emphases in Buddhist teachings and practice. But their trip to China occurred because they were sent as envoys of the Japanese state, in a government ship. Throughout this period religion was closely tied to the brilliant life of the court at the new capital of Kyoto.

The Buddhist sects founded during the Kamakura period constitute the dominant lines of Buddhist institutions down to the present day. In this setting Shinto tended to be overshadowed by Buddhism, but there was a great deal of interaction between Buddhism and Shinto, and Shinto in turn created theoretical arguments that formed the basis for a renewal of Shinto in the eighteenth and nineteenth centuries. Taoism and Confucianism persevered more as implicit influences than as distinct traditions. Christianity first entered Japan in 1549 and enjoyed a brief popularity before it succumbed to political persecution. Taken as a whole, these additions and changes to the religion of the formative period can be seen as constituting the period of development and elaboration.

9

❧

The Development of a Japanese Buddhism: Shingon and Tendai

The Heian period (794–1185) was a colorful time in the history of Japan. Chinese influence continued to dominate, but more important, a distinctive Japanese culture was flowering. In many ways Chinese culture was transformed along Japanese lines. Previously, the Japanese people tended to imitate Chinese models, especially in art; from the Heian period on, they had greater freedom to create truly Japanese forms. The writing system, which depended on Chinese ideographs, was modified so that it placed greater emphasis on Japanese phonetics. This gave the Japanese a lighter, freer means of expressing their emotions. The finest example of their new literature is the eleventh-century *Tale of Genji,* a noblewoman's tale of courtly love and sensitivity to the beauty of nature and the passing of the seasons.[1] Poetry and painting, too, developed more along Japanese lines and centered on the glittering life at court. In the countryside the emergence of the manorial system increasingly gave power to large landholders, including Shinto and Buddhist institutions. All these cultural developments are related to the emergence of new forms of Buddhism during the Heian period—new transmissions imported from China to Japan and drawn into closer contact with Japanese culture.

THE NEW BUDDHISM
OF THE HEIAN PERIOD

Buddhism in the preceding Nara period centered almost exclusively around the capital, characterized by the large temples erected by (and for) the state; by the Confucian-based government bureaucracy that not only created a form of state Buddhism but also controlled it for state benefit; and by the six formal schools of Buddhist teaching. Nara Buddhism helped centralize the Japanese state and provide the rationale for the emperor as both "the supreme priest of the worship of Shinto gods and the patron protector of the Buddhist Dharma [teaching]."[2] The combined strength of this Buddhist establishment was so great, and its rationale for the state was so crucial, that even after the capital was moved to Kyoto, Nara Buddhism continued to play a major role in both the government and in culture.

The shift from Buddhism of Nara times to Heian times can be viewed from quite different perspectives. The standard picture of Buddhism in the Heian period has been drawn mainly by the Japanese priests and scholars who have specialized in the study of their individual Buddhist sects, from the perspective of the independent, large-scale temple organizations of recent and modern times. These writers also have viewed Heian Buddhism from the end result, or "success," of the Shingon and Tendai movements toward the latter part of Heian times, and their eventual growth into sect organizations. This picture has tended to overemphasize the disjunction between the "old Buddhism" of the six schools of Nara and the "new Buddhism" of Tendai and Shingon in Heian times, and has minimized the lengthy process of both competition and cooperation with "old Buddhism" that the leaders of these two new movements had to go through to advance their cause.

Recent scholarship has found the "sectarian" perspective of Buddhism too limiting and has focused instead on placing Buddhist developments within a general historical and cultural framework.[3] This newer reading of Tendai and Shingon sees them not as supplanting the six schools of Nara, but as working alongside them; from this viewpoint, the major contribution of the two new movements was not so much the founding of independent sects (which came later), but the creation of a new relationship between Buddhism, on the one hand, and the Japanese nation and Japanese culture, on the other hand.

During Nara times the budding Japanese state supported Buddhism by creating national temples and subsidizing priests for the performance of rituals. Some of these rituals were for the personal benefit of the imperial family (in instances such as sickness and childbirth); the families of the nobility also supported temples for these purposes and for rites honoring ancestors. But the most important rites were the reading of scriptures and ceremonies for the protection of the state—both at the capital and in provincial temples established and maintained by the state. In other words, the Confucian ideas and institutions of the state used Buddhism as a tool for its own purposes. The main significance for Buddhism in the transition from Nara to Heian times was that eventually Shingon (and Tendai) succeeded in replacing "Confucianism with Buddhism as the ideology of the state."[4] The move of the capital from Nara to Kyoto was motivated, in part, by the moral decline of the priesthood at Nara and their interference in state matters, but the long-term effects of the rise of Shingon and Tendai during Heian times was the shift from Confucian control over Buddhism to a new Buddhist model of government.

The six philosophical schools of the Nara period served mainly as the religion of the capital, the nobility, and the monks. They were so concerned with Buddhism increasing their wealth and political power, rather than with propagating Buddhist teaching to the general population, that, viewed from the perspective of later Buddhist developments they are seen as corrupt, or at least as neglecting the mission of spreading the religious message of Buddhism to all social classes. These schools served at the pleasure of, and under the control of, the Confucian ideology and bureaucracy: "the primary goal of the state in promoting Buddhism was to have Buddhist priests and nuns also perform a magico-shamanistic function."[5] Therefore, it is only natural to expect that new movements would arise, with wider appeal and greater outreach. It is important to understand how the development and spread of Buddhism occurred, because it shaped the Heian period and influenced much of later Japanese religious history.

Politically, the Heian period was ushered in by the shift of the capital from Nara to Kyoto, which remained the imperial capital until 1868. It is thought that one reason for moving the capital from Nara was the political interference of the six schools of Nara Buddhism. One event highlighting the questionable state of Buddhism was the scandal of the Buddhist priest Dokyo (died 772) of the Hosso school. Dokyo gained the trust of Empress Koken (reigned 749–58) by healing her, and he may have become her lover, while he plotted (unsuccessfully) to become emperor. The move to Kyoto helped free the capital from the grip of Nara Buddhism and also helped create the possibility for the transformation of Buddhism.[6] Religiously, a major contribution of the Heian period is two new Buddhist movements, each of which originates with an outstanding religious leader. Shingon was begun by Kukai (774–835), known posthumously as Kobo Daishi. Tendai was initiated by Saicho (767–822), honored posthumously as Dengyo Daishi. (*Daishi* is an honorary term conferred by the emperor, meaning "great teacher"; Saicho was the first in Japanese history to receive the title.) For convenience, we refer to these two figures throughout their lifespans by their honorary titles, Kobo Daishi and Dengyo Daishi, even though these titles were conferred after they died.

The two movements and their creators share many features in common. Not only were they contemporaries, but also they went to China by imperial sanction at the same time in their quest of an authoritative Buddhism. Both were Buddhist priests who, dissatisfied with Nara Buddhism, traveled to China in search of the true Buddhism. Even more important, both seem to have been committed to the ideal of establishing a genuinely Japanese Buddhism. That is, they wanted to propagate a kind of Buddhism that would provide all the Japanese people with the teachings of Buddhism. We will also see some important differences between the two developments. For example, the two leaders differed in their choice of forms of Buddhism in China and in their organization of the imported traditions upon their return to Japan.

SHINGON: ESOTERIC BUDDHISM IN JAPAN

Kobo Daishi is one of the most illustrious figures in Japanese history. Within the history of Buddhism he has been credited with the founding of the Shingon sect. On the popular level, he is honored as the creator of the Japanese phonetic system of writing, and he still is venerated in many places he is supposed to have visited.[7] However, his historical and religious significance is best seen in his transmission of esoteric Buddhism from China to Japan. Esoteric Buddhism is a fascinating case of cultural interaction, illustrating how Japan has accepted incredibly diverse strands and incorporated them into the Japanese worldview: Kobo Daishi, a Japanese monk, received a complex Indian religious system in the setting of Chinese language and culture, and then transplanted it in Japan and reformulated it to become part and parcel of the Japanese spiritual heritage.[8]

The terminology of Buddhism is rather complex, and that of Shingon Buddhism is especially complicated because it is related to an elaborate symbolic and ritual system originating in India. Generally, the expression "esoteric Buddhism" refers to highly symbolic and even secret formulas and practices. More specifically, the phrase refers to the Buddhism arising out of the Tantric tradition of India from about the third to seventh centuries C.E.[9] The Tantric tradition, which influenced both Hinduism and Buddhism, takes its name from the Sanskrit word "*tantra*," a group of writings emphasizing occult rituals to control the mind and body for the purpose of realizing ultimate truth. As one scholar has summed it up, "Esoteric Buddhism teaches the *ritual* realization of the identity of nirvana and samsara, of emptiness and the world of images, of the Buddha and of every person."[10]

The Tantric tradition emphasized unconventional practices, such as the use of mystic diagrams (*mandala*), mystic syllables (*mantra*), and elaborate meditation techniques (which for initiated students might involve symbolic union and even actual sexual union). Such practices were so extreme that Tantrism was sometimes viewed with disfavor by Hindus and Buddhists alike. Nevertheless, Tantric Buddhism developed a very rich iconographic, ritual, and meditative practice, especially in Tibet, where in combination with local practices it formed the major Buddhist tradition.

Tantric Buddhism also found its way directly from India to China, where it was known as Chen-yen (or Zhenyan), a translation into Chinese of the Sanskrit term "*mantra*," or "true word." Esoteric Buddhism arrived later in China than other forms of Buddhism, so it did not have the time to become part of the Chinese tradition and to withstand the shock of government persecution like the relatively older Buddhist developments. But Chen-yen was flourishing when Kobo Daishi arrived in China, and he was able to learn and transmit the

A statue of Kobo Daishi, the founder of Shingon Buddhism, here shown as a protector of children. By borrowing a pilgrim's staff and circling Kobo Daishi's statue, a person acquires the same religious benefit as if he or she made a lengthy pilgrimage. (Kyoto, 1979)

tradition to Japan. In Japanese, "Chen-yen" is pronounced "Shingon." Thus Shingon is literally the True Word, meaning the practice of esoteric Buddhism, such as the invocation of "true words" (*mantra*) or mystic syllables. Within any religious tradition there may be tendencies to juxtapose the present, or phenomenal world, and an other or higher world; in the Tantric heritage in general, and especially in Shingon, there is a heightened sensitivity to and emphasis upon symbolic and ritual realization as the means to the highest reality or truth.

Various elements and practices of esoteric Buddhism (sometimes called "miscellaneous esoterism") had been known in Japan for some time; Kobo Daishi was attracted to this tradition and wanted to study it more completely. The imperial court was drawn to the esoteric rites, and it sent Kobo Daishi to China to learn and then return with this powerful ritual heritage. During Kobo Daishi's stay in China (804–6), he gained comprehensive knowledge of esoteric Buddhism and obtained crucial Buddhist scriptures (in Chinese translation) and ritual paraphernalia. He even studied the ancient Indian language Sanskrit. His return with the "pure" esoteric Buddhist tradition (in contrast to the prior "miscellaneous" esoterism) was a radically new contribution of Buddhism to Japan, one that was much more Indian in character than Chinese. Equally important is how Kobo Daishi nurtured and cultivated the transplanted tradition in the new "soil" of Japanese culture. He physically separated himself both from the old Buddhism of Nara and from the new capital in order to establish a monastery on the secluded mountain called "Koya." In part, Kobo Daishi imitated the mountain monasteries of China, but he also emphasized the need to bring Buddhism into a harmonious relationship with the native Japanese heritage. Even though he established his monastery far from the capital, the esoteric doctrines—and especially the rites—soon were sought after by both laity and priests. He created a synthesis between esoteric Buddhism and the schools of Nara Buddhism, and thus enabled Buddhism to escape Confucian control and become the nation's prevailing ideology.

Shingon teaching divides Buddhism into the exoteric and the esoteric. Exoteric, or public, teachings of the historical Buddha (Sakyamuni) are not wrong but are lesser forms and a lower level of Buddhism. By contrast, esoteric, or secret, teachings have their source in the Mahavairocana Buddha (Dainichi, "Great Sun" in Japanese), a kind of cosmic Buddha who is also the ultimate source of the historical Buddha; the Mahavairocana Buddha revealed the highest truths of Buddhism in the *Mahavairocana Sutra* and other sutras. Only the Mahavairocana Buddha, the writings he revealed, and the elaborate rituals and mystical teachings he taught enable a person to draw upon this higher power. In effect, this Great Sun Buddha is the source of truth and the highest realization, because not only the historical Buddha but even the entire cosmos is an emanation of the Sun Buddha. This truth is to be realized not just with the mind's apprehension of this truth, but with the vocalization of the true words (*mantra*) and with the bodily gestures (*mudra*) that express symbolically the cosmic message. The most important teachings and practices of Shingon have been handed down orally from senior to junior priests, and only in recent decades are some of these secret matters being published.

The esoteric knowledge of Shingon reveals the higher unity in the Sun Buddha, which transcends the apparent dualities of the world. Ordinarily we experience life in terms of dualities such as male and female, dynamic and static. To the ordinary person, the dualities of the world appear hopelessly split, but the esoteric knowledge of Shingon reveals that there is a higher unity to all things within their original source in the Sun Buddha. All the doctrine, art, and ritual of Shingon is based on the premise of the Sun Buddha as the original source of the cosmos.

Kobo Daishi developed Shingon teaching in an attempt to "solve the paradox of human existence" as he experienced it. In his view, human beings must face the meaninglessness of life and the futility of human knowledge. This is seen in one of his writings:

> Unknowable, unknowable
>   It is completely unknowable,
> About the Buddha and the non–Buddhists
>   There are millions of scrolls;
> Dark, dark, it is very dark
>   Of the Way that is spoken there are many paths.
> What is left
>   When the copying and chanting of scriptures stop?
> No one knows, no one knows
>   And I too do not know,
> Though they consider and speculate
>   Even the wise do not know.[11]

Here Kobo Daishi emphasizes the critical predicament of people who do not (and cannot) know the meaning of existence, but he goes beyond this dark analysis of the human situation to pose a promising solution. Although human beings are faced with a meaningless existence and even though the exoteric teachings of Buddhism do not hold absolute assurance, nevertheless, there is hope. Shingon teaching, based on esoteric doctrine and practice, reveals the integration of humanity with the cosmic Buddha (or Sun Buddha). Shingon developed the Mahayana Buddhist notion that Buddha-nature is inherent in every person and, therefore, every person can become a Buddha (or enlightened person) during one's own life and can even become a Buddha within the limits of one's own physical body. This teaching is at the heart of Shingon doctrine and practice, and even if a layperson does not have access to the secret teachings, he or she may realize enlightenment through simple practices such as reciting *mantras*.

Shingon doctrine, because of its highly symbolic and esoteric character, is one of the most complex systems in all of Japanese Buddhism. It is easier for the average Japanese layperson (and for the Westerner) to appreciate the artistic expressions of Shingon than to comprehend its intricate doctrines. The dualities of the world are often expressed in two contrasting *mandala* (in Sanskrit, *mandara* in Japanese), or symbolic representations of the cosmos. The *mandala* usually feature a square border enclosing symmetrical patterns of squares within circles and circles within squares.[12] Literally hundreds of Buddhist divinities are located within the smaller circles and squares, each identified by its particular iconographic attributes and mystic gestures. (Sometimes the divinities are represented by the symbolic [Sanskrit] letters associated with them.) Such a *mandala* presents a panorama of the Buddhist cosmos. The *mandala* were used in Shingon ordination rites: a blindfolded priest threw a flower on the *mandala* and thereby became directly linked with the particular Buddhist divinity on which the flower fell. Monks also followed the practice of meditating upon the *mandala,* which united one's life with the higher cosmic truth.[13]

Even for the average person who did not perform the most difficult practices, merely to behold the splendor of the *mandala* was to be given a glimpse of the cosmic vision to which Shingon held the key. The same can be said of the fearful statues of Shingon, which to Western eyes may appear strange, even grotesque. These statues feature a menacing countenance, glaring eyes, sharp teeth, and a brandished weapon—some even have a girdle of skulls at the waist, and their feet are stamping on demons; but they are simply the malevolent side of various deities, the counterpart of the benevolent side. Shingon does not deny the existence of evil and violence but seeks first to comprehend the duality of the world and then to affirm the higher unity that transcends worldly duality. Although many people did not necessarily comprehend the full plan of the cosmic vision, they readily brought devotion and offerings to the awesome statues, apparently because of faith in their power to protect humans from demonic forces.

The practice of Shingon centers on the great ritual treasures Kobo Daishi brought back from China, both ritual paraphernalia and the actual liturgies for performing the rituals. Within a few years, he and his followers were in demand for performing rites at court. Especially popular were rites for healing and for childbirth. Rather quickly such rites came to be practiced by all Buddhist priests as requests came from the court and nobility, and eventually from ordinary women and men. Perhaps the most fascinating of all Shingon rituals is the fire rite called "*goma,*" which is thought to be related to the Indian *homa,* or fire ritual. In the *goma* rite the priest builds up layers of wooden tablets on which prayers are written, and he then lights the wood while he chants. The symbolism of the rite is an expression of the Shingon view of the universe, burning defilements and purifying the self, and becoming transported by the wisdom of fire to the higher truth of Shingon. To sit in a dark temple, listening to the priest's chanting and watching the flames leap up, illuminating the gilded statues, elevates the viewer to another world.[14]

The quest for cosmic power in Shingon may seem alien to some forms of early Buddhism, but it was totally consistent with Tantric Buddhism. The Indian bent for elaborate iconography and complex symbolism in doctrine and ritual is expressed more within Shingon Buddhism than in any other form of Japanese Buddhism. In fact, Shingon is closer to the esoteric Buddhism of Tibet, with which it shares the common historical foundation of Tantric Buddhism, than to most other branches of Japanese Buddhism. However, the general principle that Buddhism provides power for solving immediate problems was accepted as soon as it reached Japanese shores, so Shingon shared the same principle and innovated only in providing "esoteric" means of Buddhist power.

The major contribution of Kobo Daishi was to bring to Japan the whole range of esoteric art, doctrine, and ritual in a systematic form, and to integrate Nara Buddhism and esoteric Buddhism in a comprehensive rationale for the state. For the aesthetically inclined, the artistic expressions and elaborate rituals of Shingon were overwhelming. For the intellectual, there was a comprehensive system explaining the nature of the world and criticizing all other philosophical systems. (Kobo Daishi developed a philosophy of religion that ranked all religions then known on a scale of ten levels; esoteric Buddhism occupied the highest level.) The devotionally minded could utilize the meditation, divinities, and ritual to achieve personal fulfillment and to experience the unity of Shingon's cosmic vision.

The magical formulas of Shingon provided easy access to cosmic power. So attractive were Shingon's dramatic aspects that they were quickly borrowed and used by other Buddhist schools and sects, and these aspects gradually filtered down to the ordinary people. The earlier precedent of relating and even equating Buddhist divinities and Shinto *kami* was emphasized by Kobo Daishi, reinforcing an important model for the interaction of Buddhism and Shinto. Shingon did not generate many new Buddhist sects in the fashion of Tendai, the other major Buddhist development in the Heian period. Nevertheless, even today Mount Koya is a favorite pilgrimage destination and cemetery site, made more sacrosanct by the presence of Kobo Daishi's tomb and the belief that he is not really dead but "sleeping" there, and some day will reappear.[15]

TENDAI: THE *LOTUS SUTRA*, PROPER ORDINATION FOR MONKS, AND BUDDHAHOOD FOR ALL HUMANS

During the Heian period, Kobo Daishi created the synthesis of Shingon (esoteric Buddhism) with the other forms of exoteric Buddhism that constituted the major ideology for the nation. A contemporary of Kukai (or Kobo Daishi), Saicho (later known as Dengyo Daishi) made a different but equally important contribution to the emergence of Japanese Buddhism. Within the institutional history of Japanese Buddhism, Tendai can be considered more widely influential than Shingon, for it was the direct source of most of the later Buddhist developments in Japan. Although Dengyo Daishi went to China at the same time (on the same boat) as Kobo Daishi, his experience there was quite different. Dengyo Daishi had been attracted to the few Tendai writings available in Japan; he went to China to acquire additional Tendai materials and a more complete knowledge of the Buddhist system. He viewed the esoteric Buddhism of China merely as one important Buddhist tradition along with Ch'an (the Chinese term for the Zen sect); for him the T'ien-t'ai sect was superior to the other Buddhist traditions. ("Tendai" is the Japanese pronunciation of T'ien-t'ai or Tiantai.) Dengyo Daishi spent most of his time in China at the headquarters of the T'ien-t'ai sect, on the mountain called T'ien-t'ai.

The Chinese monk Chih-i (or Zhiyi; 538–97) established the T'ien-t'ai sect, focusing on the *Lotus Sutra* and the teachings of the great Buddhist scholar Nagarjuna. Chih-i considered the *Lotus Sutra* the culmination of the Buddha's teaching and used it as the foundation for creating one grand system out of earlier Buddhist teachings. He emphasized the notion that all life was present in the mind of the historical Buddha from the moment of his enlightenment, and he related this idea to Nagarjuna's philosophical insistence on the emptiness of all phenomenal existence (that is, life here and now). Chih-i's doctrine is a threefold analysis of existence that both denies and at the same time affirms phenomenal existence.[16] For the layperson, this means that even daily life, if properly perceived and meditated on, can be the road to Buddhahood (becoming Buddha or attaining the level of a Buddha). In both China and Japan this teaching emphasized that proper Buddhist practice is dependent upon proper meditation.[17]

When Dengyo Daishi returned to Japan, he retraced his steps to the mountain called Hiei overlooking Kyoto, where previously he had been studying and meditating. There he established Tendai, emphasizing the *Lotus Sutra* and the necessity of monastic retreat for proper meditation. Of course, the *Lotus Sutra* already had a considerable history in Japan; even Prince Shotoku is said to have written a commentary on it, and the Buddhist schools of Nara had recognized its profundity. Dengyo Daishi's contribution was to teach the primary importance of the *Lotus Sutra*. He criticized earlier interpretations of it as false and proposed as the true interpretation that "all sentient beings could eventually attain Buddhahood,"[18] emphasizing the notion in the *Lotus Sutra* that all life has the potential for becoming enlightened. According to him, the *Lotus Sutra* was not a lesser teaching or one among the many writings, but the supreme message of Buddhism.

Dengyo Daishi was uncompromising not only on doctrinal matters, but also in matters of training and ordination. His criticism of Nara Buddhism and his concern for proper meditation led him to prescribe a twelve-year period of training for monks on Mount Hiei, during which time they were not allowed to leave the mountain.[19] His insistence on officially establishing the proper rite of ordination (the *bodhisattva* form of ordination, which he had received in China and which he wanted to establish in Japan) involved him in a lifelong struggle with the government, which granted his request only after his death.

Actually, Dengyo Daishi was caught between the two camps of Nara Buddhism and the government. Nara Buddhism and the state had what today might be called a symbiotic relationship: the state financially supported and controlled ordination of monks; in turn, Nara Buddhism used its religious power to protect the nation and its rituals to heal and bless the court families. Dengyo Daishi's aim in setting up new ordination procedures was a complex mix of political and religious motives. He favored a form of ordination he and his Chinese masters considered Mahayana, a form superior to the "Hinayana" ordination of Nara Buddhism. But by proposing that this new kind of ordination take place on Mount Hiei, he could escape the direct administrative authority of Nara Buddhism and establish for himself and his organization greater freedom as a religious institution. Dengyo Daishi established the precedent of a religious institution set apart from (but, of course, still dependent upon) the government. Both Dengyo Daishi and Kobo Daishi "were instrumental in establishing a new type of monasteries that were exempted from the controls and restrictions imposed by" the Nara pattern of state Buddhism. The difference between the two figures is that Kobo Daishi strove to integrate Shingon with the existing Buddhist establishment, whereas Dengyo Daishi was more isolationist, seeking to divorce Tendai from the Buddhist establishment.[20]

The mountain headquarters of Hiei symbolizes Dengyo Daishi's great hope for Japanese Buddhism. He was concerned that Buddhism in Japan be orthodox in ordination rites, scriptures, doctrine, and devotion. Having received proper ordination himself, he felt qualified to lead orthodox Buddhism in Japan. Convinced that the *Lotus Sutra* was the essential teaching of Buddhism, he upheld it as the foremost scripture. For doctrine he transmitted the T'ien-t'ai teachings based on the *Lotus Sutra,* that every phenomenal aspect of the world is filled with Buddha-nature. Determined that his monks be properly devout and disciplined, he required long periods of meditation. History rewarded Dengyo Daishi's efforts, for Mount Hiei later became the monastic and scholastic headquarters of Japanese Buddhism, regardless of sect affiliation. In spite of the ravages of time and warfare, much of the glory of this monastic headquarters survives today, and it is a popular tourist attraction just outside Kyoto. One of the distinctive architectural structures at Mount Hiei is the chapel with an image of Amida in the center of an empty room, so that priests can circumambulate Amida while in devotional meditation. The faith in Amida nurtured within Tendai later blossomed in the practices of the Pure Land sects.

The impact of Tendai on popular life is not so striking as that of Shingon (with its complex iconography). One of Tendai's greatest contributions is the placing of the *Lotus Sutra* in the center of attention, for this is one of the most influential scriptures for Japanese Buddhism. In it we find the most direct and dramatic expression of Mahayana Buddhism: all beings may easily attain enlightenment through simple acts of devotion. In the words of the *Lotus Sutra*, those who "embrace, read, recite, expound and copy the Lotus Sutra of the Wonderful Law, even only one verse, and look upon this sutra with the same reverence as they would the Buddha" will attain enlightenment.[21] This compassionate rendering of Buddhism summed up the meaning of the tradition to the majority of the Japanese people. Dengyo Daishi, by emphasizing potential Buddhahood for all people, paved the way for the geographical spread of Tendai and opened the door more widely to the propagation of Buddhism to the common people.

Tendai teaching so emphasized the penetration of Buddha-nature within the phenomenal world that in medieval times it preached the inherent Buddha-nature of the natural world: "even plants and trees are in possession of Buddha-nature."[22] Here we see how the Japanese appreciation of the natural world and Tendai teaching formed a notion central to Japanese Buddhism and to Japanese thought and arts, too. Some scholars see this emphasis on original enlightenment to be the paradigm of medieval Buddhism and the key to medieval culture: "this paradigm was characterized by . . . the conviction that enlightenment is directly accessible in the present moment, and that practice represents the expression of enlightenment, not merely the means to achieve it."[23] Shingon and Tendai notions of inherent, or original, enlightenment contrast sharply with Nara Buddhism's notions of enlightenment, which required lengthy cultivation and gradual attainment.[24]

Kobo Daishi and Dengyo Daishi were contemporaries, but they led different careers and made contrasting contributions to Japanese Buddhism. Some scholars feel that Dengyo Daishi would have been more successful if he had been more compromising in his attitude toward the schools of Nara Buddhism. Both men founded headquarters of mountain Buddhism in Japan, but their fortunes were quite different. Kobo Daishi's fame was immediate and lasting—and his synthesis of esoteric and exoteric Buddhism transformed Buddhism from a Confucian-controlled servant of the government to the major ideology; yet his movement was of lesser importance for institutional religious history. In contrast, Dengyo Daishi and Tendai are of greater importance for subsequent religious history as the direct or indirect source of later Buddhist sects.

Two major elements that Dengyo Daishi brought to Japan along with Tendai were Zen practices and faith in the *bodhisattva* named Amida. For a while these two elements had only a minor role within Tendai because Tendai gradually became heavily laden with Shingon ritualistic influence. Dengyo Daishi had learned and practiced some esoteric Buddhism, but he was no match for Kobo Daishi, the master of esoteric Buddhism in Japan; esoteric Buddhist rites were in great demand by the imperial court and aristocracy, and several of Dengyo Daishi's successors traveled to China to spend long years

there studying esoteric Buddhism and then returned to Japan and incorporated it into Tendai. These two elements of faith in Amida and Zen practices,
previously dormant within Tendai, woke to new life. They became so active
that they burst the bonds of Tendai and gave rise to new movements. (These
developments will be seen in the next chapter.)

THE DEVELOPMENT OF JAPANESE
BUDDHISM AND JAPANESE RELIGION

The Heian period was a strong affirmation of the Japanese creative ability to
mold innumerable continental borrowings. Nara Buddhism had remained
more of a foreign religion, serving both the state and the court. Kobo Daishi
and Dengyo Daishi were in agreement about the main reason for searching
out authoritative Buddhism in China: to mold it into a truly Japanese Buddhism. Because of their efforts, Buddhism in Japan took on a decidedly Japanese character, and also moved closer to the people.

At the outset of this chapter we indicated that the period of development
and elaboration was characterized by two trends: the continuation of general
patterns that had taken shape in the formative period and the appearance of
new influences such as the new importations of Buddhism. Thus far we have
surveyed only the new influences. Tendai and Shingon, however, were not
simply signs of discontinuity; on the contrary, they reinforced the earlier
religious patterns. Both Shingon and Tendai deliberately emphasized the
Japanese character of Buddhism. The headquarters of both were founded with
full cooperation of local *kami* who were considered the patron deities of the
two mountains on which the monasteries were located. Thus, the rapport between the Buddhas and *kami* became even more intimate. Tendai and Shingon
also tended to spread Buddhist teachings and build temples in areas distant
from the capital.

In addition, although the two movements had reacted against the controlling authority of state Buddhism at Nara, eventually both the ritualism of
Shingon and the ecclesiastical authority of Tendai were used to protect and
bless the state. The artistic and magical heritage of esoteric Buddhism and the
Tendai focus on the *Lotus Sutra* gradually blended with the Japanese emphasis
on purification and ritualism. Many Buddhist divinities such as Kannon, Amida,
and Jizo became increasingly important as objects of popular piety. Magical
charms and Buddhist divinities were not confined to organized Buddhism—to
temples and priests—but became a part of the living faith of the people. "All
through the Nara and Heian periods, almost all the sects of Buddhism aimed at
tangible rewards in this world and they mainly depended upon incantation and
magic."[25] All in all, the Heian period saw Buddhism take on a decidedly Japanese character as it increasingly penetrated the life of the people.

Meanwhile, the religious elements described in Part I coexisted with the
new movements. In fact, the beliefs of Taoism (especially the Koshin cult) were
more active in the Heian period than at any other time. Medieval novels such

as *The Tale of Genji* show how the people's movements were determined by the "unlucky directions" determined by Chinese customs and Taoist elements. The age was pervaded by all the implications of the *yin-yang* cosmology. The charms and incantations of earlier Buddhism, reinforced by both Shingon and its Taoistic coloring, penetrated all classes of society. The seventh-century precedent of having Buddhist priests perform funeral services had led to widespread dependence on Buddhism for death rites. The Buddhist festival of *bon* for honoring the return of the souls of the dead, probably with the help of ancient Japanese practices, became popular throughout the country. Various religious practitioners—diviners, exorcists, and ascetics—drew on all the previous traditions to serve the religious needs of the people. Shinto became more fully organized, as was evidenced by the compilation of the *Engishiki* of 927, but tended to lean on the prestige of Buddhism. The many *kami* of Shinto became even more closely identified with the Buddhas and *bodhisattvas,* and we will see that Shinto became organized around the complex philosophies of Taoism, Shingon, and Tendai. Folk religion, too, showed its vitality in the daily life of the people.

An example of the distinctively Japanese interrelationship of all these elements is Shugendo, which became organized during and after the Heian period. Building on the ancient theme of sacred mountains and festivals performed on mountains, Shugendo was a "mountain religion" that emphasized pilgrimage to the mountains and ascetic retreats within the mountains. It combined the Shinto notion of local *kami* dwelling on mountains with the

Kannon is one of the most popular Buddhist divinities in Japan. People "worship" Kannon by ladling water over the statue and using brushes (bought inside the temple grounds) to scrub the part of the statue corresponding to the part of their body that is ailing. On one fine September Sunday in Tokyo, about seventy-five people (mostly women) were patiently lined up waiting their turn to ladle water on and scrub the statue. (Tokyo, 1979)

Buddhist notion of local incarnations (avatars, or *gongen*). In addition, it borrowed the theories and charms of Chinese customs and Taoism. The legendary founder of Shugendo gained religious power by combining the aspects of several traditions: he practiced Buddhist asceticism on a Japanese sacred mountain while taking over features of the Chinese mountain wizard (*hsien* or *xian* in Chinese, *sennin* in Japanese). Many popular religious practitioners gained their extraordinary powers by climbing sacred mountains for rigorous training before descending the mountain to minister to the needs of villagers. In later periods Shugendo practitioners (called *yamabushi*) were instrumental in spreading the charms and incantations of esoteric Buddhism (mixed with Taoistic charms and Shinto elements) to the people. The *yamabushi* were important in spreading Buddhism to outlying areas of Japan. This is but one illustration of the complex religious interrelationships within the Heian period and later periods.[26]

NOTES

1. For an excerpt from *The Tale of Genji,* see my *Religion in the Japanese Experience,* 2d ed., pp. 201–4. A recent translation is Murasaki Shikibu, *The Tale of Genji,* trans. Royall Tyler (New York: Viking, 2001), 2 vols.

2. Abe, *The Weaving of Mantra,* p. 25.

3. Abe, *The Weaving of Mantra,* has summed up both a critique of sectarian studies and support of the newer "extra-sectarian" studies; see pp. 399–416 for his critique of the category of "Heian Buddhism," which he rejects as "a false category, created by the intellectuals of the Meiji period (1868–1912), among whose agendas was to legitimize the status quo of Buddhism in their society in which the imperialist state and its nationalist Shinto ideology subjugated" Buddhism (p. 16).

4. Ibid., p. 13.

5. Ibid., pp. 24–25.

6. The usual reasons given for the move of the capital from Nara are the ancient practice of avoiding pollution at the death of the previous emperor, the contemporary fear of the overpowering influence of Buddhism, and the scandal of the monk Dokyo's attempted usurpation of the throne; Ronald P. Toby has added to these reasons the politics of the "gradual transition from 'court to capital.' " See his "Why Leave Nara? Kammu and the Transfer of the Capital," *Monumenta Nipponica,* vol. 40, no. 3 (Autumn 1985), pp. 331–47. For details surrounding Dokyo, see Bender, "The Hachiman Cult and the Dokyo Incident." Both articles contain useful documentation.

7. See the folk legend "Saint Kobo's Well" in my *Religion in the Japanese Experience,* 2d ed., pp. 135–36.

8. For an introduction to the life and thought of Kobo Daishi, with translations of his writings, see Yoshito S. Hakeda, trans., *Kukai: Major Works* (New York: Columbia University, 1972). See also the materials on Kobo Daishi and Shingon in Wm. Theodore de Bary et al., *Sources of Japanese Tradition,* 2d ed. (New York: Columbia University, 2001), vol. 1, ch. 7.

9. For a general work covering the whole range of Shingon, from the origins of esoteric Buddhism in India to its thought and practice in Japan, see Taiko Yamasaki, *Shingon: Japanese Esoteric Buddhism,* trans. Richard and Cynthia Peterson (Boston: Shambhala, 1988).

10. Charles D. Orzech, *Politics and Transcendent Wisdom: The Scripture for Humane Kings in the Creation of Chinese Buddhism* (University Park, PA: Pennsylvania State University, 1998), p. 48. See also his discussion of *chen-yen, shingon,* and *mantra* on pp. 135–36.

11. *Hizo-hoyaku,* as translated and quoted by Minoru Kiyota, *Shingon Buddhism: Theory and Practice* (Los Angeles: Buddhist Books International, 1978), p. 30. This book is a convenient introduction to Tantric Buddhism, and Shingon doctrine and practice.

12. For a detailed study see Adrian Snodgrass, *The Matrix and Diamond World Mandalas in Shingon Buddhism* (New Delhi: Aditya Prakashan, 1988), 2 vols.

13. For a lavishly illustrated book on esoteric Buddhist temples and art, see Takaaki Sawa, *Art in Japanese Esoteric Buddhism,* trans. Richard L. Gage (New York: Weatherhill/Heibon-sha, 1972). For comparison-contrast of Shingon and Tendai meditation on *mandala,* see Michael Saso, *Tantric Art and Meditation* (Honolulu: University of Hawai'i, 1990).

14. For a description of these rites, see Richard K. Payne, *The Tantric Ritual of Japan: Feeding the Gods: The Shingon Fire Ritual* (New Delhi: Aditya, 1991).

15. For a view of the varying conditions but constant popularity of Mount Koya, see Hirochika Nakamaki, "Religious Civilization in Modern Japan: As Revealed Through a Focus on Mt. Koya," in *Japanese Civilization in the Modern World, VI, Religion,* ed. Tadao Umesao et al. (Osaka: National Museum of Ethnology) pp. 121–36.

16. For a brief interpretation of this doctrine, see de Bary et al., *Sources of Japanese Tradition,* 2d ed., vol. 1, ch. 6. For a more comprehensive treatment, see Paul L. Swanson, *Foundations of T'ien-T'ai Philosophy: The Flowering of the Two Truths Theory in Chinese Buddhism* (Berkeley, CA: Asian Humanities Press, 1989). See also Paul L. Swanson, ed., *Tendai Buddhism in Japan,* vol. 14, no. 2–3 of *Japanese Journal of Religious Studies* (June–Sept. 1987).

17. For a concrete description of Tendai meditation—a feast of iconography and a banquet of ritual details—see Saso, *Tantric Art and Meditation.*

18. Paul Groner, *Saicho: The Establishment of the Japanese Tendai School* (Berkeley, CA: Berkeley Buddhist Studies Series, 1984), p. 101. This work provides a "biography of Saicho" as well as a study of Saicho's view of Buddhist precepts.

19. For the text of this proposal for government approval of the twelve-year training (excerpted from Groner, *Saicho*), see my *Religion in the Japanese Experience,* 2d ed., pp. 83–85.

20. Abe, *The Weaving of Mantra,* pp. 402–3.

21. *The Lotus Sutra,* trans. Burton Watson (New York: Columbia University, 1993), p. 161. An excerpt from this scripture is included in my *Religion in the Japanese Experience,* 2d ed., pp. 54–60.

22. William R. LaFleur, *The Karma of Words: Buddhism and the Literary Arts in Medieval Japan* (Berkeley: University of California, 1983), p. 22. LaFleur treats at length the notion of *hongaku,* or "original enlightenment": "Hongaku expressed the insight that the nature of *kaku* or *satori* (usually translated 'enlightenment' or 'realization') is of something already in existence rather than envisioned as a future possibility" (p. 20). For an excerpt from this work, see my *Religion in the Japanese Experience,* 2d ed., pp. 60–65.

23. Jacqueline Ilyse Stone, *Original Enlightenment and the Transformation of Medieval Japanese Buddhism* (Honolulu: University of Hawai'i, 1999), p. 302. This book is a comprehensive treatment of "original enlightenment" in comparison and contrast with Buddhism in Nara, Heian, and Kamakura times.

24. Ibid., pp. 11, 31.

25. Hajime Nakamura, *Ways of Thinking of Eastern Peoples: India, China, Tibet, Japan* (Honolulu: East-West Center Press, 1964), p. 363.

26. For Shugendo, see my *A Religious Study of the Mount Haguro Sect of Shugendo: An Example of Japanese Mountain Religion* (Tokyo: Sophia University, 1970); and Hitoshi Miyake, *Shugendo: Essays on the Structure of Japanese Folk Religion.*

10

❧

Elaboration Within Japanese Buddhism: Pure Land, Nichiren, and Zen Buddhism

uddhism went through many changes in India and other countries before arriving in Japan, but the Indian and Chinese developments were most important for Japanese Buddhism. During the Heian period (794–1185), the grand philosophical systems of India were continued in the six schools of Nara Buddhism, and Shingon and Tendai were freshly imported from China. With so many varieties of Buddhism already present in Japan, we may wonder why the Kamakura period (1185–1333) saw such a vigorous expansion of Buddhist groups. The Kamakura period has usually been associated with three Buddhist movements that later became some of the largest and most influential of all Buddhist sects in Japan: Pure Land, Nichiren, and Zen.

These three movements, and in general the shift from the Buddhism of Heian times to Kamakura times—much like the transition from the Buddhism of Nara to Heian—can be viewed from different perspectives. It is not surprising that the priests and scholars of the sects that emerged from Kamakura times have taken a "sectarian" position, thus treating the period as a point of "sacred origins" and emphasizing the "success story" of Kamakura Buddhism, reading the later institutional prominence of their respective sects back into Kamakura times, and viewing the founders of these Kamakura movements as rejecting Nara and Heian Buddhism for a more authentic (or more Japanese) Buddhism. In earlier Japanese and Western writing the leaders of Kamakura Buddhism have been depicted as reformers, and the era as a whole has been compared to the Reformation in sixteenth-century Christianity in Europe.

The recent work of Japanese and Western Buddhologists has questioned the sectarian, or success story of Kamakura Buddhism as well as its character as a reform movement.[1] What emerges from this revisionist viewpoint is a more complex picture of Buddhism in Kamakura times, when all forms of Buddhism in Japan underwent dramatic changes: some priests attempted to reform and renew the six philosophical schools, other priests tried to expand the influence of Shingon and Tendai temples, and at the same time a number of leaders and movements sought new ways of bringing Buddhism to the Japanese people. All of these Buddhist leaders and their movements competed vigorously with one another, and at the time it was not clear which developments would continue and "succeed" in the future. Because the three new developments did not actually dominate Kamakura times, some scholars have preferred not to use "Kamakura Buddhism" in its former sense as the success story of the Pure Land, Nichiren, and Zen sects.[2]

Sectarian treatments, which have viewed Kamakura Buddhism as a rejection of Heian Buddhism because the latter was elitist and corrupt, are not without some historical foundation. As Shingon and Tendai became successful, the popularity of their esoteric rites for "magical achievement of worldly ends . . . led to widespread patronage of Mikkyo [Shingon and Tendai] ritualists by the court and by powerful aristocrats." Also, even within Kamakura times, "There is abundant contemporary evidence for widespread monastic laxity and misconduct" regarding Buddhist precepts and ethical conduct. However, sectarian views do injustice both to Heian Buddhism, which did not amount to a "thorough-going decadence" and was not totally elitist, and to Kamakura Buddhism, which was complex in character and cannot be explained simply or primarily in terms of a rejection of Heian Buddhism.[3]

The elaboration of new Buddhist movements during Kamakura times was made possible by the previous history of Buddhism in Japan and by the rise of creative Buddhist leaders in the midst of new social conditions. In fact, although the major Kamakura movements criticized earlier Buddhism, they also built upon and continued the previous Buddhist foundation, especially Heian precedents. Shingon and Tendai had moved away from the Nara model of elite Buddhism controlled by and for the state, to a model of enlightenment here and now for all people (and even for grass and trees!) through faith and simpler practices, within new temple institutions not controlled by the state. The Kamakura sects selected different aspects of the Chinese Buddhist heritage to develop, especially to make simpler Buddhist practices available to more people, and focused on faith (or devotion) and a single or "exclusive" practice. To appreciate the character and contribution of these newer forms of Buddhism, we need to place them within their historical setting.

BUDDHISM: FROM
HEIAN TO KAMAKURA TIMES

Following the relative peace of the Heian period came the troubled times of the Kamakura period (1185–1333), in which there was a major shift in political power from the court at Kyoto to ruling feudal groups headed by a generalissimo (*shogun*). The period draws its name from the site of Kamakura where this feudal government was first established. Actually, struggles between rising feudal powers had occurred in the Heian period, but in the Kamakura period they dominated the entire scene. The large Buddhist temples also figured as major economic and military forces, contributing to the general unrest of the times.

The shift from the Heian period to the Kamakura period, and the uncertainty of life in these trying times, called for a more immediate resolution of religious questions—particularly questions about personal faith and practice. A number of natural catastrophes occurred at the same time as these social disturbances, and their significance was magnified by their perception through new currents of Buddhist thought. One of the Buddhist theories that resounded throughout the Kamakura period was the theory of the "decline of the law." Here "law" (*dharma* in Sanskrit, *ho* in Japanese) means the Buddha's teachings, or Buddhism. This theory presupposed three major Buddhist ages of increasing decline or degeneration: first, the ideal age when people followed the teaching of the Buddha and could attain enlightenment; second, a relatively degenerate age when people practiced the teaching of Buddha even though they knew enlightenment was impossible; and, third, a completely degenerate age when no one even bothered to practice the Buddha's teachings. Japanese Buddhists, following the Chinese interpretation of this theory, understood that the first two ages were already past and they were living in the third and final age.[4] The people who lived through the all-too-frequent warfare and bloodshed of the Kamakura period feared an imminent end of the world. Moreover, they realized that the decline of the law necessitated special measures to help them escape their worldly and personal dilemmas.

This concern within Buddhism about the "degenerate age," however, did not bring about its extinction. On the contrary, the philosophical schools of Nara survived, the Heian sects of Shingon and Tendai continued to develop (and create their own denominations), and furthermore, the Kamakura period stimulated latent features of Japanese Buddhism, which flourished as never before. A number of great teachers appeared, each giving his own version of the authentic Buddhist message and its proper practice by laypeople,[5] especially women.

If the innovation of the Heian period was a more *Japanese* Buddhism, then a major Kamakura contribution was Buddhism more for the Japanese *people*.[6] Shingon and Tendai laid down the precedent of removing Buddhism from the monopoly of the state and the nobility and making Buddhist enlightenment available to the people. The leaders of Pure Land, Nichiren, and Zen Buddhism built upon this Heian precedent by developing specific practices for the pursuit of Buddhist fulfillment.[7]

THE PURE LAND SECTS: FAITH IN AMIDA
AND THE RECITATION OF THE *NEMBUTSU*

The term "Pure Land" (or "Pure Realm") is a translation of the Japanese term "*Jodo.*" It can refer to one particular group of Buddhist sects, the Pure Land sects, but in a broader sense it refers to the Pure Land of Amida (an object of worship in the Buddhist pantheon). The "Pure Land" is where the Buddhas and *bodhisattvas* reside, and it sharply contrasts with the impure and polluted world in which humans live. Amida (Amitabha or Amitayus in Sanskrit) was an important Buddha in Indian (Mahayana) Buddhism, although never the focus of a distinct sect. By contrast, Amida in China (O-mi-t'o or A-mi-tuo) became one of the most important objects of Buddhist devotion. The Chinese founders of Pure Land Buddhism and their writings became the foundation for Pure Land developments in Japan.

In Pure Land teachings, Amida has compassion on and wants to save all human beings. To rescue them Amida brings humans to the Buddhist realm called the Pure Land. All people can avail themselves of Amida's saving grace simply by invoking or chanting the name of Amida. In Japan this practice is known as *nembutsu;* the actual phrase is *namu Amida Butsu,* or the shortened form *namu Amida,* meaning "I take refuge in Amida Buddha." Originally the *nembutsu* was a form of silent meditation on Amida by individual monks, but this was replaced by a combination of fervent devotion and chanting the name "Amida" by groups of laypeople. In earlier Japanese Buddhism some aristocrats practiced devotion to Amida, and some itinerant Buddhist monks preached faith in Amida and repetition of the *nembutsu,* but this was mostly outside formal Buddhist institutions. The later development of the Pure Land sects expressed the shift from meditation to faith, and from individual devotion to formal institutions. In Japan, as in China, the cult of this Buddhist divinity became closely associated with memorials for the dead.

The simplicity of faith in Amida helped spread this cult throughout the land. All people sought their own Buddhist realization and the repose of their ancestors, and no comprehension of subtle doctrines was required in Pure Land Buddhism. The founders of the Pure Land sects were thoroughly trained in the monasteries of Mount Hiei and elsewhere, but they emphasized an easy path to rebirth in the Pure Land for everyone, even illiterate peasants. The reason Amida Buddhism won the day was not because people intellectually chose to follow Pure Land doctrine instead of other Buddhist teachings. Rather, they chose popular devotion to Amida because it was a readily available solution to pressing religious needs. Eventually, reliance on Amida through *nembutsu* became one of the most important Japanese forms of the popular practice of Buddhism.

During the Heian period some of the nobility had engaged in devotion to Amida as an individual practice, and some of the forerunners of Honen had preached faith in Amida to the common people, but there was no separate organization of believers in Amida or formal institutions. In the Kamakura period Pure Land faith was organized and spread more widely among the common people.[8]

Other Buddhist priests within the Tendai sect had cultivated belief in Amida as one element of Buddhist practice, especially Kuya (903–72), who is known as the "Patriarch of the Nembutsu."[9] But Honen (1133–1212) is most remembered as the founder of Pure Land as a separate sect, even though he did not intend to establish a separate institution. The earlier priests who preached faith in Amida did so within the context of Tendai or meditation, without forming a separate sect. The career of Honen is a good example of the changing religious atmosphere. Honen studied Buddhism at Mount Hiei and gained fame as a scholar. He devoted his life to studying the many systems of Buddhist thought, but he did not see how these complex doctrines could help a person attain religious peace during such troubled times. At the age of 42 he became convinced of the truth of the Pure Land teachings.

Honen was able to clearly distinguish between the earlier Buddhist teachings in Japan and the newer teaching of faith in Amida. In doing so, he followed the precedent of Chinese Amidist writings by calling previous Buddhist teachings of right conduct and religious exercises the "holy path" and ascribing them to the first two ages of Buddhist history. Nevertheless, Honen, who lived during the third and final age, believed that it was too much to expect women and men to achieve enlightenment through their own efforts, or "self-power." The only hope in such evil times was the possibility of rebirth in Amida's Pure Land, made possible by the "other-power" of Amida.

Like his Amidist forerunners, Honen distinguished sharply between the overly "difficult" holy path of earlier sects and the need for an "easy" means of religious fulfillment in the age of the decline of the Buddhist law. Honen proposed an easy means of Buddhist liberation available to all: rebirth in Amida's Pure Land by invoking Amida's name. Honen maintained that all human beings were so wicked that they could never win their own release, even if they followed the holy path perfectly. They would be much better off to acknowledge their imperfection and throw themselves upon the mercy of Amida. Honen differed from earlier Amidists in advocating *nembutsu* as the exclusive Buddhist practice, not just one practice among many—and as the practice assuring birth in the Pure Land. By setting up an independent movement, Honen challenged the policy that a new school could be established only with the permission of the state and the recognition of the Ritsu sect (one of the original Nara sects, or schools). Generally, Honen also departed from the tendency of Buddhist institutions to be closely involved with the state; he was more concerned with spreading faith in Amida among the common people.

Advocates of Pure Land Buddhism taught that people would be saved by the power of Amida, but interpretations of Amida's saving power differed considerably. There was disagreement over whether good works were a necessary precursor of the *nembutsu* or whether good works were unimportant for being reborn in the Pure Land. Another area of disagreement was whether a person was saved absolutely by just one recitation of the *nembutsu* or whether one's spiritual fulfillment depended upon constant repetition of the *nembutsu*.

After Honen's pioneering work, several priests elaborated different themes of Pure Land teaching but did not found separate sects. One who did establish a new sect was Shinran (1173–1263), who rivals Honen in Pure Land history and was considered by his followers to be the founder of the Amidist sect called Jodo Shinshu (True Pure Land sect). Shinran, too, received his Buddhist training at Mount Hiei but was converted to Honen's teaching of devotion to Amida. Shinran was even more zealous than Honen in propagating Amidism. He said that the all-important thing was faith in Amida, especially the moment of the awakening of faith as the gift of Amida. With his stress on faith, Shinran tended to deemphasize repetition of Amida's name. He maintained that just "one calling" on the name of Amida was sufficient for rebirth in the Pure Land, in opposition to Honen's teaching that emphasized repetition of Amida's name.

Shinran turned Honen's teaching to the extreme of absolute trust in Amida, completely rejecting the ability of men and women to work for their own liberation. Honen had said that even an evil man will be received in the Pure Land, and how much more a good man. Shinran placed such trust in Amida and such distrust in human goodness that he turned this saying around: "Even the good person can be born in Pure Land. How much more so the evil person."[10] Shinran's emphasis on faith in Amida alone led his followers to reject other Buddhist divinities and especially Shinto divinities (*kami*). Families belonging to the Jodo Shin sect were exceptional in that their homes featured only the Buddhist altar (*butsudan*), excluding the customary Shinto altar (*kamidana*).

The followers of Honen became the Jodo (Pure Land) sect; the followers of Shinran became the Jodo Shinshu (True Pure Land sect), which is known by its abbreviated name Shinshu (True sect). The Pure Land movements experienced varying degrees of success. After the death of Shinran, the Jodo Shinshu tended to decline. One of Shinran's successors, Rennyo (1414–99), is credited with restoring the sect by helping to shape its doctrine and organizational structure. Shinshu became the largest Buddhist sect, with Honen's Jodo sect the second largest.[11]

Shinran's importance is not limited to his status as a founder of Jodo Shinshu. According to tradition, Shinran was contemptuous of the celibate life required of monks because that lifestyle presupposed the individual monk's ability to attain enlightenment on his own and, furthermore, the monastic life implied a lack of faith in the Buddha's grace, which could erase all imperfection. Shinran supposedly wanted to show that the Buddhist life could be practiced by even the ordinary householder, so he married and raised a family. One account says that Honen himself arranged the marriage. Whether or not this story is true, Shinran is popularly honored for establishing the precedent for a married priesthood: earlier priests had married, but Shinran justified it and made it into a virtue. In later times, all Japanese Buddhist sects allowed priests to marry. This is a distinctive feature of Japanese Buddhism, one that sets it off from the Buddhism of countries such as Sri Lanka (Ceylon) and Burma, where Theravada Buddhism adheres to a celibate monasticism, and also from traditional China and Korea, where Mahayana Buddhism also insisted on celibacy for monks and nuns.

Pure Land priests were active both in spreading Buddhist faith in the heart of the cities and in building temples in rural areas.[12] Even the pattern of temple organization was an innovation to Japanese Buddhism. In the past, temples had been founded and maintained mainly by government sponsorship. Shinran gathered together practitioners of the *nembutsu,* along the lines of popularly organized congregations. Rennyo and others later solidified this network of believers into a tight organizational system, especially attracting the peasants of farm villages who at the time had gained greater freedom and power. It is no accident that Pure Land groups in general, especially Jodo Shinshu, not only have the largest memberships, but also are among the most tightly organized of all Japanese Buddhist institutions.

In Japan and in the West, Pure Land faith and practice has usually been associated with charismatic founders such as Honen and Shinran, and major cities such as Kyoto. But the extent of Pure Land influence can be seen in the cult of Zenkoji, a network of temples, each of which houses a triad of Amida sculptures. Combining assurance of rebirth in the afterlife and material benefits in this life, devotion to the image or "icon" of Amida was important for medieval warriors and rulers. This devotion was spread by *hijiri,* or itinerant religious practitioners, from the original Zenkoji in Nagano prefecture to most areas of Japan. Although the Zenkoji cult lacked the charismatic founder of other Pure Land movements and developed in a provincial area, faith in its object of worship and distinctive rituals has made it a popular pilgrimage site from medieval times to the present.[13]

Amidism is one of the most pervasive of all religious movements within Japanese history. Faith in Amida preceded the founding of the Pure Land sects and later overflowed the boundaries of those sects. The *nembutsu* was something that people accepted and practiced regardless of their own temple affiliation. Amida was responsive to all who called on the name of Amida, and men and women and children looked to Amida for help in time of need. It is said that on medieval battlefields the dying warriors sent up their loud pleas for Amida to take them to the Pure Land.

NICHIREN: FAITH IN THE *LOTUS SUTRA* AS THE EXCLUSIVE NATIONAL BUDDHISM

Nichiren (1222–82) is one of the most forceful personalities in Japanese history. By his opponents he was despised; by his followers he was emulated. Nichiren, with his humble origins in a small fishing village, stands in sharp contrast to other Buddhist leaders of Kamakura times, most of whom came from the upper classes of society. Nichiren began his Buddhist career, as did most eminent Buddhists of his time, at Mount Hiei. However, Nichiren's religious experience at Mount Hiei was very different from that of his contemporaries. At an early age he became convinced that the *Lotus Sutra* contained the essence of the historical Buddha's teachings. Eventually he believed himself to be the only reformer who recognized the true teaching of Tendai and its founder Dengyo Daishi. In fact, Nichiren identified himself with the Bodhisattva Jogyo, to whom Sakyamuni entrusted the *Lotus Sutra.* In his critique of other Buddhist movements and in his reinterpretation of the *Lotus Sutra,* he established the basis for a new, powerful sect.[14]

Passages in the *Lotus Sutra* claim that the *Lotus Sutra* is the one true channel of Buddhism. Nichiren accepted this claim and established the *Lotus Sutra* as the basis of his inspiration and as an object of veneration. He interpreted the turmoils of the times and the very age of the decline of the law as a falling away from the truth of the *Lotus Sutra,* which teaches that the Buddha is revealed in three bodies: the historical Buddha (Sakyamuni), the cosmic or universal Buddha, and the Buddha of bliss (which appears in various forms). Nichiren used his understanding of the Buddha concept to criticize the central doctrines of both Shingon and Amidism as fragmentary. He thought that they neglected the historical Buddha and overlooked the threefold character of the Buddha. His religious convictions also clashed with the other sects on the basic issues of the true object of worship and the true goal of religious life. Nichiren ridiculed the esotericism and ritualism of Shingon as superstitious folly. He was specifically critical of Shingon ritualism because it had invaded Mount Hiei and overshadowed the original Tendai teaching.

Nichiren criticized Amidism for several reasons. In the first place, he objected to the cult of faith in Amida Buddha and repetition of the *nembutsu.* This was not just a minor doctrinal criticism, for Nichiren said the true object of worship was the teaching of Sakyamuni in the *Lotus Sutra.* Later he composed a graphic representation, or *mandala,* of the title of this sutra, making this *mandala* a primary object of worship. He encouraged his followers to venerate and praise this scripture with the phrase "namu Myoho Renge Kyo" ("I give praise to or take refuge in the wonderful *Lotus Sutra*"). Critics of Nichiren and his polemical statements have "pointed out that Honen's exclusive *nenbutsu,* which Nichiren denounced, influenced his positing of the *daimoku* [chanting the title of the *Lotus Sutra*] as an exclusive practice," and noted that "while harshly criticizing Taimitsu [Tendai esoteric Buddhism], he nonetheless made use of mandalas."[15] Obviously, Nichiren did not totally object to the principle of gaining religious power from magical pictures or from devotional recitation. (This is a good example of how forms of Kamakura and Heian Buddhism interacted.) Nichiren's real objection was not the mode of practice, but the fact that Shingon and Amida Buddhism did not recognize the proper object of devotion, which was the *Lotus Sutra* of Sakyamuni.

Nichiren was also contemptuous of the Pure Land stress on absolute trust in Amida at the expense of human initiative. He was just as convinced as the Amidists about the decline of the Buddhist law (or teaching), but he reacted in a different way. He emphasized the active responsibility of every person to change this deplorable situation by a return to faith in the *Lotus Sutra.* Some other Buddhist priests thought that the disturbed times and corrupt Buddhism could be corrected by a return to the proper monastic rules—a revival of the Ritsu (Vinaya) expression of Buddhism. Nichiren dismissed this movement, too, for he measured everything in terms of the *Lotus Sutra*. At the same time, Zen was becoming a major factor in Japanese Buddhism, but Nichiren had no use for the Zen form of Buddhist meditation.

Nichiren's uncompromising character is evident in his unbending criticism of other contemporary Buddhist groups, but this trait is much more strongly accentuated in the founding of his own movement. In Japan, religion and country have always been closely associated. Nichiren did not stop with criticism of other sects; he went so far as to say that the religion of the *Lotus Sutra* should be adopted as the state religion and all other Buddhist sects should be eliminated. This is one of the most extreme expressions of the Japanese association of religion and nation. In reality, Nichiren was as much a patriot as a religious leader. His whole life can be seen as a valiant attempt to save Japan, through exclusive trust in the teachings of the *Lotus Sutra*. He suffered severe persecution for his outspokenness, several times narrowly escaping execution. But he thought little of this, because it was in the service of Buddhism and his country. He is well remembered for having made the prediction that the Mongols would attempt to invade Japan, a prophecy that came true in his lifetime. The Mongol invasion was interpreted by Nichiren as a punishment for Japan's (Japanese Buddhism's) evils and another sign of the age of the decline of the law.[16]

Although the Nichiren sect is not the largest Buddhist group, it has been one of the most active, and the main disciples of Nichiren developed their own variations on his teachings in their own movements. Not every follower of Nichiren had the founder's sense of mission, but this exclusive faith in the *Lotus Sutra* had great significance for later history. It fed into nationalistic streams before World War II and also gave rise to important New Religions, such as Soka Gakkai and Rissho Koseikai, which focus on the *Lotus Sutra*. Nichiren Buddhism can be seen both as a distinctive Japanese form of Buddhism and as a Buddhism for the Japanese people and the Japanese nation.

THE ZEN SECTS:
ENLIGHTENMENT THROUGH MEDITATION

In the West Zen is the most widely known but not necessarily the most understood aspect of Japanese Buddhism. Because of its attractiveness as an existential insight or mystical practice, many Westerners, both scholars and the general public, have been led to believe that Zen tells the entire (or at least the essential) story of Japanese Buddhism and the Japanese spirit. This view of Zen, first advocated by writers such as D. T. Suzuki and Alan Watts, has left an impression of a "pure Zen" that was a very austere meditation denying the efficacy of icons, rituals, magic, miracles, occult powers, relics, and deities (*kami*), as well as the existence of a soul—even the existence of the Buddha. Scholars have always known that Zen, like other forms of Japanese Buddhism, was deeply involved in the practice of these supposedly inefficacious or nonexistent elements. Two avenues have been followed to explain such inconsistency: either these forbidden practices were deviations or corruptions of "pure Buddhism," or they were examples of the Buddhist resorting to skillful means (*hoben*) to bring the masses into the fold of Buddhist enlightenment. More recent scholarship, however, has shown that the story of Zen is more complex than this: while Zen denied or rejected many notions and practices, at the same time it affirmed and accepted them.[17] Though we cannot explore all facets of Zen, we should keep in mind that it is much richer and more complex than popular notions of a "pure Zen."

In the present work, the treatment of Zen must be limited to its role in Japanese religious history. To understand Zen historically, we must recognize that in Japan it first rose to prominence during the Kamakura period. Therefore, it shared the same religious and cultural atmosphere as Pure Land and Nichiren Buddhism. The roots of Zen, as in the case of other Japanese Buddhist movements, can be traced back to its Indian and Chinese origins. As one earlier Japanese scholar has summed up the subject, "*Zen* combined the intellectual culture of India, the pragmatic culture of China, and the esthetic culture of Japan."[18] The word "*zen*" derives from the Sanskrit word "*dhyana*," meaning "meditation." Yet, the practice of meditation did not form the basis of a separate school until this stream had entered China, where it became related to Taoist and other conceptions and practices. The Chinese sects of Ch'an (Chinese for *dhyana*) formed the basis for the Japanese sects of Zen (the Japanese pronunciation of *Ch'an* or *Chan*).

Zen was known in Japan several centuries before Kamakura times without becoming a major movement. Several of the priests who went to China on imperial order brought back Zen. For example, Dengyo Daishi, the founder of Tendai, visited Zen monasteries in China and brought back Zen practices of meditation. Nevertheless, Zen at Mount Hiei could not hold its own against the combined strength of Dengyo Daishi's teaching of the *Lotus Sutra,* the dominant esoteric Buddhism (which overshadowed Heian times), and the emerging Amidist beliefs. In effect, Zen had to be reimported by forceful personalities who made a special effort to propagate it. The two most important figures are Eisai (1141–1215) and Dogen (1200–53).

Eisai received a thorough training in Buddhism at Mount Hiei, but he was not satisfied with the current forms of Buddhism. He wanted to go to India to search out the true Buddhism but was able to travel only as far as China, making two trips there. In China he found the T'ien-t'ai (Tendai) headquarters dominated by Ch'an (Zen); Eisai received the full training of the Lin-chi sect and was ordained a Ch'an priest. Although he did not formally establish a sect himself, his second return to Japan is considered the point of origin for the Japanese Zen sect of Rinzai. ("*Rinzai*" is the Japanese pronunciation for *Lin-chi* or *Linji*.) Kobo Daishi brought tea from China to Japan four centuries earlier, but popular lore credits Eisai with the introduction of tea. Eisai had little luck in advocating Zen practice around the capital city of Kyoto, where the older sects were still entrenched. However, he found continuing support from the military warlords at Kamakura.

In China, too, Zen (Ch'an) had been partly a reaction against the scholasticism and formalism of some imported forms of Indian Buddhism. In place of innumerable abstract doctrines, Zen set forth the simple notion that every person could attain enlightenment by insight into one's own experience and the surrounding world. The Lin-chi sect placed emphasis on a sudden enlightenment that might be triggered by an accidental circumstance. Zen became influential in Japan during the Kamakura period, when Buddhism was appealing to the masses in simpler terms. Whereas the Amida cults stressed devotion to Amida and Nichiren advocated reliance on the *Lotus Sutra,* Zen priests replaced other doctrines with the notion of immediate enlightenment through meditation.[19]

People were attracted to Zen for various reasons. Some priests were drawn to the quest for immediate enlightenment, while other priests and the educated class of society were equally if not more impressed with the Chinese culture brought back by Japanese Zen priests and Chinese (Ch'an) priests who permanently settled in Japan. The Kakamura military leaders who provided major financial support for Zen temples were influenced as much by Chinese cultural and aesthetic practices as by Zen meditation techniques. Lower-ranking, less-educated warriors did not adopt the pure meditation techniques, but accepted Zen in its intermixture with other Buddhist prayers and practices. From the time Zen entered Japan it was subject to political and social pressures. Eisai himself had to make certain compromises to the military rulers and to established Buddhists in order to have Zen accepted, even though he emphasized Zen was nothing new—it dated back to the Buddha—and even though he did not try to establish an independent Zen sect.

DOGEN: SITTING IN MEDITATION

Dogen reportedly went to see Eisai after being disappointed in his own studies of Buddhism at Mount Hiei—he was satisfied neither with the "old" Buddhism, nor with the "new" Buddhism's emphasis on the degenerate age of the "decline of the law." After Eisai's death, Dogen traveled to China but could find no answer in the Buddhist teachings there. Finally he attained enlightenment under the guidance of the Chinese Ch'an master Ju-ching and received the training of the Ts'ao-tung sect. He returned to Japan to spread this new version of Zen. (Ts'ao-tung or Caodong is pronounced "Soto" in Japanese.) Unlike Eisai, Dogen was uncompromising, and he objected to the combination of Zen with other practices (such as the *nembutsu*); nor could he bring himself to serve the military rulers. This made his life difficult, but eventually his Soto sect of Zen flourished.

The difference between Rinzai Zen and Soto Zen is roughly the same in Japan as with the comparable groups in China. Rinzai favors the use of techniques such as meditation on *koan* ("public cases" or paradoxical statements) to achieve sudden enlightenment. Soto gives some weight to study of the scriptures and emphasizes the gradual entry into enlightenment. The Soto sect is famous for its practice of *zazen,* "sitting in meditation." Within Japanese society, Rinzai came to be identified with the ruling class, Soto with the common people.

Dogen's system of thought is considered by some Japanese scholars to be one of the most creative developments within Japanese Buddhism, and increasingly Western scholars have become attracted to Dogen's analysis of human existence and the nature of time. A distinctive feature of Zen teachings, both in China and in Japan, has been to emphasize a direct, intuitive transmission of the Buddha's enlightenment, and this is equally true for the transmission of Buddhist teaching about enlightenment from one master to his disciple. Dogen's meeting in China with Ju-ching was crucial in bringing Dogen to a realization of the direct, intuitive nature of enlightenment. According to tradition, Dogen was enlightened when he heard Ju-ching scolding a monk sleeping. Ju-ching said that instead of sleeping, the monk should "drop off the body and the mind." This brought home to Dogen the fact that true enlightenment meant leaving behind completely both mind and body. When Dogen set up his own monastic retreat, he emphasized loyalty to one's Zen master and meditation that went beyond the usual process of thinking. For Dogen, this form of meditation was the true *dharma,* or teaching, of the Buddha.

Dogen was critical of the Rinzai tradition of Zen Buddhism, which stressed meditation on *koan.* Dogen did not completely reject *koan,* but he objected to the mechanical way they came to be used, and he feared that monks meditating on *koan* would become so engrossed in intellectual reflection on the *koan* that they would be deluded into just *thinking* about enlightenment, rather than actually realizing enlightenment. For Dogen, attaining enlightenment was not a rational process or a solution to an intellectual puzzle. Enlightenment was more likely to be achieved by the total realization of the whole person than by intellectual activity alone. More than the *koan,* Dogen emphasized *zazen.* Although even sitting in meditation requires the use of the body and mind, Dogen stressed that the disciplining of body and mind in meditation facilitated the dropping off of body and mind. In other words, enlightenment is beyond matter and spirit. In fact, according to Dogen, one can enter enlightenment only after any thought of attaining enlightenment, or even any thought about enlightenment, has been eliminated. The way to free oneself from any such thoughts is just "to sit," to practice *zazen.* In a sense, one does not actually attain enlightenment, for there is no enlightenment to attain: one realizes the enlightenment that lies within each person.

From the time Dogen first studied Buddhism at Mount Hiei, he had pondered the apparent contradiction of "original enlightenment" and "attained enlightenment." A person had to have some original potential for enlightenment or else one could not become enlightened. But if a person possessed the original enlightenment, then why did Buddhists find it so hard to strive to attain what they already possessed? Dogen's solution, reached through his own enlightenment experience, was that the contradiction appears because people think about enlightenment rather than practicing the way to enlightenment, *zazen*. A person who meditates in the proper fashion realizes that the practice of meditation and enlightenment are the same. In proper *zazen*, body and mind disappear automatically.

Dogen emphasized the importance of *zazen*, saying it superseded everything else. The experience of enlightenment within *zazen* reveals that the entire world is filled with the Buddha-nature. This is something the unenlightened eye does not see, but the enlightened eye is able to grasp immediately and intuitively. According to Dogen, only the present moment of enlightenment has "reality." He places so much emphasis on *zazen* that he incorporates its significance in his radical view of time: he collapses both past and future into the immediate experience of the present moment of sitting in meditation. This does not mean that a person who has attained enlightenment can stop practicing meditation. Quite the contrary, for Dogen believed that life is most important and most real when a person sits in meditation. His creative genius brought the discipline of meditation to a mature fruition.

ZEN: INSTITUTIONAL AND ARTISTIC DEVELOPMENTS

Zen eventually assumed major importance in the Buddhist world. One landmark of Zen's success was the *shogun's* decree of 1338, which led to the building of Zen temples in sixty-six localities. The temples, called *ankokuji*, or "temples to pacify the country," were similar in function to the earlier *kokubunji*, or provincial temples. Just as the *kokubunji* of the Nara period spread Buddhist teachings, so the *ankokuji* of the fourteenth century helped to spread Zen to the various regions of the country and to people of lower classes. The government recognized the top-ranking Zen temples (of the Rinzai sect), and the priests of these temples led the way in the study of Chinese classics and Neo-Confucianism.[20]

Even Zen was no exception to the general tendency of Buddhist sects to undergo fluctuating periods of strength and weakness. For example, Dogen's thought and practice were very lofty, and he trained important disciples, but the development of Soto Zen into a major Buddhist denomination in Japan was mainly the work of Keizan (1268–1325), who lived shortly after the time of Dogen. Keizan was more willing than Dogen to compromise and blend Zen with other ritual practices. The simple funeral and memorial practices that he developed helped Soto Zen spread among the people much more thoroughly than Rinzai Zen. Later, the aristocratic Rinzai tended to lose its vigor, but in the eighteenth century, Hakuin (1686–1769) did much to revive Rinzai and meditation on *koan*. Hakuin is the author of the famous *koan* "Listen to the sound of the single hand"[21]—that is, to realize the sound of one hand clapping.

The seventeenth-century poet Basho (1644–94), who also practiced Zen Buddhism, did much to further the aesthetic expression of Zen in his beautiful short poems called *haiku*. During Basho's last illness, while he was on a trip, his followers asked him to give them a final poem or "death poem." At first, Basho refused. But he lived through the night, and the next morning he gave them a poem based on his dreams during the night:

> On a journey, ill,
> and over fields all withered, dreams
> go wandering still.[22]

Zen had its roots in India, emerged as a sect in China, and first flourished in Japan as the imported Rinzai and Soto sects. But Zen is much more than a sectarian expression of Buddhism or a personal experience of enlightenment. In both China and Japan, Zen had a strong impact on the arts. Shingon contributed to the graphic arts and provided icons for ritual and devotion; Zen pervaded the whole culture. Zen (colored by Taoism's love of nature) is the spiritual inspiration of much Chinese and Japanese painting; its influence can be seen in arts such as flower arranging (*ikebana*). Unlike Shingon art, which favors the esoteric and borders on the grotesque, Zen favors a quiet simplicity.

It is difficult to say whether the Chinese tradition of Ch'an (Zen) taught quiet simplicity to the Japanese or whether the Japanese brought a cultural tradition of quiet simplicity to their understanding of Zen. From ancient times the Japanese have cultivated a tradition combining aesthetic and religious appreciation of nature. This can be seen as early as the eighth-century anthology of poetry, *Manyoshu*. Many Westerners have come to appreciate Zen through translations of *haiku*, which express the spirit of Zen. Also, the drinking of tea and the cult of tea have been closely associated with Zen.

Zen has pervaded Japanese culture far beyond the realms of what Westerners ordinarily understand as art. Zen practitioners cared less for learning abstract doctrine than for mastering the complete training of mind and body. There was a relationship between emphasis on the instant of enlightenment and tuning the mind and body to every instant of experience. Therefore, even military techniques or sports such as swordsmanship, archery, and wrestling were pursued for the sake of Zen. The object was not simply to defeat the opponent, but to tune one's whole being to a naturalness and freeness that transcended the formalities of prescribed movements. Kamakura warriors adopted Zen both for its utilitarian and its spiritual benefits. In the modern period, Zen continues to be a major inspiration for philosophical thought and religious cultivation.

One common theme that runs through the teaching and practice of the Pure Land, Nichiren, and Zen sects is the greater openness and even encouragement for women to actively participate in Buddhism. For example, "Honen notes the practice of the temples of the Nara- and Heian-period sects of strictly excluding women from participation in their activities and even from entry into their sacred precincts: 'In this land of Japan the most sacred and exalted holy places all forbid women to enter.' " [23] Honen wrote at length on the fact that "Amida made a special vow to save women" as the basis for his conviction that women eventually (after being reborn as men) could achieve rebirth or salvation. Dogen, too, "harshly criticized the traditional centers of

Offering incense at temples is one of the most common acts of religious devotion in Japan. In the top photograph is the courtyard of a large Zen temple in Tokyo, where people are offering incense in a large metal brazier in front of a seated statue of Jizo (featuring a large pilgrim's hat). Below, people take advantage of the curative powers of incense at another nearby temple by placing their hands in the smoke and rubbing the afflicted parts of their bodies. The woman in front is holding her hand into the smoke, while the women behind the incense brazier are rubbing their bodies. (Tokyo, 1979)

Buddhism for discriminating against women, [and] preached the equality of the sexes with regard to practice and the attainment of enlightenment." Nichiren based his views on the enlightenment or Buddhahood of women on the scriptural authority of the *Lotus Sutra:* " 'even should all the women in Japan be despised and rejected by all the other sutras in the canon, what does it matter as long as salvation is assured by the authority of the Lotus Sutra?' " [24] These three movements, each in its own way, elevated the attitude of Japanese Buddhism toward females, and by welcoming women helped broaden and strengthen their own institutions.

To explain the development and elaboration of Buddhism in Kamakura times, it has been necessary to describe new sects and doctrinal variations. However, one should not infer that all the Japanese people who accepted Buddhism were aware of all these developments. Buddhism made its impression on the lives of ordinary laypeople in a direct fashion. We must not forget, amid these discussions of doctrine, that Japanese Buddhism has always been important for carrying out indispensable memorials for family ancestors. Even Nichiren, seen by some as a religious fanatic and superpatriot, is said to have spent much time in prayer for the departed souls of his parents and teacher. One way of viewing the development of sects is to recognize that they created special channels within which practical functions could be carried out. In addition to the memorial services, temples held regular festivals and issued various protective amulets. The people who had memorial services performed at a temple or went there for other reasons might not be familiar with the peculiar doctrines of that sect. The sects that came into being in the Kamakura period later became the major Buddhist institutions of the modern era, and since their founding they have combined theoretical doctrine with popular practice.

NOTES

1. James Foard, "In Search of a Lost Reformation: A Reconsideration of Kamakura Buddhism," *Japanese Journal of Religious Studies,* vol. 7 (Dec. 1980), pp. 274–81.

2. See Payne, ed., *Re-Visioning "Kamakura" Buddhism,* especially his "Introduction," pp. 1–23.

3. Stone, *Original Enlightenment,* pp. 20, 60. Payne, in his "Introduction," p. 11, suggests, following Sir George Sansom, that the "rhetoric of decadence" directed by warriors (*bushi*) against the contemporary court aristocracy may have been motivated by a combination of superiority/inferiority complex: "the *bushi* felt virtuous in their austerity, superior to the decadence of the court, and simultaneously inferior to the cultural achievements of the court. . . ."

4. The third and final age is known in Japan as *mappo,* a compound term formed by the two words *matsu* (last or final) and *ho* (the Buddha's teachings). For a historical overview of the notion of *mappo* in Japanese Buddhism see Michele Marra, "The Development of Mappo Thought in Japan (I)," *Japanese Journal of Religious Studies,* vol. 15, no. 1 (Mar. 1988), pp. 25–54; "The Development of Mappo Thought in Japan (II)," *Japanese Journal of Religious Studies,* vol. 15, no. 4 (Dec. 1988), pp. 287–305.

5. See Yusen Kashiwahara and Koyu Sonoda, eds, *Shapers of Japanese Buddhism,* trans. Gaynor Sekimori (Tokyo: Kosei, 1994) for "twenty major biographies" of Buddhist leaders and "brief biographies" of many Buddhist figures. This work is a convenient reference for both major and lesser known Buddhist innovators.

6. Payne, in his "Introduction," p. 9, rejects the notion that the new Buddhism of Kamakura was "'more Japanese,'" or reached out "to a broader portion of the populace, 'the common people,'" emphasizing the economic factor: "the rising prosperity of the peasants made it possible for the new Buddhisms to establish productive connections with them."

7. See de Bary et al., *Sources of Japanese Tradition,* 2d ed., vol. 1 for selections of translated documents concerning the Pure Land sects (Chapter 10), the Nichiren sects (Chapter 13), and the Zen sects (Chapter 14).

8. For an introduction to Honen and his work, and a translation of Honen's key work outlining faith in Amida and salvation through the *nembutsu,* see *Honen's Senchakushu: Passages on the Selection of the Nembutsu in the Original Vow (Senchaku Hongan Nembutsu Shu),* "Translated and Edited with an Introduction by *Senchakushu* English Translation Project" (Honolulu: University of Hawai'i; Tokyo: Sogo Bukkyo Kenkyujo, Taisho University, 1998).

9. Yuishin Ito, "Kuya," in *Shapers of Japanese Buddhism,* p. 52.

10. James C. Dobbins, *Jodo Shinshu: Shin Buddhism in Medieval Japan* (Bloomington, IN: Indiana University, 1989), p. 71. This book includes accounts of Honen and Shinran, as well as the formation of Shin Buddhism (the True Pure Land sect). See also Dennis Hirota, trans., *The Collected Works of Shinran* (Kyoto: Jodo Shinshu Hongwanji-ha, 1997), 2 vols.

11. For the significance of Rennyo, see Minor and Ann Rogers, *Rennyo: The Second Founder of Shin Buddhism: With a Translation of His Letters* (Berkeley, CA: Asian Humanities Press, 1991).

12. For an account of the itinerant *nembutsu* practitioner called Ippen, see Dennis Hirota, trans, *No Abode: The Record of Ippen* (Kyoto: Ryukoku University, 1986).

13. See Goodwin, *Alms and Vagabonds,* and Donald McCallum, *Zenkoji and Its Icon: A Study in Medieval Japanese Religious Art* (Princeton: Princeton University, 1994).

14. See *Selected Writings of Nichiren,* Burton Watson et al.; trans.; edited and introduced by Philip B. Yampolsky (New York: Columbia University, 1990).

15. Stone, *Original Enlightenment,* p. 297.

16. The Mongol fleet was destroyed by a storm that was perceived as a "divine wind" (*kamikaze*). Thus, the Shinto interpretation stressed that native *kami* or gods had driven out the foreigners. The World War II airplanes of the suicide pilots who crashed their planes into Allied ships have been called *kamikaze.*

17. For a critique of Suzuki's view of Zen, see Robert Sharf, "The Zen of Japanese Nationalism," in James W. Heisig and John C. Maraldo, eds., *Rude Awakenings: Zen, the Kyoto School, and the Question of Nationalism* (Honolulu: University of Hawai'i, 1994), pp. 107–60. The English-language publications on Zen, both popular and scholarly, are quite extensive; for a critical treatment attempting to balance Zen's rejection/acceptance of various practices, see Bernard Faure, *The Rhetoric of Immediacy: A Cultural Critique of Chan/Zen Buddhism* (Princeton: Princeton University, 1991).

18. Reiho Masunaga, *The Soto Approach to Zen* (Tokyo: Layman Buddhist Society, 1958), p. 34.

19. The notions of "gradual" and "sudden" enlightenment are the focus of Faure's *The Rhetoric of Immediacy.*

20. The actual system of ranks of five temples, or *gozan,* is probably Chinese in origin. See Toshihide Akamatsu and Philip Yampolsky, "Muromachi Zen and the Gozan System," in *Japan in the Muromachi Age,* ed. John Whitney Hall and Takeshi Toyoda (Berkeley: University of California, 1977), pp. 313–15. For a comprehensive study, see Martin Collcutt, *Five Mountains: The Rinzai Monastic Institution in Medieval Japan* (Cambridge: Harvard University, 1981).

21. Philip B. Yampolsky, trans., *The Zen Master Hakuin: Selected Writings* (New York: Columbia University, 1971), p. 163.

22. *An Introduction to Haiku,* translated by Harold G. Henderson. Copyright © 1958 by Harold G. Henderson. Reprinted by permission of Doubleday & Company, Inc. For an excerpt from this work see my *Religion in the Japanese Experience,* 2d ed., pp. 176–79.

23. Kazuo Kasahara. "Women and Buddhism," in *A History of Japanese Religion,* ed. Kazuo Kasahara, trans. Paul McCarthy and Gaynor Sekimori: (Tokyo: Kosei, 2001), p. 285.

24. Ibid., pp. 294, 297.

11

❧

The Development of Medieval Shinto

In our historical account of Japanese religion we seem to have lost sight of the tradition that has come to be known as "Shinto." Our last direct view of this tradition was in Chapter 4, where we saw that from about the sixth century, prehistoric Japanese religious practices related to rice agriculture, seasonal celebrations, and the imperial line became more formally organized, partly in reaction to the influx of continental traditions such as Buddhism. In subsequent chapters we followed the path of the imported traditions of Buddhism, Confucianism, and Taoism, and also folk religion. Chapters 9 and 10 explored the vitality and innovation within Japanese Buddhism from the ninth through thirteenth centuries.

It may appear that the formation of Shinto has been crowded out of the historical picture from the sixth through the thirteenth centuries by the discussion of foreign importations such as Buddhism. As a matter of fact, in early Japan formative Shinto tended to be overshadowed while Buddhism was flourishing. Most of the emperors and the nobility favored Buddhism, and the court was primarily concerned with Buddhism. Thus, if we look at the capital and the formal organization of the state, Buddhism appears to have almost completely overwhelmed the native beginnings of Shinto.

However, the "great tradition," which dominated political and literary life, is only one side of Japanese religious history. There is also the "little tradition," which expressed the cultural and religious life of the people. The common people outside of the capital lived out much of their religious lives in annual festivals connected with agriculture and other vocations. Many shrines and festivals existed before the entry of Buddhism and continued with or without the influence of Buddhism. While Buddhism dominated the court and centralized institutions, Shinto, with its loosely organized religious life gathered around local shrines, flourished in the countryside. Shinto was not as highly organized and institutionalized as Buddhism, which had the advantage of a long scriptural, doctrinal, and monastic history spanning the Asian continent from India to China. During Heian and Kamakura times the local customs and practices of incipient Shinto were not as conspicuous as the dramatic developments of Buddhism, with its innovative leaders, continental imports, and remarkable institutions. Nevertheless, the distinctively Japanese heritage that became Shinto was important both in local seasonal rituals and in the prayers and rituals handed down in major shrines. The imperial family also was a repository of prehistoric ceremony and Shinto ritual, even though events such as annual rites and enthronement ceremonies were not open to the common people.

What happened to the formation of Shinto after the sixth century was a complex process of preserving and transmitting the prehistoric Japanese heritage, influencing and being influenced by the continental culture and religion (especially Buddhism), and undergoing development and codification. The *interpretation* of what happened to Shinto is complicated by a variety of vantage points, each providing its own version of the story. To better understand the ambiguity of different treatments of Shinto, we need to interrupt the historical narrative and consider different viewpoints leading to contrasting interpretations.

Two major Japanese perspectives that provide an overview of Japanese religion are those of Shinto and Buddhism. Although each tradition includes a wide range of attitudes and commitments, for the purpose of our discussion we can assume two contrasting "voices" that highlight the problem of conceptualizing Japanese religion. Generally, Shinto priests and scholars in modern times have viewed Shinto from the vantage point of the post-Meiji era when Shinto was legally isolated from Buddhism and became much more highly organized as a distinct institutional "religion" than in pre-Meiji times. From this viewpoint, Shinto is seen as the "unique" Japanese religious heritage, with direct continuity from prehistoric times down to the present, temporarily dominated by foreign traditions such as Buddhism, but throughout history representing the "authentic" national spiritual heritage. In this perception, Shinto's modern identity and more organized character have been considered as present in much earlier times; however, even more important, Shinto is perceived not so much as a formal religious institution, but rather as a permanent and indelible feature of Japanese culture and religion. Therefore, following this line of reasoning, because the *kami* created the Japanese islands and the *kami* are the source of Japanese people and all life (such as the all-important rice), implicitly or unconsciously all Japanese are considered to "naturally" be a part of Shinto.

Generally, Buddhist priests and scholars in modern times share with Shinto priests and scholars a post-Meiji conception of Shinto and Buddhism as two separate religions. But there is considerable divergence between the two groups of priests and scholars and their notions of the differences and relationships between the respective traditions. Buddhism's modern viewpoint is shaped even more by the perception of religion and Buddhism gained from sophisticated Buddhist studies focusing not only on Buddhism as a philosophical tradition but also on each Buddhist sect as a separate ecclesiastical and doctrinal heritage. In other words, Buddhism and religion in general are viewed as highly organized institutions with elaborate doctrine and ecclesiastical structures. From this vantage point, Buddhist spokespeople have often looked down on early Shinto as a "primitive" religion without a complex organizational form and as holding implicit and uncritical "animistic" beliefs in spirits rather than explicit bodies of codified doctrine and systematic philosophy. In fact, from the viewpoint of Buddhism and a highly formal view of religion, it has been argued that Shinto did not exist as a full-fledged religion until quite recently, and that Buddhism provided the main Japanese religious heritage from ancient and medieval times down to about the Meiji period.[1]

These two polemical, almost contradictory, viewpoints present us with a dilemma. Should we see Shinto as the implicit or unconscious spiritual heritage of the Japanese people, in other words, the unique religious tradition of the Japanese nation? Or should we consider Shinto a loose set of primitive beliefs not organized as a religion until the nineteenth century? Before we make a choice between these two alternatives, we should recognize a hidden assumption within this critical view of Shinto. If the critique of "Shinto" as a concept is that it is not highly organized, but rather a loose set of animistic or "primitive" beliefs, does this mean that the concept of "Buddhism" is a set of formally organized institutions with abstract doctrines? We need only return to the Nara period to remember that Buddhism, for all its institutional and doctrinal complexity, was accepted and practiced for various magical techniques and worldly benefits. Throughout its history in Japan, down to the present, Buddhism has been received, believed, and invoked by people mainly for its practical benefits, not for its institutional strength or doctrinal superiority.[2] This makes the choices more complex: we can view Japanese religion through Shinto theory *or* Buddhist doctrine; turning this upside down, we could view Japanese religion through Shinto practice *or* Buddhist practice.

Before we commit ourselves to choose between these either-or Shinto or Buddhist alternatives, it is important to remember that, as scholars and students, we do not need to choose a Shinto viewpoint or a Buddhist viewpoint. We are not forced to make an either-or choice: *either* Shinto as the unique and unbroken indigenous heritage, *or* Shinto as "primitive" beliefs not qualifying as religion. Nor are we bound to select an either-or option of Shinto/Buddhist theory or practice. As "outsiders" to the Japanese religious scene, we may opt for other interpretations.

Nevertheless, as scholars and students, we must assume a vantage point, realizing that each point has its own limitations as well as its own advantages. The approach assumed in this book is Japanese religion as a whole way of life or unified worldview (rather than seen from within an individual religion, such as Shinto or Buddhism), and as expressed and lived by the Japanese people (rather than as idealized by religious elites). One advantage of this approach is the ability to grasp, in textbook fashion, the generalities that enable us to study and learn about the unity of what we call Japanese culture and Japanese religion. Another advantage is not having to "choose sides" and favor *either* a Shinto *or* a Buddhist perspective. An obvious limitation of this position is that such *generalities* do not live in historical time so much as in the minds of those of us who look back and try to make sense out of history: we must be careful not to assume that these generalities are historical facts and not to think that the category "Japanese religion" has an essential or eternal existence.

There are two good lessons from this consideration of how to interpret Shinto, something to keep in mind throughout our consideration of Japanese religion. One lesson is to remember that our contemporary notion of religion as an area of life separate from other areas, and as discrete traditions rather compartmentalized one from another, was not present in premodern Japan. Another lesson is that whenever we view Shinto, or Buddhism, or Japanese religion, we should ask ourselves what viewpoint we are using, and the advantages and limitations of that viewpoint. We should take these lessons with us as we leave this discussion of the problems of interpretation and return to the historical narrative of Japanese religion.[3]

For much of Japanese history down to the Meiji era for most of the people, Shinto and Buddhism were integral parts of a religious life that usually did not clearly compartmentalize the two. This close interrelationship has been seen earlier, for example, in the *honji suijaku* correspondence of Buddhist divinities and *kami*. The intimate association between Shinto and Buddhism comes into focus, or becomes obscured, depending not only on the viewpoint we assume but also on the material we happen to study.

When we looked at Heian Buddhist leaders and their idealized messages, which emphasize doctrinal arguments and institutional forms, the interaction between Buddhism and Shinto was not so evident. But especially for Shingon and Tendai, the founding of mountain temples was closely associated with obtaining the blessing of the local *kami* and maintaining Shinto shrines in close proximity and in intimate relationship with Buddhist temples. Most major temples have been built with the blessing of *kami,* housed in nearby shrines. Shinto priests and Buddhist priests often used the rites of both traditions at shrines as well as temples. In some cases Buddhist sutras were recited before Shinto *kami,* for the express purpose of "converting" the *kami* and saving them from endless transmigration. Yet, Shinto was not simply a recipient of Buddhist influence. Although much of the formal rationale and ritual for the Shinto-Buddhist interaction was Buddhist, it should be remembered that the preexisting background of *kami* was the cultural perception within which Buddhist divinities were accepted. As one scholar has summed up this interaction of traditions, "In order to penetrate Japanese culture and to be assimilated by it, Buddhism needed to interpret the nature of divinities other than its own in such manner that they might fit its cosmography and cosmology, and that it thus be able to offer a comprehensive interpretation of the world."[4] Most of the Buddhist objects of worship were received and embraced not as representatives of a universal Buddhist pantheon, nor even as transplanted Indian and Chinese divinities, but as the *Japanese* manifestations of Buddhist figures that appeared in the context of a miracle or revelation. The setting for these miraculous tales was the coexistence and cooperation of shrines and temples that dominated the medieval scene. One scholar has insisted that rather than using the rubrics of "Buddhism" and "Shinto" in premodern times we should focus on "shrine-temple multiplexes."[5] "Most of the temples of these multiplexes did not belong exclusively to one or another sect, nor could most of the shrines be said to be purely Shinto. Rather, the shrines expressed the local character of creeds and practices with which Buddhism joined to produce in the course of time combined Shinto-Buddhist cults in these religious centers."[6]

These major shrine-temple complexes, or multiplexes, preserve traditions or stories (often listed in short form on sign boards in front of the temple and/or handed out in pamphlets) of the miraculous appearance of the Buddhist divinity worshiped there. These stories (*engi*) have a general pattern of introducing a cosmogony featuring *kami* such as Izanagi and Izanami and "related structures of sacred time and space" for the context to introduce the local miracle tale.[7] In this setting, Buddhas and *bodhisattvas* became interchangeable with *kami,* shrines and temples were located and acted together, and Shinto and Buddhist priests (sometimes one man serving both functions) offered Shinto and Buddhist services at these sites. Each religious site had its own local version of this mixture, which also might include Chinese customs, Taoist elements, and Confucian notions. In medieval times pilgrimage to these holy centers became popular, first for the nobility and then for the common people.[8]

In summary, on the formal and institutional level Buddhism seemed to overwhelm Shinto, but on the informal and local level Buddhism never superseded Shinto. In fact, Shinto's appropriation of Buddhist symbols and rites helped enhance Buddhism's popular appeal. As Buddhism was accepted by the Japanese people and they were converted as Buddhists, Buddhism itself was transformed into a Japanese religious reality. It can be argued that although Buddhism seemed to triumph on the surface, the religious life of Shinto persevered—even within Buddhist forms, beneath the surface. One Buddhologist, writing mainly about Kamakura Buddhism, has made a point that applies generally to Buddhism in the premodern period: "the truly unique character of Japanese Buddhism seems to have been the institutional, doctrinal, and ritual integration of Buddhism and Shinto."[9]

MEDIEVAL BUDDHISM
AND MEDIEVAL SHINTO

Buddhism never completely dominated or replaced Shinto. Even at the capital, Shinto lived on in the imperial rites led by the emperor. In fact, as long as Buddhism was centered at the capital, it tended to remain the religion of the aristocracy. Nara Buddhism made little direct impact on the people. The Tendai and Shingon sects of Heian Buddhism began the process of creating a Japanese

Buddhism, a process continued by Kamakura leaders. People eventually came to accept various Buddhist *bodhisattvas* on much the same level as their Japanese *kami*. Therefore, although Buddhism seemed to triumph on the surface, the religious life of Shinto continued—even within Buddhist forms. While Buddhism was being transformed into a Japanese movement, Shinto was quietly incorporating the multiple strands of continental influence.

The continual development of Shinto resulted from more than a simple encounter with Buddhism. In the Heian and Kamakura periods, when Chinese culture was so highly esteemed, Shinto tended to draw into itself features of Confucianism, Taoism, and Buddhism—especially speculative philosophy and cosmology from Buddhism. In general, Shinto accepted religious expressions from the three traditions: ethical concepts came from Confucianism; Chinese notions and Taoist elements provided cosmology, a religious calendar, divinities, and festivals; Buddhism furnished philosophy, cosmology, rituals, objects of worship, and formulas.

Shinto's practice of borrowing must be seen from two viewpoints. On the one hand, Shinto never ceased to be the transmitter of the older Japanese traditions: borrowed foreign concepts usually complemented or elaborated Shinto traditions. In this sense, Shinto remained Shinto in spite of the borrowings. On the other hand, the borrowings became so much a part of Shinto that eventually their foreign origin was forgotten. In this sense, Shinto's complexity increased to the extent that Shinto cannot be called simply the indigenous religion of Japan. Imported traditions added to the richness of Shinto and enabled it to become more systematically organized.

"Medieval Shinto" is an approximate term referring to Shinto when it was actively borrowing from other traditions and organizing itself along the lines of borrowed patterns, especially from about the twelfth through the sixteenth centuries. The outside limits of medieval Shinto are difficult to fix, for at this time it was not completely set apart as a distinct tradition; the precedent for Shinto's borrowing from other traditions was already established in the Nara period, and medieval Shinto began to take shape and flourish from the Heian period onward. The terminal date for medieval Shinto may be put at 1868, the date of the Meiji Restoration, about the time when Shinto and Buddhism were forcibly separated. Shinto purists, however, had been working for this separation for several centuries before 1868.[10]

Perhaps the best way to introduce medieval Shinto is to discuss it in terms of the traditions that influenced it. Although Buddhism was not the only influential tradition, it was undoubtedly the most important. The Buddhist theory of *honji-suijaku* ("original substance manifests traces") pervaded practically the whole of Shinto.[11] The theory of *honji-suijaku*, transmitted from China to Japan, became the theoretical foundation for considering Japanese *kami* as "manifest traces" (*suijaku*) or counterparts of the "original substance" (*honji*) of particular Buddhas and *bodhisattvas*. For example, as early as the Nara period, Hachiman was considered both a *kami* and a *bodhisattva* without a clear distinction of Shinto or Buddhist identity. In later periods almost every Shinto shrine considered its enshrined *kami* as the counterpart of some Buddha or

Buddhist divinity. It was customary to enshrine statues of these Buddhist counterparts in Shinto shrines, and this practice further encouraged the interaction of Buddhist and Shinto priests.

It should be noted that the Japanese practice of mixing Buddhism with local religion is not unique in the history of Buddhism. For example, the Buddhist pantheon had been closely associated with other divinities in India, and was blended with other spirits and deities in southeast Asia; then in China it developed a pattern of interrelated Buddhist and Chinese deities.

One reason medieval Shinto is difficult to outline is the fact that it was never uniformly systematized. For example, the theory of *honji-suijaku* was put into practice in many local shrines throughout the country, linking particular local *kami* with specific Buddhist figures, but there was no uniform nationwide set of counterparts for Shinto *kami* and Buddhist divinities. Shinto shrines might be dedicated to the worship of divinities that were Buddhist, Chinese, or Indian in origin. Shinto priests (and Buddhist priests and the people) could participate religiously in this ambiguous context without making precise relationships or sharp distinctions. This informal sense of harmony among the several religious traditions is present throughout Japanese religious history, especially at the level of popular practice.

THE RELATION OF TENDAI
AND SHINGON TO MEDIEVAL SHINTO

When the "way" of Buddha (Butsudo) first entered Japan about the sixth century C.E., it stimulated the formation of the "way" of *kami* (Shinto): in each term the "way" is represented by the same Chinese character, pronounced *"tao"* or *"dao"* in Chinese, *"to"* or *"do"* in Japanese. Thereafter Buddhism and Shinto were always in informal contact with one another, but more formal interaction between the two traditions began in the Heian period when the Tendai and Shingon sects promoted a mutual interrelationship. Medieval Shinto arose in the Heian period, and borrowed especially from the Tendai and Shingon sects for two apparent reasons. First, these two Buddhist sects actively assumed a Japanese character, making them more readily available to Shinto. Second, both sects possessed the richer cosmology, philosophy, and ritual that Shinto sought. The early precedents for Shinto-Buddhist cooperation were used by Shinto scholars in the Heian period to justify borrowing from Tendai and Shingon in building up a more elaborate Shinto system. This set the stage for significant cross-fertilization between Shinto, on the one hand, and Tendai and Shingon, on the other hand.

One significant system of borrowing between Shinto and Buddhism was at Mount Hiei, the mountain headquarters of Tendai. (The basic mode of borrowing was similar at Mount Koya, the mountain headquarters of Shingon.) In the Heian period, Shinto shrines and Buddhist temples stood side by side, and priests of Shinto and Buddhism sometimes participated in each other's rites. The founders of the two Buddhist sects, Dengyo Daishi and Kobo Daishi, thought it only natural that shrines should be erected to honor the local *kami* of their respective mountains. Gradually there emerged at each locale individual forms of thought and practice that related the Shinto *kami* and Buddhist doctrine. Because the Tendai headquarters was modeled after the Chinese mountain headquarters by the same name (T'ien-t'ai in Chinese), the Tendai scholars had a Chinese precedent to follow in recognizing local deities. The collective name for the local Japanese *kami* and Buddhas at Mount Hiei, adopted from the Chinese, was "mountain king" (pronounced *"Sanno"* in Japanese); they were worshiped at the Shinto shrine Hie Taisha at the foot of Mount Hiei. "Grounded in both local and elite native traditions, the Shinto shrines of Hie came to be seen as the protectors of the Buddhist institutions of Mount Hiei with which they gradually evolved systematic relations at all levels of their existence."[12]

The theoretical foundation of the system, according to Tendai, was found in the highly revered *Lotus Sutra*. This text states that all the Buddhas that come into the world are only "one reality" (*ichi jitsu*)—the Tendai concept of an absolute reality behind the whole universe. The theory was used to argue that the various *kami* are Japanese historical appearances that correspond to Buddhist divinities, all of which are subsumed in the "one reality." This form of Shinto was called either "Sanno Shinto" or "Ichi-jitsu Shinto."[13] The *honji-suijaku* theory set up a general framework of correspondences between *kami* and Buddhist divinities; Ichi-jitsu Shinto developed a particular theory of correspondences based on Tendai teaching.

This brief presentation may have given the impression that borrowing was mainly intellectual. The contrary, however, is true. At the popular level, there was a ritual and devotional union of Shinto and Buddhism. Officially, Shinto was separated from Buddhism after 1868, but today many Sanno shrines still survive. Although explicit Buddhist influence has been removed from the shrines, their very existence is a continuing reminder of the earlier Shinto-Buddhist interweaving.

In the same vein, we can see Shinto absorbing the Shingon notion that the whole world can best be understood through two *mandala*. The symbolic pictures of the cosmos represented the bipolar character of existence evident in the mutually opposing forces of matter-mind, male-female, and dynamic expression-static potential. Within this ideological framework, Shinto priests could coordinate Japanese *kami* and Buddhist divinities, for they could place some *kami* within the womb *mandala* and other *kami* within the diamond *mandala*. Because this style of Shinto emphasized the two *mandala* of Shingon, it was called Ryobu Shinto. *Ryobu* means "two parts" or "dual," and sometimes Ryobu Shinto has been called "Dual Shinto." A famous example of the rationale of Ryobu Shinto is found at the Ise Shrines, the most venerated shrines in Japan. Amaterasu, the Sun Goddess and ancestress of the imperial family, is enshrined at Ise. In later times the Sun Goddess came to be equated with the Sun Buddha (Dainichi or Birushana or Vairocana) of the *Mahavairo-*

cana Sutra, which is the main scripture of Shingon. The Ise Shrines, which include the Inner Shrine and Outer Shrine, came to be considered representations of the two *mandala* of Shingon.

It should not be overlooked that Shinto influenced Buddhism, even in the highly developed religious art form of the *mandala;* in fact, a Shinto version of the *mandala* appeared. Often it portrayed a kind of aerial view of a shrine compound. Shinto adopted the form of the *mandala* but gave it a typically "this-worldly" Shinto coloring.[14] Shinto transformed the abstract Buddhist *mandala,* which represented an ideal otherworld, into a picture of the actual Japanese landscape. This is a good example of how Shinto emphasis on the sacredness of nature and the presence of *kami* in this world influenced the abstract Buddhist symbolism that it adopted.

Shinto also received Shingon rituals such as the fire *(goma)* rite, architectural forms, and theoretical elements. A shrine that inherited the influence of Ryobu Shinto can be identified even today by the unusual *torii* (sacred arch) in front of it. There are numerous kinds of Shinto *torii,* all of which feature two upright poles with a crosspiece connecting the poles. In Ryobu Shinto the *torii* was modified so that each upright pole had attached to it two smaller poles. The two smaller poles indicate the dual character of the world, which is transcended by an overarching unity.

MEDIEVAL SHINTO: INDIVIDUAL
SCHOLARS AND FAMILY TRADITIONS

During medieval times the tradition that we now call Shinto was present in at least three different forms of expression, none of which existed completely apart from the other forms. First were the age-old beliefs, customs, and practices inherited from prehistoric times and continued both at the emperor's court and on the local level. Second were the elite developments of shrine-temple multiplexes, in which the native heritage was the basis for the acceptance of continental traditions and at the same time the receiving vessel of these imported elements and systems. Third were the specific formulations handed down in priestly families and developed by individual thinkers.

As an example of this third form, the Japanese tradition of *yin-yang* divination (Onmyodo) entered medieval Shinto through the Shinto families who had carried on the traditions formerly within the government Bureau of Divination. Naturally, this school emphasized the important role of divination. Even outside these hereditary families, the influence of *yin-yang* notions and Chinese cosmology were already apparent as early as the writing of the eighth-century *Nihongi.* Medieval Shinto inherited the influence of Chinese customs and Taoist elements from the time of their first appearance in Japan, both directly from these hereditary families and indirectly from the Taoistic traditions incorporated within Buddhism (especially Shingon). The amulets and divinities of Taoism penetrated both Buddhism and Shinto. Confucianism was an indirect influence on Shinto thinkers because their education was still heavily Confucian.[15]

From the very moment when Shinto arose, we see a general picture of Shinto appropriating as much as it could of the continental traditions. But Shinto was not a passive recipient of these influences; rather, it actively adapted the new elements. The apparent reason for this appropriation and adaptation was to strengthen and organize Shinto. Then, as Shinto became more self-confident, it attempted to reassert its distinctiveness and superiority.

A good example of Shinto adaptation is the Yui-itsu (or Yui-ichi) school of Shinto. This school set forth a reverse *honji-suijaku* theory (*han-honji-suijaku*), making the Japanese *kami* the "original substance" (*honji*) and the Buddhist divinity the "manifest trace" (*suijaku*) and giving the superior position to the Japanese *kami*. The Yui-itsu school of Shinto, sometimes named after the Urabe or Yoshida family, developed a comprehensive pantheistic system on this basic principle, making Shinto into an all-embracing philosophy and religion. The Yui-itsu school and other Shinto scholars used similar schemes to try to set themselves apart from Buddhism, Confucianism, and Taoism. However, from our historical vantage point we can see that they could not escape from the received influence. The pantheistic system was pervaded by the very Buddhist influence that Shinto scholars were trying to escape. Nevertheless, these movements are important for understanding the growing Shinto concern to "purify" itself and to regain its former position of glory.

A long line of writers from medieval times onward supported the cause of a purified Shinto. The most famous of the early writers is Kitabatake Chikafusa (1293–1354), who supported the theory of the divine descent of the imperial line and argued for the superiority of Shinto over the foreign traditions.[16] A more systematic writer, the foremost proponent of Yui-itsu Shinto, is Yoshida Kanetomo (1435–1511). A modern Japanese scholar of Shinto has written, "From this inexhaustible intellectual fountain-head of Kanetomo's theology almost every later Shinto theological school of the Tokugawa period takes its source."[17] Kanetomo depended heavily on *Gobusho,* a thirteenth-century writing of the Ise priests. The *Gobusho,* a collection of five writings, is a good example of how Shinto became organized partly in reaction to Buddhism and other influences. Shinto writers composed the *Gobusho* so that they, too, would have a scripture.

A number of nebulous Shinto schools formed themselves around one or more of these traditions. But they remained schools (lines of teaching) and did not become separate sects (organized religious institutions) until about the nineteenth century. The Shinto schools never had the distinct existence that Buddhist sects enjoyed. Perhaps this is a significant clue to medieval Shinto. Shinto possessed distinctive Japanese traditions that were very important for the life of the country, yet Shinto did not establish a highly codified system by which to express these traditions. Shinto did not have the philosophical subtlety and completeness of Buddhism. The motive for medieval Shinto's borrowing, evidently, was not to create a new tradition, but to elaborate Shinto into a full-blown system equal to any foreign tradition.

We must never forget the vitality and broad base of Shinto. As early as 927 the Institutes of the Engi period (*Engishiki*) recorded more than six thousand Shinto shrines where annual offerings were made by officials of the court or provincial government.[18] This was a big step in organizing and ranking the loosely affiliated shrines. Gradually local shrines became more closely related to the regional community and more directly related to the formal Shinto pantheon. Although many early shrines were actually the possession of individual families and their blood relations, these shrines eventually became places of worship for all the local people. This set the pattern for the traditional village shrine with the village or village subdivisions as the geographical parish. During medieval times when powerful families began to open up the northeast part of Japan, they established branch shrines in their new homes in the north. The branch shrines, too, became important regional worship centers for the surrounding people. At the same time there was a tendency for Shinto scholars to insist that the object of worship in local shrines correspond to one of the *kami* in the *Kojiki* or *Nihongi*. These *kami* were specified as the official objects of worship at local shrines, yet this change did not really alter the rituals at the shrines and the faith of the worshipers.

At the end of the medieval period, three forms of Shinto still existed: the ancient beliefs and practices still handed down in the emperor's rituals and local observances, the elite "combinatory" traditions of the shrine-temple multiplexes, and the hereditary family practices and individual thinkers. We will see that in late medieval and early modern times the influence of some thinkers—individually and collectively—led to the notion of Shinto not only as distinct from, but also superior to, other traditions.

NOTES

1. Toshio Kuroda has provided an influential statement of the Buddhist view that "Shinto" both as a linguistic term and as an institutional religion is a relatively recent development. See Kuroda, "Shinto in the History of Japanese Religion." William LaFleur as a Western scholar has developed in his book *The Karma of Words* an argument for the notion of Buddhism as the foundation for the medieval worldview, and as providing a theodicy or philosophy of life, especially in literature. For an excerpt from LaFleur, see my *Religion in the Japanese Experience,* 2d ed., pp. 60–65. For a broader discussion, see James C. Dobbins, ed., *The Legacy of Toshio Kuroda,* vol. 23, no. 3–4, of *Japanese Journal of Religious Studies* (Fall 1996). Scholars and advocates of Shinto, not surprisingly, have not accepted the view of Shinto as a recent development and have proposed other ways of viewing "religion," "Japanese religion," and "Shinto." For one moderate view, see Minoru Sonoda, "Foreword," and "The Religious Situation in Japan in Relation to Shinto," in *Studies in Shinto,* vol. 51 of *Acta Asiatica* (Tokyo: The Toho Gakkai, 1987). Sonoda argues against defining "religion" narrowly as an institutional organization, preferring to see religion more generically as a "communal religion," and "Japanese religion" as a kind of "ethnic religion" or "natural religion." Within this context, "The term Shinto refers to that ethnic religion found within traditional Japanese culture"; "Shinto may be defined historically as the system of *kami* worship observed under the emperor system of the ancient Japanese state" (pp. iii, iv).

2. The most complete argument for viewing Buddhism (and Japanese religion) as a lived reality is Ian Reader and George J. Tanabe, Jr., *Practically Religious: Worldly Benefits and the Common Religion of Japan* (Honolulu: University of Hawai'i, 1998).

3. A balanced assessment of Kuroda's argument by John Breen and Mark Teeuwen acknowledges Kuroda's main point that Shinto is not a uniform, unchanging entity from prehistoric times to the present, but these authors counter with the recognition of the pervasiveness of Shinto in Japanese culture and religion: "many shrines, priestly lineages, kami beliefs and rites do display a remarkable degree of continuity over very long periods of time. . . ." They also turn around Kuroda's argument of Buddhism's dominant influence upon Shinto, asking if "indigenous practice . . . did not in some profound way leave its mark . . . in the various forms of Buddhist practice adopted in Japan." See John Breen and Mark Teeuwen, "Introduction: Shinto Past and Present," in their coedited work, *Shinto in History*, pp. 1–12, especially pp. 3–7. See also Susan C. Tyler, *The Cult of Kasuga Seen Through Its Art* (Ann Arbor: University of Michigan, 1992), especially pp. 185–98, "Epilogue: Is There a Religion Called Shinto?"

4. Allan Grapard, "Linguistic Cubism: A Singularity of Pluralism in the Sanno Cult," *Japanese Journal of Religious Studies*, vol. 14, no. 2–3 (1987), pp. 211–34, especially p. 215.

5. This view has been championed by Allan Grapard in a number of articles, especially "Institution, Ritual, and Ideology: The Twenty-two Shrine-temple Multiplexes of Heian Japan," *History of Religions*, vol. 27, no. 3 (Feb. 1988), pp. 246–69, and in his book *The Protocol of the Gods: A Study of the Kasuga Cult in Japanese History*. See also McMullin, "Historical and Historiographical Issues," pp. 4–8.

6. Grapard, "Lotus in the Mountain, Mountain in the Lotus," *Monumenta Nipponica*, vol. 41 (1986), p. 21.

7. Ibid., p. 23.

8. See Ian Reader and Paul L. Swanson, eds., *Pilgrimage in Japan*, vol. 24, no. 3–4, of *Japanese Journal of Religious Studies* (Fall 1997).

9. Payne, "Introduction," p. 13.

10. See Daniel C. Holtom, *The National Faith of Japan: A Study in Modern Shinto* (New York: Dutton, 1938; reprinted, New York: Paragon Book Reprint Corp., 1965), pp. 30–52, for a historical treatment of the transition from early to medieval Shinto. See also de Bary et al., *Sources of Japanese Tradition*, 2d ed., vol. 1, ch. 15, for an introduction to medieval Shinto, with translated documents.

11. For a book on this subject see Alicia Matsunaga, *The Buddhist Philosophy of Assimilation: The Historical Development of the Honji-Suijaku Theory* (Tokyo and Rutland, VT: Sophia University and Charles E. Tuttle, 1969); for an excerpt see my *Religion in the Japanese Experience*, 2d ed., pp. 50–54.

12. Grapard, "Linguistic Cubism," p. 214.

13. Sugahara Shinkai sees Sanno Shinto and Sanno Ichijitsu Shinto as related but distinct entities: "Sanno Shinto involves devotion to the guardian deities of Mt. Hiei and is centered around the Hie Shrine at the foot of Mt. Hiei. . . . Sanno Ichijitsu Shinto, in contrast, centers on religious ritual for Tosho Daigongen, the deified soul of Tokugawa Ieyasu." See Sugahara, "The Distinctive Features of Sanno Ichijitsu Shinto," *Japanese Journal of Religious Studies*, vol. 23, no. 1–2 (Spring 1996), pp. 61–84, especially p. 65.

14. For two lavishly illustrated books on Shinto art, including Shinto *mandala*, see Haruki Kageyama, *The Arts of Shinto*, trans. Christine Guth (New York: Weatherhill/Shibundo, 1973), and Elizabeth ten Grotenhuis, *Japanese Mandalas: Representations of Sacred Geography* (Honolulu: University of Hawai'i, 1999).

15. Much later, in the nineteenth century, several Shinto sects were formed around Neo-Confucian doctrines.

16. For an excerpt of Kitabatake Chikafusa's writing about the superiority of Shinto, see my *Religion in the Japanese Experience,* 2d ed., pp. 25–28.

17. Genchi Kato, "The Theological System of Urabe no Kanetomo," *Transactions of the Japan Society of London,* vol. 28 (1931), pp. 149–50. (Yoshida and Urabe refer to the same family line). See also the more recent article by Allan Grapard, "The Shinto of Yoshida Kanetomo," *Monumenta Nipponica,* vol. 47 (1992), pp. 27–58. Grapard writes that "Kanetomo set the foundations of a movement that . . . swiftly pervaded the sacerdotal world of his country" (p. 41) and that "the Yoshida system became an orthodoxy cum orthopraxy of sorts during the Tokugawa period" (p. 45).

18. For a translation of the *Engishiki,* see Bock, trans., *Engi-shiki.*

12

⚜

The Appearance of
Christianity in Japan

By the middle of the sixteenth century, all the major traditions within Japanese religion had appeared and interacted with one another to form a distinctive religious heritage; the Japanese people, after a thousand years of blending their native beliefs and practices with a number of continental religions, had come to see their common worldview as the combination of complementary traditions. This was the general situation in 1549, when Christianity was introduced into the Japanese islands by Roman Catholic missionaries. Jesuits presented Christianity to the Japanese as a new religious tradition with exclusive and uncompromising commitment, requiring rejection of all other religious commitment in order to "convert" to Christianity. Under these circumstances, most Japanese were unable to understand Christianity or perceived it as a foreign religion incompatible with Japanese culture and religion.

Westerners, especially Christians, who have viewed the expansion of Christianity into other lands as desirable or inevitable, have asked why more Japanese did not convert to Christianity. Japanese, from the viewpoint of their own cultural and religious heritage, may beg the question of why they should be expected to give up their own tradition for a foreign tradition. We will attempt to view the introduction of Christianity to Japan from a neutral position, neither advocating Christianity nor defending Japanese tradition, but seeing this event from a comparative perspective as an example of interacting traditions.

We may recall that Buddhism, too, began its career as a form of foreign spirituality and at first was regarded with suspicion, but it soon became accepted, and after centuries was naturalized and "Japanized." It may be argued that today, after four centuries, Christianity is still seen more as a foreign religion, and with rare exceptions, has never made the transition to being considered a Japanese tradition the way in which Buddhism has. Nevertheless, an examination of "the Christian century in Japan,"[1] as one scholar has described the period of about one hundred years when Christianity first gained followers in Japan, affords us many insights into Japanese religious history.

The initial Christian missionary to Japan was the Spanish Jesuit Saint Francis Xavier, later called the Apostle of Japan. While on a missionary trip to Asia, Xavier was drawn to Japan by favorable accounts of the people, and his first impression verified the rumors. In a few years he saw an encouraging number of converts and foresaw a glorious future for the Roman church in Japan. He did not underestimate the faith of the most sincere converts, but neither did he anticipate the great trials to which their faith would be subjected. Within a century's time, the foreign priests and Japanese Christians experienced a persecution that some scholars say is unparalleled in the history of the Christian church. By about 1650, Christianity ceased to exist in Japan as a public religion, surviving only on a small scale and practiced secretly.

THE INTRODUCTION OF
CHRISTIANITY INTO JAPAN

The motives for missionary work, whether Christian or Buddhist (or in any tradition), have usually included a mixture of religious, economic, and cultural factors. The entry of Christianity into sixteenth-century Japan was no exception. The earliest missionaries were European (especially Spanish and Portuguese) Jesuits, and the ships that brought the Jesuits carried European and Chinese goods for trade.[2] The Jesuits' economic support was closely related to this trade, and it was no secret that the Japanese feudal lords desired the presence of a Jesuit priest in their domain to attract trade with the Portuguese ships. (The ships brought highly prized Chinese silk to Japan.)

Xavier at first traveled to the capital with the purpose of speaking to the "king" of Japan, and he discovered that in the mid-sixteenth century the emperor was only a figurehead; real political power was held by a military ruler and local feudal lords. In Europe, Jesuit missionaries first tried to convert members of elite groups such as the nobility, a pattern repeated in Japan. The Jesuits learned that without the cooperation—or at least the tolerance—of the feudal lords, they could do nothing. A feudal lord often would declare for Christianity more or less superficially, and his subjects would follow suit. The Jesuits were well aware of the expediency of these conversions, but they accepted the situation because it enabled them to work for genuine converts.

Xavier left Japan reluctantly after two years. A handful of priests remained to carry on the work. Gradually other Roman Catholic orders were represented, but there seldom was a great number of priests in Japan. (The unfriendly rivalry between Jesuits and other Catholic orders constituted a major obstacle to effective missionary work and may have heightened the military rulers' mistrust of all foreigners.) Nevertheless, conversions continued, and the attraction to Christianity cannot be explained simply in economic terms. In accounting for these conversions to Christianity, we can understand something about the nature of Christianity itself, the contemporary religious scene in Japan, and the Japanese people.

THE JAPANESE
ACCEPTANCE OF CHRISTIANITY

Generally, when a foreign religion enters a new area, its acceptance or rejection hinges on a host of complicated factors that are not directly related to religion. A religion is never accepted or rejected solely on the basis of its message, or "theology." In Japan, as elsewhere, an important factor influencing the acceptability of a foreign religion has been the relative instability of the social and political situation. Japanese scholars have pointed out that during periods when there was great social upheaval and the Japanese people were eager to receive a new message, the foreign character of Christianity was to its advantage in gaining Japanese converts. Christianity has been most successful during three periods of radical social change: (1) the latter part of the period of civil wars (1482–1558), (2) the Meiji era (1868–1912), and (3) the post–World War II period of Occupation (1945–52). But when the national mood swung back to emphasize national and cultural unification, the foreignness of Christianity invited criticism and even persecution.[3]

The acceptance of Christianity during the first half of the Christian century (from 1549 to 1597) was stimulated by great social changes. Japan was suffering from civil wars, which had resulted in much bloodshed and sudden swings of loyalty. In the midst of this confusion there was a great deal of immorality, particularly on the part of the warriors. Buddhism suffered from its own participation in these bloody wars, as well as from sharp sectarianism. These conditions helped persuade the Japanese to look for a new, foreign faith.

The difference that the Japanese perceived in Christianity was not simply its foreign origin, but its stark contrast with the tradition of Japanese religion. The dissimilarity can be highlighted by focusing on some central features of the two heritages at the time of their meeting.[4] Christianity emphasizes absolute faith in a transcendent deity (to the exclusion of other religious commitments). The Japanese tradition accepts the existence of many *kami* and Buddhist divinities as well as multiple affiliation by one person. The Christian tradition sees a great distance between human beings and the deity; the Japanese notion stresses the close harmony among mortals, *kami* (or Buddhist divinities), and nature. Crucial to Christian faith is the idea of human sinfulness and the need for redemption; the Japanese tradition has a higher opinion of human nature and tends to remove impurities and correct mistakes through purification ceremonies. And, to take one final example, Christianity stresses individual responsibility before God, whereas the Japanese tradition values group loyalty and group participation in religion. These differences, which were recognized by both Christian missionaries and Japanese, were not so great as to make it impossible for Japanese to accept Christianity; but they played a role both in the initial acceptance and in the subsequent rejection of Christianity.

It is well to remember that the historical circumstances of the sixteenth century sharply limited Japanese perception of Christianity. Christianity was presented to the Japanese as a unified system of Catholic faith and practice, because only Roman Catholicism entered Japan at this time and initially it was introduced only by the Jesuit order. The Jesuits deserved their reputation as the intellectual leaders of Catholicism. Their military style of organization enabled them to recruit talented men in Europe and train priests as well-disciplined defenders of the Church in the attempt to rebuild Catholic strength following the Protestant Reformation. Japanese were not aware of the Protestant–Catholic confrontation, Protestant sectarianism, and the diversity of Catholic orders in Europe, and the Jesuits chose not to tell them. All that the Japanese knew about Christianity, they learned from the Roman Catholic missionaries.

In the context of these general historical considerations, what was the attraction of Christianity? According to one scholar, "Christianity represented a double attraction: ethical to the *bushi*, the leading class of Japan; and salvationist to the masses." For the *bushi*, or warrior, who was brought up on the notion of absolute loyalty to his feudal lord, "the step to Christianity was not a large or an illogical one,"[5] because the relationship between human beings and the Christian God was also taught by the Jesuits to be one of absolute loyalty. In fact, the Jesuit preaching in Japan, which stressed both a self-sacrificing ideal and an uncompromising moral code (with stinging criticism of immorality in Japanese society), appears to have been very attractive to these highly disciplined warriors. The Jesuits, with their blend of religious and military discipline, appealed directly to the Japanese warriors.

In northern Kyushu, in particular, common people were the mainstay of the Church, and they seem to have been drawn by the combination of a guarantee of a transcendent salvation and a strong moral code. It is worth recalling here that each of the most successful Buddhist movements in Japan—the Pure Land, Zen, and Nichiren sects—had stressed an assurance of religious fulfillment or "salvation" in a distinctive fashion. Thus it is not totally unexpected that some Japanese would accept a foreign version of the notion of assurance of salvation. Some feudal lords seem to have been more concerned with patronizing Christianity (especially by allowing missionaries to preach in their domains) or with converting to Christianity for the economic benefit of attracting the Portuguese trading ships in which the Christian missionaries had a financial interest. In some cases when the feudal lord converted, he had his whole domain convert to Christianity.

As the foregoing considerations demonstrate, the historical circumstances and personal motivations leading to acceptance of Christianity were complex (as is true of almost all instances of religious conversion). But whatever the circumstances and motivations, many Japanese overcame the obstacles of difference and foreignness to gain a deep and lasting commitment to Christianity, even to the point of martyrdom. Although the exact degree of personal commitment cannot be determined, by 1579 there were about 130,000 Christians in Japan. What is surprising is that this large number of Christians was served by only fifty-five members of the Jesuit order (twenty-three of whom were priests).

At first, the Jesuit missionaries in Japan required Japanese converts to adopt Christian (and European) customs and refused to ordain Japanese as priests. This policy was soon changed, so that both the European priests and their Japanese converts followed Japanese customs wherever possible, and eventually Japanese men were ordained. The inability of the Christian mission to spread throughout Japan cannot be attributed just to an ineffective policy; the effort was severely hampered by limited manpower and meager finances. It was impossible for the Jesuits to gain enough replacements for the European priests (the journey to Japan was lengthy and hazardous), and the training of Japanese assistants was a painfully slow process. The missionaries created their own Japanese language dictionaries, because even the simplest tract had to be translated from a European language, such as Latin, to Japanese. In finances, the mission field was not yet self-supporting, and the only income was the profit from the annual trading ship (which might be lost at sea). Perhaps the miracle of the Christian century is the fact that, in the face of all these difficulties, Christianity made as much progress in Japan as it did. The Christianity of this early period is still remembered by the Japanese term *"Kirishitan,"* a Japanese pronunciation of the Portuguese word *"Christao,"* for "Christian." The Japanese perception of Christianity as a foreign religion had helped Christianity gain members. Later the foreign character of Christianity would make it the target of suspicion by the government.

THE EXPULSION OF CHRISTIANITY

The fortunes and misfortunes of Roman Catholicism in medieval Japan were closely linked to the careers of three great military leaders and unifiers of Japan: Oda Nobunaga (1534–82), Toyotomi Hideyoshi (1536–98), and Tokugawa Ieyasu (1542–1616).[6] During Nobunaga's rule, Christianity flourished with his consent. It is said that Nobunaga was motivated not so much by his love for Christianity as by his hatred toward Buddhism. Nobunaga, in trying to unify the country politically, saw the large Buddhist headquarters as political and military threats. Several times he saw fit to punish the Buddhist strongholds with military force. In 1571, for example, he completely devastated the Tendai headquarters on Mount Hiei, massacring all monks, laypeople, and even women and children on the mountain. It is thought that Nobunaga may have allowed Christianity to grow only with the ulterior motive of having it check the strength of Buddhism.

Nobunaga's successor, Hideyoshi, turned into a persecutor of the Christian church; the reasons for this change are veiled by the passage of time. The reversal of policy, however, may have been connected with a general fear that the Catholic fathers conspired with both European powers and Japanese Christians to take over Japan. Hideyoshi had destroyed the strongholds of Pure Land Buddhism (which threatened his secular power), and he did not hesitate to ban a foreign religion that seemed to demand too much loyalty of his subjects. To a pragmatic ruler like Hideyoshi, there was no room for absolute loyalty outside the state—whether it was to Amida and Pure Land priests or to Christ and Catholic priests (and certainly not to European rulers). Hideyoshi's 1587 order expelling the Catholic priests was not just antiforeign or anti-Christian. "It was part of Hideyoshi's program for the restructuring of Japan under central authority."[7] At any rate, Hideyoshi still encouraged trade with the Portuguese while proscribing the Christian faith. In actuality, his edict against Christianity was not rigorously enforced, and the result was that more converts were added to the church during this period of mild persecution.

Ieyasu, the next ruler, made good the threats of his predecessors by actually driving the foreign missionaries from Japan. Whereas Nobunaga and Hideyoshi had been antagonistic toward Buddhism, Ieyasu's personal life was influenced by Buddhist piety and his government policy was supported by Neo-Confucian ideals.[8] Ieyasu is one of the most imposing figures in all Japanese history. He was so revered that he was deified by his own priestly adviser as the Sun God of the East.[9] An imposing shrine serves as his tomb of enshrinement at Nikko, and branch shrines dedicated to him are found throughout Japan. His edict of 1614 proscribing Christianity meant the physical deportation of all foreign missionaries, including some leading Japanese Christians. (The arrival of Dutch traders in 1609 and English traders in 1613 probably provided the pragmatic motive for this edict: "Ieyasu, who had tolerated the missionaries in order to maintain the lucrative silk trade, now had other options."[10])

Although Ieyasu did not shed any blood, his successors provided many martyrs for the church. Priests who had defied the edict to stay in Japan, and the loyal Japanese Christians who hid them, were executed. The most hideous tortures were devised to make these foreign priests and Japanese Christians recant their faith and refute Christianity publicly. However, the tortures were only partially successful in gaining formal renunciation of the faith among the people. Gradually the foreign priests were hunted down, and later attempts to land missionaries resulted in immediate capture.[11]

One of the decisive events in the downfall of Catholicism was the Shimabara Revolt of 1637–38 by Japanese Christians in Kyushu. Because of the hardships of peasant life and oppressive government policy, many peasants and some warriors occasionally revolted against the government. In fact, even Pure Land and Nichiren groups had become involved in social and economic protest. In the bloody Shimabara Revolt, "The revolt was not primarily a religious uprising, but a desperate protest against the oppressive rule of feudal lords in a remote and backward region."[12] Nevertheless, in this feudal context any rival faith represented a threat to social stability, and the feudal government used the Shimabara Revolt (when many thousands were killed) as a justification for abolishing Christianity. This led to the final exclusion order of 1639, which strictly prohibited any future visits by Portuguese ships on penalty of the destruction of ship and crew. In 1640, when a Portuguese ship came to Japan on a diplomatic mission to negotiate this decree, the ship was destroyed and its sixty-one passengers executed; only the thirteen Chinese crew members were allowed to leave Japan. From 1641 contact and trade with the West was limited to the small island of Dejima (or Deshima) in Nagasaki harbor through the Dutch East India Company.

Japan in the 1640s was more highly unified and centralized than in the 1540s, when Christianity first arrived. The mood of the mid-sixteenth century was relatively favorable to a foreign religion, but in the mid-seventeenth century the emphasis on national unification made Christianity's foreign character a serious disadvantage. The initial acceptance of Christianity was made possible by complex social and political factors; the later rejection of Christianity also was brought about by a variety of circumstances. In the end, by about 1650 Christianity had become an underground religion. The Japanese authorities thought they had completely abolished this foreign religion, but in reality it was handed down as a secret tradition within certain families, particularly in the Kyushu region where it had gained its strongest foothold.

THE SIGNIFICANCE
OF THE CHRISTIAN CENTURY

It is ironic that Christianity took on a decidedly Japanese character only when it was deprived of ordained priests and went underground. Japanese customs and beliefs became naturally mixed with Christian beliefs. Interestingly enough, one of the persistent arguments against Christianity in the exclusionary edicts was that Christianity was anti-Japanese and against the Japanese religious traditions. Christianity was considered anti-Japanese because a Japanese Christian was loyal to foreign gods and to foreign priests (and possibly to foreign rulers), rather than to native *kami* and to the local Japanese feudal lord.

Christianity certainly had presented a contrast to the general trend in Japanese religion that traditions harmonize with one another rather than making exclusive claims to absolute truth. The Jesuits were very effective in their active policy of acquiring the language and customs of the country, but in matters of religious doctrine and practice they were not so flexible. A double irony of the Christian century is that Buddhism, when it first entered Japan, was seen by the Japanese as a foreign religion and for that reason opposed as offensive to the native *kami,* but eventually Buddhism had become so thoroughly assimilated within Japanese culture that it claimed the status of a "native" Japanese tradition opposing the foreign Christianity. Although they lost much of their original Indian and Chinese features, both Buddhism and Confucianism were considered full-fledged Japanese traditions having the right to reject the foreign Christian religion.[13] By contrast, Christianity has never become Japanized to the extent that it could be considered a Japanese tradition to counter foreign traditions.[14]

The Christian century in Japan may seem a relatively unimportant interval in the long stretch of several millennia of Japanese history, but it is significant for understanding later developments. The success of the Catholic missionaries is nothing to gloss over. The number of Catholic priests was always small, never exceeding two hundred, and yet they succeeded in gaining as many as 300,000 converts by the first decade of the seventeenth century. If the population of this period was between 20 million and 25 million, a higher percentage of the population was Christian at that time than Japan has ever known since. This is remarkable in light of the large numbers of Catholic and Protestant missionaries who have spent great sums of money during the past century (when conditions were never as oppressive as during the earlier "Christian century"), only to achieve a lower percentage of Christian converts, Protestant and Catholic (and Orthodox) combined.

The Christian century in Japan was influential for later developments in Japan. Some scholars feel that the threat of Christianity—real or imagined—helped shape Japan's decision to impose a "closed-door" policy, which kept Japan relatively isolated from foreign influence between the mid-seventeenth and mid-nineteenth centuries. Furthermore, in order to stamp out Christianity, every family was required to belong to a Buddhist temple. In effect, this made Buddhism an arm of the government, giving it a great advantage over Shinto. We must be aware of this imbalance in order to comprehend religious developments during the Tokugawa period (1600–1867), which will be discussed in Part III.

NOTES

1. See C. R. Boxer, *The Christian Century in Japan, 1549–1650,* rev. ed. (Berkeley: University of California, 1967).

2. For the reports written by these missionaries and other European travelers, see Michael Cooper, *They Came to Japan: An Anthology of European Reports on Japan* (Berkeley: University of California, 1965).

3. See Norihisa Suzuki, "Christianity," in *Japanese Religion,* ed. Ichiro Hori (Tokyo: Kodansha International, 1972), pp. 71–73.

4. For a critique of Christianity written by a Japanese (Fabian Fucan) who lived during the Christian century—and converted to Christianity but later recanted—see George Elison, *Deus Destroyed: The Image of Christianity in Early Modern Japan* (Cambridge: Harvard University, 1973). For an excerpt of Fucan's critique, see my *Religion in the Japanese Experience,* 2d ed., pp. 144–49.

5. Elison, *Deus Destroyed,* pp. 45–46.

6. See Tsunoda et al., *Sources of Japanese Tradition* Chapter 15, for information concerning Nobunaga, Hideyoshi, Ieyasu, and their policies with regard to Christianity; see vol. 2 of the forthcoming 2d ed.

7. Elison, *Deus Destroyed,* p. 117. See my *Religion in the Japanese Experience,* 2d ed., pp. 161–63 for Hideyoshi's "Letter to the Viceroy of the Indies," in which he outlines the religious reasons for rejecting Christianity.

8. Peter Nosco writes that "Oda Nobunaga and Toyotomi Hideyoshi . . . were more concerned with what the leaders and members of religious communities controlled, did, or threatened to do, than with what they believed or averred"; for Tokugawa Ieyasu, "the effort was redirected almost exclusively toward political control." He notes that such governmental control and public compliance were limited. See his "Keeping the Faith: *Bakuhan* Policy Towards Religions in Seventeenth-Century Japan," in *Religion in Japan: Arrows to Heaven and Earth,* ed. P. F. Kornicki and I. J. McMullen (Cambridge: Cambridge University, 1996), pp. 135–55, especially p. 136.

9. See "The Sun God of the East" in Tsunoda et al., *Sources of Japanese Tradition* Chapter 15; see vol. 2 of the forthcoming 2d ed. For remarks on this pattern of "immanental theocracy," see Joseph M. Kitagawa, *Religion in Japanese History* (New York: Columbia University, 1966), pp. 154, 161. For Ieyasu, see Conrad D. Totman, *Tokugawa Ieyasu, Shogun: A Biography* (San Francisco: Heian, 1983).

10. Christal Whelan, trans., *The Beginning of Heaven and Earth: The Sacred Book of Japan's Hidden Christians* (Honolulu: University of Hawai'i, 1996), p. 8. This translation of "the only text the Kakure Kirishitan [Hidden Christians] produced" (p. 35) is preceded by a convenient introduction to the subject and an interpretation of their "hybridized cultural heritage." For two recent overviews, see Stephen Turnbull, *The Kakure Kirishitan of Japan: A Study of Their Development, Beliefs, and Rituals to the Present Day* (Richmond, Surrey: Japan Library, 1998); and Ikuo Higashibaba, *Christianity in Early Modern Japan: Kirishitan Belief and Practice* (Leiden: Brill, 2001).

11. The Japanese Catholic novelist Shusaku Endo has written extensively on Christianity, including a novel describing a Jesuit missionary caught in the persecution of the late Christian century: *Silence,* trans. William Johnston (Tokyo: Sophia University, 1969); and a historical novel chronicling an actual sixteenth-century journey of Japanese Christians across the Pacific Ocean to Mexico, and by land across Mexico, to continue their sea voyage to Europe and then on to Rome—and back to Japan: *The Samurai: A Novel,* trans. Van C. Gessel (New York: Harper & Row, 1982). For an assessment of the life and writing of Endo, see Richard E. Durfee, Jr., "Portrait of an Unknowingly Ordinary Man: Endo Shusaku, Christianity, and Japanese Historical Consciousness," *Japanese Journal of Religious Studies,* vol. 16, no. 1 (Mar. 1989), pp. 41–62.

12. Sir George Sansom, *A History of Japan,* vol. 3 (Stanford: Stanford University, 1963), p. 38.

13. For the argument (based on Shinto, Confucianism, and Buddhism) rejecting Christianity, see my *Religion in the Japanese Experience,* 2d ed, pp. 161–63.

14. The relative success or failure of a religion may be closely connected with the political fortunes of the people supporting the religion. When Buddhism was first introduced and in subsequent centuries, the families and territories supporting Buddhism gained political power; in contrast, the feudal territories supporting Christianity lost political power, as seen in the Shimabara Revolt.

13

❧

The Five Traditions: Development and Mutual Influence

From ancient times, the five basic traditions of Japanese religion have interacted with one another. In the period of development and elaboration,
discussed in Part II, these traditions created distinctive forms within
the general context of Japanese religion. Buddhism received from China new
waves of influence that were reshaped into forms of Japanese Buddhism. Likewise, Confucianism and Taoism continued to be Japanized. Neo-Confucianism,
along with Buddhism and Shinto, provided a semiofficial rationale for the existence of the state. Chinese customs and Taoist elements played an important
role, but on the level of popular religion. Folk religion blended with the
more organized traditions and persisted in the beliefs and customs of the
people. Shinto was busy borrowing from all these religious streams with
the motive of becoming systematized and strengthened so as to compete with
the other systems.

This period has been called one of development and elaboration because,
with the exception of Christianity, no new major religious traditions were introduced. Only new streams of the older traditions were introduced, such as
the newer sects of Buddhism. Buddhism became elaborated into a truly Japanese phenomenon: Buddhist practices became more thoroughly interrelated
with Shinto practices; distinctively Japanese developments of Buddhism such
as Nichiren Buddhism appeared; and the largest Buddhist sects developed.

Shinto underwent development and elaboration when it appropriated
foreign traditions and, by incorporating them, produced a more complete religious system. Study of Confucian classics led Shinto scholars to a study of the

Japanese classics, which in turn led them to support a revival movement for "purifying" Shinto.

Chinese customs and Taoist elements, which entered Japanese history mainly in the form of a government bureau controlling the calendar and divination, spread through the countryside. This cosmology provided a rich resource for theoretical and ritual developments, especially within Shinto. On a more popular level, the adopted Chinese calendar gave rise to many wide-spread beliefs about what was lucky and unlucky. Often Taoist thoughts and beliefs were carried to the people by *hijiri,* some of whom were popular successors to the earlier officials in the government Bureau of Divination (the Onmyoryo). The *hijiri,* a combination of sage, saint, and fortune-teller, were wandering practitioners who went directly to the people to meet all kinds of religious needs.[1] Unattached to shrines or temples, they drew on Shinto and Buddhist usages as well as those of Taoism in their fortune-telling, divination, and purifications.

One popular movement that drew heavily on the influence of Taoism and the activity of *hijiri* was Koshin associations (Koshin-ko). The mythological background of the movement had become mixed with Buddhist elements in China and was blended with Japanese folk practices by people such as the *hijiri* and by local village groups. The village groups were independent associations organized for the purpose of lengthening life through all-night vigils. They met especially on the six Koshin days of the Chinese calendar, revering an image or painting of the Taoist-Buddhist divinity while holding a festive banquet. During the all-night vigils they abstained from sexual relations, because on that night a divinity observed them and reported on their conduct to a heavenly superior. These groups, their beliefs, and their practices became so thoroughly ingrained in village life that the devotees took for granted the Japanese character of the Koshin movement, completely forgetting its foreign origins.[2]

Folk religion continued in the many customs and beliefs associated with seasonal rhythms and the home, thoroughly interacting with the organized religions. The beliefs and festivities of the Chinese calendar were inseparable from Japanese seasonal and agricultural customs. For example, the New Year festivities came to be celebrated especially through Buddhist and Shinto usages. Popular religious observances connected with the growing season, too, were related to the organized religions. Often a farmer visited a shrine or temple in order to obtain an amulet or talisman, which he placed in his rice field as a blessing for his crop.

The home continued to be a major focus for folk religion. This is especially well illustrated by the religious decorations around the home at New Year's. Each household became a repository of the diverse elements of the Japanese religious tradition. For example, each family knew that physical and spiritual sickness could be caused by evil forces, which could be warded off through the help of benevolent divinities. The afflicted family might visit a temple or a shrine, or an itinerant *hijiri* or Shugendo practitioner might visit the afflicted family. These popular practitioners resorted to Buddhist rituals and formulas as well as Taoistic purification ceremonies to promote healing. Some popular religious figures specialized in the art of trance and possession for the purpose of communicating with the dead. Often a blind woman, a female shaman, communicated with the dead. All these practices illustrate the way in which folk religion continued to exist outside of organized religion at the same time aspects of the organized traditions came to be the people's common property.

Christianity's appearance on the Japanese scene was an unexpected interruption of the development and elaboration process. Indeed, in this early period Christianity could hardly be considered a *Japanese* tradition. Those who did not accept Christianity tended to see it as a threat to the Japanese traditions. Buddhism, Confucianism, and Shinto took a stand and jointly challenged the threat of the anti-Japanese, or at least non-Japanese, tradition of Christianity.

The development and elaboration in Japanese religion that took place from the eighth to the seventeenth century was a remarkable process not paralleled in more recent history. Every historical age undergoes its own sequence of transformation, including continuity/discontinuity with the past and transition to the future. However, the patterns laid down in this period of development and elaboration have been determinative for all later religious history, and new comprehensive patterns did not appear in subsequent centuries, nor are they likely to surface in the foreseeable future. The founders of Japanese Buddhism established the institutional lines of Buddhism that have continued to this day; no founders comparable to Honen, Nichiren, or Dogen have appeared, and no Buddhist denominations of the scope of the Pure Land, Nichiren, and Zen have arisen. Similarly, the grand synthesis of Shinto as a transmission of prehistoric beliefs and practices within the context of Buddhist, Neo-Confucian, and Taoist forms, has set the tone for the subsequent history of Shinto, and it is not likely that this synthesis will be replaced.

In short, the general configuration of Japanese religion that took shape during the period of development and elaboration is in fact what has come to be known as "Japanese religion," and this larger system probably will remain so long as there is Japanese culture and Japanese religion. Yet, no culture or religion ever stands still or stops—unless it dies out or is destroyed: every tradition is ever evolving, a reception of past customs, with modification and innovation, and transmission to the next generation. As we have seen, "tradition" itself means a handing down, which inevitably means not only receiving the past, but also reforming or reshaping what will in turn become the future.

Therefore, the fact that there were no new founders comparable to Honen, and no new denominations the likes of Pure Land, does not mean that Buddhism and history came to a halt. Although no new founders arose, there were dynamic figures who organized and expanded these Buddhist institutions; often competing interpretations of a founder's message and movement led to new ecclesiastical organizations. Buddhism was handed down not just as the original sects, but as a host of new institutions, and there was considerable innovation in forming these institutions.

Creativity is seen not only in the establishment of new Buddhist institutions, but also in the expansion and consolidation of Shinto shrines. However, in the life of any religion, the vital motives that impelled the founders and organizers may become crystallized in rather rigid institutional forms. By the late Tokugawa period, there were signs within both Buddhism and Shinto that the form of the institution often lived on at the expense of vitality. In other words, institutional religious life became rather formalistic. We will see how this tendency toward formalism became a major problem and how it led to movements of renewal.

NOTES

1. For an account of the *hijiri,* see Ichiro Hori, *Folk Religion in Japan: Continuity and Change,* ed. Joseph M. Kitagawa and Alan L. Miller (Chicago: University of Chicago, 1968), pp. 83–139.

2. See E. Dale Saunders, "Koshin: An Example of Taoist Ideas in Japan," in *Proceedings of the IXth International Congress for the History of Religions* (Tokyo: Maruzen, 1960), pp. 423–32. An excerpt from Saunders's work is included in my *Religion in the Japanese Experience,* 2d ed., pp. 120–25.

PART III

❦

Formalism and Renewal in Japanese Religion

Part I introduced the formative elements of Japanese religion and their initial interaction; Part II treated the further development and elaboration of these formative elements and described the reception accorded Christianity upon its introduction to Japan in the sixteenth century. Now that our historical narrative has traced the formation and development of the Japanese religious heritage, Part III will discuss subsequent changes and more recent trends, in particular formalism and renewal.

The final period, from the seventeenth century to the present, has been characterized as an era of formalism and renewal because during this time the dominant tradition of Buddhism became formalistic, and the large shrines of Shinto were not in close touch with the people. "Older, established forms of religion, serviced primarily by Buddhist and Shinto clergy, lacked the power to inspire many people in late Tokugawa Japan."[1] Throughout Tokugawa times, major trends were started by the rediscovery of Confucianism (as Neo-Confucianism), the development of new Shinto theories, and the emergence of New Religions. "Formalism and renewal" may occur within any religious tradition at any time, and there are any number of ways in which these related processes may appear.

Such processes of aging and rebirth are not unique to Japanese religion—every religious tradition experiences periods of growth and decline. New traditions may emerge gradually out of previous ones or spring suddenly from a great leader's teachings. Some budding traditions wither and soon disappear—they are not "handed down"—in other words, they do not even become traditions. Those that do survive attempt to embody the original breath of inspiration in lasting forms; that is, they become institutionalized in permanent forms that are transmitted to future generations. Then, either slowly or suddenly, comes the realization that forms are being preserved for their own sake and that the inspirational impetus has been lost. The continuation of institutional trappings out of a sense of history or custom, rather than out of feelings of enthusiasm and acts of dedication, is an indication of formalism. Renewal, the opposite of formalism, is characterized by the exciting rediscovery of an earlier tradition or the rejuvenating birth of a new tradition.

Although development and elaboration continued within Japanese religion from the seventeenth century to the present, the two most conspicuous trends are formalism and renewal. From the seventeenth century, Buddhism, dominant for so long, became formalistic for two reasons: First, its institutional ideas, rituals, and practices became rather rigid; and, second, it increasingly served as an arm of the government more than as a source of spiritual support for the people. Buddhism had experienced renewal in the Heian and Kamakura periods because of the efforts of vigorous founders of new institutions, but from the Tokugawa era (1600–1867) Buddhism tended to live on more through earlier forms than because of new developments. Many laypeople and priests were content to live within these forms. Indeed, Buddhism's ongoing vitality can be seen in such activities as flourishing pilgrimage routes (often linked in regional patterns) that support elaborate priestly institutions and temple headquarters. There were some attempts at reforming Buddhism and at reinvigorating it with dynamic preaching, but the major religious changes that took place after 1600 did not occur within Buddhism.[2]

The most dramatic changes of the Tokugawa era took place in Confucianism and Shinto. These traditions were rediscovered as means of stimulating large numbers of people to a new sense of commitment. Neo-Confucianism helped define the major rationale for the Tokugawa government in achieving the unification of Japan, thereby creating the foundation on which modern Japan rests. Confucianism had been present in Japan more than a thousand years, but Japanese thinkers rediscovered this tradition in the writings of Chinese (and Korean) Neo-Confucianist scholars. Ironically, this interest in Chinese classics encouraged Japanese scholars to study Japanese classics, resulting in a rediscovery of the ancient Shinto tradition. Renewed interest in Shinto helped shape the climactic events marking the end of Tokugawa feudalism and the rise of a modern nation-state.

From late Tokugawa times to the present, another form of renewal has been most remarkable: renewal through the creation of new movements, as exemplified by the founding of large numbers of so-called New Religions. Usually established by charismatic founders outside the framework of organized Buddhism and Shinto, and gathering hundreds of thousands or even millions of members, the New Religions have gradually developed into the most dynamic religious force on the contemporary scene.

NOTES

1. Sawada, *Confucian Values and Popular Zen,* p. 169.

2. One new form of Chinese Buddhism introduced to Japan during the seventeenth century, the Obaku sect, formally a Zen sect but also incorporating Pure Land and esoteric practices, was particularly important for a new infusion of Chinese culture. See Helen Josephine Baroni, *Obaku Zen: The Emergence of the Third Sect of Zen in Tokugawa Japan* (Honolulu: University of Hawai'i, 2000). She uses the case of Obaku to argue against "The common view that the Buddhism of the day, especially Zen, was degenerate, ossified, and in desperate need of restoration. . . ." Instead, she sees Obaku as an instance of innovation, as a "new religious movement," pp. 3, 19–23. For a rare instance of a contemporary critique of Tokugawa Buddhism, see Nakamoto Tominaga, *Emerging from Meditation,* translated with an introduction by Michael Pye (Honolulu: University of Hawaii, 1990).

14

Buddhism, Neo-Confucianism, and Restoration Shinto in the Tokugawa Period

The Tokugawa period (1600–1867) was very important for unifying Japan and establishing the basis on which a modern nation would be developed in Meiji times (1868–1912). Just before the Tokugawa period, political and social conditions were unstable. Each feudal territory was a separate domain, and there was always the danger that one feudal lord would use force to acquire neighboring territories. Even religious institutions, especially Buddhist temples, had become armed camps as priest-soldiers struggled to protect their own territories. And although past scholarship has criticized a "degenerate" Buddhism for meddling in politics, recent scholars "have come to realize that the separation of religion and politics is a distinction that the premodern Japanese never knew." From the time Buddhism entered Japan it was in close alliance with the state. In late Heian and Kamakura times, "Buddhist-Shinto monastic centers" were "important providers of rituals and support for the state," at the same time that they demonstrated keen competition and factionalism (politically, economically, and religiously).[1] The Tokugawa period's greatest achievement was joining the separate feudal territories under the power of one military leader, thereby unifying the country and creating political stability. Several military leaders began subduing the individual feudal domains and large Buddhist monasteries, but the Tokugawa line of military rulers completed the unification and carried out a thorough policy of social control. In this chapter, we will examine the important changes experienced by Buddhism, Confucianism, and Shinto during the Tokugawa period.

THE TOKUGAWA
GOVERNMENT AND RELIGION

The head of the military government was the *shogun*,[2] or military dictator, theoretically the highest general in the emperor's army but in actuality the top military leader controlling the government. The title was passed down in the Tokugawa family after Tokugawa Ieyasu seized control in 1600 and unified the country. The family acquired power over the country through warfare but later maintained its dominance through a centralized government. Administration of government policies was efficiently carried out, and the entire society was carefully organized. In general people were separated into four classes: *samurai* (warrior), peasant, artisan, and merchant. The status of the warriors was much higher than that of the three other classes, for warriors were seen as the protectors of the realm. They alone had special privileges such as the right to wear swords, and they received government stipends of rice. The other three classes were the economic mainstay of the country. Considered particularly important were the peasants (farmers), the providers of rice, which was the measure of economic income. Artisans were valued for their service or work; merchants were of least value, providing neither protection nor food, nor even service— and deriving their profit at the expense of the other classes.

The political stability achieved by the Tokugawas lasted for two and a half centuries and made possible considerable social and economic development. With the cessation of warfare, industry and life in the cities generally flourished. Early in the seventeenth century the Tokugawa rulers severely curtailed trading with Europe, so there was no extensive trade with foreign countries. Within Japan, however, trade and business developed so rapidly that commerce soon outranked agriculture in economic importance. Life in the cities began to determine new cultural styles, and popular culture thrived in a wide variety of forms. The wealth of merchants supported popular theater, and generally cities gave rise to art forms for the masses, such as woodblock prints. Many impoverished peasants risked punishment to leave the countryside and work for wages in the city. The increasing secularism of the cities is seen in the emergence of ribald novels and woodblock prints featuring both daily life and sensual delights.[3] Both the rich merchant and the average worker were at least as interested in the sensuality of this world as in the spirituality of the other world.

Religion was not unaffected by the Tokugawa policies of unification and social control. The great religious centers, especially the powerful Buddhist monasteries, had been subdued in the bloody fighting of the sixteenth century that preceded the Tokugawa rise to power. From the mid-seventeenth century, as part of a program to eliminate Christianity and control the people, every family was required by the government to belong to a Buddhist temple. The Tokugawas used the temples for the purposes of social control. However, the major rationale for social control came not from Buddhism, but from the Chinese commentaries on Confucian teaching known as Neo-Confucianism.

Japanese thinkers not only adopted Neo-Confucian teachings but also associated them with Japanese thought (especially Shinto), and expressed them in terms of a practical rationalism in tune with the social and economic developments of the time. Overall social stability was apparent even in the villages, which developed residential patterns of affiliation to local Shinto shrines.

TOKUGAWA BUDDHISM: STATE PATRONAGE AND WEAKENED VITALITY

The Tokugawa period was a time of peace and order thanks to the unification of the country achieved by Oda Nobunaga, Toyotomi Hideyoshi, and Tokugawa Ieyasu. Government policy was characterized by stability and unification. The tone of the period was set by the need to safeguard this unity with a strong central government. A consistent Tokugawa goal was to eliminate religious strife, which threatened to divide the country into warring factions. Whereas Nobunaga had favored Christianity, later in the Tokugawa period—partly in order to counteract the power of Buddhism—Christians were persecuted and Buddhism came to be patronized.

During the Tokugawa period, when Christianity was a proscribed religion, the government used Buddhism in enforcing the proscription. Every family was legally required to belong to a Buddhist temple and had to be questioned periodically by the temple priest. "At one stroke, all Japanese were incorporated administratively into the existing Buddhist structure."[4] Births were registered and deaths were recorded in the local temple to which the family belonged. (Prior to the Tokugawa period, there was individual membership in temples.) The Tokugawa government was even responsible for rebuilding many temples destroyed in earlier warfare, including temples at the Tendai headquarters of Mount Hiei, which had been ruthlessly razed by Nobunaga. However, the state money that flowed freely into the Buddhist temples cost them much of their autonomy and religious vitality. Nobunaga and Hideyoshi had punished the larger temples with military force because the temples were their most powerful political rivals. The Tokugawa government, by unifying the country, controlled all the Buddhist sects from the top. Buddhist priests became subordinates of the government, and the government strictly forbade any inter-sect quarrels. Buddhism was practically the established religion of Japan; the separate sects remained under direct government supervision. Buddhism, to a large extent, was constrained by monastic institutions and formal sermons stressing the value of the monastic life and looking down on "worldly occupations as an interim phase on the path to a higher religious state." Popular preaching on daily life themes related Buddhism more directly to the lives and needs of the people; these "talks," given in informal everyday language, "became more widely read than the Buddhist scriptures themselves"[5] (which were written in Chinese). These talks were the model for popular Neo-Confucian teaching.

The general situation tended to stifle religious devotion, especially at parish Buddhist temples where family membership was obligatory; temple members' "relationship with Buddhism often came to be more formalistic and pragmatic rather than a matter of individual religious conviction."[6] The Japanese historian Anesaki has described the general situation: "For the people at large religion was rather a matter of family heritage and formal observance than a question of personal faith."[7] The vitality of grassroots Buddhist piety is seen in such activities as the flourishing of pilgrimage to sacred sites, the purchase of amulets, and the widespread use of practices such as *nembutsu* recitation. To the present day, the organized sects of Japanese Buddhism have not been able to escape completely the unfavorable stigma of disinterested affiliation. Both enlightened priests and devout laypeople have often deplored the inertia of Tokugawa "feudal" patterns of Buddhist ancestor worship and have lamented the lack of a strong, personal Buddhist faith in the setting of parish temples.

NEO-CONFUCIANISM: POLITICAL STABILITY AND SOCIAL CONFORMITY

The Neo-Confucianism of the Tokugawa period must be distinguished from the initial period of Confucianism in Japan. Before Tokugawa times, Confucianism made significant contributons to Japanese culture but was not distinctly set apart as a separate school. Confucian scholarship had been kept alive within Buddhist temples, however, where Buddhist priests studied Confucian classics as well as Chinese Buddhist scriptures. From the thirteenth to seventeenth centuries, the scholar monks of the Zen sects were most influential in preserving and transmitting Neo-Confucian thought.

Neo-Confucianism is a general term for the Confucian revival that took place in China especially during the Sung (Song) dynasty (960–1279).[8] Confucianism in China underwent various periods of development. During the Sung dynasty, it borrowed from Taoism and Buddhism to create a comprehensive philosophy for interpreting every aspect of the world and of human life in the world. This philosophy, called Neo-Confucianism, offered a profound understanding of cosmology, humanistic ethics, and political ideals in a unified system. It enjoyed great success not only in China, but also in Korea and Japan. Although there were several schools within Neo-Confucianism, the Chinese philosopher Chu Hsi (Zhu Xi, 1130–1200) developed the most famous system of thought. (In Japan, Chu Hsi is called Shushi.)[9]

According to Chu Hsi, there is a rational principle in the universe, and this principle works in the material world to give rise to human beings and all things. This Neo-Confucian teaching provided Japan with a rational and secular philosophy that served to both unify the country from within and provide a common front for dealings with foreign countries. The feudal order of Tokugawa times, with its agrarian economy and hierarchical social system, was reinforced by this Neo-Confucian worldview.

In ancient Japan, Confucian classics were adopted as a solid foundation for education, and they were studied from Nara times up to the Tokugawa period. However, these studies became very formal and scholastic, especially because they continued to depend upon Chinese commentaries rather than the actual Confucian "classics." Gradually the tradition of Neo-Confucian studies maintained within the Japanese Zen temples began to attract attention outside Buddhist circles, influencing even Confucian and Shinto scholars. Neo-Confucianism was supported and patronized both by the shogunate and the feudal domains, and Neo-Confucian philosophy assumed preeminence when the shogunate banned heterodox Confucian teaching and recognized the philosophy of Chu Hsi (Shushi) as the prevailing rationale of the state.

The Tokugawa government was interested more in the organizational powers of Neo-Confucianism than in its cosmological theories. Tokugawa Ieyasu apparently saw in Neo-Confucianism a suitable philosophy for stabilizing and ordering the state. What the Neo-Confucian tradition amounted to was a heavenly sanction for the existing political and social order. Neo-Confucianism in this period served as the main intellectual rationale justifying the existence of the four social classes and their support of the Tokugawa government. The rulers or superiors were advised to be just and benevolent; subordinates were taught to be obedient and respectful.

The harmony of the universe was thought to depend upon a reciprocal relationship of justice from the superior and obedience from the subordinate. One venerable Confucian plan for ensuring this harmony was based on the bond of five human relationships: (1) ruler and subject, (2) parents and children, (3) husband and wife, (4) elder and younger, and (5) friend and friend. The last relationship, friendship, is characterized by mutuality; the other four are characterized by the obedience of the subordinates to superiors (and benevolence of superiors to subordinates). This philosophy supported the feudal ethics of Tokugawa times. Neo-Confucianism did not create the feudal situation, but it provided a rationale for legitimating and strengthening it.

The political use of the Confucian or Neo-Confucian tradition has been criticized for justifying the status quo. However, there is no doubt that Neo-Confucianism in Japan helped to maintain peace during this time, contributing especially to social mores and education. A famous example is the Neo-Confucian contribution to the philosophy of life called Bushido, the "way of the warrior," a model of training and a code of ethics that emphasized self-control and duty to one's master. Bushido also included a philosophical or spiritual dimension of self-cultivation. At first it was limited mainly to the warrior class, but Bushido's combined sense of honor and unswerving loyalty later had wide influence among the people. The personal qualities of loyalty and filial piety had been stressed in earlier Japanese history, but Neo-Confucianism reinforced them. The Japanese *samurai* (warrior), too, drew upon several traditions simultaneously. "The typical Tokugawa samurai saw some value in each of the three worldviews that competed for his allegiance. Buddhism and Shinto provided for his religious needs; Confucianism gave him a rational cosmology and a social ethic; Confucianism and Shinto both contributed to his conceptions of the political order."[10]

Under Tokugawa patronage, Neo-Confucianism became a combination of state cult and state educational system. By this time there were independent scholars of Neo-Confucianism outside the Buddhist temples. The *shogun* and feudal lords gave some of these scholars land on which to found Neo-Confucian schools, which not only taught the Chinese classics by means of the Neo-Confucian commentaries but also trained bureaucrats for the Tokugawa government. The cult, or ritual, aspect is seen in the fact that these scholars were ordered to perform old Confucian ceremonies such as the annual sacrifices, and Confucian temples were built for their observance of the sacrifices. Eventually, the Chu Hsi school of Neo-Confucianism enjoyed such privileged protection by the government that other schools of Neo-Confucianism were banned. In general, Neo-Confucianists exerted a widespread influence, tending to move attention away from Buddhism and combining forces with those who sought to purify Shinto from Buddhist influence. In late Tokugawa times, in spite of government opposition, popular teachers established new schools in which great numbers of people from all social classes were instructed in a heavily Neo-Confucian philosophy of life. In contrast to China, which had a long tradition of using the Confucian tradition as the basis for a civil service system (to train bureaucrats), Japan's early experiment with a Confucian-styled civil service system had been brief and unsuccessful. During the Tokugawa period, Neo-Confucianism was crucial for the development of independent scholars as charismatic teachers, and also the development of popular schools (*terakoya*), which provided basic educational needs such as literacy along with moral instruction.[11]

NEO-CONFUCIANISM: THE DEVELOPMENT OF PUBLIC AND PRIVATE ETHICS

Although Neo-Confucianism generally served to legitimate the state, it was much more than a monolithic rubber stamp of government policies. A long line of creative thinkers was attracted to several forms of Neo-Confucian thought, and these minds were instrumental in developing systems of public ethics and personal philosophies of life. One of the first was Fujiwara Seika (1561–1619), who had studied Confucian teachings while he was a Buddhist priest. Seika was the first Buddhist priest to give up Buddhist orders and concentrate his life solely on Confucianism. His shift from Buddhism to Confucianism is symptomatic of Tokugawa times generally, for during this period a number of leading thinkers became concerned more with secular rationales for the social and political order than with religious solutions such as Buddhist enlightenment. Fujiwara Seika met with the great ruler (*shogun*) Tokugawa Ieyasu, who invited him to serve in his government, but he declined the invitation, preferring to live as a recluse devoted to his studies and writings.

One of Fujiwara Seika's students, Hayashi Razan (1583–1657), was the first of a line of hereditary Confucian advisers to the *shogun*. Razan was given money and land to build a private school where he taught students his version of Neo-Confucianism. The Hayashi family was faithful to Chu Hsi philosophy in pursuing a rational and secular order, in the process criticizing Buddhism as being antisocial and also developing anti-Christian polemics. Nevertheless, the direction and results of Confucian teaching were not easy to control. For example, Neo-Confucianists emphasized a study of *Chinese* classics and a dislike for *Buddhism* as a "foreign" tradition. Eventually this emphasis was reinterpreted by Japanese scholars to pursue a study of *Japanese* classics and a distaste for *Confucianism* itself as a tradition foreign to Japan.

One of the transitional stepping stones to the revival of the Japanese tradition was Yamazaki Ansai (1618–82), who took a moderate position, balancing Confucianism with the native Shinto tradition. Yamazaki Ansai attempted to blend the ethical teachings of Confucianism with the religious aspects of Shinto. He equated Shinto stories of creation with Chinese cosmology. Later Shinto scholars such as Motoori Norinaga (1730–1801) were extremely critical of Yamazaki's compromising of the Shinto tradition with Neo-Confucian rationalism, but Yamazaki in his own way helped build a bridge from Confucianism to Shinto and thereby helped promote the rediscovery of Shinto; his blending of Shinto themes and Confucian ethics, known as Suika (or Suiga) Shinto, was an important influence on the Meiji Restoration.

Neo-Confucianism was much more than formal philosophy, as demonstrated clearly in the life and work of Kaibara Ekken (or Ekiken, 1630–1714). This man lived a simple life and tried to convey to common people the Neo-Confucian principles in informal Japanese language (rather than in the highly formal style of early Japanese Neo-Confucianists), setting forth a personal plan of self-transformation (or self-cultivation) to realize social harmony and, eventually, union with heaven and earth. Instead of stressing abstract metaphysical doctrines, he taught people that they should obey their parents and respect Heaven and Earth as their parents on a grander scale, a kind of "cosmic filiality."[12] For Kaibara Ekken, respect for nature meant not just love of nature but the actual study of nature. His extensive studies of plant life were pioneering works that attracted Western attention. He enjoyed a happy married life, and wrote extensively on family values and education. His views on women have led some to attribute to him authorship of *The Great Learning for Women* (*Onna Daigaku*), a classic feudal statement of the subjugation of women to men; it had a strong influence on the popular mentality and its use until recent times helped to shape women's sense of themselves as inferior and subordinate to men. In modern times such works have been criticized—by both men and women—for their negative attitudes toward women.[13]

The Tokugawa rulers brought unity and order to a Japan that had been torn by strife and disorder, and they felt their destiny was to continue in power and maintain their control. Neo-Confucianism was seen by its advocates as a rational and moral force in society (particularly in politics) that corresponded to the structure of the universe and the nature of life. The rulers may have had personal preferences for Buddhist piety and some sympathy for Shinto teaching, but the government support of Neo-Confucian teachers and advisers was an expression of political duty, in the interest of preserving the social order. The intention of the government policy supporting an official school of orthodox Neo-Confucianists (who taught people the nature of the moral order) was to create moral citizens and thereby preserve social stability. The government sought to tie the political system and social stability to support for Confucian (Chu Hsi) principles, and banned heterodox teachings.

However, currents of thought generated by the new social conditions of Tokugawa times and stimulated by Neo-Confucian scholarship could not be stopped by government order. The Neo-Confucian teachers of the early Tokugawa period, especially the Hayashi family, had set forth a rather slavish restatement of Chu Hsi's philosophy, which became viewed as mechanical repetition rather than inspired teaching. A number of thinkers dared to challenge the government prohibition of unorthodox teaching.

Even in China, the Neo-Confucianism of Chu Hsi had been criticized by contemporaries and later Chinese philosophers. One of the most influential later critics of Chu Hsi was Wang Yangming (1472–1529), who first studied Chu Hsi philosophy and then rejected Chu Hsi's notion of abstract reason in favor of a more subjective or intuitive reason within the human mind. The philosophy of Wang Yangming (known as Oyomei or Yomeigaku in Japan), with its stress on a strong moral sense and actual deeds (rather than intellect and words), appealed to Nakae Toju (1608–48) so much that he advocated it over Chu Hsi's rational philosophy.

Nakae Toju is considered the founder of the Wang Yangming (or Oyomei) school in Japan, but his fame was due not so much to his brilliant intellect as to his example of a highly moral life. He resigned a government post to return to his native village and care for his aging mother, thus putting into action his teaching about filial piety. His writings have the highest praise for this virtue: "Filial piety is the summit of virtue and the essence of the Way in the three realms of heaven, earth, and man. What brings life to heaven, life to earth, life to man, and life to all things, is filial piety. . . . Where is filial piety to be found? In one's own person."[14] He took very seriously the notion of cultivating the mind, not only by scholars and officials, but by all men and women. In contrast to Kaibara Ekken, who thought a woman's education should be limited to serving her future husband and in-laws, Nakae Toju held that cultivation of mind is important for both men and women, and he favored the proper education of women.

Other Confucianists opposed Neo-Confucian orthodoxy. For example, Ito Jinsai (1627–1705) studied the works of both Chu Hsi and Wang Yangming before turning to the Confucian classics such as the *Analects;* Ito Jinsai lived as a private teacher emphasizing the values of loyalty, faithfulness, and sincerity.[15] Yamaga Soko (1622–85), trained in the school of Hayashi Razan, later rejected Neo-Confucian orthodoxy, advocating a return to classical truth. Yamaga Soko felt that even the Neo-Confucian teachings of the Sung dynasty were not the truth but pointed back to the original teachings of Confucius himself. Yamaga

Soko saw in Confucius's teaching a strong ethical principle, and he criticized Neo-Confucian teachings such as the philosophy of Chu Hsi for making metaphysical notions more important than ethical principles. Like earlier thinkers of the Tokugawa period, Yamaga Soko worried about the inactivity of the warriors (*samurai* or *bushi*) in the prolonged peace of Tokugawa, and he proposed a code of personal ethics for warriors. His work entitled *The Way of the Warrior* is considered the first systematic attempt to set forth what later was called Bushido. The notions of self-discipline and loyalty in this code of life were very influential for popular ethics in subsequent centuries.

Yamaga Soko was so outspoken in his criticism of orthodox Neo-Confucianism that he was ordered into exile; but this experience only deepened his conviction that people should return to the true ethical teaching of Confucius, and he gave a nationalistic turn to this idea. He insisted that the Japanese people were truer to Confucius than were the Chinese because the Japanese practiced a more complete loyalty of son to father and subject to lord than had the Chinese.

The controversy between the orthodox Chu Hsi school and other schools continued. In 1790 the government issued an edict forbidding Confucian teaching other than the ideas of the Chu Hsi school. Yet, it was impossible to stop minds from thinking, and one after another thinkers appeared who developed their own blend of Confucian and Japanese systems of thought. Although each thinker had his own message, some similarities are found in the works of many writers of the seventeenth through the nineteenth centuries. Confucian and Neo-Confucian studies had invigorated historical and philological studies of the Chinese classics, and this carried over to a study of Japanese classics. Interest in Japanese history led to a heightened nationalism and a revival of Shinto studies.

There was a serious concern for developing a total rationale for the social and political order, to be offset by a deeper pursuit for a personal philosophy of life. This philosophizing was not idle speculation but was concerned with the actual management of government and the practical affairs of daily life (including family relations and farming). Not restricted to scholars and philosophers, these teachings formed the basis of lectures by popular scholars who drew large followings of warriors, merchants, and even common people. These lectures, heavily Neo-Confucian in content, were modeled on the long tradition of popular preaching in Buddhism, and included elements of Shinto. As these teachings spread to the common people, they tended to provide a broad rationale for the social order and to reinforce hierarchical social values generally, especially in the family.

In several regards, the Japanese institutional forms justified by Confucian ideals differed from their counterparts in China. For example, in China the relationship between a soldier and his master was a formal tie that could be formally broken; in Japan the loyalty of a warrior to his master was absolute and lifelong and could not be broken. In China the family took precedence over other social institutions; in Japan the family was a kind of "prototype of social organization" for other institutions.[16] The Japanese family was the training ground and model for loyal participation in larger social and political units—villages, businesses, and even the state.

All these teachings and social institutions helped shape the mental framework of the Japanese people as they left the Tokugawa period and entered the modern world. Some scholars think that such value systems have played an important part in the formation of modern Japan.[17] But the assessment of Neo-Confucianism has been sharply divided between views of its positive and negative significance for later history, viewing "the role of Neo-Confucian ethics as containing either the seeds of modernization of Japan or antecedents to the authoritarian structures of pre-war Japan."[18]

As we leave this long line of illustrious Confucian thinkers of Tokugawa times, we can learn a great deal of the mood of this period by looking at another Confucian-influenced thinker, little known during his lifetime, who offers a rare voice of dissent against the feudal establishment and even against the religious establishment. Ando Shoeki (1703?–1762), who apparently studied in a Zen monastery before becoming a physician, was conversant with the whole range of Buddhist philosophy as well as Confucian thought and Shinto writings. However, rather than supporting any of these teachings, over the years he developed his own philosophy, a "thoroughgoing egalitarianism,"[19] which severely criticized the exploitative and parasitic nature of both the feudal system and all the traditional forms of religion. In one of his radically satirical writings, *The Animal Court,* he uses the voices of animals and other creatures to parody the greed and corruption of especially government officials and religious leaders. As reported by the modern translator of this "political fable," "Most of *The Animal Court* is a critique of the philosophies and religions, dogmas and 'isms' that reigned in [Ando's] day," including Confucianism, Buddhism, and Shinto.[20]

Insisting that all people should earn their own way, he was equally critical of political and religious leaders who do not cultivate the land, but live parasitically off the fruit of their subordinates: "the master eats the labors of his servants, as do the Buddhist monks, doctors, shrine priests, and mountain ascetics."[21] Ando uses the voice of a reed warbler to launch one of his most scathing denunciations of "thieving" religionists: "The Buddha, the bodhisattvas, the arhats, and the monks of every sect preach all sorts of teachings; lost in illusion themselves, they seek to lead the rest of the world there. The preachings of Confucius, the Buddha, Laozi, Zhuangzi, the doctors, and Prince Shotoku are no more than teachings that promote the selfishness, mental confusion, and reckless behavior that are the basis of the World of Law, and those teachings are no different from my ceaseless warblings."[22]

It is not surprising that Ando's writings got him in trouble with the censors of the feudal government; in spite of this he did gather around him some disciples, but after his death this circle of followers broke up, and his writings were rediscovered only in the twentieth century, and were studied especially after World War II when traditional thought and feudalism were criticized more freely. Ando's thought is a complex fabric of mainly Neo-Confucian thought—even though he turns it against Confucianism; his trenchant criticism pits individualism and egalitarianism against all the hierarchical authorities of government and religion. A single writer's views cannot be taken as characteristic of a whole era, but his rare voice of protest reminds us that if one person was willing to challenge the authorities and criticize the forms and formalism of government and religion, it is likely that many others harbored these views without taking the risk of expressing them openly.[23]

RESTORATION SHINTO:
THE MOVEMENT FOR A PURIFIED SHINTO

Ever since the eighth century, Shinto had been overshadowed by the more highly systematized foreign traditions favored at court and among nobility, but it had remained a vital part of popular religious life in the local communities. Even during the most flourishing periods of Buddhism, there were Shinto scholars who remained true to their Shinto heritage and produced theoretical writings. In medieval times Kitabatake Chikafusa wrote a theological defense of the divine ancestry of the emperor and the centrality of Japan based on Shinto ideas. Indeed, the medieval schools of Shinto thought, although borrowing heavily from foreign traditions, pursued the ultimate goal of improving Shinto's status in Japanese religion. "Loyalists"—those around the imperial court who favored the emperor's return to power—had always supported Shinto. It is only natural that they were opposed to rule by a military leader and his warriors. There were religious commitments on both sides of this issue. In Tokugawa times, the several lines of Shinto support were united and reinforced by a powerful movement called "Restoration Shinto."

Restoration Shinto was not a simple resuscitation of Shinto, for Shinto had never died out; nor was it a sudden awakening. It was the cumulative result of the attitudes and writings of Shinto thinkers spanning several centuries, stimulated by several unique conditions of Tokugawa times. The relative isolation of Japan from foreign influence for about two centuries had positive as well as negative results. While foreign influence was excluded, national pride and national strength grew. Another stimulus for Restoration Shinto came from Neo-Confucianism. It must be remembered that Neo-Confucianism had to divorce itself from the Buddhist temples in order to become an independent movement; thus it was more favorably disposed to Shinto than to Buddhism. In addition, Neo-Confucianism had become so thoroughly Japanized that its main goal became support for the Japanese tradition and the political system. Neo-Confucianism encouraged and supported the policy of isolating Japan from the world. Shinto and Neo-Confucianism shared a common goal of glorifying the Japanese nation. Interest in the Chinese classics stimulated interest in the Japanese classics. Eventually Shinto developed such a high degree of self-consciousness that it formally rejected all foreign influence, including even Neo-Confucianism.

From the seventeenth through the nineteenth centuries, an illustrious line of Shinto theorists advanced the cause of Shinto as a "native" tradition—a cause that had been neglected too long in favor of the "foreign" traditions of Confucianism and Buddhism. The interest in Japanese classics was placed on firm ground when Kada Azumamaro (1669–1736) founded a school of National Learning for the purpose of studying Japan's own literature; he proposed National Learning (Kokugaku) as a replacement for Confucianism as the state rationale. This led the way for two leading scholars of Japanese language and literature, Kamo Mabuchi (1697–1769) and his disciple Motoori Norinaga (1730–1801). A systematic treatment showing Shinto to be superior to all religions was developed by Hirata Atsutane (1776–1843), who used arguments borrowed from other religions (including Christianity) to prove Shinto's superiority. These scholars helped to renew interest in ancient Japanese culture and to stimulate the development of Japanese nationalism.

The arguments of these Shinto scholars have been of great religious importance, and they have influenced the course of the nation and its cultural identity. These scholars' appeals for a return to the pure Japanese spirit were a significant factor in the momentous political change of the Meiji Restoration (to be discussed in Chapter 15). The rediscovery of Japanese literature and poetry is equally important, for the scholars paved the way for modern appreciation of Japanese classics.

Ancient Japanese writings, especially the *Kojiki,* but also valuable poetry and novels, had been neglected for so long that few people could read or understand them. In fact, the ancient literature had been smothered under a mantle of Chinese and Buddhist interpretation. But Mabuchi and Motoori discarded the prevailing Buddhist and Chinese cliches used to interpret and criticize these writings. They succeeded in showing that the early poetry and other writings should not be criticized because they do not conform to abstract Buddhist or Confucian ideals; rather, they should be recognized and appreciated for reflecting the "true" Japanese spirit before it had become "spoiled" by foreign influences. Implicit in Mabuchi and Motoori's argument was the idea that everything Japanese had been natural, spontaneous, and pure, but foreign influence had destroyed that naturalness and purity. The tone of their argument was often irrational, even mystical, advocating a return to the original state of purity from which the Japanese had fallen.[24]

MOTOORI NORINAGA
AND RESTORATION SHINTO

Of all the Shinto thinkers of this period, Motoori's scholarly achievements still command the greatest respect. He laid a permanent foundation for studying ancient Japanese writings on the basis of sound linguistic principles, and he elaborated his viewpoint into a perceptive view of human life and artistic creativity. Motoori used systematic linguistic evidence to show that the Chinese ideas in the *Nihongi* (written in Chinese) were later additions to Japanese culture; and he focused attention on the study of the *Kojiki,* which was written in a form clearly reflecting ancient Japanese language.[25] Because the study of ancient Japanese writings had been neglected, few people could read and understand the ancient language of the *Kojiki.* Most scholars simply superimposed abstract Confucian and Buddhist notions on both the *Kojiki* and the *Nihongi,* as well as on other writings such as the ancient poetry of the *Manyoshu* and the long medieval novel *Tale of Genji.* Motoori completed a thorough analysis of the language and ideas of the *Kojiki,* comparing it with other ancient Japanese writings. He spent thirty years writing his commentary on the *Kojiki,* and the scholarly value of this monumental work is still appreciated today.[26]

Motoori also led the way to a new awareness of the artistic achievement of the *Tale of Genji* by stripping away the layers of Chinese and Buddhist ideas that had been applied to it. He insisted on reading and interpreting the *Tale of Genji* through its own dramatic unity rather than in the light of abstract notions borrowed from Chinese and Buddhist philosophy. Motoori preferred the freshness and honesty of the *Tale of Genji,* which paints a very lifelike picture of the Japanese court's events in the eleventh century. The hero of this tale, Genji, is involved in many amorous intrigues, which conflict with notions of Buddhist ethics and Confucian conduct. Motoori, however, did not shrink from this apparent literary inconsistency with ethical ideals; instead, he applauded the *Tale of Genji* for showing that human emotions do not always follow the dictates of reason. He went beyond his own time in advancing the notion of the primacy of the emotions over intellect in art, developing a theory of art that is relevant for contemporary literary criticism. "In his study of literature, he developed the concept of *mono no aware,* the idea that the true value of literature lies in its ability to convey human sensitivity and emotion, and not in the transmission of didactic moralization."[27] Motoori wrote:

> Since novels have as their object the teaching of the meaning of the nature of human existence, there are in their plots many points contrary to Confucian and Buddhist teaching. This is because among the varied feelings of man's reaction to things—whether good, bad, right, or wrong—there are feelings contrary to reason, however improper they may be. Man's feelings do not always follow the dictates of his mind.[28]

The idea of art as a reflection of the imperfections of human life seems quite modern; yet it was deeply imbedded in the ancient Japanese worldview, including the notion of the *kami.*[29] Motoori directly criticized the overly intellectual and rational views of Confucianism and Buddhism, favoring instead the more direct appreciation of life—with all its ambiguities—found in ancient Japanese writings and in Shinto generally. He praised the *Kojiki* for its honesty in depicting evil *kami,* claiming that all life is a mixture of good and evil, right and wrong. Motoori believed that people should learn from accounts of evil deities and avoid the impurity or pollution that gave rise to them, thereby avoiding much evil. Also, he argued that it is better to accept Shinto views of the coexistence of good and evil than to follow the "false" and "deceptive" views of Confucianism and Buddhism, which paint an untrue picture of life in terms of abstract ideals—impossible for ordinary mortals to attain.

Motoori was especially contemptuous of Buddhist teachings that humans can transcend death and therefore should not be sorrowful at death. He wrote that such teachings are deceptive because they are contrary to human sentiment and fundamental truths of life. Motoori insisted that life is sorrowful and that people must be true to their emotions by marking death with sorrow. This inherent emotional life of human beings is not limited to reflection on mortality but touches all aspects of life and nature: this is what Motoori called "*mono no aware.*" The term is so emotionally charged that it is difficult to translate, but it is often regarded as central to the worldview of Japanese art and religion. This pure, emotional response to the beauty of nature, the impermanence of life, and the sorrow of death is similar to the religious attitude toward *kami*. The *kami* are behind and within nature and one's life, and a person should revere the *kami* immediately and directly without stopping to evaluate intellectual arguments about their existence. Motoori was a complex figure, "highly rational in unraveling linguistic problems in the text, yet highly irrational in his literal belief of the myths described therein."[30] The combination of literal belief in Shinto myth, and the notion of the superiority of Japanese culture and religion, was at the heart of Kokugaku, providing an important source for the Meiji Restoration and the nationalism and militarism leading up to World War II.

Motoori was too much a man of his time to escape completely from the "foreign" influence that he criticized. He read Confucian and Taoist materials and participated in Buddhist ceremonies. But he approached these imported traditions with the same depth of emotional response that he felt toward the *kami*. This idea is expressed in one of Motoori's poems:

> Shakyamuni[31] and Confucius
> Are also kami;
> Hence their Ways are branch roads
> Of the Broad Way of Kami.[32]

Generally, the movement known as Restoration Shinto was not limited to religion but influenced cultural and political developments as well. In terms of organized religious institutions, Restoration Shinto sought to reinstate Shinto as the true Japanese religion, purified of its foreign borrowings. Culturally, Restoration Shinto leaders tried to revive interest in Japanese classics for their own sake. In politics, the movement contributed to the growing support for a "restoration" of imperial rule. Most of these developments within Shinto were theoretical writings for the limited circle of intellectual elite and political leaders, but there also appeared at this time popular Shinto preachers, who drew upon the precedent and patterns of popular Buddhist preachers and Neo-Confucian teachers.[33]

In late Tokugawa times the patterns of thought in Restoration Shinto became linked to a general dissatisfaction with the Tokugawa government, and they gave rise to nationalist and ultranationalist forces. Restoration Shinto and these related forces play a significant role in the complex events of the Meiji Restoration, the subject of the next chapter.

NOTES

1. Mikael S. Adolphson, *The Gates of Power: Monks, Courtiers, and Warriors in Premodern Japan* (Honolulu: University of Hawai'i, 2000), p. 347. Neil McMullin has discussed at length "The change that came about in Buddhism in the sixteenth century," noting the severe critiques of Buddhist institutions both by medieval commentators and by modern Japanese and Western scholars; his own conclusion is that "In this new milieu Buddhism was on the wane," but "although it is true that many Buddhist temples had become corrupt by the sixteenth century, it is doubtful that the factor of corruption can account for the profound change in the religious dimension of Japanese society at that time." See his *Buddhism and the State in Sixteenth-Century Japan* (Princeton: Princeton University, 1984), especially "'Post-Buddhist' Japan," pp. 264–83.

2. The term *shogun* has become familiar to many Westerners through the popular novel and television program by the same title—*Shogun,* written by James Clavell (New York: Dell, 1980).

3. For a glimpse of this glittering world, see Howard S. Hibbett, *The Floating World in Japanese Fiction* (London: Oxford University, 1959).

4. Kenneth A. Marcure, "The *Danka* System," *Monumenta Nipponica,* vol. 40, no. 1 (Spring 1985), pp. 39–67; see p. 42. *Danka,* usually translated as "parishioner," is defined by Marcure as "a household (or households) affiliated to a temple" (p. 40).

5. Sawada, *Confucian Values and Popular Zen,* p. 21.

6. Marcure, "The *Danka* System," p. 45.

7. Masaharu Anesaki, *History of Japanese Religion,* p. 260. Some recent scholars disagree with this criticism of religion (especially Buddhism) in Tokugawa times. See Stone, *Original Enlightenment,* p. 366. Although there is difference of opinion on the nature and extent of "corruption" in Tokugawa religious institutions, there is consensus that popular religion or "lived religion" was active and vital in Tokugawa times. See Barbara Ambros and Duncan Williams, eds., *Local Religion in Tokugawa History,* vol. 28, no. 3–4, of *Japanese Journal of Religious Studies* (Fall 2001).

8. For translated materials and general discussion of Neo-Confucianism in China, see de Bary and Bloom, eds, *Sources of Chinese Tradition,* 2d ed., Part Four.

9. For a convenient introduction to Neo-Confucianism in Japan and translations of the writings of major Japanese Neo-Confucian thinkers, see Tsunoda et al., *Sources of Japanese Tradition,* paperback ed., vol 1, pp. 384–433; 2d ed. forthcoming.

10. John Whitney Hall, "The Confucian Teacher in Tokugawa Japan," in *Confucianism in Action,* ed. David S. Nivison and Arthur E. Wright (Stanford: Stanford University, 1959), p. 291. An early modern advocate of Bushido was Inazo Nitobe, *Bushido: The Soul of Japan* (rev. and enl. ed., Rutland, VT: C. E. Tuttle, 1969; reprint of the 1905 ed.). For a brief overview, see Martin Collcutt, "Bushido," *Kodansha Encyclopedia of Japan,* vol. 1, pp. 221–23.

11. Ronald Philip Dore, *Education in Tokugawa Japan* (Berkeley: University of California, 1965).

12. For a comprehensive treatment of Ekken, see Mary Evelyn Tucker, *Moral and Spiritual Cultivation in Japanese Neo-Confucianism: The Life and Thought of Kaibara Ekken;* for comments on the Neo-Confucian tradition of cosmic filiality, see pp. 54–56, 380.

13. Tucker, *Moral and Spiritual Cultivation in Japanese Neo-Confucianism,* p. 119, writes that "Ekken was simply codifying and developing the contemporary ethical practices of the period," but "In his interest in education for women he was ahead of many of his contemporaries."

14. Tsunoda et al., *Sources of Japanese Tradition,* paperback ed. vol. 1, p. 375.

15. See John A. Tucker, *Ito Jinsai's Gomojigi and the Philosophical Definition of Early Modern Japan* (Leiden: E. J. Brill, 1998).

16. Mitsuo Tomikura, "Confucianism," in *Japanese Religion,* ed. Ichiro Hori, pp. 110–11.

17. For the account of one teacher, Ishida Baigan (1685–1744), and the influence of his teachings (Shingaku) on the formation of modern Japan, see Robert N. Bellah, *Tokugawa Religion: The Values of Pre-Industrial Japan* (Glencoe, IL: Free Press, 1957; reprint ed., Boston: Beacon Press, 1970; reprinted as *Tokugawa Religion: The Cultural Roots of Modern Japan,* with a new introduction by the author, New York: The Free Press, 1985). Bellah was the first Western scholar to emphasize the role of religion in Japan's modernization; see his second thoughts in the introduction to the 1970 edition. For a more recent work on the significance of Shingaku, with comments on Bellah's work, see Sawada, *Confucian Values and Popular Zen.*

18. Tucker, *Moral and Spiritual Cultivation in Japanese Neo-Confucianism,* p. 25 (and note 46, p. 370, for the scholars who hold these disparate views).

19. Masahide Bito, "Ando Shoeki," *Kodansha Encyclopedia of Japan,* vol. 1, pp. 55–56.

20. Jeffrey Hunter, *The Animal Court: A Political Fable from Old Japan* (New York: Weatherhill, 1992), pp. viii–ix. See also the larger study from which this book is taken, Toshinobu Yasunaga, *Social and Ecological Philosopher of Eighteenth-Century Japan* (New York: Weatherhill, 1992). The first Western treatment of this figure (as a critique of feudalism) was by E. Herbert Norman, *Ando Shoeki and the Anatomy of Japanese Feudalism, Transactions of the Asiatic Society of Japan,* 3d ser., 1949, vol. 2; (reprinted, Washington: University Publications of America, 1979).

21. Hunter, *The Animal Court,* p. 5. Mountain ascetics are *yamabushi,* members of Shugendo.

22. Ibid, p. 15. "The World of Law" is what Shoeki calls, with disgust, the artificial laws of corrupt government and religion. Shoeki goes on to direct his scathing critique of religion against every major Buddhist sect.

23. A Russian observer of Japanese customs during his "captivity" in Japan from 1811 to 1813, when quizzed by his keepers about his own and fellow countrymen's fervent Christian faith and practice, asked the return question about the practice of religion in Japan. The gist of the answer was that they found the traditions in Japan to be ridiculous and incredible but thought they might be useful to the state. Though differing from Ando's outright cynicism, this attitude of indifference seemed widespread in Tokugawa Japan. See Vasilii Mikhailovich Golovnin, *Memoirs of a Captivity in Japan, During the Years 1811, 1812, and 1813; with Observations on the Country and the People,* 2d ed., 3 vols. (London: H. Colburn, 1824; reprinted, New York: Oxford University, 1973); see vol. 3, p. 13. I thank my son David for bringing this work to my attention. In his wider discussion of the abstract thought in all languages and cultures, and the presence of "philosophy" in some individuals, Paul Radin also recognized the possibility of "skepticism and critique" in apparently uniform cultures. See his *Primitive Man as Philosopher* (New York: D. Appleton, 1927; 2d rev. ed., New York: Dover, 1957).

24. For two studies of Kokugaku viewed as "nativism," see H. D. Harootunian, *Things Seen and Unseen: Discourse and Ideology in Tokugawa Nativism* (Chicago: University of Chicago, 1988), and Peter Nosco, *Remembering Paradise: Nativism and Nostalgia in Eighteenth Century Japan* (Cambridge: Harvard University, 1990).

25. For additional comments on the *Kojiki* and *Nihongi,* see Chapter 4.

26. For a sample of this lengthy commentary, see Motoori Norinaga, *Kojiki-den, Book 1,* "introduced, translated, and annotated by" Ann Wehmeyer (Ithaca, NY: Cornell University, 1997); see especially pp. 213–47 for Motoori's views of *kami* and the superiority of the way of the *kami* and things Japanese over Confucian, Chinese, and Buddhist ideas.

27. Wehmeyer, in Motoori, *Kojiki-den, Book 1,* p. 1.

28. Tsunoda et al., *Sources of Japanese Tradition,* paperback ed., vol. 2, p. 29; 2d ed. forthcoming.

29. For a lengthy quotation of Motoori's view of *kami,* see p. 8 above.

30. Makoto Ueda, "Motoori Norinaga," *Kodansha Encyclopedia of Japan,* vol. 5, p. 258.

31. Shakyamuni is another name for Buddha.

32. "Way of Kami" is Motoori's expression for Shinto. The poem is quoted from the translation of Shigeru Matsumoto, *Motoori Norinaga, 1730–1801,* p. 164. This book is a useful study of Motoori, including many translations.

33. See Peter Nosco, "Masuho Zanko (1655–1742): A Shinto Popularizer between Nativism and National Learning," in *Confucianism and Tokugawa Culture,* ed. Peter Nosco (Princeton: Princeton University, 1984), pp. 166–87; this article also provides a convenient overview of the "the major examples of Confucian-Shinto prior to Masuho Zanko."

15

🌿

The Meiji Restoration
and State Shinto

For more than two hundred years, the Tokugawa rulers maintained peace based on a feudal system of government, but gradually the effectiveness of their regime declined. Economically, the heavy taxes imposed on peasants to support the feudal government led to widespread suffering and thousands of local uprisings, especially among rural people, but also among urban workers (who suffered from high rice prices). In addition, toward the end of the Tokugawa period the foreign insistence upon open trade with Japan was a constant political threat. This situation presented a formidable combination of internal unrest and external pressure. Internally, the common people—both peasants and laborers—were dissatisfied with economic conditions and were open to popular movements calling for a "world renewal" (a "renewal" not only in personal rebirth but also in social reform). Externally, the European and American ships bearing demands for trade threatened the sovereignty of Japan, and at the same time their presence intensified the patriotic calls to defend the country and restore the emperor (particularly among some *samurai*).[1] The *shogun* made repeated attempts to unite the *daimyo* (feudal lords) and resolve both the internal problems and external threats, but failed to forge a consensus.

As the *shogun* became increasingly ineffective in handling these problems, more and more people came to favor the restoration of the emperor: their campaign against the *shogun* used the slogan "revere the emperor, expel the barbarians." Some groups supported the emperor against the Tokugawa ruler, and now their political agenda was reinforced by these new developments. An attempt to link the Tokugawa government and the imperial family was unsuccessful. Japanese intellectuals, dissatisfied with Neo-Confucianism as a means of regulating the country and opposing foreign threats, increasingly turned their attention to the study of Western science. "The regime fell because the imperialist intrusion of the mid-nineteenth century presented it with a set of political tasks that it could handle neither then nor at any time in its past."[2] As a result of all these factors, in late 1867 the last Tokugawa *shogun* resigned, and in early 1868 Tokugawa rule came to an end when the emperor was "restored," at least in name, to his position as head of state.

THE POLITICAL AND RELIGIOUS SIGNIFICANCE OF THE MEIJI RESTORATION

Those groups—primarily *samurai* and prominent merchants—who had successfully called for the emperor's "restoration" as Japan's political leader were quick to proclaim a new age of "Enlightenment and Restoration" (that is, Meiji). In this fashion, the Meiji Restoration drew its name from the movement for the return or restoration of the emperor as symbolic head of state. In actuality, this was no simple "restoration" of an earlier period of Japanese history, but, nevertheless, this stated intent of returning to the emperor's mythical origins and to the age of the gods did provide a sacred legitimation for the innovations of Meiji (which to a certain extent survive even today in the form of the modern nation-state that evolved out of Meiji developments).

Not exactly a restoration, at the same time it marked the appearance of new beginnings in many areas of government and religion. In government, the Meiji period (1868–1912) divides feudal Japan from modern Japan. From ancient times the Japanese people had a general sense of collective unity, but through most of Japanese history, especially in the medieval feudal setting, individuals and groups identified themselves more as belonging to a specific geographical region and to a particular social unit (such as a feudal domain). After 1868 the new government's main priority was to establish a much stronger national identity, which required the refashioning of individual identity as citizens within a nation-state. Much of Japanese history from 1868 to 1945 is the story of the creation of the nation-state and the rationale of nationalism to support it (nationalism will be discussed later in the chapter). "The sense of nation, of being Japanese, was transmitted to the whole of the *kokumin* [citizens, countrymen] for the first time in the Meiji period and is not much diminished today."[3]

After 1868 the new Meiji government set about centralizing and reorganizing power, along the lines of a nation-state, and established entire governmental institutions, such as education, banking, and a modern army and navy. Most significantly, the office of the *shogun* was abolished. Technically, from the twelfth century the *shoguns* had been authorized by the imperial court to rule the country; the Meiji transformation was a clever strategy to remove the *shogun* by going back more than a millennium (long before the *shoguns*) to Japanese imperial origins in order to go forward to the radically new developments of a Western-style nation-state.

From Meiji times the emperor formally headed a centralized state, which actually was ruled by officials (who held power in the *name* of the emperor), in conjunction with a constitution and elected legislators. At first, both the electorate and the legislators came from a rather limited elite group, but gradually the common people gained greater recognition and power—as seen in the permitting—and then the requiring—of surnames for commoners. The system of feudal lords and domains was abolished (as well as *samurai* status) and a nationwide network of prefectures (similar to states in America) was established; prefectures administer local government as branches of the central authority. A new capital was established at Tokyo (formerly known as Edo). To finance the government, a national tax system was adopted. It was obvious that if the central government was to be sovereign, competing regional feudal armies would have to give way to an imperial or national army. These radical transformations in politics and economics took time, as well as many adjustments, in the fitting of noble ideals to realistic possibilities.

The political and economic transformations of the Meiji Restoration were matched by significant changes in the religious arena. The transition of religion from Tokugawa times into the Meiji era, put simply, may be described as the replacement of state support of Buddhism with state support of Shinto (or State Shinto). Changes in religion, too, took time and involved considerable trial and error. In general there was a negative purpose (the demotion of Buddhism) and a positive purpose (the elevation of Shinto).

The general motive for demoting Buddhism is easily understood, because Buddhist temples had been, in effect, branches of the Tokugawa feudal government, and Buddhist sects lost favor due to their association with the former government. Furthermore, this privileged position had enabled Buddhist temples to accumulate wealth from a captive audience, making Buddhism an easy target for the Meiji architects' reforming zeal. The main purpose of promoting Shinto is obvious, too. The reasoning of Shinto leaders and some government officials was that, just as the emperor had been restored to his rightful status as (titular) head of the state, so should Shinto be restored to its rightful position as the old imperial religion—and new state religion. During Tokugawa times Buddhism (and Neo-Confucianism) had provided the primary rationale for the *shogun's* rule; in early Meiji the new ideal of the emperor and Shinto provided the central rationale for the new government.

In the transitional years of early Meiji an exaggerated discrediting of the old regime and persecution of Buddhism was accompanied by an inflated enthusiasm for the newly restored Shinto.[4] Prior to the Meiji period, most Shinto shrines had come under Buddhist influence. The close relationship between the two religions was natural, because from ancient times Shinto shrines and Buddhist temples were built side-by-side and the priests of the two traditions cooperated in the worship within both edifices. However, especially during the Tokugawa period, high-ranking Buddhist priests often came to control Shinto shrines. In reaction to this situation, many Meiji reformers were outspoken in their desire to "purify" what they perceived as "native" Shinto from the foreign influence of Buddhism. The viewpoint of the Restoration Shinto representatives (who had extraordinary influence in early Meiji) was that, from the time Buddhism entered Japan from foreign lands, it had diluted the purity of the original Japanese tradition, and therefore was inherently evil. Confucianist critiques of Buddhism joined Shinto in advocating the destruction of Buddhism, based on the Confucian complaints that Buddhist teachings incorporated useless elements of magic and that Buddhism preyed parasitically on the people's money.

For Shinto leaders the remedy was very simple—to eliminate an evil foreign religion and replace it with a return to the pure native Japanese religion of Shinto. Such a drastic measure was not acceptable to many government officials, and was impossible to carry out once Buddhist priests mounted a powerful opposition. Many compromises and temporary provisions were made before arriving at satisfactory arrangements for the coexistence of Buddhism and Shinto.

Japan has always presented a mixture of the old and the new. The Meiji Restoration attempted its own blend, seeking to return to the ideal of an ancient age in which government and religion were inseparable, while breaking a path to the future by boldly opening Japan to all kinds of new foreign ideas and usages.

THE ATTEMPT TO RESTORE SHINTO
AS THE ONLY JAPANESE RELIGION

"Restoration Shinto" was an attempt to purify Shinto shrines and the Shinto priesthood from Buddhist influence. Buddhist statues were removed from shrines, and Buddhist priests were ejected. However, the proximity of the two traditions and their priesthoods is further illustrated by this very move: many Buddhist priests simply renounced their Buddhist ordination and overnight became Shinto priests. For a while Buddhism suffered from severe persecution. There was a widespread cry to eliminate Buddhism and Buddhist monks. Many priceless Buddhist treasures were wantonly destroyed, while others were bought for a pittance to become the nucleus of museum collections in the West.

In general, as Buddhism was disestablished, Shinto was reestablished (or newly established). The goal was to return to the earlier period when Shinto had played a prominent role in government. Accordingly, in 1868 Shinto was proclaimed the sole basis of the government. Not only was the emperor the head of the state (and the imperial rituals were state rituals), but there was also a Ministry of (Shinto) Rites within the government, superior to other ministries. In addition to cleansing Shinto from Buddhist domination, the ministry began to regulate Shinto on a centralized, nationwide basis. For example, the hereditary succession of Shinto priests was abolished so that Shinto priests could be appointed by the state as government officials. Shinto priests were used to propagate purified Shinto, especially in districts where Buddhist influence was strongest. There was even a brief (and unsuccessful) attempt to prohibit Buddhist funerals and to require all funerals to be Shinto rites.

An imperial rescript, or proclamation, in 1870 explained the rationale for such policies. According to the rescript, the Japanese nation had been founded by the gods (*kami*) and preserved by an unbroken line of emperors who maintained "the unity of religion and state." This unity was considered indispensable for the restoration agenda of the Meiji era. By 1871 the official policy of using Shinto parishes for registration purposes replaced the Tokugawa practice of relying on Buddhist parishes.[5] After the expulsion of Christianity in the mid-seventeenth century, the government had required every family to belong to a Buddhist temple to ensure the prohibition of Christianity. In similar fashion, in the early Meiji period, the new government required registration at a local Shinto shrine. The main purpose of the Shinto parish system was to unify the state, rather than to attack Buddhism or Christianity. One carryover from Tokugawa government policy was the Meiji government's attempt to control, and persecute if necessary, people and groups engaging in religious practices not consistent with state goals; in early Meiji the government prohibited various "superstitions" and "wasteful" practices.

Because today we are familiar with Japan as a highly unified and centrally organized nation-state, it is difficult to imagine the turmoil and disorder that accompanied the transition from feudal to modern times. The Meiji government, or at least one major faction within the government, sought to reduce the chaos by returning to Shinto's ideals. Yet, neither intellectual persuasion nor even government order was able to transform the complex religious history of Japan into a completely Shinto affair. Some people feared (and some hoped) that Buddhism was destined for extinction, joining the doomed Tokugawa feudal regime with which Buddhism had been closely linked. Despite the widespread criticism of Buddhist priests and temples, many people maintained their Buddhist piety and practice. Also, the criticism and persecution of Buddhism had a purging effect. Although caught at a low ebb of spiritual resources, the major sects of Japanese Buddhism rallied to fight for their own role in the creation of the new modern state. During the Meiji era, Buddhism became more active than Shinto in developing a systematic critique against Christianity, and was just as forceful as Shinto in supporting the emperor and state, as well as its military policies.

Two major factors persuaded the new government to back down from its focus on Shinto as the sole foundation of the state: first, within Japan, the renewed strength of Japanese Buddhism; second, internationally, the insistence of Western spokespeople for religious freedom in Japan. Popular support for Buddhism and the revitalization of Buddhist institutions made it impossible for the Ministry of Rites to control both Shinto and Buddhist affairs. Therefore, the Ministry of Rites was abolished, and between 1872 and 1875 there was a brief attempt to administer both Shinto and Buddhism within the more neutral setting of the newly created Ministry of Doctrine, and to use both Shinto and Buddhist priests (and even artists and entertainers) for educating people about citizenship and their obligations to the emperor and the state. But it was impractical to try to handle Shinto and Buddhism in the joint administration of the Ministry of Doctrine. After the Ministry of Doctrine was abolished, there were temporary measures for handling shrines and temples, until the official designation of "Shrine Shinto" in 1882.

Buddhism took on a new appearance during the first decade of Meiji. In Tokugawa times Buddhism was practically the official religion, and as the arm of the government had thrived under state support and mandatory participation by all people. But in early Meiji, as the tables turned, and Shinto became the main pillar of the new nation-state, Buddhism suffered greatly from persecution; some Buddhist scholars who traveled to America and Europe found the notion of separation of religion and state as an external argument for supporting this principle in Japan, and also as a way of easing their own persecution. Ironically, within a decade, prominent Buddhist thinkers shifted from supporting the close alliance of state and religion (establishing Buddhism), to a new standpoint advocating separation of state and religion (disestablishing all religion). This new position allowed greater freedom of religion for Buddhism and—unintentionally—for Christianity as well.

The second major factor making it impossible—or politically unwise—to recognize Shinto as the only religion in Japan was the Westerners' demand that Japan allow freedom of religion and accept Christian missionaries. Christian missionaries (both Catholic and Protestant) entered Japan even before the official opening of Japan to foreign intercourse in 1868. To the surprise of both Christian missionaries and the Japanese populace, some Japanese people approached Western missionaries and said they had kept alive the Catholic faith for more than two centuries by practicing secretly in homes and small groups. The Tokugawa proscription of Christianity had not yet been lifted, and the government swiftly prosecuted these "Christians," seizing their property and exiling them to remote areas. The desperate plight of these Christians soon became known not only among Westerners in Japan, but also in Europe and North America.

Japan, emerging from two and a half centuries of seclusion, was very sensitive to foreign criticism. Government-sponsored groups went abroad to observe the functioning of Western countries so that the Meiji government could learn from Western precedents. Japanese officials wanted to adopt Western practices they thought would be beneficial to Japan, and they actively sought to establish relations with Western nations. Western diplomats argued for lifting the ban on Christianity and its reintroduction into Japan. Against this background of Western insistence for the recognition of Christianity, and Buddhism's new position supporting separation of religion from government (supported by the more liberal minds of the Meiji era), in 1873 the ban against Christianity was lifted.[6] Christianity was now a recognized religion and

Christian missionaries could legally enter Japan and recruit converts. The regulation for compulsory registration at Shinto shrines was dropped, and from about 1875 the government attitude toward religion shifted to a new direction.

THE ESTABLISHMENT OF
NONRELIGIOUS SHRINE SHINTO

Early Meiji attempts to make Shinto the exclusive national religion shaping the new state proved impractical, and gradually government officials who were less enthusiastic about Restoration Shinto found ways of using Shinto to unify and support the state without following the agenda (especially the anti-Buddhist program) of Restoration Shinto. In effect, officials of the new government recognized that if it was not feasible to make Shinto the sole religion of the state, then it would be more effective to make the state into a semi-Shinto institution.

Shinto remained deeply involved in state matters, but the state declared Shinto to be nonreligious in character. To be more precise, an 1882 law divided Shinto into Shrine Shinto (*jinja shinto,* sometimes called nationalistic or State Shinto by Western writers) and sect Shinto (*kyoha shinto*). Under the category of Shrine Shinto, the law included most of the Shinto shrines throughout the country, excluding only those that had developed special sect forms. (This government action did not create any new shrines, but it changed the status of most local shrines.) From 1882, only adherents of Shrine Shinto could call their buildings shrines (*jinja*), for they alone were state institutions. A special Bureau of Shrines was set up in the Department of Home Affairs to administer the shrines as state institutions. In this subtle shift of events, rather than Shinto controlling the state, the state came to control Shinto.[7]

Thirteen groups that had developed as sects of Shinto—or had accepted Shinto supervision in order to gain government recognition as independent sects—came to be included in the category of sect Shinto. These thirteen sects were considered separate religions by the government. The buildings of sect Shinto could not be called shrines (*jinja*); they were labeled *kyokai,* a term usually translated as "church." Sect Shinto had the same religious status as the sects of Buddhism and Christianity. In fact, all these religions (Shrine Shinto by its new definition being excluded from "religion") were supervised directly by the government, shifting control from one agency to another.

This policy, on the surface a separation of religion and state, was of great utility and convenience to the Meiji government. It paid lip service to religious freedom, because technically no religion was required and the Constitution of 1899 guaranteed the Japanese people freedom of religious belief "within limits not prejudicial to peace and order, and not antagonistic to their duties as subjects." At least in principle freedom of religion was upheld, while in practice there was legal precedent for controlling and suppressing any religious group seen as a threat to "peace and order." At the same time this policy provided a free hand for using the supposedly nonreligious Shrine Shinto to unify and mobilize the country through patriotic support of the state. The claim of freedom of religion rested on the political decision to consider Shrine Shinto "nonreligious"; meanwhile, the Imperial Rescript on Education of 1890 ensured that Shinto and Confucian principles would be included in the people's moral education and thus unify the nation.[8] This rescript, invoking loyalty to the state as a corollary of reverence for the imperial ancestors who founded it, did not advocate a completely novel message, but it instituted new practices: this proclamation was displayed with the emperor's portrait and recited in every Japanese school to instill reverence for the emperor and un-questioning loyalty to the state. "Religious" teaching as defined by the state, meaning especially Buddhist and Christian teaching, was excluded from schools, while Shrine Shinto (as a "nonreligious" national tradition) was sup-ported politically and economically by the government.[9]

In theory all religions were free to manage their own affairs, but in prac-tice they were restricted or even suppressed. For example, in the early 1900s the government was attempting to more effectively unify the nation by using local shrines to encourage loyalty to the emperor and patriotism toward the state. The government therefore required small local shrines to "merge" into single village shrines, so that the government could control shrine activities and inculcate patriotism more efficiently. Although the local people did not want to "merge" their small shrines, they could not ignore the government or-der, so they reluctantly dismantled their small shrines. After World War II, many local groups reestablished the small shrines they had been forced to abandon in the merger process.[10] Whether as merged or reestablished shrines, one of the Meiji era's enduring legacies is the shaping of Shinto as a modern religion, the way we see it today, formally separate from Buddhist institutions.

JAPAN AS A NATION-STATE—
NATIONALISM IN WORLD PERSPECTIVE

The political and religious developments of early Meiji—some experiments soon replaced by more successful attempts, some innovations lasting much longer—may be seen as part of the trial and error process that takes place in the creation of any nation-state. The rationale for creating, legitimating, and maintaining this nation-state, which we may call "nationalism," also went through a process of provisional measures before arriving at more permanent arrangements. "Nation-state" and "nationalism" are two concepts that may help us better understand both recent Japanese religious history and religious history around the world, particularly the problem of religious nationalism, or nationalistic religion.

The term "nation-state" is usually reserved for the highly centralized gov-ernments of the past few centuries. Although in many parts of the world peo-ple in earlier times felt bound together by shared linguistic, ethnic, cultural, and religious identity, they were not citizens of a common state. The term "nation-state" is best applied to the countries with well-developed political institutions and fixed boundaries. "Nationalism," like its companion term "nation-state," may build on various characteristics, such as shared linguistic, ethnic, cultural, religious, or even economic identity, but most of the time it is viewed as the perception or awareness of the shared identity—or the awakening or conscious creation of this identity. Scholars disagree about which came first, the nation or nationalism, but we cannot take for granted the common notion that the nation came into existence first and then generated the nationalism to legitimate it. In fact, some scholars have even argued that "nationalism is not the awakening of nations to self-consciousness; it invents nations where they do not exist."[11] However we view the "chicken-or-egg" question of whether the nation-state or nationalism came first, this statement reminds us that much of what happened from Meiji times on was not just the extension and revision of past forms, but also the creation or "invention" of new structures and institutions. If the Meiji Restoration led to the Japanese invention of the nation-state, then this process may also have so thoroughly refashioned or remade modern Shinto and Buddhism that they emerged as "reinvented" traditions.

The development of the nation-state in Japan has much in common with the formation of nation-states in other times and places: the replacement of more local practices, identities, and institutions with more inclusive national identity and centralized governmental institutions covering all people. Yet, the formation of every nation-state has its own particular history, and Japan's national development is no exception to this rule.

Japan is both older and newer in the world history of nations. If the nation-state in Japan is dated at the first year of Meiji in 1868, and the nation-state of the United States was formally established in 1776, we see that Japan is a rather young nation-state. The origins or roots of Japanese identity, however, reach much farther back on Japanese soil than those of North and South America (whose identities were forged in recent centuries by peoples of highly diverse geographical and cultural origins). Japan, by contrast, even has its own prehistoric myths of the sacred origin of its land, people, and ruler.

Scholars have long recognized the combination of factors that made the creation of the nation-state and nationalism in Japan more feasible than in other parts of the world.[12] National identity may be fostered by one or more common factors, such as language, ethnic descent, religious beliefs, and geographical separateness. Few nations have been influenced by all of these factors, but all were both present and strong in Japan. The insular character of the Japanese islands has been important in isolating and shaping these factors into a national identity. In this regard, Japan is more comparable to the English experience of an island country, than to the development of nation-states in continental Europe, the Americas, and Asia.

Japan also stands in sharp contrast to the many nation-states that arose out of colonial histories or the breakdown of empires. The United States itself remembers a colonial period, when it was a colony of England; and both nineteenth-century South America and twentieth-century Africa have seen the transition of former colonies to nation-states; more recently the Soviet Union has given way to a number of new nations. Japan was never a colony or territory of another country or empire. Japan as a nation-state is also quite different from the eastern Europe nation-states whose boundaries were determined by political decisions after World War I; Japan became a nation-state by its own decisions and actions, and its boundaries were determined more by its insular isolation than by particular political decisions.

This brief overview of nation-states and nationalism offers us clues into why and how Japan developed as it did. In short, Japan's journey into a nation-state and nationalism was quite different from the path followed by European and American countries. Although in premodern times Japan had been threatened by a Mongol invasion, and Japan itself had harbored the ambition of conquering Korean and continental territory, Japan was neither a colony nor a colonizer before the Meiji Restoration. Japan's self-imposed centuries of isolation during Tokugawa times was rudely interrupted by European powers who sought to "open" Japan, either with trade or with military force, or both. Japan's emergence from isolation in the Meiji period found Japan competing against well-developed Western nation-states with their own colonial lands and ambitions. Japanese leaders, intellectuals, and even common people perceived the Western intrusion as a threat that Japan, like other Asian and non-Western lands, would become a colony or territory of Western nations. Japan's solution was to become a nation-state itself and to compete directly against Western nations, using some of their own nation-building strategies. The Japanese, learning from the lesson of Western colonialism (and from government missions to the West), saw that the key to being a powerful nation-state was to develop an effective centralized government backed by a strong military and an efficient industry, which in turn required universal technical education. The success of the Meiji experiment is seen in the fact that Japan prevented European countries from making it a colony; the tragedy of the Meiji success, as it bore fruit from the late nineteenth to the mid-twentieth century, is that Japan did not avoid the pitfall of becoming a colonizer of other Asian countries.

How, then, should we view "nationalism" as a part of Japanese history and world history? Historians and other scholars disagree sharply over this highly controversial issue. One rather neutral definition of nationalism is: "the belief in the primacy of a particular nation, real or constructed."[13] For our purposes, considering nationalism in general, we may single out three divergent views of the rise of nationalism: as inevitable, as beneficial, and as malevolent.

Nationalism may be viewed as inevitable—as part of the historical process—as an unavoidable side-effect (or perhaps one of the motivating forces) in the transition from loose groups of people to citizens unified within a nation-state. Or nationalism may be viewed as beneficial to a nation, in the sense of patriotism, praised as instilling values of courage and loyalty in supporting and protecting its land, people, and government.[14] In contrast, nationalism may be seen as malevolent (and then labeled as ultranationalism or chauvinism), as a powerful motivation for the people of one nation to destroy another nation, occupy its land, and subjugate its people.

Those who see nationalism as beneficial may have vested interests in support of a nation that has not experienced military defeat. Conversely, those with vested interests in support of a nation that has suffered military defeat, colonization, or economic domination may view nationalism as inherently evil and a source of great suffering—as malevolent. And while some scholars and historians may adopt a neutral, "objective" view of nationalism as the result of an inevitable historical or developmental process, in reality no contemporary person can completely escape involvement in (and responsibility for) the manifold ramifications of nationalism.[15] Probably nationalism in any country has features that allow it to be seen in all three views, although a particular view may be much more evident and appropriate in a specific historical period.

Nationalism, obviously, is an ambiguous phenomenon, and religion's close relationship to nationalism is equally ambiguous. Although religion is usually thought of in the ideal terms of the pursuit of lofty goals such as enlightenment and salvation, in actual historical practice religions support and become identified with the material interests of individuals, groups, and nations. In fact, with the exception of some pacifist movements opposing all war, the historical record of religions is that most often they have been the supporters—the spiritual cheerleaders—for nationalism and militarism (and in some cases may be seen as a major motivation for militant nationalism). As politicians and generals have long known, there is no better way of gaining support for a nationalistic or military cause than to argue that it is a holy cause, legitimated or sanctified by sacred principles.

It is worth recalling that, even in early Tokugawa times, the feudal government recognized the danger of the alliance of religion and nationalism (and economics) posed by the sixteenth-century Catholic missionaries, who were brought to Japan and funded by European trading ships. The feudal authorities suspected the Christian missionaries of supporting European (especially Portuguese) political ambitions against the Japanese feudal government, and of being more concerned with changing Japanese people's political loyalties than with converting their religious faith. This is one of the reasons the feudal government proscribed Christian missions and drove out the missionaries.

Nowhere is the ambiguity of religion more obvious than in its conjunction with nationalism. Religious nationalism, like nationalism itself, is not necessarily all good or all bad. In their best light, cast by their own ideals, government officials protect and promote national interests; entrepreneurs develop the economy and the nation's financial interests; religious leaders advocate their tradition's message and help laypeople realize that message as being in their and others' best interests. Some individuals in government, business, and organized religion deserve to be seen in this favorable light, but other individuals and their institutions did not live up to their own ideals. In their worst light, altruistic interest was compromised by self-interest, and this is revealed in the colonial record: religion provided the sacred justification for military conquest, political subjugation, and economic domination.

Every instance of religious nationalism has its own historical circumstances, such that it is not possible to generalize for all cases. To take up just one instance of the early history of Western colonization in the Americas, political and economic conquest usually was justified as the means for conversion to Christianity. However, in the conquest of the Aztecs (in present-day Mexico) during the sixteenth century—about the same time as the so-called Christian Century in Japan—there was actually a heated debate among Catholic monks about whether the natives (called "Indians") were actually human and capable of conversion to Christianity. One monk, Juan Gines de Sepulveda, held that the natives could not be converted because they had no souls and were not humans; the monk Bartolome de Las Casas took the opposite view, that natives were humans possessing souls, and could indeed be converted.[16]

Such a theological dilemma could hardly arise in the practice of Japan's colonialism, which was much more concerned with political subjugation and economic domination, and *religious conformity* as an expression of subjugation, rather than with actual "conversion" to Japanese religious traditions. Nevertheless, we will see that Japanese nationalism falls within the previously quoted definition of "the belief in the primacy of a particular nation," and that views of primacy of one's own nation could mean (as they did with the Christian monks' treatment of Aztecs) denying other people's humanity or their right and ability to self-determination. The principle that remains the same in these two instances of colonization is the triple alliance of political, economic, and religious subjugation.[17]

How we view religious nationalism in Meiji and post-Meiji Japan is important not only for how we look back at Western colonialism and Japanese colonialism, but how we interpret religious nationalism in the present and future. In the past few decades religious nationalism has been one of the pressing problems throughout the world—from Ireland and the former Yugoslavia, to the Middle East and South Asia. In these and other areas too numerous to mention, religion conjoined with nationalism has supported militarism and violence. Political leaders and international negotiators (such as United Nations officials) are hard pressed just to maintain the coexistence and tolerance of people of different religious and political identities. Those of us who are not professional politicians or negotiators, and cannot resolve such huge problems, nevertheless have the responsibility and opportunity, as we study history, to ask where nationalism is inevitable, and understand it; to see where nationalism is benevolent, and encourage it; and to find out where nationalism is malevolent, and discourage and oppose it.[18] The question we put to ourselves is: as we study the Japanese record of the close alliance between religion and state, what lessons do we learn that can help us better understand the ambiguous role of religion in other times and places? We should keep this overview of religious nationalism in mind as we reenter the story of Japanese religion and the treatment of Shrine Shinto and nationalism.

SHRINE SHINTO AS AN EXPRESSION OF NATIONALISM AND MILITARISM

Religious nationalism was, undeniably, a major force in modern Japanese history, especially in the Meiji period through the end of World War II.[19] Shrine Shinto has been called nationalistic or State Shinto by Westerners because it was used as a main support to the Japanese nationalism that preceded World War II. Nearly all Japanese people who grew up after 1890 received a public education of nationalistic ethics emphasizing absolute loyalty to the emperor and to the state that he symbolically ruled. Those who questioned absolute loyalty to the state were definitely in the minority: some liberal intellectuals, a few members of the so-called New Religions, and a few Christians. The 1890 Rescript on Education had been prompted by a reaction to what some officials and intellectuals saw as excessive Westernization; by 1930 another surge of anti-foreign feeling was sweeping through the country. Especially after Japan invaded Manchuria in 1931 and Japan's relations with foreign countries deteriorated—Japan withdrew from the League of Nations in 1933—it became a serious matter to question the state's authority. In 1938 all schools were required to use an ultranationalistic textbook that emphasized the uniqueness and supremacy of Japan as a political and religious unity; in Japanese this "national entity" was called *kokutai*.[20] According to the Japanese historian Ienaga, "Every facet of the curriculum was permeated with emperor worship and militarism. . . . Young children were indoctrinated to believe that the Greater East Asia War was a holy war."[21]

The rationale for Japanese nationalism, however, did not appear for the first time in the twentieth century, and its religious justification was not taken exclusively from Shinto. The term *kokutai* was used in the Tokugawa period by scholars combining Neo-Confucian and Shinto thought. As we saw in Chapter 14, Neo-Confucian and Shinto thought became closely linked in the late Tokugawa period: one expression of the relationship was emphasis on *kokutai* as "an inner essence or mystical force residing in the Japanese nation as a result of Amaterasu's" divine revelation. A modern Western scholar has defined "*kokutai* thought" in Tokugawa times in this way:

> According to *kokutai* thought, Japan is a patriarchal state, in which everyone is related and the imperial house is the main or head family. The emperor is the supreme father, and loyalty to him, or patriotism, becomes the highest form of Filial Piety. Because of the command of Amaterasu, this structure is both sacred and eternal; compliance with its requirements is the obligation and deepest wish of every Japanese.[22]

The Tokugawa roots of nationalism, including features such as absolute loyalty to the emperor, form the background for Meiji developments of nationalism and Shinto.

The question of nationalism is a delicate one because the painful memories of World War II endure, and some Western treatments have tended to depict Shinto (and the emperor) as the main source of Japanese nationalism and the cause of the war, a perception that persists today. According to this view, the war arose because Shinto commanded worship of an emperor-god, and Japanese soldiers were bound to follow commands issued in the emperor's name in order to extend the Japanese empire into foreign lands. This scenario is more a carryover from American wartime fears than a description of the actual situation in Japan at the time.

Since the end of World War II, there has been a reassessment of Shinto and its relationship to nationalism and militarism. Earlier Western notions probably placed too much emphasis on the nationalistic aspects of Shinto and linked it too closely to its manipulation by the government, viewing the essence of Shinto as the unity of state and Shinto during the past century. But to call this tradition "State Shinto" and then to think of it as indicating the nature of Shinto through its long history is obviously a mistake. It is more difficult, but more true to the facts, to try to distinguish between the perennial tie of Shinto to the Japanese identity, on the one hand, and the modern manipulation of this tie for militaristic purposes, on the other hand. The widely respected Shinto scholar Muraoka refused to support nationalistic interpretations of Shinto before and during World War II. But in the freedom of the postwar period, he rejected the notion that Shinto by nature is militaristic. In a balanced assessment of Shinto he concluded that, "judging from the overall character of the legends of the *Kojiki* and *Nihongi,* it is clear that no militaristic or ultranationalistic intent" existed in the notion of a sacred country.[23]

Another inadequacy of "State Shinto" as a blanket term is that it is too abstract and nebulous, failing to differentiate between the intentions of government officials, shrine priests, and the people at large: the intentions of these different groups may have coincided, or overlapped, or perhaps significantly diverged. It is quite likely that these three groups often participated within the same governmentally controlled shrines, but not necessarily with identical intentions: the government officials might have been concerned mainly with ideological control of the populace; the shrine priests might have had in mind ritual and theological concerns; and the people may have looked for simple blessings of their homes and welfare.[24] The possibility of multiple intentions within the same religious practice is illustrated in the following personal anecdote.

Some years ago, while I was visiting a country Shinto shrine with a Japanese scholar, he picked up from the ground around the shrine a piece of wood with writing on it. It was a form of prayer or petition for the protection of a son in the military during World War II, actually a "bullet-protector" amulet, offered by parents to the shrine and its *kami;* the upper end of the piece of wood had a hole through which a cord had been passed to hang the tablet (over a nail driven into the shrine). The petition stated it was one instance of a "hundred-shrine" pilgrimage, meaning the parents had paid visits and hung petitions at a hundred shrines, seeking greater safety in a greater number of petitions. After decades of swinging in the wind, the cord holding the petition had frayed and eventually worn through, letting it drop to the ground. But even a half century later this wooden amulet has much to tell us—in fact, it bears testimony to so many possibilities that at this late date we can only imagine how to reconstruct them.

No doubt this amulet is an example of how government officials encouraged and welcomed the "ideological" benefit of religion, which helped promote the participation of young men (and their families) in military campaigns. Probably for the priests overseeing this country Shinto shrine, this was but one more of the countless petitions and sources of income (because they were customarily presented with a monetary offering) for blessing and protection by the shrine's *kami*—which in this case was for protection in war.

Certainly the parents, whatever their ideological persuasion and "theological" views of Shinto or this shrine, had foremost in their intentions the protection of their son (rather than the national agenda or the shrine goals). Whether or not the parents were enthusiastic supporters of the war (which they may have been),[25] and even if they did not subscribe to the contemporary versions of religious nationalism and State Shinto (which was a distinct possibility), their explicit faith in the local *kami* surely transcended their political allegiances and their general notions about religion.[26] There is no point arguing the accuracy of this or any other reconstruction, but such concrete items are a good reminder that religious behavior is always concrete, complex, and ambiguous. Religious nationalism is not just an abstract theory, it is also quite specific, practical, and personal.

One of the problems in reassessing twentieth-century Shinto is the lack of precise terms differentiating traditional Shinto from its nationalistic involvement. One scholar attempting to reappraise Shinto has proposed separating the discussion of the "*Kokutai* cult" from the topic of Shinto as such. The "*Kokutai* cult" is defined as "Japan's emperor-state-centered cult of ultranationalism and militarism," which "included elements of Shinto mythology and ideology and . . . utilized Shinto institutions and practices" but "was not a form of Shinto." Defined in this manner, the Kokutai cult consisted of six elements compulsory for all Japanese: (1) "acceptance of the doctrine that the Emperor was 'sacred and inviolable'"; (2) veneration of spirits of the imperial ancestors and imperial rescripts; (3) unquestioned acceptance of ancient myths and their chauvinistic interpretation in modern works such as the nationalistic textbook *Kokutai no Hongi;* (4) the observance of national holidays, centering in the glorification of the imperial line; (5) worship of *kami* at shrines and in the home (before the *kamidana*); and (6) financial support of local shrines and festivals.[27] This interpretation highlights the complexities of the relationship of Shinto to nationalism; it also demonstrates the need to understand nationalism in Japan.[28]

Factors that gave rise to nationalism in Japan, like the causes of war, are many and complex, including the whole context of economic, political, and social conditions in prewar Japan. And Shinto was but one factor contributing to Japan's ultranationalism. The pioneer Western scholar of Shinto nationalism, Daniel C. Holtom, has shown that Japanese Buddhism competed with Shinto in claiming to support and protect the nation: "If . . . Buddhism has never declared a holy war, it has nonetheless proclaimed all Japanese wars holy."[29] Even Japanese Christians were quick to announce their support of the state program. The ironies of history present a much stranger case. The Chinese tradition of Confucianism had become so Japanized through the centuries that the Japanese could appeal to Confucianism as their own rationale for their "benevolent rule" of Manchuria, Korea, and China. Especially after 1933, Confucianism in Japan became an important rationale for supporting ultranationalism and militarism.[30]

During the first four decades of the twentieth century, Japan's energies were heavily concentrated on the strengthening of nationalism and militarism;

and religion, especially Shinto, was used to further these aims. However, proper historical perspective is crucial if we are to understand Shinto. We must see Shrine Shinto as a modern development within a tradition possessing a long history. We should avoid the temptation to view Shinto's whole history in terms of its modern nationalistic phase. Although Shrine Shinto captured the limelight in the modern period, in the countryside Shinto shrines preserved much of the traditional religious life. The major activities at local shrines repeated the age-old pattern: events such as annual festivals for spring and fall associated with agriculture, the elaborate New Year's celebrations, and special villagewide festivities invoking the blessing of the *kami*. Nationalism pervaded even these local Shinto shrines, thus representing the central government, but it did not eliminate the religious life of the shrines. As Muraoka has described the situation: "Instead of the doctrines and thought of Shrine Shinto causing the Imperialism and expansionism of the politicians and the military, it was rather Imperialism and expansionism that enhanced the doctrine of Shrine Shinto."[31]

Shinto (in its modern form of Shrine Shinto) tended to dominate other religious traditions in the period from 1868 to 1945—a period in which nationalism and then ultranationalism combined with militarism as the keynotes of Japanese life. Because of Shrine Shinto's dominance over Shinto as a whole and Shrine Shinto's close association with the war effort, many Japanese people lost faith in Shinto after the surrender of 1945. Nationalistic religion was not the problem of Shinto alone. In early Japanese history as well as before World War II, Buddhism and Confucianism were equally aligned with the national welfare. In the next two chapters we will see how formalism heightened the perception of the need for a renewal of religious life.

NOTES

1. George M. Wilson, *Patriots and Redeemers in Japan: Motives in the Meiji Restoration* (Chicago: University of Chicago, 1992), p. ix. See also Carol Gluck, *Japan's Modern Myths: Ideology in the Late Meiji Period* (Princeton: Princeton University, 1985).

2. Conrad Totman, *The Collapse of the Tokugawa Bakufu 1862–1868* (Honolulu: University Press of Hawaii, 1980), p. xiii.

3. Gluck, *Japan's Modern Myths,* p. 286.

4. For a detailed description of the "persecution" of Buddhism, as well as the conditions leading up to it and the general significance for religion in Meiji times, see James Edward Ketelaar, *Of Heretics and Martyrs in Meiji Japan: Buddhism and Its Persecution* (Princeton: Princeton University, 1990). For briefer treatments see Allan Grapard, "Japan's Ignored Cultural Revolution: The Separation of Shinto and Buddhist Divinities in Meiji (*shimbutsu bunri*) and a Case Study: Tonomine," *History of Religions,* vol. 23, no. 3 (Feb. 1984), pp. 240–65; and Martin Collcutt, "Buddhism: The Threat of Eradication," in *Japan in Transition, from Tokugawa to Meiji,* eds. Marius B. Jansen and Gilbert Rozman (Princeton: Princeton University, 1986), pp. 143–67.

5. See Torao Haraguchi et al., *The Status System and Social Organizaton of Satsuma: A Translation of the* Shumon Tefuda Aratame Jomoku (Honolulu: University Press of Hawaii, 1975).

6. For the variety of Japanese thought, especially liberalism and nationalism, from pre-Meiji times to 1945, see Tsunoda et al., *Sources of Japanese Tradition* Chapters 24–27; 2d ed. forthcoming.

7. For historical details of this complex period, see Helen Hardacre, *Shinto and the State 1868–1988* (Princeton: Princeton University, 1989). For a Shinto view of the situation, emphasizing the role of Buddhist interests in the creation of Shinto as a "non-religion," see Hitoshi Nitta, "Shinto as a 'Non-religion': the Origins and Development of an Idea," in John Breen and Mark Teeuwen, eds., *Shinto in History: Ways of the Kami* (Surrey: Curzon, 2000), pp. 252–71; for a Shinto view of the various stages and roles of State Shinto, see Koremaru Sakamoto, "The Structure of State Shinto: Its Creation, Development, and Demise," in Breen and Teeuwen, pp. 272–94. See his remarks on the term "State Shinto" as "not a natural consequence of scholarly endeavour so much as a result of the occupation policies," p. 268.

8. For a translation of "The Imperial Rescript on Education," see my *Religion in the Japanese Experience,* 2d ed., pp. 236–37.

9. Any document, such as the Imperial Rescript on Education, can be viewed from very different time periods and perspectives. Here it is placed within the historical context of Meiji nation-building, which may throw light on its positive or unifying role for the new nation. A critical or negative assessment of this document is given by a survivor of the atomic bomb in Hiroshima, who reflects on the upbringing of his generation: "We were taught to believe in the Imperial Rescript on Educaton, with loyalty to the emperor and love for the country, and in selfless devotion to the nation. We were also made to believe in the slogan, 'we will not desire anything until we win'; and many were killed even without having been provided with sufficient food. In the eyes of these individuals, the names of those responsible for the war have not yet been disclosed." Go Matsuda, quoted in Lisa Yoneyama, *Hiroshima Traces: Time, Space, and the Dialectics of Memory* (Berkeley: University of California, 1999), p. 130.

10. See Wilbur M. Fridell, *Japanese Shrine Mergers, 1906–12: State Shinto Moves to the Grassroots* (Tokyo: Sophia University, 1973). See also Haruo Sakurai, "Tradition and Change in Local Community Shrines," *Acta Asiatica,* no. 51 (1987), pp. 62–76.

11. Ernest Gellner, *Thought and Change,* p. 169, quoted in John A. Hall, "Nationalisms: Classified and Explained," *Daedalus* (Summer 1993), p. 4.

12. An earlier work is Delmer M. Brown, *Nationalism in Japan: An Introductory Historical Analysis* (Berkeley: University of California, 1955; reprint ed., New York: Russell & Russell, 1971); for a more recent study, see John C. Maraldo, "Questioning Nationalism Now and Then: A Critical Approach to the Kyoto School," in *Rude Awakenings: Zen, the Kyoto School, & the Question of Nationalism,* eds. James W. Heisig and John C. Maraldo (Honolulu: University of Hawai'i, 1995), pp. 333–62. Both studies point to the multiple sources of Japanese nationalism.

13. Hall, "Nationalisms: Classified and Explained," p. 2.

14. Wm. Theodore de Bary cites "the obvious lack of a unified national consciousness" in China as a major reason for its "inability to mobilize its human resources against the challenge of the West and Japan." He concludes that "Some contrasted this perceived weakness of China to the unifying power of nationalism in Japan and the West, and some saw the power of the latter to mobilize peoples' energies as further linked to the religious dynamism of Shinto and Christianity. . . ." See de Bary, *The Trouble with Confucianism,* p. 92.

15. For a discussion of Japanese nationalism in comparative perspective, and for a Polish activist's condemnation of all nationalism, see Maraldo, "Questioning Nationalism Now and Then," pp. 333–34.

16. See Benjamin Keen, *The Aztec Image in Western Thought* (New Brunswick, NJ: Rutgers University, 1971), especially pp. 71–104. One of the philosophical justifications of slavery was the argument of Aristotle that some people are "slaves by nature."

17. Our focus on this chapter is on nationalism and religion in Japan, but it is well to remember that the holy (or unholy) alliance of political, economic, and religious subjugation is found throughout world history. One reason we study and analyze this as an academic problem is to better recognize and deal with it in the world at large.

18. Maraldo in "Questioning Nationalism Now and Then," while criticizing Japanese nationalism, also levels his criticism at American nationalism; see pp. 351–55.

19. Some scholars who focus on Asia consider the term "World War II" as too narrow, reflecting the rather short war experience of the United States from 1941 to 1945; they prefer the term "Asia-Pacific War," which emphasizes the lengthy campaign in Asia from 1931 to 1945 (which some have called the "fifteen-year war").

20. See John Owen Gauntlett for a translation of this text, *Kokutai no Hongi: Cardinal Principles of the National Entity of Japan,* ed. Robert King Hall (Cambridge: Harvard University, 1949). Excerpted in my *Religion in the Japanese Experience,* 2d ed., pp. 238–42. See also the succinct treatment in Graham Healey, "Kokutai," *Kodansha Encyclopedia of Japan,* vol. 4, pp. 262–63.

21. Saburo Ienaga, *The Pacific War: A Critical Perspective on Japan's Role in World War II,* trans. Frank Baldwin (New York: Pantheon, 1978), p. 107.

22. David Magarey Earl, *Emperor and Nation in Japan: Political Thinkers of the Tokugawa Period* (Seattle: University of Washington, 1964), pp. 236–37. For other definitions of *kokutai,* see Richard H. Minear, *Japanese Tradition and Western Law: Emperor, State, and Law in the Thought of Hozumi Yatsuka* (Cambridge: Harvard University, 1970), pp. 65–71.

23. Tsunetsugu Muraoka, "Separation of State and Religion in Shinto: Its Historical Significance," in his *Studies in Shinto,* p. 242.

24. For an analysis of Shinto and shrines "from the perspective of the contrast between the view of shrines held by the state and the view of shrines prevalent in village society," see Haruo Sakurai, "The Shrine Cult and Local Society in Modern Japan," *Acta Asiatica,* no. 75 (1998), pp. 53–72.

25. According to Ienaga (*The Pacific War,* p. 248), "The conflict was acclaimed as a 'holy war' and enthusiastically supported in Japan. The great mass of the people sincerely believed in the cause."

26. This tentative reconstruction of faith in amulets is supported by the actual record of amulets in the diary of "Corporal Ashihei Hino" during the Japanese army's battles in China 1937–38. This corporal wore a "thousand-stitch belt" (*sennin-bari*—a cloth with a stitch made by each of a thousand well-wishers) and carried various charms. In his own words, he wrote, "I do not understand the symbolism connected with each. Some are Buddhist and others Shinto. It makes no difference, of course. All are supposed to afford protection from wounds." He also had an embroidered charm with various amulets from his mother, and a "bullet-proof vest . . . made of nine strips of dried cuttlefish" given to him by a friend. See Ashihei Hino [Katsunori Tamai], *Wheat and Soldiers,* trans. Baroness Shidzue Ishimoto (New York: Farrar & Rinehart, 1939), pp. 20–27. This book is a firsthand account of the war in China from the viewpoint of the ordinary conscripted Japanese soldier.

After writing this personal anecdote about amulets, I read Emiko Ohnuki-Tierney's *Kamikaze, Cherry Blossoms, and Nationalisms: The Militarization of Aesthetics in Japanese History* (Chicago: University of Chicago, 2002). This work records a more bizarre tale involving amulets, religion, and nationalism. In 1944 a Japanese woman who was a Christian and had refrained from visiting Yasukuni Shrine, apparently as a "protest against the war," nevertheless, because she was the mother of a *kamikaze* pilot in training, went to another shrine and purchased "an amulet from the shrine [that] would protect a soldier from bullets." In a letter to his mother the *kamikaze* pilot son, also a "peace-loving Christian" who "wished to go to Heaven and wait for his mother" (pp. 238–39), wrote "It was this amulet that . . . he would carry with him at the time he plunged into a vessel"

(p. 177). This book describes and analyzes the complex factors and motivations not only of *kamikaze* pilots, but also of nationalisms in Japan—cultural nationalism, political nationalism, and military nationalism. A major point of the book is to "dispel the image of the *tokkotai* [*kamikaze*] pilots as simple-minded ultra-nationalists who were in lockstep with the military ideology, and who happily died for the emperor" (p. 193); "these men 'volunteered' to reproduce the ideology *in action* while defying it *in their thoughts*" (p. 300).

27. William P. Woodard, *The Allied Occupation of Japan, 1945–1952, and Japanese Religions* (Leiden: E. J. Brill, 1972), p. 11.

28. For a discussion of *kokutai* and ideology, see Gluck, *Japan's Modern Myths,* especially pp. 3–16, 279–86.

29. Daniel C. Holtom, *Modern Japan and Shinto Nationalism: A Study of Present-Day Trends in Japanese Religions,* rev. ed. (Chicago: University of Chicago, 1947; reprint ed., New York: Paragon Book Reprint Corp., 1963), p. 148.

30. See Smith, *Confucianism in Modern Japan;* an excerpt from Smith (which illustrates the role of Confucianism in Japanese nationalism) is included in my *Religion in the Japanese Experience,* 2d ed., pp. 115–19.

31. Muraoka, "Separation of State and Religion in Shinto," p. 243.

16

✿

Religious Currents
from 1868 to 1945

In the period from 1868 (the beginning of the Meiji Restoration and the reopening of Japan to the West) to 1945 (the end of World War II), nationalism was prominent in every aspect of Japanese life. In general, after 1890 the government exerted increasing control over organized religion; prior to World War II the government laid down strict rules for the consolidation of denominations (both Buddhist and Christian) in order to control them more effectively. Shinto, especially Shrine Shinto, was a main channel for this nationalism, but other religious traditions were also involved. Indeed, one scholar feels that after 1933 Confucianism played an even greater role than Shinto in supporting the national polity (*kokutai*): the Confucian virtue of loyalty, redefined as loyalty to the Japanese state and the emperor, provided the central theme of *Kokutai no hongi,* the nationalistic textbook that was required reading in all schools after 1938.[1] In Chapter 15, Buddhism and Christianity were also cited as being heavily influenced by nationalistic trends. But the religious history of this period was much more than nationalism. A brief description of Buddhism, Christianity, and the New Religions reveals important religious undercurrents in addition to the major current of nationalism. These undercurrents are important not only for understanding the prewar period, but especially for comprehending the critical spiritual mood of postwar Japan.[2]

BUDDHISM: THE QUEST
FOR RENEWAL, ESPECIALLY
WITHIN BUDDHIST SCHOLARSHIP

The Meiji Restoration presented Buddhism with an unexpected crisis. The preceding centuries of patronage by the Tokugawa government (1600–1867) had led many Buddhist priests and temples to take for granted their superior positions of wealth and leisure. Priests of local temples became so firmly entrenched in their role of providing government-required rites and supervision for every family that acquisition of wealth often outstripped cultivation of spirituality. Then in a flash the Tokugawa government fell, the legal obligation to support Buddhism vanished, and temple income dropped. It was bad enough that the Meiji Restoration did not stop with a mere reform of Buddhism but instead chose to disestablish Buddhism and establish Shinto in its place. Even worse, perhaps, was the severe criticism and persecution of Buddhism stimulated by the zeal to restore Shinto. On the one hand, some of the destruction of Buddhist temples during the transitional period can be attributed to the misplaced enthusiasm that accompanies any radical social change. On the other hand, much of the criticism against the institutions and practices of Buddhism—financial and moral corruption—was justified.

At first the Buddhist priests could comprehend neither the social and political transformation nor the criticism against Buddhism. As a whole, Buddhism tried to maintain in the Meiji period the same role and position it had known during the Tokugawa period: religiously, preoccupation with ancestral rites; politically, subservience to the state. Buddhist priests were so totally concerned with funerals and masses that they had come to be referred to jokingly as the "undertakers of Japan";[3] they strove to be at least second to Shinto as supporters of the state. However, implicit in the Meiji criticism of Buddhism was a call for a spiritual as well as a moral renewal of Buddhism. Japanese Buddhism today is still wrestling with the problem of spiritual awakening—a quest shared by Shinto and New Religions.[4]

The vitality of folk Buddhist piety in the early Meiji period was illustrated by the fact that the government was forced to recognize Buddhism as a religion of the people. Nor did Buddhist institutions lack devout and far-sighted priests. Some priests, rather than lamenting the persecution of Buddhism, recognized Buddhism's disestablishment as a blessing in disguise. They had the courage to acknowledge the criticisms leveled against Buddhism, and they advocated its spiritual rebirth. An example of the attempt to reform Japanese Buddhism is Kiyozawa Manshi (1863–1903), who openly criticized Buddhism's traditional pattern of hereditary family membership in temples. He advocated a renewal of personal Buddhist faith and a reorganization of Buddhism as a "brotherhood" based on small groups of believers. He viewed the Jodo Shinshu religious organization as "feudalistic" or authoritarian; he favored giving more power to local temples and lay Buddhists, and, although he was unsuccessful, his ideas provided inspiration for postwar reform of Buddhist institutions.[5]

In actuality, Japanese Buddhism was challenged from several sides simultaneously. Shinto strove to abolish or suppress it as a decadent and foreign religion. Christianity attacked it on doctrinal grounds. Confucian scholars criticized Buddhism as deceiving people with magical rites, and as a parasitic drain of people's money. In addition, Buddhism, like Confucianism, was charged as being outmoded and premodern by those who accepted the "modern" teachings of Western science and philosophy. Buddhism's competition with Shinto can be seen in the more familiar pattern of nationalistic religion. Buddhism's encounter with Western learning and Christianity, however, must be seen as a remarkable innovation in Japanese religious history.

Buddhist priests accepted the challenge of Western learning by sending priest-scholars to Europe. As early as 1876 Nanjo Bun'yu[6] went to England to study Sanskrit texts with F. Max Muller. This marked an important meeting of East and West, because Muller was the founder of the "science of religion" in Europe, and Nanjo was one of the first Japanese Buddhists to adopt Western methods of historical and philological scholarship. From this time forward, the Buddhist priest-scholars of Japan who studied in the best European universities (and published in French, German, or English) strengthened their native erudition with the critical methods of European scholarship (especially history and philology).[7]

On the Japanese side this scholarly cooperation had two positive results. First, the reforming motive of devout Buddhists was rewarded with a direct knowledge of early Indian Buddhism. Formerly their knowledge of Buddhism had been filtered through Chinese Buddhism. A second positive result was a growing confidence in Western methods of critical scholarship and Western philosophy. The Buddhist scholars were competent in discussing comparable philosophical movements in the European and Buddhist traditions. Also, they were fully capable of using one philosophy to criticize another. During this upsurge of scholarly activity, monumental publishing ventures were undertaken, among which were the printing of the Buddhist canon (in Chinese), compilation of documents from Japanese Buddhism, and publication of erudite encyclopedias and reference works on all aspects of Buddhism. Japanese Buddhist scholars were some of the most well-received participants in the World's Parliament of Religion held in Chicago in 1893; they returned to Japan confident that Japanese Buddhism was a major religious tradition in Japan and a successful competitor on the global scene of world religions.

On the whole, Buddhist priests have been much more in touch with Western culture than Shinto priests. With the establishment of Western-style universities in the Meiji era, Buddhist priests came to be trained in departments of Indian and Buddhist philosophy where the classical languages of Buddhism (Pali and Sanskrit, as well as Tibetan and Chinese) and modern European languages were emphasized. Buddhist appropriation of Western learning and co-operation with Western scholars represented one of the most remarkable possibilities for the renewal of Buddhism in the prewar period. Indeed, only decades after Japanese scholars traveled to Europe to learn Western methods of studying Buddhism, "Japan had surpassed Europe in virtually every major area of inquiry" into Buddhism. Now the tables were turned, and "Japan, recipient of Western enlightenment in the Meiji period, becomes the country that shall bring enlightenment to the world."[8]

This possibility for renewal, however, only further complicated an already complex Japanese Buddhism, which was split between traditional piety and modern intellectualism. Popular Buddhism continued in the same patterns as in Tokugawa times, while some Buddhist priests and intellectuals tended to think in terms of appropriated Western concepts. Buddhist studies in Japan is a huge field, covering almost every imaginable doctrinal and philosophical aspect of Buddhism's history throughout Asia, such that it is difficult to characterize briefly. However, one general feature of Buddhist studies in Japan has been a tendency to focus on the "original" Buddhism of India or the Chinese foundations for Japanese Buddhism. Buddhist scholars have concentrated more on historical aspects of scriptures, doctrines, and philosophy rather than living Buddhism today (which often is looked down on as inferior to the original Indian or classical Chinese Buddhism).

The success story of post-Meiji Buddhism is that it was able to survive severe persecution and perceptions of corruption, and then go on to reconstitute Buddhism not only as a modern religion separate from Shinto, but also as an equal partner in the support of the emperor and the state. However, such worldly success has its price, and serious questions have been raised about many leading Buddhist scholars who uncritically linked the spiritual goals of Buddhism with the political goals of the imperial state in its colonial foray into Asia, especially during the 1930s and 1940s. To rephrase this in Buddhist terms, such scholars praised Japanese Buddhism as the guiding light of Japanese culture, able to liberate Asians from Western colonialism and enlighten them— but they failed to express the basic Buddhist virtue of compassion for the large number of Asians (many of them Buddhists) who were mistreated and killed by the Japanese military in countries such as China, Korea, Burma, and Indonesia.[9] In the words of the Japanese historian Ienaga, commenting sadly on academics who sold out to the government and did not criticize the war, "The same words applied to organized religion. Buddhism had always lacked the capacity to challenge the state, and Japanese Buddhism rallied behind the war."[10]

About the same time that Buddhist studies were being developed in the Meiji period, the systematic, or "scientific," study of religion was founded in Japan. This established the academic study of religion apart from the practice and propagation of religion, and distinct from other academic fields such as Shinto studies, Buddhist studies, and Chinese studies. Anesaki Masaharu was the first to occupy the chair of the science of religion at Tokyo University in 1905. Some Shinto scholars, notably Kato Genchi, furthered the Japanese study of the science of religion by pioneering Shinto studies in the light of comparative research.[11] These new currents of thought did not greatly affect the people at large, but they did raise problems about religious faith and practice for many intellectuals, especially the scholars and students who had accepted Christianity.

CHRISTIANITY: STRENGTH AND WEAKNESS SINCE 1868

The story of Christianity in Japan from 1868 to 1945 shows some similarities with the Christian century of Roman Catholic missions from about 1550 to 1650. In both periods early phases of Christian success linked with Japanese acceptance of Western culture were followed by phases of Christianity's decline due to Japanese reaction against the West. Apart from these general parallels, there were remarkable dissimilarities in the two periods. For example, one significant difference is that, in the latter period, Protestant as well as Roman Catholic missionaries came to Japan. Christian missionaries arrived in Japan in the late 1850s, soon after the signing of treaties with Western powers, but they were unable to openly missionize and achieve results until 1873, when the Tokugawa ban on Christianity was lifted.

After 1873, Christianity tended to gain followers. However, the career of Christianity in Japan was shaped by three major factors that presented obstacles to gaining individual converts, but at the same time made Christianity an important contributor to the formation of the new Japanese government. The first factor is that the official attitude of Christianity toward other traditions (especially in modern times) has been to favor conversion rather than compromise and synthesis. Of course, Christianity has blended with other traditions, but usually on an unofficial basis and over a long period of time. Thus the Japanese had to make a radical leap from their own tradition to accept Christianity and its insistence on renouncing other traditions. (In contrast, both Buddhism and Confucianism were more open and flexible in their contact with Japanese culture and religion.) The second factor is that the Japanese people were not only aware of, but proud of, their long, rich heritage. To be Japanese meant to accept the plurality of religions, and to hold the worldview and follow the beliefs and customs of the Japanese tradition—including semireligious activities such as respect for (or veneration of) the emperor and ancestors; some customs such as visiting shrines and temples at New Year's were followed even by people who did not consider themselves very "religious." Missionaries discouraged or forbade Japanese Christians from following these practices. From the late nineteenth century to 1945 there was an active discussion among Japanese Christians about whether they could be both devout Christians and loyal Japanese. The third factor was that Japanese officials looked to the West for models of government and science. This meant an initial acceptance of Christianity as the spiritual culture of the West, until the Japanese realized that they could be Westernized (and industrialized) without becoming Christian.

Social turmoil after 1868 turned many disempowered warriors of the feudal lords to Christianity. Having lost their effort to maintain the Tokugawa government and state Buddhism, the warriors saw Christianity as a means of ordering Meiji society and government. Some scholars have thought that the religious fervor and courageous loyalty of these early Christians was as much a carryover from their Confucian warrior training as it was a product of their Christian conversion.[12] But the attraction of Christianity was different for those not of warrior background: "'wealthy farmers and merchants found in Christianity a new religio-ethical concept that emphasized the equality of all humanity, created by God and redeemed by Jesus Christ.'" Also, some converts to Protestantism saw a continuity from the ethics of Confucianism to the ethics of Christianity: "Confucianism prepared the way for [some] early converts . . . to accept Christianity, and Christianity in turn served to perfect Confucian values."[13] At any rate, the Christian faith spread to the middle classes of the cities, so that in the 1870s evangelism was being carried out by Japanese Christians. These sincere Japanese Christians were eager to avoid the strife of denominationalism, favored financial self-support by Japanese churches, and tried to eliminate Western customs hindering the development of a truly Japanese Christianity.

They quickly attained almost complete financial independence, but the problems of denominational conflict and difficulties in developing a distinctively Japanese Christianity have persisted to the present. For example, the famous Japanese Christian Uchimura Kanzo (1861–1930) is noted for his statement about his love for the "two J's": "I love two J's and no third; one is Jesus, and the other is Japan."[14] His example of blending the Christian and Japanese traditions was a rare exception. For many Japanese Christians the

Advertisement at a Tokyo store for the "Christmas cake" that has become popular throughout Japan. Santa Claus, represented as a Caucasian man in a red and white outfit, is aided by a smiling Japanese girl. They encourage shoppers to "please order early." (Tokyo, 1979)

imitation of countless foreign national customs and denominational practices in Japan seemed superfluous. Nevertheless, Christmas became quite popular for many Japanese people, apart from its specific Christian significance, especially after World War II. It is still celebrated as a children's festival and is nearly as commercialized as it is in the West.[15]

Christianity gained many of its followers from the young people who attended Christian schools. Christian missionaries made a great contribution to Japanese education, particularly in girls' schools and in the teaching of foreign languages such as English. Young people were encouraged to attend these schools and thus came into contact with Christianity, which was taught openly or privately. In fact, until the late 1880s, the tendency for uncritical acceptance of anything Western, including Christianity, alarmed both the government and the priests of Shinto and Buddhism. In the late 1880s, however, Japan's humiliation by Western powers through unequal treaties stimulated reactionary support for Japanese independence from foreign missions. The 1890 Imperial Rescript on Education cleverly removed religious instruction from education on the pretext of religious freedom. In reality, it was a result of the new government policy to counteract Western (and Christian) influence by supporting Shrine Shinto and the emperor.

The early Japanese Christians who studied abroad in Europe and the United States were greatly influenced by modern education, movements for women's rights, socialism, and liberal politics. These men played very important roles in shaping the more humane aspects of Meiji government. Nevertheless, even though Christianity provided the rationale for these social and political reforms, social issues and socialism were increasingly conceived apart from Christianity.[16]

Although Japan's rulers became committed to Western models in education and industrialization, they could do so without accepting Christianity. Furthermore, well before 1900, several developments caused strife within Japanese Christianity. Factional disputes—"denominationalism"—caused dissension within a minority tradition in need of unity. Theological disagreement between the new liberals and older conservatives further fragmented Japanese Christianity. In addition, the evolutionistic and atheistic philosophies of the West presented challenging and attractive options for many intellectuals. As the quality of government schools equaled and then surpassed that of Christian schools (run by missionaries and Japanese Christians), more Japanese found they could accept Western knowledge without accepting Western religion. Japanese philosophers, for example, are at home with all periods and schools of Western philosophy. As a result of these factors, Christianity did not become a major religion in Japan despite the presence of some devout Japanese Christians.

After 1890, the youth came under the influence of nationalistic education, and the mood of the country gradually changed from nationalism to ultranationalism. Victories in the Sino-Japanese War (1894–95) and the Russo-Japanese War (1904–05) greatly heightened nationalistic fervor and militarism. From this time through 1945 Japan's primary focus was strengthening the country against Western powers. Christianity no longer attracted converts just because it was a Western religion.

Most Japanese Christians supported all aspects of nationalism and militarism. For example, they supported both the Sino-Japanese and Russo-Japanese wars, not only by praying for victory but also by sending aid for the combat troops. By the time of the Russo-Japanese War, some Christian intellectuals had become pacifists, but they were the exceptions. Later, in the 1930s, Japanese Christian ministers were sent to Manchuria at the request of the Japanese soldiers who were Christians. The Japanese historian Ienaga, who criticized Japanese Buddhism's support of the war, was just as critical of Japanese Christianity: "A very few Christians withheld support [of the war]—the Non-Church Christians . . . and a very few others. . . . Nearly all other Christian groups enlisted in the 'holy war.'"[17]

Statistics of religious affiliation are particularly difficult to determine in Japan, but by the turn of the twentieth century there were about seventy-five thousand church members and by the late 1930s about three hundred thousand Christians. Because the total population was about eighty million at this time, the percentage of Christians—both Protestant and Roman Catholic—was lower than it had been at the high point of Roman Catholicism in the early seventeenth century. Of course, one can argue that in the sixteenth and seventeenth centuries mass conversions of feudal domains took place, whereas in the nineteenth and twentieth centuries conversions were individual and probably more sincere. Nevertheless, before World War II, the total number of church members constituted less than 1 percent of the total population. This number is small even when compared with the individual New Religions of the same period.

THE NEW RELIGIONS:
NEW VARIATIONS FROM OLD TRADITIONS

The rubric "New Religions" (*shinko shukyo*) has been given to a number of religious movements that first appeared in late Tokugawa times, gained strength after the Meiji Restoration, and became a powerful force after World War II. The term "*shinko shukyo,*" which translates more accurately as: "newly arisen religions," was first used by journalists to imply that the newcomers were up-starts. Leaders of the New Religions prefer the more neutral term "*shin shukyo,*" literally "new religions." The term "New Religions," however, is somewhat misleading because these movements are neither completely new nor necessarily complete religions in the Western sense. Every New Religion contains elements from one or more of the preexisting traditions: folk religion, Shinto, Buddhism, Confucianism, Taoism, and even Christianity. Therefore, these religious movements are as much renovation as innovation, as much renewed religious traditions as new traditions. These new religious movements can be seen as splinters or branches of the main Japanese traditions. The new movements are not necessarily "complete" religions because often they did not break age-old religious patterns such as having Buddhist priests perform funeral and memorial rites. In other words, the New Religions do not always insist on their followers' exclusive attention, nor do they automatically meet all of a person's religious needs. They may be viewed as religious movements or religious societies rather than as independent religions with exclusive claims. It is well to remember that throughout Japanese history, most people relied on several religious traditions, and did not depend on a single tradition for all their spiritual needs. Only the Jodo Shin sect and Nichiren sect among Japanese traditions (and some New Religions deriving from Nichiren Buddhism) have expressed an exclusive claim to absolute truth.

To understand the emergence of the New Religions, it is necessary to recognize the context of Japanese religion and society from which they sprang. By late Tokugawa times, when the first New Religions appeared, popular piety was flourishing, but much of organized religion in Japan had become rather formalistic, losing its ability to hold the interest of many people. From late Tokugawa times through the prewar period, social and economic conditions were very depressed for poor farmers and city laborers. Although one factor contributing to the Meiji Restoration was peasant revolts, the money economy and tax system of the Meiji era only increased the tendency for small peasants to become helpless tenants. Rural people who became city laborers suffered from the low wages and harsh working conditions of the early stages of the new capitalistic system. The New Religions drew many of their leaders and members from the depressed classes, those who had suffered together and now shared their religious experiences. Economic and social crises stimulated a spiritual renewal of the older traditions, but the renewal was more likely to occur within newly formed religious movements than within the older religious organizations. In fact, New Religions are remarkable not only as religious phenomena, but also as "unquestionably the largest and fastest-growing popular movement" of all mass movements in Japan from World War I to World War II.[18]

The New Religions got their start in the early nineteenth century but were not allowed complete freedom of organization and practice until 1945. Both the Tokugawa authorities and the Meiji government maintained strict control over all popular movements, including religious activity. During the late Tokugawa period, the new religious movements were forced to define and organize their activities to fit within the traditional forms of Shinto or Buddhism. They continued with varying phases of recognition or suppression until 1882, when State Shinto was separated as a government institution from sect Shinto. Eventually, thirteen religious movements were recognized and supervised as religious subdivisions of Shinto. Several of the thirteen sects preserved special Shinto traditions and were actually sect developments of Shinto. Other sects were organized around elements of folk religion and blendings of Buddhism, Confucianism, and Taoism. Their origins are so diverse and their later doctrinal systems so complex that it is difficult to make general statements about all of them.[19]

One of the distinguishing features of the New Religions is that usually a living person served as either founder or organizer. In most cases the impetus for organizing a religion came from the charismatic quality of the founder, who was considered semidivine or divine; his or her utterances became revealed scripture. Even the sect developments of Shinto selected special *kami* from the *Nihongi* and *Kojiki* as objects of worship. The New Religions offered specific objects of faith and appealing forms of worship. They usually promised the solution of all problems through faith and worship. Some of the founders were led to their crucial religious experience (or revelation) by a personal dilemma that was solved by the discovery of a new faith. Often the New Religions practiced faith healing but also promised solutions to personal crises such as financial and marital difficulties.

It may be argued that no religious movement at any time or place is completely new, because everything in human history is influenced and conditioned by the past. (The same argument can be made even for world religions; Christianity emerged out of and was influenced by Judaism, and Buddhism arose out of and was colored by Hinduism.) The New Religions of Japan certainly demonstrate continuity with earlier Japanese traditions. This is borne out by the fact that the persistent themes of Japanese religious history can be found in the New Religions. Yet, these movements also display originality and distinctive features. One hallmark of New Religions is that they made a more direct appeal to individual faith, whereas organized religion in Japan in recent times tended to depend upon family membership along hereditary or geographical lines. Each new movement picked up a spark from one of the old traditions and fanned it into a dynamic spiritual force. For example, in the twentieth century, Nichiren Buddhism was revived by a number of sects (such as Soka Gakkai) that placed their trust in the *Lotus Sutra* and in Nichiren practices. Once a New Religion gained followers, it tended to be codified in organized scriptures, doctrine, worship, and priesthood.

THE FORTUNES OF RELIGION
1868–1945: FROM FREEDOM OF
RELIGION TO STATE ORTHODOXY

Japanese religion from 1868 to 1945 went through an unusually large number of radical changes, most of which were linked to the growing pains of the developing nation-state. We have seen that in early Meiji, Buddhism was persecuted and Christianity was still banned, but the persecution was dropped and the ban was lifted; and with the Constitution of 1889 freedom of religious belief was promised while Shrine Shinto was considered "nonreligious" and those religious organizations deemed a threat to "peace and order" were constantly threatened with suppression.

At the end of the Meiji era (1912) religion followed several different paths, one more liberal and tolerant, the other more restrictive and intolerant; the dual track for religion in part mirrors conflicting tendencies within Japanese society and government at this time. Some aspects of the constitutional government had advocated democratic procedures and individual liberties; yet, such individual "freedom" was restricted by the demands of absolute loyalty to the state and unquestioned respect for the emperor. During the first few decades of the twentieth century, some intellectuals actively pursued a philosophy of liberalism, including individual rights and freedoms, over what they saw as an authoritarian state. Others saw liberalism as a dangerous, even subversive, program of individualism that threatened the fabric of society and the state (*kokutai,* Japan's "unique" national polity). Gradually, especially from the 1930s, when Japan became locked in "expansionist" military campaigns in Asia, the government effectively suppressed liberal dissent in all areas of society, including newspapers and universities.[20]

In the previous and present chapter we have viewed the trends in individual religions; now we turn to the general fortune of religious life that cuts across all traditions. This period moved from the relative religious freedom of Meiji times to the suppression of religion and enforcement of a kind of state "orthodoxy" in the 1930s.

Though the *guarantee* of religious freedom was never removed, the Constitution's limitation of freedom of religion "within limits not prejudicial to peace and order, and not antagonistic to their duties as subjects," came to be interpreted so strictly as to suppress or even openly persecute any religious group the state saw fit to target. Actually, two kinds of groups, one secular—communism, the other religious—New Religions, were increasingly the scapegoat of state attacks. As capitalism developed, labor unions and communism were seen as a threat not only to industry but also to the nation, and openly opposed by the government. In a similar fashion, just as the "radical thought" of communism was attacked, so were the New Religions, which were seen as misleading the people with superstitions that led them astray from the "imperial way." In fact, in the 1920s and through the early 1940s, the government arrested leaders of several New Religions and even destroyed some buildings. The charges against one of the attacked New Religions, Omotokyo, was that its leader had committed *lese majeste,* or challenged the emperor's supremacy, by riding a white horse (a prerogative of the emperor) and that the group had disrupted "peace and order" by teaching a version of Japan's founding myth that did not square with the official view of the national polity. Some Omotokyo leaders and members were arrested, and its major shrines destroyed with dynamite on government orders.

Although the government as a political institution was the agency carrying out this suppression, most of the organized religions were active, enthusiastic supporters of this policy and its implementation. Generally the leaders of Shinto, Buddhism, and even Christianity (and some New Religions) publicly praised the military expansion of the Japanese empire across Asia and openly supported the suppression of communism, labor movements, and New

Religions within Japan. In other words, the relationship of organized religion to state policy followed self-interest: "Religious leaders welcomed state intervention when it advanced the interests of their own organization, but single-mindedly resisted intrusions that did not."[21] Organized religions supported the state program of suppressing communism and New Religions, but as one scholar has phrased it, the state had its own broad interpretation of "orthodoxy," which he defines negatively as the exclusion of communism and New Religions. By contrast, the state viewed "heterodoxy" in terms of four major threats to orthodoxy: (1) *lese majeste;* (2) irrationality, superstition, and faith healing; (3) corruption of public morals (especially upsetting the traditional family); and (4) organizational autonomy (outside the state-approved established religions). Although these linked notions of orthodoxy and heterodoxy most frequently were used to suppress the New Religions, from the late 1930s some popular Shinto groups and some Christian groups were also persecuted. The same scholar concludes that "Led by the military, the state increasingly equated orthodoxy and 'peace and order' with a rigid interpretation of Japan's 'national polity' (*kokutai*)."[22]

Another way of looking at "orthodoxy" is not through the negative lens of what was excluded and persecuted, but through the positive lens of what was promulgated and taught. In 1937 the Ministry of Education published *Kokutai no Hongi* (Cardinal Principles of the National Entity of Japan) as the official government view of the national entity (and as the actual textbook) to be used in all schools. Drafted by leading university professors and edited by government officials, this work viewed Western influence as the threat of individualism destructive to Japanese society. To counter this threat, the textbook advocated patriotism based on "a mystical belief in the divine origins and absolute authority of the imperial line . . . and willingness to accept blindly any command or demand for sacrifice alleged to have come from" the imperial line.[23] In short, this textbook set forth the mythical uniqueness of Japan, and the racial and ethical superiority of the Japanese people.[24]

The principles in this textbook define the legacy of the prewar and wartime policy toward religion—and supported by much of organized religion—directed at the external threat of Western influence, the internal threat of communism, and the danger of home-grown New Religions. We will return to this legacy in a later chapter when we view the postwar religious scene.

For the moment, if we focus just on the perceived threat of New Religions, we note that they were attacked by the combined force of intellectuals, competing religious organizations, and the state. To be sure, throughout much of their history, the New Religions have received much criticism as unrefined, superstitious, and interested mainly in acquiring money. However, if they were so "evil," how can their popularity and "success" be explained? Their vitality is demonstrated by the number of followers they attracted. Even in prewar Japan, before they received their biggest stimulus, many sects could claim from several hundred thousand to several million members.[25] In postwar Japan, it is remarkable that Soka Gakkai could gain millions of members in a few decades, at the time when the total number of Protestant and Catholic

Christians did not exceed a half-million members (after almost a century of mission work). The New Religions represent the greatest possibility for religious renewal up to the present day. In the next chapter we will look briefly at two New Religions, attempting to gain a more complete picture of their activities and dynamism.

NOTES

1. See Smith, *Confucianism in Modern Japan,* pp. 156ff. See also Gauntlett, trans., *Kokutai no Hongi: Cardinal Principles of the National Entity of Japan;* an excerpt is included in my *Religion in the Japanese Experience,* 2d ed., pp. 238–42.

2. For a general overview, see Iichi Oguchi and Hiroo Takagi, "Religion and Social Development," in *Japanese Religion in the Meiji Era,* ed. Hideo Kishimoto, trans. John E. Howes (Tokyo: Obunsha, 1956), pp. 311–57.

3. During five years of living in a rural Buddhist temple, Marcure noted that "several of the villagers voiced a general diminished respect toward monks, and the latter were occasionally referred to as . . . 'funeral salarymen' or . . . 'funeral entrepreneurs.'" See Marcure, "The *Danka* System," p. 64.

4. For an evaluation of Zen Buddhism in Meiji times, see Richard Jaffe and Michel Mohr, eds., *Meiji Japan,* vol. 25, no. 1–2, of *Japanese Journal of Religious Studies* (Spring 1998). In their "Editors' Introduction: Meiji Zen," the editors conclude "that Buddhism in general and Zen in particular were neither stagnant nor without political influence." They also point out that Zen (Soto) clerics were diverse in their response to state policies: one "pro-colonization advocate" and one "anarchist" "show how Zen doctrine and practice were used both to justify murder and aggression and to resist such tendencies" (pp. 8, 6). See also in the same volume Ishikawa Rikizan, "The Social Response of Buddhists to the Modernization of Japan: The Contrasting Lives of Two Soto Zen Monks," pp. 87–115.

5. For a brief overview of Kiyozawa and his role in Meiji Buddhism, see Yusen Kashiwahara, "Kiyozawa Manshi," in *Shapers of Japanese Buddhism,* pp. 230–40.

6. This scholar's name is also spelled Nanjio Bunyiu.

7. Proficiency in language and translation was not limited to Buddhist scholars. From Tokugawa times, and especially from Meiji times, the Japanese were quick to learn Western languages and translate into Japanese important Western books. By contrast, Western translation of Japanese works appeared much later.

8. Jacqueline Stone, "A Vast and Grave Task: Interwar Buddhist Studies as an Expression of Japan's Envisioned Global Role," in *Culture and Identity: Japanese Intellectuals During the Interwar Years,* ed. Thomas J. Rimer (Princeton: Princeton University, 1990), pp. 225, 227.

9. Heisig and Maraldo, eds., *Rude Awakenings.* The articles in this book carry on a heated debate over Japan's larger motives in World War II (or the Pacific War, which for Japan started in 1931): was it to combat Western (European and American) imperialism; was it to combat Western colonialism and at the same time promote Japanese colonialism; or was it just to further Japanese imperialism and colonialism? The comments of one Japanese Zen monk, limiting his remarks to Zen Buddhism, are worth quoting: "Not a few Zen priests joined hands with State Shinto and its imperialist view of history in order to promote the war. None of the historical arguments brought forth in their defense (for example, the indignation at the West's colonization of the East referred to earlier) can justify their simple failure to speak out on the Buddhist ideal of nonbelligerence, much less their active support of the war effort." See Seiko Hirata, "Zen Buddhist Attitudes to War," in *Rude Awakenings,* pp. 3–15; especially p. 11.

For the full story of "Zen at war," see the book by this title, Brian (Daizen) A. Victoria, *Zen at War* (New York: Weatherhill, 1997). This work describes in great detail the complicity of most Buddhist sects with the war effort, and especially the unquestioning support of the war by Zen sects: three categories discussed are "imperial-way Buddhism, imperial-state Zen, and soldier Zen." Victoria claims that "By the 1920s, Japanese institutional Buddhism, as a whole, firmly supported Japan's military and colonial policies," while only a small group of "freethinkers formed the Youth League for Revitalizing Buddhism," refusing "to accept the stance of their sectarian leaders" (p. 66). A 1931 declaration by this group proclaimed: "when we look to already existing sectarian organizations for reform, we are forced to recognize just how serious their corrupt traditions and degeneration are" (p. 67). This work contains a wealth of information on the statements and actions of Buddhist clerics and institutions supporting militarism and colonialism (including Buddhist arguments for a "just war"); it also chronicles the postwar situation and the attempt of some individuals and groups to repent earlier policies and actions, and the silence and inaction of others choosing to forget the past. This retrospective includes a variety of opinions from D. T. Suzuki on Shinto's, Buddhism's and his own involvement in the war. Victoria's conclusion is worth quoting: "It is difficult to know who we ought to be if we cannot recognize who we have been" (p. 193).

10. Saburo Ienaga, *The Pacific War, 1931–1945,* p. 123. The mention of academics raises the interesting question of the relationship of the university, academics, and research to war, especially because this book is written from the vantage point of an academic in a university setting. Unfortunately, history teaches us that professors and institutions of higher learning are often part of the problem, rather than the solution, of nationalism and militarism. University science professors in Japan and Germany cooperated with the military to perform experiments on prisoners as human guinea pigs; and it is well known that American scientists won the race to create the first atomic bomb. For Japan, see Sheldon H. Harris, *Factories of Death: Japanese Biological Warfare, 1932–1945, and the American Cover-up* (London: Routledge, 1994); for Germany, see Robert Jay Lifton, *The Nazi Doctors: Medical Killing and the Psychology of Genocide* (New York: Basic Books, 1986); for the United States, see Ira Chernus, *Nuclear Madness: Religion and the Psychology of the Nuclear Age* (Albany: State University of New York, 1991). The advice suggested here is not to disparage all academic work (which would make the present book a self-contradiction!), but to bring academics and academic work under the same critical questioning and vigorous cross-checking that we expect of religious/political leaders/programs.

11. Naomi Hylkema-Vos, "Kato Genchi: A Neglected Pioneer in Comparative Religion," *Japanese Journal of Religious Studies,* vol. 17, no. 4 (Dec. 1990), pp. 375–95.

12. See Irwin Scheiner, *Christian Converts and Social Protest in Meiji Japan* (Berkeley: University of California, 1970).

13. Akio Dohi, quoted in A. Hamish Ion, "Essays and Meiji Protestant Christian History," in Aizan Yamaji, *Essays on the Modern Japanese Church: Christianity in Meiji,* "translated by Graham Squires, with Introductory Essays by Graham Squires and A. Hamish Ion" (Ann Arbor: Center for Japanese Studies, University of Michigan, 1999), p. 34, and pp. 36–37.

14. "Two J's," in Tsunoda et al., *Sources of Japanese Tradition* Chapter 29; 2d ed. forthcoming. This translation is included in my *Religion in the Japanese Experience,* 2d ed., pp. 150–52.

15. See David Plath, "The Japanese Popular Christmas: Coping with Modernity," *Journal of American Folklore,* vol. 76 (1963), pp. 309–17. This article is abridged in my *Religion in the Japanese Experience,* 2d ed., pp. 308–12.

16. For an interesting firsthand view of women's rights from the perspective of an upper-class woman in the early twentieth century, see the autobiography of Shidzue Ishimoto, *The Story of My Life.* (Stanford: Stanford University, 1984, first published 1935).

17. Ienaga, *The Pacific War,* p. 123.

18. Sheldon M. Garon, "State and Religion in Imperial Japan, 1912–1945," *Journal of Japanese Studies,* vol. 12, no. 2 (Summer 1986), p. 273. (These materials are incorporated in

his book, *Molding Japanese Minds: The State in Everyday Life* [Princeton: Princeton University, 1997]).

19. See Daniel C. Holtom, *The National Faith of Japan: A Study of Modern Shinto* (New York: Dutton, 1938; reprint ed., New York: Paragon Book Reprint Corp., 1965), pp. 189–286, for a description of the thirteen "Shinto sects" in prewar times.

20. For a critical overview of Japanese religion and the problem of freedom of religion after 1868, see Shigeyoshi Murakami, *Japanese Religion in the Modern Century,* trans. H. Byron Earhart (Tokyo: University of Tokyo, 1980).

21. Garon, "State and Religion in Imperial Japan, 1912–1945," pp. 282–83.

22. Ibid., pp. 296–300.

23. Robert King Hall, "Kokutai no hongi," *Kodansha Encyclopedia of Japan,* vol. 4, p. 264. For a complete translation see Gauntlett and Hall, *Kokutai no hongi;* an excerpt is included in my *Religion in the Japanese Experience,* 2d ed., pp. 238–42.

24. For other examples of the unity of the ancient mythology of divine descent of the emperor, and the modern ideology of absolute loyalty to the emperor (as military indoctrination), see quotations from the Field Service Code carried by every soldier, in John W. Dower, *Embracing Defeat: Japan in the Wake of World War II* (New York: W. W. Norton, 1999), p. 277. Dower also has described and interpreted the racism in American propaganda during World War II, which was more virulent and exaggerated against the "yellow" Japanese than against white European enemies. See John W. Dower, *War Without Mercy: Race & Power in the Pacific War* (New York: Pantheon Books, 1986).

25. See Holtom, *The National Faith of Japan,* p. 285, for membership figures of the thirteen "Shinto sects" in 1937.

17

❦

Two New Religions:
Tenrikyo and
Soka Gakkai

Of all the New Religions that have arisen in Japan since the early nineteenth century, Tenrikyo and Soka Gakkai are two of the most important; their stories serve to highlight similarities as well as differences among New Religions. Both are new movements, founded and organized outside the established religions. Tenrikyo has been more closely associated with Shinto; Soka Gakkai comes out of the Nichiren Buddhist tradition. Both movements arose during the active period of the New Religions, in the past century and a half, but at opposite ends of this time span.

Tenrikyo was a pioneer New Religion, the first to succeed on a large scale, and served as a model for later movements. Soka Gakkai arose about a century later in the prewar period and flourished only after World War II, yet its rapid success has made it the envy of other groups. Although both were founded by the deliberate actions of specific individuals, the religious dynamics of their respective foundings differ. Tenrikyo is oriented around its foundress, who is seen as a living *kami* who created her own sacred scriptures and rites. Soka Gakkai reveres as absolutely powerful the medieval Buddhist saint Nichiren and the *Lotus Sutra,* which its founder rediscovered, but does not place nearly so much trust in its founder. Tenrikyo flourished in the countryside and has maintained its strength there while moving into the cities; Soka Gakkai emerged in the city and has been strongest among urban people while making some inroads in the rural areas.

THE MANY NEW RELIGIONS:
DIFFERENCES AND SIMILARITIES

Our brief look at Tenrikyo and Soka Gakkai highlights several important features of New Religions, but it is well to point out some characteristics of the many New Religions that differ from these two major movements. Some New Religions were not founded so decisively by one person but tended to coalesce around distinctive regional traditions; this is the case with several nineteenth-century movements originally included among the thirteen members of Sect Shinto. Not all the New Religions can be traced clearly to either Shinto or Buddhism; a number of them are highly complex in origin and character. Healing is important for several New Religions, much more important than for Tenrikyo and Soka Gakkai. Some are more closely related to the Western tradition, through spiritualism and a spiritualistic interpretation of Western science. Although both Tenrikyo and Soka Gakkai practice mission work, many New Religions are active only in Japan. And, of course, not all the New Religions are as large as Tenrikyo and Soka Gakkai.

Founded in 1838, Tenrikyo today is practically an established religion, because it is one of the oldest New Religions with more than a century and a half of its own tradition. Soka Gakkai also may qualify as an established religious institution: although formed a century later, it is the largest New Religion—with an extensive membership, a highly efficient organization, and branches throughout the world. Each of these two New Religions has its own university, another indicator of their "established" status. By contrast, a number of new religious movements appearing in Japan from the 1970s, with special appeal to college students and young people through emphasis on miracles and the occult, are sufficiently different from the previous New Religions that some scholars have called the more recent groups "New-New Religions."

The most famous—or infamous—of the New-New Religions is Aum Shinrikyo, organized in the 1980s by Asahara Shoko around a mixture of yoga, rigid asceticism, and mystical realization. Although Aum Shinrikyo was relatively successful in attracting followers and amassing an impressive capital base, its growth did not come close to that of some of the other New-New Religions, and it failed to attract members from other groups. Aum's leaders, frustrated by the group's inability to develop a large movement and its failure in electing political candidates, resorted to extreme measures. Asahara and members of his group were implicated in abduction, murder, and the 1995 poison gas attack in the Tokyo subway system that killed twelve people and injured thousands.[1] In mentioning so briefly such a controversial subject, we must stress two points: first, Aum Shinrikyo shares many features with the New Religions, especially the New-New Religions—including the presence of a charismatic leader, faith healing, and adaptations of Indian forms of meditation; second, Aum Shinrikyo represents a rare instance of a New Religion resorting to violence against the people and the government to further its ends. Historical perspective reminds us that until postwar times, New Religions were the frequent target of government restrictions, persecutions, and prosecutions. (Both Tenrikyo and Soka Gakkai suffered from persecution by the government.)

What we discover in Tenrikyo and Soka Gakkai, then, is a sampling from two of the hundreds of active New Religions, but a sampling that in its own diversity displays the amazing variety within the panorama of individual movements.

TENRIKYO: A LIVING
KAMI AND A JOYOUS LIFE

The religious nature of Tenrikyo (literally, "the religion of divine wisdom") is reflected in the dramatic events surrounding its founding by Mrs. Nakayama Miki (1798–1887, usually referred to by her given name of Miki). Up to the age of 40, Miki led a rather uneventful life as a farmer's wife until 1838. Miki's son had been ill, and in 1838 she had called in an exorcist to cure him. In premodern Japan, illness was usually seen as due to the presence of evil spirits, which were driven out by exorcists; some of these beliefs and practices are still followed even today. In such cases the exorcist (a *yamabushi,* or practitioner of Shugendo) used a woman as a medium; after he put the medium into a trance she would identify the evil spirit to be exorcised. But when the exorcist was called to heal Miki's son, the exorcist's regular medium was absent, so Miki herself served as the medium.

Miki's trance experience was unusual. Instead of the customary, brief possession and "diagnosis" of illness, Miki received a divine revelation in the form of permanent possession by a *kami* who claimed to be the true original *kami.* This divinity was Tenri O no Mikoto, literally "Lord of Divine Wisdom." (Tenri means "heavenly wisdom" and O no Mikoto is equivalent to "royal divinity.") The deity is also known as Oyagami, "God the Parent." This divinity gave a rather new message through Miki's mouth: the *kami* had loaned Miki her body, but now was reclaiming it and demanding that Miki spend the rest of her life spreading the divinity's message. Her family reluctantly yielded to the demand. This 1838 event marks the traditional founding of Tenrikyo, the religion of divine or heavenly wisdom. From this point Miki is viewed as a kind of living *kami.*

Quickly Miki's fame as a living *kami* spread, and people came to ask her for spiritual help, particularly for protection against smallpox and for safe childbirth. Gradually those who had received such help from Miki gathered around her as a group of followers. A carpenter (whose wife had been healed by Miki after childbirth) built a small worship hall and eventually helped bring the teachings of Miki into a more highly organized form. As Miki attracted a larger following and began to hold religious services, she drew the authorities' attention and was harassed and even arrested. In late Tokugawa times religious organizations were closely supervised, and unrecognized religious movements were subject to prosecution. Nevertheless, Miki persevered in her mission of proclaiming faith in Tenri O no Mikoto, and her family spread the message to the surrounding area, as far as the nearest metropolis, Osaka. The earliest worship phrase, *Namu Tenri O no Mikoto,* is comparable to the Pure Land phrase *Namu Amida Butsu* and to the Nichiren phrase *Namu Myoho Renge Kyo.* (*Namu* translates roughly as "praise be" or "I put my faith in.") Eventually, as her following became larger and as Miki devoted more time to her group (especially after the death of her husband in 1853), there emerged all the features of an organized religion.

Central to this movement's ethos was the founder as a living *kami;* her life was a kind of divine model. What she wrote was considered revelation and came to be the scripture of Tenrikyo. The songs she composed became hymns, and the dance she created was transformed into Tenrikyo liturgy. The gestures she used in the dance became standard ritual gestures. Her scripture indicated a nearby spot as the place where the world and human beings were created (by Izanagi and Izanami); this location, considered the center of the world, became the site for the main shrine of Tenrikyo. The shrine was built in accordance with Miki's revelation: there is a square opening in the roof and a wooden column underneath. The corporate worship and elaborate liturgies that Miki established continue to be performed around this column under the open roof. Although these features have assumed a mysterious symbolism within later Tenrikyo, they signify a channel for continued communication between Heaven and humans.

As Tenrikyo gradually developed into a larger organization around the central figure of Miki, it also developed a message, or philosophy of life, based on her teachings. Miki taught that "At the very beginning of the world, God the Parent created mankind out of an earnest desire to make them live a *yokigurashi,* a joyous life. Mankind, however, ignoring the will of God the Parent Who created them to live a life of *yokigurashi* in the truest sense of the word, has come to abuse their minds which were granted to them as their own, and becoming self-willed, come to regard life as a gloomy world."[2] According to this teaching, because people have become self-centered and selfish, they are surrounded with gloom. But when an individual recovers oneness with God the Parent, he or she once again participates in the joyous creation of the world. The means to this joyous life is faith in God the Parent and "sweeping away" one's evils through the worship services instituted by Miki. From a historical viewpoint, we might say that this religious reform is based on a return to traditional Japanese peasant values: gratitude to the sacredness of the cosmos and ethical obligation to place social good before individual interest.

Miki herself worked hard at manual labor and the menial tasks of farming, and her family successors continue this practice, though more as a formality on ritual occasions. For the average member of Tenrikyo, much emphasis is placed on voluntary labor for the erecting of Tenrikyo buildings, and it is customary for these people to spend long sessions at the Tenri headquarters in unpaid labor. Many Western visitors to Tenri headquarters have been so impressed with the infectious happiness and energetic enthusiasm of these voluntary laborers that they compared Tenrikyo's atmosphere to the accounts of Christianity's vitality in its first century of development.

When Miki died in early 1887, Tenrikyo had already emerged as a rather well-organized religion, so it suffered no critical shock due to the loss of this charismatic leader. The founding site (later called the city of Tenri) became a kind of mecca for pilgrimage, with the model of Miki's life and teaching as the compass for the individual believer. The first religious shrines had been erected and the liturgical patterns developed. Hereditary succession in the leadership was taken over by a line of patriarchs descended from Mrs. Nakayama. At the turn of the twentieth century, Tenrikyo was so highly organized that it had divisions for training ministers, propagation, and missions, and later these divisions approached the complexity of their counterparts in Protestant denominations.

As Tenrikyo became more organized, it was forced to accept supervision from other recognized religious bodies; finally in 1908 it was granted relatively independent status as one of the thirteen sects of Sect Shinto. By assuming the subordinate role of a Shinto sect, Tenrikyo was thereby able to operate more freely. Only after World War II, with complete freedom of religion, was Tenrikyo able to separate itself from Shinto and become a fully independent organization. Tenrikyo now boasts a large publishing house, issuing works not only in Japanese but in other Asian and Western languages. Tenri University, formally established in 1948, is a leading private institution with an internationally recognized library. The highly efficient central headquarters at the modern city of Tenri is backed up by a large nationwide network of local branches and a number of overseas branches, especially in North and South America (where Japanese have emigrated).

The success story of Tenrikyo is a good example for understanding the dynamic power of the New Religions and their impact on the religious scene. Tenrikyo is firmly rooted in traditional Japanese religion, as evidenced in the revelation to Miki through a kind of shamanistic possession. Centering on Miki's charismatic leadership and relying on established religion only for the expediency of government recognition (until the end of World War II), Tenrikyo developed its own scriptural, liturgical, ecclesiastical, and social forms. By creating the model for the formation of a New Religion, Tenrikyo became the first movement to proceed from individual revelation to large-scale religious organization. According to a Tenrikyo publication, by 1899 "the whole number of the churches was 1,493; that of the missionaries, 18,150; and that of the believers, about 2,000,000."[3]

There is no doubt that Tenrikyo's success encouraged other groups to form and to look upon Tenrikyo's precedent as a model for their development. But if Tenrikyo has the distinction of being the pioneer or model New Religion, it is also the first New Religion to become fully organized, or "established." Tenrikyo started with every member a convert drawn into a rather loose unity, but eventually second-, third-, and even fourth-generation members were participating in a highly elaborate ecclesiastical framework. The fate of many would-be New Religions is rather brief because they are unable to move from charismatic leadership and the initial followers to the creation of a fully institutionalized organization. Tenrikyo made the transition with relative ease, translating the charisma of Miki into institutional lines of authority and liturgy. Compared with other New Religions, Tenrikyo has had rather few movements splitting away from it.[4] Like all larger religious organizations, it has received some criticism for increasing formalism and for pressuring believers financially to support the bureaucracy. Such is the dilemma of all organized religion: how to preserve the founding inspiration and the initial vitality within the framework of permanent institutions.

SOKA GAKKAI: FAITH IN THE *LOTUS SUTRA* AND A HAPPY LIFE

Makiguchi Tsunesaburo (1871–1944), the founder of Soka Gakkai, was a teacher from Hokkaido who developed a new theory of education or theory of value. Makiguchi contrasted the usual philosophical triad of truth, beauty, and goodness with his own triad of beauty, benefit (or gain), and goodness. He held that truth is objective and absolute, whereas values are subjective and relative; in other words, truth has to be discovered, but values have to be created. (The literal meaning of Soka Gakkai is "Value Creation Society.") This theory, too complicated for simple summary, was developed out of Makiguchi's work in education, but it took on specifically religious significance when he linked it to belief in the Nichiren Shoshu branch of Buddhism. This meant, roughly, that the absolute truth was identified with Nichiren and the *Lotus Sutra;* the values to be created were identified as aspects of the happy life available through this absolute faith.

During the 1930s, Makiguchi and Toda Josei (1900–58), a teacher in the school where Makiguchi was principal, made the first efforts to propagate the new message. They had attracted only several thousand members by 1941 when World War II began. During the war the movement was suppressed because Makiguchi and Toda refused to comply with wartime directives ordering unified religious support for the military; in particular, they refused to enshrine in their homes talismans from Ise Shrine (which was a symbolic action supporting State Shinto and the war effort). To comply with this directive, for Makiguchi and Toda, would have meant compromising the absolute truth of Nichiren and the *Lotus Sutra* with other Buddhist groups and Shinto. The two leaders were arrested, and Makiguchi died while in prison; Toda survived and was released in 1945 shortly before the end of the war. The original movement was so completely destroyed that it is safe to say Toda is the second founder.

In 1951 Toda decided to devote all of his time to transform Soka Gakkai from a membership of several thousand families to his goal of 750,000 families before he died; the goal was achieved in 1957. This phenomenal success was due in part to Toda's organizational ability, for he mobilized a large youth division that enthusiastically converted great numbers. Also he was helped by the close ties he renewed with Nichiren Shoshu. After Toda's death in 1958, his protege Ikeda Daisaku (1928–), who had been in the forefront of the youth division, in 1960 became Soka Gakkai's third president (and in spite of some controversies, has continued to be a prominent international spokesperson for the group).

Toda's aggressive conversion policies and the confrontational tactics of the youth division led by Ikeda had given Soka Gakkai a bad reputation, which Ikeda attempted to improve. He favored expansion of membership by peaceful persuasion, and he oversaw the development of cultural and political activities within Soka Gakkai. Ikeda consolidated this movement into a sophisticated and highly efficient modern organization. Ikeda, the able disciple of Toda, proved more attractive as a charismatic leader. He has traveled extensively through major countries of the world and is equally at home with Japanese and non-Japanese dignitaries. There is a constant flow of his publications, not only on Buddhism, but also on social and international issues, in Western-language editions. In 1979 he left the presidency of Soka Gakkai for the position of honorary president, but he has retained much influence.

To understand the traditional religious background of this dynamic modern movement, we must review the inspiration of the founder Nichiren and the history of his movement. Nichiren emphasized absolute, exclusive faith in the *Lotus Sutra* and recitation of faith in the *Lotus Sutra* through the phrase *Namu Myoho Renge Kyo* (or *Nammyoho Renge Kyo,* the form preferred by Soka Gakkai). After Nichiren's death, his followers split into groups that in time turned into hard denominational lines. By the late Tokugawa period, people devoted to Nichiren as a model of religious faith and to the *Lotus Sutra* as a source of religious guidance were increasingly frustrated with Nichiren denominations. Some people turned away from these denominations and formed voluntary organizations called *"ko,"* which eventually developed into New Religions. Other New Religions (such as Soka Gakkai and Rissho Koseikai) also emphasize faith in the *Lotus Sutra* but emerged directly from the general current of popular faith in Nichiren and the *Lotus Sutra,* without the intermediate development of voluntary organizations.

Soka Gakkai is more recent than the earliest Nichiren-derived New Religions but is by far the largest, most dynamic, and most efficiently organized. Its ethos is defined by the solution of all personal and societal problems through absolute faith in the *Lotus Sutra.* Soka Gakkai holds to absoluteness not only in the commitment of the believer, but also in the truth of its message. Therefore, it follows that all other religions are false. Likewise, all personal and cultural values must be dependent on this absolute truth. A positive aspect of this absolute faith in an absolute truth is its promise to solve all personal and cultural problems. A negative aspect is the frequent accusation that, especially during the aggressive conversion campaign started in the 1950s, absolute faith in the *Lotus Sutra* led believers to use *any* means to convert people.

One of the controversial means was the use of the conversion technique called *"shakubuku."* Controversy surrounds even the translation and interpretation of this term. In Buddhism, particularly in the tradition of Nichiren

Buddhism, two contrasting approaches have been used for conversion: *shakubuku*, "to break and suppress" or "to defeat evil"; and *shoju*, "to embrace, or welcome good." Both aggressive and persuasive attitudes are accepted in Buddhism.[5] *Shakubuku*, used to implement the aggressive conversion campaign of 1950s Soka Gakkai in the hands of zealous youth members, sometimes involved a number of Soka Gakkai members pressuring or intimidating a potential convert. Some Western scholars writing at the time or shortly thereafter have rendered *shakubuku* as "browbeating."[6] It is well to remember that religious organizations, somewhat like human beings, usually outgrow the excesses of youth. And although Soka Gakkai no longer practices such an aggressive form of conversion, many scholars and journalists remember this more mature organization by its youthful indiscretions.

The dynamics of early Soka Gakkai's strength and numbers can best be seen by the way in which a new member, usually a person experiencing some life difficulty, was taken into the organization. Soka Gakkai's grassroots strength was derived from small discussion groups of twenty to thirty people who met informally in members' homes to share testimonials, discuss personal problems, and study Soka Gakkai doctrine. Most nonmembers made their first contact with Soka Gakkai when a member who happened to be a friend, relative, or coworker persuaded them to attend a meeting (often for the purpose of helping the newcomer handle his or her difficulty). After several meetings, the nonmember might seek to solve his or her problems in the context of such a group with faith in Nichiren and the *Lotus Sutra;* but to become a member of Soka Gakkai, the person had to be formally admitted into Nichiren Shoshu. This necessitated removing all traces of other religions from his or her home— throwing out or burning the Shinto and Buddhist elements and images that traditionally were an integral part of most homes (Christian elements, if present, also were forbidden). Only then could the individual go to a Nichiren Shoshu temple for the official conversion rites, at which time he or she was given a wooden tablet with the title of the *Lotus Sutra* carved in it. The tablet was patterned after the one Nichiren made and was a sacred object to be placed in the now-empty family altar. Twice every day, morning and night, the member expressed faith in the *Lotus Sutra* by chanting the phrase including the title of this sutra (*Nammyoho Renge Kyo*) and reciting passages from it before the sacred object. From this time the member participated in the discussion groups and the other activities of Soka Gakkai. The new member also was required to be active in proselytizing others and was expected to make a pilgrimage to the head temple of Nichiren Shoshu, Taiseki-ji near Mount Fuji. Several million members made the trip annually.

The organizational structure of this lay movement has been amazingly effective and tight-knit, with several interlocking and overlapping subgroups. On the lowest level, there was an inviolable link between a member and the person who converted him or her, completely apart from geographic or organizational ties. The member also belonged to the small "unit" of ten or twelve families; from five to ten units constituted one "group"; a number of groups made up a "district." The next structural element was the "chapter," including from one to two thousand families; several chapters formed a "general chapter"; next came "headquarters," followed by "joint headquarters," which was directly controlled by Soka Gakkai's leadership. After 1955, Soka Gakkai also introduced the "block" system of geographical units. Every family belonged to the smallest geographical block, and subsequent larger blocks included all Soka Gakkai families. Not only did every family belong to both a "unit" and a "block," but every individual also belonged to the men's, women's, or youth division.[7] It was also possible for one to take competitive examinations on Soka Gakkai doctrine and achieve the academic rank of instructor, assistant professor, or full professor.

The movement published its own religious materials in Western and Asian languages, conducted highly successful fund-raising campaigns, and completed phenomenal building programs in Tokyo and at Taiseki-ji. Its Soka University, which opened in 1971, may be seen as the apex of its organizational and building programs. But most of Soka Gakkai's notoriety has come from its participation in politics.

In 1964 Soka Gakkai developed the Komeito (Clean Government Party) as a full-fledged party with a large number of local and national candidates; it has been highly successful in electing candidates. Due to the nature of the Japanese political system, many political offices are filled by voting in the top several candidates out of a large field. Soka Gakkai has been able to judge accurately how many votes will be needed to elect a candidate and then, based on how many votes it can command in that area, put up only as many candidates as their votes can elect. Komeito, the only religiously based party in Japanese history, has already become a major national force. Komeito and Soka Gakkai have been accused of attempting to gain religious control over the state—a charge they deny. However, after an incident in 1969 and 1970 when both were charged with suppressing publication of a book criticizing Soka Gakkai, there was an investigation in the National Diet (the legislative branch of the Japanese government).[8] Afterward, Soka Gakkai officially separated itself from Komeito. As the second largest opposition party (after the Japan Socialist Party), Komeito has played an important role in discussing political issues and forming coalition governments.

Our focus on Soka Gakkai, as with Tenrikyo, has been mainly on its formation and early development. Yet, the more recent history of Soka Gakkai includes a reversal that is crucial for appreciating its present situation and future possibilities. In 1991, following an increasingly intensified power struggle between the New Religion Soka Gakkai as a lay organization, and the Buddhist denomination Nichiren Shoshu as the formal parent body and priestly institution, the two bodies permanently separated. From the Nichiren Shoshu viewpoint, this parting was excommunication of a recalcitrant subgroup. From Soka Gakkai's vantage point, their departure from Nichiren Shoshu was voluntary, an active choice to free a lay Buddhist movement from the restraints of an irrelevant and outmoded priestly establishment.[9]

This reversal actually amounts to a double-reversal. Makiguchi founded this movement in 1930 as an educational reform body, under the earliest name

Soka Kyoiku Gakkai, "Kyoiku" for education, in other words, the Value Creation Education Society. Makiguchi began with an educational group, and "backed into" Nichiren Shoshu, in the process dropping "Kyoiku" from the group's name and transforming Soka Gakkai into a lay Buddhist movement. More than a half century later, Soka Gakkai has "backed out of" Nichiren Shoshu, retaining its name and status as a lay religious organization (but of course not reverting to an educational mission). At this point it does not seem likely that these two bodies will renew their affiliation; it is more probable that Soka Gakkai will demonstrate its organizational strength by existing and thriving outside the umbrella of Nichiren Shoshu.

The true test of a New Religion is not just its initial ability to make the transition from the original founder to an institutionalized structure, but its enduring power and flexibility to adapt and even transform its institutional character to survive under changing circumstances. Both Tenrikyo and Soka Gakkai have encountered and survived varying political and social conditions through their ingenuity and resilience in the face of adversity: as in most human endeavors, past success is the best predictor of future success, and the track record of these two groups shows great promise for their prospects.

THE SIGNIFICANCE OF THE NEW RELIGIONS: OLD WINE IN NEW BOTTLES

The lessons of Tenrikyo and Soka Gakkai throw much light on the New Religions. For example, we remember that Tenrikyo moved from charismatic leadership of a living *kami* to a large-scale organization. Soka Gakkai also has had charismatic leadership, but its primary focus has been on the *Lotus Sutra;* this demonstrates the ability to revive a traditional sacred treasure and develop a large-scale religious organization around it. This is like putting old wine in new bottles: the old wine is Nichiren and his interpretation of the *Lotus Sutra;* the new bottle is the lay organization of Soka Gakkai. The "old bottles" of organized religion have tended to break apart under the pressures of modern life, especially in cities where secularism and alienation are high. The dilemma of balancing "old" and "new" in such a modern situation is whether traditional religions or the newer movements can speak more meaningfully to human lives.[10]

NOTES

1. Susumu Shimazono, "In the Wake of Aum: The Formation and Transformation of a Universe of Belief," *Japanese Journal of Religious Studies,* vol. 22, no. 3–4 (Fall 1995), pp. 381–415. This article is included in a volume of essays, *Religion and Social Crisis in Japan: Understanding Japanese Society through the Aum Affair,* eds. Robert J. Kisala and Mark R. Mullins (Houndmills: Palgrave, 2001). The controversy has resulted in a number of books on the subject: Ian Reader, *Religious Violence in Contemporary Japan* (Honolulu:

University of Hawai'i, 2000); Helen Hardacre, *Aum Shinrikyo and the Japanese Media: The Pied Piper Meets the Lamb of God* (New York: East Asian Institute, Columbia University, 1995); Haruki Murakami, *Underground: The Tokyo Gas Attack and the Japanese Psyche,* trans. Alfred Birnbaum and Philip Gabriel (London: The Harvill Press, 2000); Robert J. Lifton, *Destroying the World to Save It: Aum Shinrikyo, Apocalyptic Violence, and the New Global Terrorism* (New York: Metropolitan Books, 1999).

2. *A Short History of Tenrikyo* (Tenri, Japan: Tenrikyo Kyokai Honbu, 1956), pp. 79–80.

3. Ibid., p. 158.

4. For an "inside" account of one split from Tenrikyo, see Yoshi Sugihara and David W. Plath, *Sensei and His People: The Building of a Japanese Commune* (Berkeley: University of California, 1969).

5. *Japanese-English-Buddhist Dictionary,* "Shakubuku-shoju" (Tokyo: Daito Shuppansha, 1965), p. 267; Hisao Inagaki, *A Dictionary of Japanese Buddhist Terms,* 3d ed., "Shakubuku" (Kyoto: Nagata Bunshodo, 1988), p. 286.

6. Soka Gakkai prefers a gentler phrasing: "A method of propagating Buddhism by refuting another's attachment to heretical views and thus leading him to the correct teaching." See "shakubuku," *A Dictionary of Buddhist Terms and Concepts,* 1st ed. (Tokyo: Nichiren Shoshu International Center, 1983), pp. 376–77.

7. See the "Organizational Chart" in *The Nichiren Shoshu Sokagakkai* (Tokyo: Seikyo Press, 1966), p. 19. This 1966 publication and the organizational chart describe Soka Gakkai during its early period of rapid growth, when it was still formally part of the Buddhist denomination Nichiren Shoshu.

8. This episode is described in Hirotatsu Fujiwara, *I Denounce Soka Gakkai,* trans. Worth C. Grant (Tokyo: Nishin Hodo, 1970).

9. For several views of this controversial split, see Jane Hurst, "A Buddhist Reformation in the Twentieth Century: Causes and Implications of the Conflict between the Soka Gakkai and the Nichiren Shoshu Priesthood," in David Machacek and Bryan Wilson, eds., *Global Citizens: the Soka Gakkai Buddhist Movement in the World* (Oxford: Oxford University, 2000), pp. 67–96; and Daniel A. Metraux, "The Dispute Between the Soka Gakkai and the Nichiren Shoshu Priesthood: A Lay Revolution against a Conservative Clergy," *Japanese Journal of Religious Studies,* vol. 19, no. 4 (Dec. 1992), pp. 325–36.

10. A volume of essays discussing various aspects of these newer movements is *New Religions,* ed. Nobutaka Inoue, trans. Norman Havens (Tokyo: Institute for Japanese Culture and Classics, Kokugakuin University, 1991). For their presence outside Japan, see *Japanese New Religions in Global Perspective,* ed. Peter B. Clarke (Richmond, Surrey: Curzon, 2000).

18

❦

Religion in
Postwar Japan

When World War II ended in 1945, a new age dawned in Japan. For the first time in history the nation had been defeated, her soil occupied. These events precipitated a reversal of the nationalistic and militaristic mood that prevailed from 1868 to 1945. All areas of Japanese life, including religion, changed remarkably after World War II.[1] And even after more than a half century, it is safe to say Japanese religion still has not fully recovered from the disorientation and reorganization brought about by the defeat. One of the ironies of modern Japan, and Japanese religion, is that most Japanese living today were born after the war, and have little knowledge of or interest in World War II (partly due to the Ministry of Education's refusal to approve textbooks critical of the war), but the spiritual buildup toward the war and the reaction to defeat were crucial for the reshaping of the religious landscape. In this chapter we will survey Shinto, Buddhism, Christianity, and New Religions in the postwar period; in the next chapter we will comment on recent changes in Japanese life and see how they help us to understand the religious situation.

SHINTO: DISESTABLISHMENT
AND POPULAR DISFAVOR

The most obvious religious effect of the defeat was the official disestablishment of Shrine Shinto by order of the Allied Occupation forces. The emperor, whose voice had never before been broadcast, announced defeat over the radio. In 1947 he issued a public statement that he was not a *kami* or god but was only human.[2] The Occupation forces did not intend to change Shinto insofar as it was a religion of the people but insisted that neither Shinto nor any other religion should be the tool of militaristic nationalism. This immediately brought an end to Shinto's "nonreligious" status and special role in government. In effect, Shinto shrines throughout the country once more were treated as religious institutions, the same as Buddhist temples and Christian churches. Shinto priests ceased being government officials, and government subsidies to shrines stopped. As Muraoka has interpreted this postwar change of events, "the removal of all state prerogatives was a heavy blow for Shrine Shinto," but "this was a just and inevitable retribution."[3] Even more important was the removal of religious nationalism from school textbooks and the mass media.

It is hard to fathom what happened in the minds of the Japanese people at the time of defeat and thereafter. During the war some Westerners, on the basis of the tenacious resistance of Japanese soldiers and civilians, and their refusal to surrender, predicted that every Japanese town would put up a last-ditch defense. (This perception informed the American government's decision to use atomic bombs to end the war quickly.)[4] Yet after the emperor's broadcast announcing surrender, there was almost no resistance. Even in defeat the emperor's authority commanded obedient respect. "What defeat showed, to the astonishment of many, was how quickly all the years of ultranationalistic indoctrination could be sloughed off."[5]

Shinto had profited the most from government support between 1868 and 1945, so of course it suffered the most from the removal of support. Although Shinto experienced great financial loss, even greater was the loss of the people's sympathy. When they lamented the war's destruction, many tended to blame Shinto as the tradition most closely allied to the war machine. Another setback was the disorganization of Shinto. Government control of Shinto before World War II was disliked by some Shinto priests and parishioners, but at least it welded Shinto into a national religious force. After the war there was complete religious freedom for the first time. Any religious group was able to organize and qualify for tax exemption as a religious body. Ironically, this meant even greater freedom for local Shinto shrines. As was mentioned in Chapter 15, in the early 1900s some local groups had been forced by the government to abandon small shrines and "merge" with centralized village shrines. After World War II, many local groups were free to reestablish the shrines they had been forced to abandon. These reestablished shrines preserve some of the close relationship to village groups and regional customs that have been the heritage of Shinto for centuries.[6] Most of the postwar Shinto shrines reorganized as the Association of

Shinto Shrines, but the prewar groups of Sect Shinto declared their independence from Shinto control. Both Shinto shrines and Buddhist temples were divested of much of their land holdings, removing a main source of income.

A delicate problem of the postwar period has been the exact relationship of the emperor to the state and to Shinto. There has been disagreement about what it means for the emperor to be the symbolic head of the state. On the one hand, are those few who would like to abolish the emperor even as a symbol; on the other hand, are those few who would like to give the emperor a more important role in government. In the middle are the majority, who seem to be indifferent or passively respectful (but not worshipful) toward this national symbol.[7] The emperor's rituals are considered his private religious activity, but the ceremonies' great expense is a troublesome matter. (This controversy surfaced publicly in 1989 with the death of the Showa Emperor and disagreements over the arrangements for and financing of the funeral; a similar controversy surrounded the enthronement ceremonies for his son, the present emperor.) Also, Shinto priests feel that the emperor still should function as the chief priest of Shinto and the nation. A further complication is the problem of state financing for certain shrines, such as Ise, which until 1945 received state funds.

Yasukuni Shrine in Tokyo, founded in early Meiji times and developed into a national shrine for the war dead, has been a controversial institution since 1945. Some people have favored more state support for the shrine, even financial support, seeing the shrine as a harmless patriotic monument, somewhat like the Tomb of the Unknown Soldier in America.[8] Others have feared that explicit state support for the Yasukuni Shrine would be the first step toward reviving the unity of state and religion that gave rise to ultranationalism and militarism before and during World War II. People who object to state support of the Yasukuni Shrine point out that the Tomb of the Unknown Soldier is a poor comparison because it is not a religious institution, does not have priests in attendance, and does not conduct religious rites.[9]

BUDDHISM: THE CONTINUING
QUEST FOR RENEWAL

Although most Buddhist sects had supported the war effort, they did not suffer as much as Shinto shrines from the stigma of defeat. Nevertheless, Buddhist institutions were hard pressed due to the loss of temple lands, and Buddhist sects, too, felt the disorganization that resulted from complete religious freedom. Even after 1868 the lines between main temples and subtemples had been strictly maintained, and before World War II the government had required all Buddhist temples to conform to narrowly defined denominational ties. The Allied Occupation removed such government restrictions. After 1945, temple affiliations became more flexible. Additionally, when land revenues were lost and branch temples became financially independent, the Buddhist sects' headquarters were at a disadvantage. These are some of the practical problems, but basically Buddhist leaders had not fully responded to the earlier voices calling for spiritual renewal, and they continued the Tokugawa heritage of hereditary family affiliation to parish temples. The primary religious function for Buddhist priests and temples was to provide funeral and memorial services for family members, and also to hold annual celebrations and sell amulets, but opportunities for the spiritual development of the people were few.

Of course, the sense of need for religious renewal was not limited to Buddhism, but was recognized throughout Japanese society, especially after the war. Even during the war, graffiti on the wall of a public toilet asking for various reforms went so far as to include religious reform, and this lone voice may have spoken for many who remained silent: ". . . in my opinion, individuals should find God for themselves."[10]

Since the war, some renewal of Buddhism has taken place through increasing participation by laypeople, and there has been some attempt to change Buddhism from the traditional affiliation by families to a more personal commitment. (One Pure Land denomination used the slogan "From a Household Religion to a Personal Religion.")[11] The challenge for Buddhism to deal with changing family patterns, particularly the trend away from extended families and toward nuclear families, is documented by a recent sociological study, which reports that in one metropolitan residential area of white-collar workers, "only about 30% of the nuclear families as against 90% of the extended families have Buddhist altars in their homes."[12] However, attempts to change the pattern of hereditary family membership in Buddhist temples ("household Buddhism") have been the exception rather than the rule, and typically parish temples have continued their major activity of funerals and rites for the dead. The national expenditure for the Buddhist funeral "industry" is so great that it ranks with the annual revenue for major corporations.

The major postwar innovations for temple Buddhism (not unlike those for Shrine Shinto) are priests taking outside jobs (such as part-time teaching jobs) and the use of temple buildings for financial gain by such means as kindergarten classes and tourism. Some intellectuals, especially the internationally known scholars of Buddhism, have actively propagated the message of Buddhism as a pan-Asian or even a worldwide religion, and one of Japan's oldest Buddhist sects has become a proponent of international peace activism.[13] Still, such activities have had little effect on the lives of Japanese Buddhists or the patterns of Buddhist temples. In the postwar period, the greatest popular interest in Buddhism has been in the New Religions based on Buddhism (such as Soka Gakkai and Rissho Koseikai).

CHRISTIANITY: THE PROBLEMS
OF DENOMINATIONALISM

After World War II, widespread dissatisfaction with Shinto and general indifference toward Buddhism might have provided a great opportunity for Christianity to gain converts. Such was not the case. Christianity was somewhat suppressed by the government during the war years, but because it was led by

Japanese ministers without the aid of foreign missionaries, it was never banned. Christian churches suffered a greater proportional loss from wartime bombing than Shinto shrines and Buddhist temples because most Christian churches were in large cities. The reentrance of foreign missionaries after the war did not result in the conversion of many Japanese. Christianity was still at a distinct disadvantage because of denominational splintering, theological disagreement, and the perennial problem of developing a truly Japanese Christianity. To this day, Christianity is viewed by most Japanese as a foreign religion. Furthermore, the crisis of defeat forced both Shinto and Buddhism to reconsider their basic foundations, giving them greater strength in meeting Christianity intellectually.

No longer was there a simple choice between native and foreign philosophies of life. Long before the war, Japanese intellectuals had become acquainted with Western agnostic and atheistic philosophies, and the extreme crisis of the postwar years pushed some to the materialistic philosophy of Marxism. In fact, in Japan, Christianity and Marxism possess some unusual similarities. Both tend to appeal to intellectuals on the basis of a universal message seeking to transform the Japanese social order.[14] Especially in the postwar period, some Christians and Marxists have cooperated in opposing right-wing political movements such as the attempt to restore pre–World War II nationalism. Immediately after the war there was a serious food shortage, followed by the combined problems of reconstruction and inflation. These conditions did not make the ethical monotheism of Christianity any more attractive to the Japanese than it had been before the war, and most of those who made a decision of faith as individuals turned to the New Religions. In postwar Japan, Christians still represent less than 1 percent of a total population of more than 100 million.

They represent a tiny minority in Japan's religious world, but Japanese Christians have been very creative. On the intellectual side, Japanese Christian theologians have studied in the best North American and European schools, and not only are conversant with the latest trends in Western theology, but recently have advocated a truly "Japanese theology" not dependent on Western models. On the popular level, charismatic leaders relied on their own personal religious experience to boldly blend Christianity with Japanese customs and practices, forming Christian movements more comparable to the New Religions than to the Western-style denominations. These theological tendencies and the popular movements are attempts to soften or eliminate the stigma of "foreignness" that has always disadvantaged Christian missions in Japan.[15]

THE POSTWAR BOOM OF NEW RELIGIONS

Whereas Buddhism and Confucianism dominated the Tokugawa period, and Shinto dominated the period from 1868 to 1945, the New Religions have captured the limelight since World War II, for several reasons. First, they, more than any other religious tradition, escaped the stigma of association with the nation's defeat. Although the leaders of some New Religions supported the war effort, a number of these groups came into conflict with the government's control of religion both before and during the war. Several leaders of New Religions had suffered through wartime incarceration as "subversives," and their groups, persecuted during the war, emerged almost victorious amid the general sense of defeat. Thus the religions that sprang up after the war made a clean break with the recent past and looked forward with hope to the future. (Depending on how they are counted, several hundred New Religions have arisen since the war.)

Second, the new movements profited the most from religious freedom after World War II. They were able to attain complete independence for the first time, and the "old" religions of Shinto and Buddhism were forced to compete with them on their level of popular appeal because of the loss of revenue from land and government support.

Several other reasons can be advanced for the phenomenal success of the new groups in postwar Japan. The newer movements, by virtue of the fact that they were new, possessed no commitment to outmoded forms and spoke immediately to the nation's religious needs. In the postwar period, the population balance reversed from being 70 percent rural and 30 percent urban, to 70 percent urban and 30 percent rural. Great mobility tended to dissolve traditional ties to Shinto and Buddhism, and made joining a New Religion all the more likely. Moreover, the New Religions represented a thoroughly Japanese response to the many challenges, spiritual and material, posed by the recent defeat at the hands of foreign powers. Equally important, the new movements reflect all the persistent themes in Japanese religious history. This helps to explain how a single New Religion—Soka Gakkai—during just one decade—the 1950s—could develop a membership larger than the total number of all Christians (Catholic, Protestant, and Orthodox combined) after almost a century of intense missionary efforts. Another point of strength was the tendency for the New Religions to be open and accepting, often taking the best features from Buddhism, Shinto, and even Christianity. A theme emphasized by some of the new movements is the unity of all religion. Not only do they make universalistic statements about religion, but some even send missionaries abroad to spread their faith.

There is considerable speculation about the future role of the New Religions in Japan. Some people fear their growth and increasing power, especially the largest New Religion, Soka Gakkai, and the political party it established, Komeito. The implication of Aum Shinrikyo, a small New Religion (or New-New Religion) in the 1995 poison gas attack in the Tokyo subway raised again, much more urgently, suspicions and fears of new religious movements. There were public demands to disband Aum Shinrikyo, and the government passed legislation for stricter regulations and supervision over religious organizations.

If we take the long view of more than a hundred and fifty years of New Religions, however, they were frequently the target of government persecution and prosecution until 1945, and only rarely were a threat to the public and the state. Indeed, most of the New Religions most of the time have promoted some of the same family, work, and national values as traditional religion—they have just been more effective in the context of voluntary organizations. Inevitably the New Religions themselves have become fully institutionalized, for which they have been criticized by some "New-New" Religions. The New Religions have developed to the point that, for all practical purposes, they now constitute organized, or "established," religions like the older Buddhist and Shinto groups: after World War II they formed their own Association of New Religions. Most of these groups have great financial resources and impressive headquarters in Tokyo or at religious centers elsewhere.

At the same time, it is worth noting that some of the recent movements are not complete religious organizations. For example, members of many New Religions still rely on Shinto marriage ceremonies conducted by Shinto priests, and funeral and interment ceremonies conducted by Buddhist priests. Thus, it would be a mistake to think that Buddhism and Shinto are defunct. Japanese history shows many cases where a slumbering tradition was revitalized, and it is quite likely that, as time passes, the differences between new and old religions will diminish. The newer movements may become more highly organized and institutionalized, and Buddhism and Shinto may adopt some of their successful activities (such as discussion groups) and organizational forms (such as lay participation).

NOTES

1. For a work emphasizing the theme of continuity between prewar and postwar Japan, see *Total War and 'Modernization,'* ed. Yasushi Yamanouchi et al. (Ithaca, NY: East Asia Program, Cornell University, 1998).

2. See Daniel C. Holtom, *Modern Japan and Shinto Nationalism: A Study of Present-Day Trends in Japanese Religions,* rev. ed. (Chicago: University of Chicago, 1947; reprint ed., New York: Paragon Books Reprint Corp., 1963), pp. 215–18, for a translation of the "Directive for the Disestablishment of State Shinto"; see pp. 219–20 for a translation of the "Imperial Rescript on the Reconstruction of New Japan," including the so-called renunciation of divinity. These translations can also be found in my *Religion in the Japanese Experience,* 2d ed., pp. 38–44. For the role of Allied Occupation staff in this so-called renunciation, and its different significance as perceived by the Occupation officials and the emperor and his advisors, see Dower, *Embracing Defeat,* pp. 308–18. Dower says that "Neither on this occasion, nor later, did the emperor unequivocally repudiate his alleged descent from the gods" (p. 316). Dower has told the complicated tale of how the Occupation helped preserve the office of emperor and the actual person of the Showa Emperor (Hirohito) as the "symbol of the country," thereby absolving him from responsibility for the war and removing him from the threat of trial with war criminals—in order to support the Occupation policy of controlling the country and fostering "democracy."

3. Tsunetsugu Muraoka, "Separation of State and Religion in Shinto: Its Historical Significance," in his *Studies in Shinto,* pp. 239–40.

4. The atomic bombing of Hiroshima and Nagasaki, certainly one of the most controversial events of World War II (and some would say of all times), has generated a huge body of materials describing and interpreting its military, political, legal, ethical, and humanitarian significance. For a critical treatment of Hiroshima and the ambiguities of the "memory" of Hiroshima—questioning both the consideration of "crime against humanity" on the part

of the United States and a major tendency in Japan to view Hiroshima as "national victimology"—see Lisa Yoneyama, *Hiroshima Traces,* p. 13; the bibliography contains a comprehensive list of English and Japanese writing on Hiroshima and atomic bombing.

5. Dower, *Embracing Defeat,* p. 122. Almost overnight, *kamikaze* pilots became black market entrepreneurs: "Even survivors from suicide squadrons, who had been prepared to take off on their sublime one-way missions when the war ended, leaped into the wild scramble for goods" (p. 59).

6. See Sakurai, "Tradition and Change in Local Community Shrines." For the dynamics of a contemporary shrine, see John K. Nelson, *A Year in the Life of a Shinto Shrine* (Seattle: University of Washington, 1996).

7. Scholars, politicians, and journalists in Japan have tended to avoid the touchy subject of the emperor: Norma Field describes the circumstances of the mayor of Nagasaki who, due to his remarks including the Showa Emperor (Hirohito) in his own admission of responsibility for the war, was shot in a failed assassination attempt. See her *In the Realm of a Dying Emperor,* (New York: Random House, 1991), pp. 177–266, which takes the emperor's death as the occasion for a critical look at contemporary Japanese society. A number of recent Western works have focused on the life and role of Emperor Hirohito, especially his involvement in and responsibility for the Pacific War of 1931–45. For two of these studies, see Herbert P. Bix, *Hirohito and the Making of Modern Japan* (New York: HarperCollins, 2000), and T. Fujitani, *Splendid Monarchy: Power and Pageantry in Modern Japan* (Berkeley: University of California, 1996). See also Peter Nosco, ed., *The Emperor System and Religion in Japan,* vol. 17, no. 2–3, of *Japanese Journal of Religious Studies* (June–Sept. 1990).

8. See the viewpoint and personal comments of Terumichi Kiyama, a main priest of Yasukuni Shrine, "Meeting at Yasukuni Shrine," in Haruko Taya Cook and Theodore F. Cook, *Japan at War: An Oral History* (New York: The New Press, 1992), pp. 447–53. For the official view of Yasukuni Shrine, see the translation by Richard Gardner, "Nationalistic Shinto: A Child's Guide to Yasukuni Shrine," in *Religions of Japan in Practice,* ed. George J. Tanabe, Jr. (Princeton: Princeton University, 1999), pp. 334–39. This "guide" is a "defense" of war: "to protect the independence of Japan and the peace of Asia surrounding Japan, there were . . . several wars with foreign countries" (p. 337); and "The gods of Yasukuni Shrine gave their noble lives on the battlefield with the hope that Japan might continue forever in peace and independence. . . ." (p. 339).

9. See David M. O'Brien, *To Dream of Dreams: Religious Freedom and Constitutional Politics in Postwar Japan* (Honolulu: University of Hawai'i, 1996), for detailed descriptions and analyses of court cases about religious freedom.

10. Ienaga, *The Pacific War,* p. 226.

11. Kiyomi Morioka, "The Changing Family and Buddhism in Postwar Japan," in his *Religion in Changing Japanese Society* (Tokyo: University of Tokyo, 1975), p. 11.

12. Ibid., p. 106.

13. Tendai Buddhist leaders have sponsored the Hieizan Peace Summit, started in 1987 and held annually. For a comprehensive treatment of the relationship between Japanese religions (especially New Religions) and the ideal of peace, see Robert Kisala, *Prophets of Peace: Pacifism and Cultural Identity in Japan's New Religions* (Honolulu: University of Hawai'i, 1999).

14. See Norihisa Suzuki, "Christianity," in *Japanese Religion,* ed. Ichiro Hori, p. 73.

15. For a recent treatment of Japanese theology, see Yasuo Furuya, ed. and trans., *A History of Japanese Theology* (Grand Rapids, MI: Eerdmans, 1997); for a look at "indigenous Christianity," see Mark Mullins, *Christianity Made in Japan: A Study of Indigenous Movements* (Honolulu: University of Hawai'i, 1998); for comments on "Japanese Christianity," see David Reid, *New Wine: The Cultural Shaping of Japanese Christianity* (Berkeley, CA: Asian Humanities, 1991).

19

❦

Religious Life in Contemporary Japan

In the previous chapter, we surveyed the general situation of *institutional* religion in postwar Japan as religious organizations attempted to recover from the physical and spiritual ravages of World War II. But this survey of institutional strength is only one aspect of the contemporary religious scene; it excludes the personal and individual dimension of religion. For example, a question that Westerners often ask is whether the Japanese are religious. This question refers to personal religious commitment and cannot be answered with a simple "yes" or "no." By looking briefly at interpretations of this question, we can gain a better vantage point for understanding religious life in Japan today.

ARE THE JAPANESE RELIGIOUS?

When Westerners ask whether the Japanese are religious, they may be wondering whether the Japanese are religious in the same way that Americans and Europeans are religious. And this, in turn, begs the question of whether or not the Japanese belong exclusively to one religious organization as a Protestant, Catholic, or Jewish person would. For most Japanese, the answer must be "no," for usually they participate in several religious traditions. Because, at least in theory, all the families living in the vicinity of a local Shinto shrine may be considered "parishioners" of that shrine, and because most families have some

214

ties to a parish Buddhist temple, the same family may be counted as belonging to both Shinto and Buddhism. Thus the number of people "belonging" to any of the religions in Japan may be almost twice as large as the nation's total population. In the modern period, the exceptions to the general practice of simultaneous participation in several religions are members of some New Religions, and Christians, who choose not to participate in other religious traditions.

Another implicit aspect of the question about the religiosity of the Japanese is how they identify themselves religiously. An American might say, "I am Christian" or "I am Jewish," or might be more specific and say he or she is Catholic, or a member of a Protestant denomination, or a member of a Judaic branch. However, in Japan a person is not likely to identify exclusively with one religion unless he or she is a Christian, or a member of some New Religions.

An individual Japanese is not apt to say, "I am Shinto" or "I am Buddhist" (or even "I am both Shinto and Buddhist"). If a Japanese person is put in a situation where the direct question "What is your religion?" must be answered, the response may be, "I have no religion." This does not necessarily mean that the person is against or indifferent to religion; it may simply mean that he or she does not identify exclusively with one religion the way a Christian or Jew might. Even if the Japanese person responds, "I am a Buddhist," the answer does not necessarily mean that the person is committed to exclusive affiliation with (and regular attendance at) one Buddhist institution. More likely it means that the person's family has a *butsudan* (Buddhist altar) and observes Buddhist rituals for the family ancestors in their home.

A contrast of Japanese with Muslims may highlight some hallmarks of religious identification that do *not* apply to Japanese people. For example, most Muslim students on American campuses identify themselves religiously as Muslims. Not only will they state, "I am a Muslim," but they may specify the meaning of this affirmation with a creedal statement about belief in Allah, and they will implement the belief by attending weekly prayers on Friday; also they observe dietary restrictions against eating pork.

It is in this sense that most Japanese are *not* religious: they do not identify with a particular creed, do not attend weekly religious services, and do not observe religiously based dietary restrictions. (Nor do they observe any religiously based customs of dress, such as are seen in some religions.) On large American campuses it is now common to see special buildings for Muslim students to observe religious prayers. But even if the number of Japanese students in Western countries greatly increased, we would not expect to see special buildings for religious use by Japanese students, because Japanese religion does not readily lend itself to these kinds of creedal and institutional forms.

Japanese religion is not usually expressed in creeds (which are more characteristic of monotheistic religions), and it is not organized into exclusive organizations. Therefore, as we have seen, a simple counting of members is misleading. Also, standard questionnaires on religion, used in Europe and America, are not always relevant in Japan. Questions about whether the Japanese "believe in God" cannot be answered with a simple "yes" or "no," or given a numerical percentage. Instead, one must recognize that the Japanese do not emphasize belief in God in the way that monotheistic religions do. If we want to understand Japanese religion, rather than looking at it through "monotheistic" eyeglasses, we should try to view it in terms of Japanese notions such as *kami*.

It may be worth mentioning that posing the right questions about religion is also a problem for Japanese trying to understand Western religion. Recently when I was in Japan studying a New Religion and gave the members a chance to ask me (in Japanese) about American religion, one of the first questions was, "Is it true that Americans don't venerate their ancestors, and if so, why?" This was a difficult question to answer, because the Japanese person assumed that the core of religion is defined by worshiping ancestors, an assumption not found in America. However, the person was eventually satisfied when I explained that in America ancestors do not constitute the central social and religious fact that they do in Japan. In other words, the central religious importance that the Japanese place on ancestors, Americans tend to place on God.

Are the Japanese religious? We might as well ask whether they are social, political, and economical. The answer to all of these questions, obviously, is "yes." The catch, of course, is that the Japanese are religious, social, political, and economical in their own way. Some *general* features of Japanese life are common to all other cultures. For example, Japanese religion, like the religions of all other cultures, consists of symbols, beliefs, and practices that provide an orientation to reality and a means of celebrating participation in that reality— all of which is treasured and handed down to the next generation. Similarly, social, political, and economic aspects of Japanese culture share *general* features with other cultures.

To rephrase the issue: If we say that society has to do with the organization and interaction of human relationships (such as kinship and territorial units), that politics has to do with national identity and the securing and administering of power, that economics has to do with the creation and distribution of wealth—then certainly the Japanese are social, political, and economical. In each of these human dimensions, however, the Japanese have developed distinctive notions and practices.

In the social realm, kinship (family) and group identity have special significance for Japanese. In the political realm, traditional notions of power and authority have led to strong loyalty to political parties and a form of parliamentary government that are distinctively Japanese. In the economic realm, the Japanese have forged their own pattern of cooperation for labor, business, and government. In the religious realm, too, they have created their own particular tradition, with emphasis on notions such as *kami* and nature (and other persistent themes). In other words, all aspects of Japanese culture—the social, economic, political, and religious—share some features with all cultures while maintaining distinctively Japanese characteristics. The heart of the matter, then, is not *whether* the Japanese are religious but *in what way* the Japanese are religious. We should never conclude that the Japanese (or any other people) are not religious just because their beliefs and practices differ from those of our own culture. Such differences should challenge us to seek wider concepts of religion—and society, economics, and politics—that include other cultures as well as our own.

PERSISTENT THEMES IN CONTEMPORARY JAPANESE RELIGION

Two features that Japanese religion shares with all other religions are continuity with the past and discontinuity with the past. In this section we will focus on continuity, in the next section on discontinuity. Perhaps the most convenient way to highlight continuity of contemporary Japanese religion with the past is to investigate the present status of the persistent themes identified in Chapter 2: the closeness of human beings, gods, and nature; the religious character of the family; the significance of purification, rituals, and amulets; the prominence of local festivals and individual cults; the pervasiveness of religion in everyday life; and the intimate bond between religion and the nation.

Even today the age-old pattern of the interrelationship of human beings, the gods, and nature lives on. Although in 1945 the emperor formally renounced his divinity, and although the notion of *kami* is not taken so literally today, the presence of *kami* remains important. New Religions still honor founders and their descendants as living *kami*. The fact that family ancestors still constitute the most widely venerated objects of ritual ceremonies is further testimony to the ease with which men and women bridge the gap to the realm of the *kami*. In Japan the natural environment may be seriously polluted, but nature is still revered and extolled, particularly in graphic art and literature.

The family has changed considerably in recent years but is still considered the basic religious unit. This is evident from the fact that statistics of religious membership are still given in households rather than as individual members. The extended family is not so important as it once was, the nuclear family becoming more important. This change has meant fewer observances before Shinto altars (*kamidana*) and Buddhist altars (*butsudan*) in homes. But family ancestors remain important in the lives and minds of the Japanese people. Contemporary Japanese still have a sense of identity with and obligation toward their family ancestors and usually do not fail to observe memorial services for their immediate ancestors. (Foreigners are advised not to travel on the overcrowded transportation system during the annual season of visiting family graves.)

The proliferation of purifications, rituals, and amulets that Japan once knew has greatly diminished, but many are still found in present-day Japan. Most traditional amulets, although not used as extensively as before, are readily available. At many temples and shrines one can buy time-honored amulets to ensure safe childbirth and avoid sickness. The most widespread contemporary example is the amulet for traffic safety, conspicuously displayed in taxis, buses,

The reflective sticker above the Toyota emblem on the trunk of a car is a "traffic safety" charm from the Omiya Hachiman Shrine. (Tokyo, 1979)

and private cars. This protective device has even been "modernized" in the form of a yellow reflector that is attached with adhesive to the back of an automobile. Another modern variation of amulets is a good-luck amulet to ensure success in school exams, purchased either for oneself or for a family member. Recent surveys show that about half of the Japanese population "often" use amulets, and from 70 percent to 80 percent (depending on the age group) "sometimes" use amulets.[1]

Local festivals have become abbreviated or curtailed, but festivals in cities and regions have prospered. Festivals in small villages have suffered because of the loss of manpower, money, and interest. City and regional festivals that attract tourists have flourished. This trend is influenced and colored by differences in local practice. For example, the widespread festival on November 15 for girls age 3 and 7 and boys age 5 (called Shichi-go-san) was formerly celebrated by parents dressing their children in elaborate traditional clothing and taking them to a nearby Shinto shrine. Recently, ease of travel has made it possible to take children to more distant shrines, and the innovations are as interesting as the continued custom. On November 15, 1979, I visited a mountain shrine an hour south of Tokyo. The cable car from the foot of the mountain to the shrine was free for families participating in the Shichi-go-san festival, and many young girls wore Western formal dresses (such as long velvet dresses) instead of the more costly *kimono*. The "same" festival is celebrated, but perhaps at a distant mountain shrine rather than a neighborhood shrine, and the dress may be "modern" rather than "traditional."

Individual pilgrimage sites or religious centers reflect the same pattern: some centers are languishing, while others are bustling and wealthy. The visitor to Japan who has extra time at Narita airport outside Tokyo may verify the popularity of such "holy places" by taking a taxi to the nearby Narita-san, a temple complex dedicated to the popular Buddhist divinity Fudo. This "traditional" pilgrimage site for venerating Fudo is complete with "modern" lodging facilities. (As we will note later, "traditional" and "modern" are closely associated in contemporary Japan.)

As social and economic conditions have changed, probably the persistent theme that has changed most is the role of religion in everyday life. In the past, religious observances were closely tied to the cultivation of rice by hand; now that most rice is transplanted by machine, such festivals are rarely seen. Radical changes in occupations and crafts have also meant a sharp drop in religious activities related to specific occupations. However, Japanese religion is still very much related to the problems of daily life. As previously noted, probably the most popular amulet in all Japan is the one for traffic safety. And in a recent nationwide questionnaire distributed to members of a New Religion, for "motive of joining" many replied with answers such as healing of sickness and resolving family difficulties. The New Religions have brought problems such as financial and marital difficulties into the context of religious counseling, especially in small discussion groups. In other words, as the circumstances of daily life have changed, so have the means of relating religion to daily life.[2]

The intimate bond between Japanese religion and the Japanese nation lives on today, though not so much in explicit terms as in implicit understandings. Not all Japanese accept the literal or historical account of the divine founding of Japan, yet many (including intellectuals) have argued for the "uniqueness" of things Japanese—which indirectly expresses the sacredness or superiority of Japan and the Japanese, and echoes in modern idiom the ancient mythological themes.[3] Similarly, some would interpret the high degree of cooperation between labor, business, and government in Japan as a religious commitment because such cooperation calls for a sacrifice of individual benefit for the good of the nation as a whole. Usually this tie is implicit, but in some cases the tie becomes explicit, as when a Shinto priest "purifies" or dedicates a new airplane for an airline. And conservative religious groups still view filial piety and loyalty to the state as integral parts of worshiping the *kami* and *bodhisattvas*.

As the culture has changed, so has the way in which religion is related to it. Viewed in terms of continuity, however, the themes of Japanese religion are still abundantly present in contemporary Japanese life.

APPROACHES TO RELIGIOUS CHANGE

In the remainder of this chapter, we will examine some major changes Japanese religion has undergone in recent years. This subject is complicated not merely by the complexity of events but also by the varied approaches to the subject of social change generally and religious change specifically. Some approaches are not so profitable for interpreting cultural change in Japan. The tendency to juxtapose too sharply the traditional and the modern wrongly suggests that the two categories are mutually exclusive—as if we would have to step across the boundary of traditional Japan to "enter" modern Japan. Phrased a little differently, this approach assumes that the traditional is an element that is discarded when the modern element is accepted. One Japanese scholar has criticized this artificial division of Japanese culture into "pieces of two kinds" and suggests that "the 'traditional' is one aspect (not element) of the same social body which also has 'modern' features."[4] To the extent that this insight is valid for Japanese culture, it probably holds true for most societies, which are mixtures of traditional and modern aspects. We will better understand change in Japanese culture if we see it as a combination of old and new, not as a replacement of the old with the new.

Another temptation we should resist is the notion that transformations in Japanese culture are simply due to Western influence, or "Westernization." "Modern" Japan is not equatable to "Westernized" Japan. It is true that Western influence, especially American influence, has been very important during the past century and a half. But we should not forget that Japan's shift from an agricultural-rural society to an urban-industrial society started long before Western contact. And Japan's present industrial and commercial organization has been so innovative and effective that Western leaders have become interested in learning lessons from Japan.[5] Therefore, it would be just as misleading to call this process "Japanization" as it would be to put labels such as "Westernization" or "Americanization" on the earlier interaction between Japan and the West. Many of Japan's changes resulted from a combination of Japanese institutions and selected Western borrowings that were modified according to Japanese specifications. In other words, the changes should be seen as a combination of Japanese and Western models, not as a replacement of Japanese models with Western models.

Indeed, transformations are taking place on a global scale that defy any simple labels such as "Westernization" and "Japanization." Two good examples are Japan's fascination with and importation of Walt Disney's artistic creations, culminating in the opening of Tokyo Disneyland in 1983, and America's (and the West's) craze for Japanese comics (*manga*) and animation (*animé*), climaxing in the "invasion" of Nintendo games (especially the handheld electronic Pokemon games) into one out of every three American households. In each case, we can assume that the mythic worldview of the respective countries has been significantly altered, even though we are too close to the event to evaluate exactly how and to what extent the earlier mentality has been transformed. Young people in Japan are blending Disney characters with both Pokemon characters and traditional folklore (such as demons). Young Americans are merging Pokemon characters with Disney characters and their traditional views of fantasy and reality. This does not mean that the result in each country will be the same—even though both Japanese and American young people will have a much more cosmopolitan or international mythology—but it certainly will be quite different from the worldviews of previous generations.[6]

The question of religion and change, also, is a matter that can be approached from widely diverging viewpoints. One view is that religion is part of traditional life, and when people become "modern," they reject the traditional in favor of the "rational," thus causing religion to decline or even disappear. A second view is that religion is an integral part of the worldview and behavior of a culture, so that when the culture undergoes basic change, religion also changes significantly. (And religion is never just passive, but also an active agent of change: when religion undergoes basic change, culture also changes significantly.)

This complex theoretical problem is not limited to Japanese religion, but our discussion must be restricted to the Japanese situation. The first view is not without merit, for it is clear that in some discernible ways (which we will examine shortly), the role of Japanese religion is less than it once was. But this approach is too narrow because it tends to consider the traditional as an element that is replaced by the modern. This makes the first viewpoint less useful than the second: the first tends to look at decline and disappearance, whereas the second looks at change in terms of both loss and reformulation. Although we cannot solve the larger theoretical issue here, the basic point to remember is that the questions we ask determine the answers we get.[7] If we ask, "How has religion declined in modern Japan?" we will tend to learn only about the decline. If, on the other hand, we ask, "How has religion changed as it continued or persisted into the present?" we will also learn how religion has been modified and handed down today. This second view is the approach taken in this chapter, in keeping with the viewpoint throughout this book, of tracing continuity and change in Japanese religious history.

It is well to remember that life is always changing, so the change that we observe in contemporary Japan is not basically different from changes that have occurred throughout Japanese history. All aspects of Japanese life have shifted from time to time, though the transformation that has occurred in the past century or so, especially after World War II, has been more sudden and sweeping. Most immediate were dramatic legal changes after World War II: freedom of religion, greater rights for women, more "democratic" rights overall. The transition from a rural-agricultural lifestyle to an urban-industrial lifestyle, however, had been taking place for a long time, but became more pronounced after the war. For several centuries, people had been leaving the countryside for the city; in the postwar period the population became overwhelmingly urban. Even the "farm" population, which in recent years has been about 5 percent, is only marginally involved in farming; few young and middle-age men consider themselves full-time farmers. Most farm families have full-time and part-time jobs off the farm, and farming itself has become highly mechanized, with the majority of work done by women and older men.

These are the kinds of long-term, basic changes that are important for consideration in connection with religious changes. For as the economic pattern shifts, social institutions such as the family are modified, and the religious activities of the family are altered. Especially in the villages of the countryside such economic and social changes have had a devastating effect on religion. With so many young people migrating to the cities, local festivals become difficult to carry out, especially if a number of participants are required to pull or carry a heavy portable shrine. With economic life following a factory schedule rather than the seasonal rhythms of nature, even the remaining "farm" people can hardly take time off from their side jobs to participate in an agricultural festival. This is one sense in which religion has declined or, we might say, has a lesser role in contemporary Japan: Fewer people participate in local festivals; less time is spent in these festivals; the timing of them is adjusted to fit economic schedules; and the rituals themselves may be abbreviated or even disappear.[8]

TRANSFORMATIONS OF RELIGIOUS LIFE IN CONTEMPORARY JAPAN

The "decline" of traditional village religion can be illustrated by some of the results of two related studies of the village of Kurusu (on the island of Shikoku), carried out first in 1951 and then twenty-four years later. The 1951 date of the initial study is in the immediate postwar period, by which time many "traditional" customs had already been greatly modified or curtailed. Twenty-four years later, in 1975, the pattern of change was much more noticeable. The dominance of the six-day work week is seen in the fact that shrine festivals and memorial services are held mainly on Sundays. The obvious reason, of course, is that this is the only time the villagers have free; in addition, village and family rituals are no longer major junctures of an annual cycle. To put it bluntly, "color television has long outshone the gilt and jollity of village festivals."[9]

Americans sometimes joke that the television set is the central altar in American homes and that family activities and attention center around television viewing. There is reason to believe that in Japan television viewing as a leisure activity is replacing former religious practices in the Japanese family. In 1951, only one out of the twenty Kurusu homes did not have a Shinto-style home altar (*kamidana*); the other homes adorned their altars with various sacred objects and observed daily offerings. In 1975 the altars had not been removed, but few made offerings at the altars except at New Year's. *Kamidana* were included in two new homes that had been built recently, but the old men who built the homes were not sure their children would maintain rituals at the altars.

Buddhist rituals for family ancestors, too, have been adjusted to fit modern convenience. Although the day for a funeral is still determined by the old (Chinese) ceremonial calendar (with "lucky" and "unlucky" days for funerals), the memorials for ancestors are often held not on the annual anniversary of death but on a Sunday that is close to the anniversary. This obviously works a hardship on the Buddhist priest, who must rush from house to house on the Sundays that fall close to the annual ceremony for the dead (*bon*). The three Buddhist priests in the Kurusu area, however, have secular part-time jobs to supplement their religious occupation as priests.

In traditional times, and even as late as 1951, a funeral was conducted mainly by the Buddhist priest and the hamlet association in cooperation with the bereaved family. There was a procession in which the corpse was carried from the home to a nearby cremation ground. Members of the hamlet association lit the funeral pyre and kept the wood fire burning all night long to reduce the body to ashes, which the family would collect the next morning. By 1975 professionalism had taken over. In 1960 an electric crematorium with an oil furnace back-up had been built in a nearby town, and an undertaker assumed many of the functions of the hamlet association, transporting the body in a hearse to the crematorium. Before 1960, the coffin was in the shape of a cask and the body was seated in an upright position (which is the posture of Buddhist devotion or meditation); but since neither the automobile hearse nor the door of the crematorium furnace could accommodate such a tall coffin, corpses have had to be laid out prone in long narrow boxes called "sleeping coffins."[10] In the decades from the 1950s through the 1970s village life and religious practices changed remarkably; in the decades since the 1970s, as Japan has moved through the rapid growth known as the "economic bubble," earlier "traditional" practices have come under increasing pressure (but at the same time the New-New Religions have arisen and flourished).

Events in the village of Kurusu are signs of religion's "decline" in Japan. However, while some forms and aspects of religion are declining, other forms and aspects are growing or increasing. Two examples will be used to illustrate the growth of religion in contemporary Japan—a new festival in Kobe and activities in the New Religions. The Kobe festival may be considered the antithesis of developments in Kurusu.

Whereas local festivals and religious activities are declining and disappearing, some older festivals in cities are becoming more elaborate and a few new

The "bird boat" in a harbor festival of the Shiogama-Matsushima area. A sacred palanquin (omikoshi) can be seen in the center of the boat. (About 1963)

ones are being developed. Kobe, a city of more than a million people just south of Osaka, is well known in the modern period as a major seaport. Kobe has an international flavor; many non-Japanese live there, and the Kobe festival reflects this cosmopolitanism. The Kobe festival was created in 1971 by combining the port festival, which had been held thirty-eight times between 1933 and 1970, and the Kobe carnival, held four times between 1967 and 1970. The inspiration for both festivals had been foreign. The port festival was patterned after the Rose Festival of Portland, Oregon; the Kobe carnival was patterned after the carnival of Rio de Janeiro.

The specifically religious elements of the Kobe festival are overshadowed by the kinds of activities associated with American parades. Shinto priests still pray for the harbor's prosperity, and the mayor presents offerings to the sea, but these activities are not as important as the parade, which features Japanese "queens," and "princesses" from the foreign community residing in Kobe. Like other Japanese cities, Kobe is divided into wards, and each ward has its separate celebrations (especially prayers for traffic safety), which are more traditional in character.

Japanese scholars who have studied the Kobe festival have called it "a festival with anonymous *kami,*" because from the beginning its religious character was underemphasized. The people who plan and carry out the festival actually state that the festival is "without religious ceremonies" and "without divinities." We might be tempted to view it as a kind of secular festival, lacking most of the traditional religious elements. However, the scholars analyzing the festival are quick to point out that it is not the case that traditional "elements were merely withdrawn; instead, new values were attached to the festival in a positive way." These new values are a clear sense of community consciousness (in a city that more than doubled its size in the postwar recov-

Young men preparing to shoulder a sacred palanquin (omikoshi) *in a small local festival in the city of Sendai. (About 1963)*

ery period), the symbol of Kobe as a sort of sacred space replacing traditional *kami,* and internationalism.[11]

If the Kobe festival appears to the non-Japanese reader to be a confused mixture of traditional features and borrowed elements, a similar sense of confusion is found among Japanese participants. Some Japanese liked it because it was full of pleasure, gaiety, and relaxation; they overlooked the surviving religious elements. Some Japanese disliked it, criticizing it as an "imitation of foreign festivals" and claiming that "without the *kami* it is nothing at all like a real festival." Anyone who has seen a more traditional Japanese festival must sympathize with those who criticize the Kobe festival as "*kami*-less," not simply because of its nonreligious character, but also because it tends to be gaudy and commercialized. Such urbanized festivals must be understood in historical perspective. As early as the fifteenth century, "the focus of interest shifted to the para-festival activities"[12] such as parades and public entertainment. Therefore, it would be a mistake to view the Kobe festival merely as an instance of "Westernization." It is not just an occasion of borrowing non-Japanese elements; it may also be seen as an extension of urban festivals dating back five centuries.

The second example of how religion has grown or increased in contemporary Japan is the pattern of activities of the New Religions. In the traditional setting, participation in religious life was narrowly limited to the family, village, and regional centers, with perhaps an occasional pilgrimage to a distant shrine or temple. As we have seen, various factors have weakened family and village institutions and celebrations. A conspicuous change that has taken place in the last century, especially in the postwar period, is the proliferation of religious activities on the part of the New Religions. We have already examined two New Religions—Tenrikyo and Soka Gakkai—which illustrate a typical, dramatic expansion of religious life, both in the nature and in the extent of participation.

In the traditional religious practice of most Buddhist temples and Shinto shrines, people participated mainly by virtue of birth in a residential area and membership in a specific family. A person took part in the rites of a local Shinto shrine because being born in the "parish" of that shrine made him or her a parishioner: the *kami* of the local shrine was a tutelary deity, and the person was under the protection of the *kami*. A person participated in the rites of a Buddhist temple because it was the hereditary family temple of the man's family (married women joined the temple of their husbands). A family was tied to a local Buddhist temple, particularly through funerals and rites for the spirits of the (patrilineal) family dead. (When a person or family had a special need, such as healing, or a request for a specific blessing, an individual went to a temple or shrine known for meeting that need.) The general pattern of residential and hereditary participation contrasts sharply with membership in a New Religion.

To be a member of a New Religion requires a conscious choice, at least for the first generation of believers. Groups formed without regard to kinship and territorial considerations, on the basis of a voluntary decision, are called voluntary organizations. The difference between traditional religious groups and voluntary organizations goes further than a decision to join. In former times there was no nationwide network of believers, and even religious institutions such as temples were only loosely linked. New Religions, however, provide a commonality of belief, practice, and social cohesion that is shared by Japanese throughout the Japanese islands, and in some cases by Japanese and non-Japanese in other countries. Although the number of foreign members is rather small, it is emphasized in the literature of these New Religions because it demonstrates that the Japanese member is part of an international organization, a universal religion.

The sense of identity experienced as a member of a New Religion is quite different from that felt as a member of a traditional family and village (although the two are not mutually exclusive). The core of a New Religion is not found within its large organizational size but in each of its clusters of small groups, which often meet in homes. As we have seen, the small discussion groups are the recruiting base for the New Religions: an acquaintance, friend, or relative extends the invitation and leads in the new member; then a person joins after his or her personal problem has been resolved through the religious faith and practice of the group. The discussion group is more intimate than the traditional village and more democratic than the traditional family. Members of discussion groups meet regularly to share daily experiences, worship, and simple refreshments. Most New Religions provide the social context for counseling about personal problems and the ritual means for specific needs. From time to time, members travel to regional meetings or to national headquarters and sacred centers, where huge, colorful festivals are held. The fact that individuals from distant regions can travel to their New Religion's national headquarters and share social and religious experiences is a remarkable change from the relative isolation of traditional festivals. It represents a dramatic expansion of religious organization on a national, and even international, level.

The example of Kurusu demonstrates religious decline. The Kobe festival and the social organization of the New Religions are examples of religious growth or expansion. These are but three instances of the changes that religion has undergone and continues to undergo in contemporary Japan. They show not only the "more" and "less" of religion in present-day Japan, but also what is new. For example, in the village of Kurusu it is a relatively new pattern for most celebrations to be on Sunday; and even small matters, such as the new shape of the coffin, should not be overlooked. The Kobe festival was deliberately designed as a "new kind of festival." And the very term "*New* Religion" indicates that it is a new form of socio-religious organization.

Two other brief examples of religious innovation show the flexibility of contemporary Japanese religion to create special rituals at both ends of the life cycle: masses for aborted fetuses, and prayers for the aged to have a peaceful death. There had long been special prayers for the repose of the spirits of infants in the case of stillbirth or miscarriage. Then in postwar times the trend was toward smaller families, and abortion became a major means of limiting family size. With the dramatic increase in induced abortions (legalized in 1948) during the past few decades, many women have sought religious rituals after

Byakko Shinkokai, a New Religion stressing international peace, has erected pillars advocating universal peace in Japanese and English. This pillar in front of an old Buddhist building on Mount Oyama gives some idea of the mixture of national tradition and international currents found in contemporary Japan. (1979)

an abortion, and some Buddhist temples have specialized in so-called abortion masses: their temple grounds are literally filled with plaques or small stone statues bought and placed there as part of the service.[13] These rites—and the laypeople and clerical people involved—have their critics, both within the world of religion and in general publications, but their practice continues.

At the other end of the life cycle, the combination of greater longevity and smaller families (and smaller houses or apartments) has made aging grandparents less welcome in their children's homes. One religious response has been the rise to popularity of some Buddhist temples nicknamed "sudden death-temples" (*pokkuri-dera*) where individuals or even busloads of old people go to pray for a quick and painless death (and usually rebirth in Amida's paradise).[14] This is a good example of how changing social conditions have turned a little known custom into a popular practice: old people (especially women) want to avoid being burdens on their families, and to escape prolonged and painful illness. These last two instances are somewhat unusual; however, they point up the fact that religion in Japan is not static but is ever changing.

Organizationally, too, new possibilities are arising. Just as we saw the new wave of internationalism in the Kobe festival, so democracy is another major thrust of postwar Japan. The Otani branch of Pure Land Buddhism, once considered one of the most "feudal" institutions of contemporary Japan, has been wracked by internal change. Partly because of early social reformers, who insisted that the personal faith of *individuals* was the basis for Pure Land Buddhism (rather than ancestral memorial rites for *households*), and partly because of postwar democratic trends, a concerted drive has been made to remove absolute power from a hereditary abbot and place it in the hands of a lay board of devout members. The result has been rather ugly litigation in the civil courts, but whatever the outcome, this bold new move may lay down the precedent for more democratic representation by lay members in the established Buddhist denominations and prepare the way for reorganizing Buddhism on the basis of individual faith.[15]

Another change is the shift from religious to nonreligious patterns. For example, in Kurusu, professional undertakers have assumed part of the Buddhist priests' traditional role. In Kobe, a new kind of festival based on secular models rather than religious foundations was created. The same religious-to-secular change can be seen in more subtle and distant shifts. For example, youth groups and participation in festivals in traditional villages have greatly diminished, but in the city a young man's "initiation" into a business organization in some ways corresponds to the more explicitly religious initiation in the countryside. Companies and offices often observe morning routines of exercises, statements of company slogans, and even singing of company songs. The obvious purpose of such activities is to stress loyalty to the company and encourage hard work. They are not explicitly religious, but they are in some ways analogous to the local village rites for achieving identity. Some companies perform, or have performed, explicitly religious rites.[16]

These brief illustrations of recent and contemporary practices cannot cover the entire range of Japanese religion today, but they may serve to highlight its richness and complexity. However we perceive Japanese religion at present, it is too complex to be seen simply as a move from the "traditional" to the "modern." Nor can it be grasped by relying just on notions of "decline" or "increase." These examples have served their purpose if they help us recognize how incredibly diverse Japanese religion is—in fact, these examples may stretch our minds and persuade us to rethink the usual Western conception of religion as exclusive affiliation to one organization.

NOTES

1. Jan Swyngedouw, "Religion in Contemporary Japanese Society," in Mark Mullins et al., eds., *Religion and Society in Modern Japan: Selected Readings* (Berkeley, CA: Asian Humanities, 1993), p. 53.

2. For a brief description of Shinto ritual purification of a boiler for a factory, and purification of a Kentucky Fried Chicken franchise by a Shinto priest, see Dorinne K. Kondo, *Crafting Selves,* excerpted in my *Religion in the Japanese Experience,* 2d ed., pp. 306–7.

3. An early critique of Nihonjinron, the notion of Japanese uniqueness, is Peter Dale, *The Myth of Japanese Uniqueness* (Oxford: University of Oxford, 1986).

4. Nakane, *Japanese Society,* p. ix.

5. See Ezra F. Vogel, *Japan as Number One: Lessons for America* (Cambridge: Harvard University, 1979; reprint ed., New York: Harper & Row, 1980). With Japan's more recent economic downturn, there is less enthusiasm today for modeling American business after

Japanese business. See Ezra F. Vogel, *Japan As Number One: Revisited* (Singapore: Institute of Southeast Asian Studies, 1986).

6. For Tokyo Disneyland, see Raz, *Riding the Black Ship: Japan and Tokyo Disneyland;* for *manga,* see the work of Frederick L. Schodt, especially *Dreamland Japan: Writings on Modern Manga* (Berkeley, CA: Stone Bridge Press, 1996); for Nintendo, see David Sheff, *Game Over: How Nintendo Zapped an American Industry, Captured Your Dollars, and Enslaved Your Children* (New York: Random House, 1993). A doctoral dissertation waiting to be written is a comparative study of the mythic/fantastic/religious worldviews of Japanese and American (or other Western) children. Japanese and American children, for example, share the imagery of Disney and Pokemon, intermixed with "traditional" elements of religion and cosmology for each respective country. (Even a preschooler in Japan knows how amulets "work," and the significance of ancestors; an American kindergartner knows how sin "works," and the significance of God.) It would be fascinating to learn how Disney/Pokemon/*manga* (and Japanese folk tales) are folded into the Japanese youngster's mental map of the world, and how Pokemon/Disney/cartoons (and Bible stories) are merged in the American child's picture of the cosmos.

7. For a volume of essays discussing the notion of "secularization" and how it might be applied to Japanese religion, see *Proceedings of Tokyo Meeting of the International Conference on Sociology of Religion, 1978;* reprinted in *Japanese Journal of Religious Studies,* vol. 6, no. 1–2 (Mar.–June 1979), pp. 1–386, especially Noriyoshi Tamaru, "The Problem of Secularization," pp. 89–114.

8. For a treatment of "The Festival and the Local Social Order" in recent Tokyo, see Theodore C. Bestor, *Neighborhood Tokyo* (Stanford: Stanford University, 1989), pp. 224–55. Festivals may also be recreated. See Jennifer Robertson, *Native and Newcomer: Making and Remaking a Japanese City* (Berkeley: University of California, 1991), especially "New Festivals for Old," pp. 38–71.

9. R. P. Dore, in Robert J. Smith, *Kurusu: The Price of Progress in a Japanese Village, 1951–1975* (Stanford: Stanford University, 1978), pp. xi–xii.

10. Smith, *Kurusu,* pp. 212–24.

11. Nobutaka Inoue et al., "A Festival with Anonymous Kami," in *Proceedings of Tokyo Meeting of the International Conference on Sociology of Religion, 1978;* reprinted in *Japanese Journal of Religious Studies,* vol. 6, no. 1–2 (Mar.–June 1979), pp. 163–85.

12. Ibid.

13. For this highly controversial practice, see William R. LaFleur, *Liquid Life: Abortion and Buddhism in Japan* (Princeton: Princeton University, 1992), and Helen Hardacre, *Marketing the Menacing Fetus in Japan* (Berkeley: University of California, 1997). This controversy has sparked some lively debates; see the series of exchanges between George J. Tanabe and LaFleur in *Japanese Journal of Religious Studies,* vol. 21, no. 4 (Dec. 1994), pp. 437–40, and vol. 22, no. 1–2 (Spring 1995), pp. 185–200.

14. See Fleur Woss, "*Pokkuri*-Temples and Aging: Rituals for Approaching Death," in Mark R. Mullins et al., eds., *Religion & Society in Modern Japan,* pp. 191–202.

15. For an early discussion of this dispute, see Gerald Cooke, "Traditionalist Buddhist Sects and Modernization in Japan," *Japanese Journal of Religious Studies,* vol. 1, no. 4 (Dec. 1974), pp. 267–330; for an overview of postwar Buddhist developments, see Kasahara, ed., *A History of Japanese Religion* Chapter 23, "The Established Religions Today," especially pp. 586–93.

16. See the excerpted materials on religious values in blue collar and white collar work settings, in my *Religion in the Japanese Experience,* 2d ed., pp. 298–307.

20

❧

Conclusion:
The Challenge for
Japanese Religion

We have viewed Japanese religion through three major historical periods, but the story does not end here. Throughout this span of several thousand years, Japanese religion developed a distinctive tradition, yet it also underwent significant change. It is difficult for historians to predict the future, but the best basis for discussing the future prospects of Japanese religion is a review of the recent transformations and their implications for continuity and innovation.

Contemporary Japan presents a complex challenge to every tradition and form of religion. Both Shinto and Japanese Buddhism developed in the context of a premodern culture and were closely related to an agricultural lifestyle (as well as to income from land). As the nation became increasingly industrialized and urbanized, both religions have been tested by changing conditions. The heart of Shinto, defined by agrarian rhythms of planting and harvesting, is threatened in an industrial-urban setting. Buddhism is hard hit by social mobility, which has upset its parish system. The economic base of such institutions is uneven: there is great disparity in the financial condition of individual shrines and temples. Those that depended mainly on government subsidy or income from land have suffered financially, and some have disappeared (especially in the rural areas). In contrast, some temples and shrines flourish because of other sources of participation and income. Some receive money by virtue of being sites of popular devotion and pilgrimage. Those that are older historical landmarks or are located in scenic resort areas draw more money from visitors who put leisure, sightseeing, and vacationing ahead of religious devotion and practice.[1] One might expect that Buddhism and Shinto will reorganize on the basis of a more dynamic faith, recruiting individual members and developing new devotional activities, imitating the recent success of the New Religions. However, more than a half century after the momentous changes brought about by the end of World War II, it is still not clear what religious leaders are willing and able to do to reconsider and reshape their practices and institutions.[2]

Some Shinto and Buddhist leaders are investigating these problems. Shinto scholars especially are probing the meaning of Japanese culture in an attempt to maintain the Shinto heritage in the modern world. Buddhist scholars have become more active in the worldwide Buddhist movement. The New Religions are Japanese at heart, but some are making an earnest bid to become world religions. Taoism and Confucianism are inconspicuous survivals within other traditions, popular beliefs, and (for Confucianism) social values. Folk religion is still important, but its influence has been severely attenuated by industrialization and urbanization. A general dilemma is the movement away from religious practice and toward secular interests.

But we should not make too much of the "modern" dilemma of religion— already by the beginning of the Tokugawa period, growing cities and expanding commercialism were shifting attention to the glitter of city life, which provided both secularism and hedonism as strong competitors to traditional religion.[3] In the twentieth century, industrialism and urbanization experienced unprecedented growth, and secularism became much more pervasive. Religious devotion remained strong in the countryside, but indifference to organized religion became a fact of city life. To a certain extent, the New Religions have capitalized on this indifference, attracting the bored or troubled urban worker (or homemaker) with the promise of a vital message able to solve the immediate human problems of everyday existence. Yet, even the New Religions are unable to change the nature of city life. For example, leisure is a problem in any modern city, and the Japanese man (and, increasingly, the Japanese woman) in the street is likely to spend much idle time (and much loose cash) in a *pachinko* parlor, a kind of slot-machine gallery. Many people with nothing useful to do have little interest in religion.

On the other hand, many intellectuals and writers have gone beyond indifference to religion to express a pessimistic view of the meaninglessness of life. Japan regards its novelists and artists as cultural heroes, and some of Japan's most respected novelists have committed suicide.[4] If religion at its best represents a positive affirmation of life and the world, then secularism at its best views life as an opportunity for hedonism. In the shadow cast by secularism is the "negative ideal" of suicide, an act that both acknowledges and attempts to negate meaninglessness. Perhaps this extreme form of secularism represents the most serious challenge to religion, for it rejects any traditional religious answer.

In the past few chapters we have focused closely on the prewar and postwar Japanese experience, partly because World War II was so important in the formation of modern Japan, partly because it was crucial for reshaping Japan's contemporary religious situation. However, the main tendency in Japan has been to ignore or forget about World War II, and until very recently the Ministry of Education's policy on history textbooks for public schools has been to silence any critical treatment of the war.[5]

One result of decades of educational neglect of World War II has been that people who grew up after the war know little about it. In line with this practice of ignoring World War II, the field of religion has had little to say about the war.[6] Some exceptions to this pattern of "collective amnesia" include: first, New Religions, which after the war gained both religious freedom to organize and political freedom to describe the persecutions they suffered at the hands of the government; second, left-wing writers such as Communists, whose critical voice was also allowed to speak without punishment in the postwar era;[7] and, third, Okinawans—whose triple burden of being viewed as not "really" Japanese, having suffered through the devastating Allied invasion at the end of World War II, and after a lengthy postwar occupation (even today being overwhelmed by a large American military presence)—have been outspoken both against Japanese militarism and the Japanese government's acquiescence to American military bases in Okinawa.[8] If we return to mainstream Japanese society, no matter how religious leaders assess their respective group's support of and involvement in World War II, it is difficult to imagine these leaders critically and creatively returning to their traditions' roots without passing through and coming to terms with this more recent history.[9]

For our historical purposes, a close look at prewar and wartime conditions is very important, but most Japanese today are much more aware—and proud—of the postwar economic miracle that has propelled Japan to the forefront of the industrial and commercial world. Japan has become one of the most affluent countries, and soul-searching by Japanese is usually future-oriented rather than past-directed. Two prominent concerns are how Japan can keep up the competitive pace, especially how Japanese youth can thrive in the highly successful but equally stressful school system, and how people will live and make their peace with affluence.[10]

In the aftermath of the Aum Shinrikyo poison gas attack of 1995, there was unusual openness and concern for the health of education, the youth, and the country as a whole. This anxiety was prompted not merely by the shock of such devastating violence in such a low-crime country, but especially by the combined facts that a religious group was responsible for planning the attack and that some of the brightest university students were involved in producing and releasing the gas. Aum Shinrikyo's ability to attract a significant number of promising young intellectuals has forced many people to reconsider the direction and pace of education and of the country as a whole. Obviously, in the glaring light of extensive media coverage, it is easy to make too much of one incident—horrible as it may be—and to take it as a barometer reading for the entire Japanese scene. But in the long run, it may well be that the *reaction* to the Aum Shinrikyo incident by the media and the public is even more important than the incident itself. The inability to come to terms with the catastrophe, the lack of critical response from the field of religion,[11] and the general confusion over blaming either a renegade religion or an ineffective educational system or incompetent government supervision—all these factors have heightened concern about the "real" Japan, where the Japanese people are headed, and how religion can play a constructive role in helping direct the country and individual lives.

For some women the challenge to religion is not that it is irrelevant but that it is unfair in its organization and in its treatment of females. In "A Feminist Critique of Japanese Religions," a Japanese feminist claims "there are probably no feminists who would deny the fact that within the patriarchal framework of Japanese society, the values of Shinto, Buddhism and Confucianism cast deep shadows," and she raises the question of "whether sexual discrimination is a strategy or structural necessity of religion in the first place. Is there a different underlying cause for discrimination in each separate religion, or is there some hidden broad-based cause of a completely different nature?" She laments the fact that "sexual discrimination in Japan becomes multi-layered and opaque" due to the fact that it is not individual males, but the combination of family and state, that supports the status quo of an androcentric society; and religion helps support this status quo.[12] We cannot resolve the complexities of these pointed questions, but we can see two interesting corollaries of this feminist critique: first, the "status quo" of Japanese religion is not accepted as a given, and may be further questioned; second, feminist theologians in other countries may find significant the arguments of Japanese feminists about culture-specific and universal factors in religiously based sexual discrimination.

The religion problem in Japan today is not so different from the same problem in the West,[13] and has been recognized by perceptive Japanese, scholars and writers, from the time they recognized the ambiguity of modern life. What remains unresolved is the question of how cultural, spiritual, and religious values can be articulated and perpetuated in the modern world.[14] Japan must find a way to maintain her cultural and religious heritage while contributing to a world culture. What is at stake is not simply a matter of making Japanese religion conform to new social and economic conditions. This is not just a "modern" question, it is the perennial quandary of how people define the human condition, and how they may live meaningful lives. At the heart of the problem is a human and spiritual question that asks what it means for a Japanese person to live in the present world. This raises the question of how men and women relate to their national history and to the world at large. It also implies the question of how they define themselves in relation to the natural world and to other people. Answering these questions is the task of the Japanese people, and this task presupposes a reassessment of Japanese religion.[15]

As we watch the drama of Japanese religion unfold, we perceive the richness of this tradition as well as the serious problems it faces. We see that the Japanese people are proud of their tradition, and we empathize with their attempt to use traditional resources to face the modern world and contemporary problems. We empathize with them because in the final analysis all people in today's world are facing a common dilemma: relating one's own religious traditions to current questions. As we study Japanese religion and other religious traditions, we realize, however, that the challenge of modernity presents an opportunity for creativity. This study gives us the chance to see ourselves not just as members of the Western tradition, but as participants within the worldwide history of religious experience. People of different cultures invariably have somewhat different perceptions of human experience, the world at large, and the nature of reality. We are not Japanese, and therefore our cultural perceptions will never coincide completely with Japanese perceptions. But we do not have to be Japanese to appreciate the richness of their tradition and recognize our common humanity as we face the perennial question of how to live a meaningful life.

NOTES

1. Often in Japanese religion there is a mixture of categories spiritual and recreational, for example, combining religion with play and pilgrimage with sightseeing. See Nelson Graburn, *To Pray, Pay and Play: The Cultural Structure of Japanese Domestic Tourism* (Aix-en-Provence: Centre des Hautes Etudes Touristiques, 1983).

2. Indifference to religion and skepticism toward religious institutions are widespread. An interview with a contemporary elderly Japanese woman, terminally ill, echoes this skepticism: "I can't say for sure there's no life after death, but I've never heard of anyone who went to that world and returned. . . . I don't believe a lot of what Buddhist priests say. Priests are only human. They've never been to the other world; what they preach they've only learned from books!" See Mathews, *What Makes Life Worth Living?*, p. 135. Usually Japanese people are reserved in their comments about controversial subjects such as religion, but once when I gave a talk in Japanese to a group of wealthy women, I was surprised by their strong anti-clerical remarks. As a visiting professor, my agreed subject was how "Japanese religion" is taught in American universities. My talk emphasized that the center of Japanese religion is in the home more than in shrines and temples. These women not only heartily agreed with this notion, but were openly critical of the Buddhist priests who, they claimed, thought people come to their temples because of the priests and temples. These women insisted it was their own *ancestors* who were important, not the priests and their temples. Anecdotes such as these help us see the spiritual problems behind the facade of the institutional strength of organized religion. Fumio Tamamuro, a noted scholar of local religion in Tokugawa times, is quoted as having been led away from the usual perspective of priests and institutions to the ordinary people when as a boy, after helping his Soto Zen priest father conduct a funeral, he "overheard the group of women complaining about how expensive temple memorial services had become at his father's temple. . . . For the first time he noticed that villagers questioned the authority of the Buddhist temple, while maintaining a respectful relationship to it in front of the priest." See Barbara Ambros and Duncan Williams, "Local Religion in Tokugawa History: Editors' Introduction," *Local Religion in Tokugawa History*, vol. 28, no. 3–4, of *Japanese Journal of Religious Studies* (Fall 2001), p. 211.

3. The novels of Saikaku Ihara (1642–93) provide dramatic evidence of the colorful and hedonistic lifestyle of Tokugawa cities. In *The Life of an Amorous Man* (Rutland, VT: Charles E. Tuttle, 1963, translated by Kengi Hamada), the main character Yonosuke had been leading a profligate life, squandering the family fortune on his passion for drinking and women, until finally his family disowned him. Penniless, exhausted physically, and abandoned by his women, he retreated to a mountain hut and took up the life of a Buddhist hermit. But not for long. As the novel describes his situation:

Doubts entered his mind. "No one has ever actually seen the promised hereafter," he argued with himself. And his past life of sin, from which the stern spirit of the Buddha seemed to have conspicuously kept away, now appeared in retrospect to be more desirable than ever.

So in a fit of impious disgust he sold the coral beads of his rosary, all of them. Silver coins jingled on his palm. And now again he thought of the life of the flesh (p. 55).

This dramatic struggle between worldly sensuality and otherworldly spirituality, some three centuries later, is still relevant for our consideration of the Japanese situation, and the human situation generally. In 1989–91, when Gordon Mathews was interviewing Americans and Japanese about how they "make sense of their worlds," one Japanese man expressed his doubts about the "hereafter" in almost the same words as the character in Saikaku's seventeenth-century novel: "I don't know about a world beyond this one. After all, no one's ever come back from there" (Mathews, *What Makes Life Worth Living?*, p. 202).

4. See Howard S. Hibbett, "Akutagawa Ryunosuke and the Negative Ideal," in *Personality in Japanese History,* eds. Albert M. Craig and Donald H. Shively (Berkeley: University of California, 1970), pp. 425–51, especially p. 449. Since the time of the writing of this article, a number of prominent artists and intellectuals have committed suicide.

5. Ienaga, *The Pacific War,* pp. 254–56, and Ienaga, *Japan's Past, Japan's Future.* Translated and introduced by Richard H. Minear (Lanham, MD: Rowman & Littlefield, 2001). See also Lisa Yoneyama, *Hiroshima Traces,* pp. 5, 7. The "textbook" issue is a highly controversial subject for Japan and her Asian neighbors. The Japanese government, through its Ministry of Education, approves all textbooks for public schools. At the time of the revision of this edition, in early 2001, Koreans in Seoul demonstrated in protest against a Japanese "junior high school text that maintains that Japan's colonization of South Korea, which ended in 1945, was legal and helped 'stabilize East Asia against the advance of the Anglo-Saxon world'" (Michael Zielenziger, "S. Korea, Japan at odds over revisionist history book," *San Diego Union-Tribune,* Friday, March 2, 2001, A-21). Koreans and other Asian peoples see Japan's colonial and military campaigns as acts of aggression.

6. Because 1995 marked the fiftieth anniversary of the end of World War II, some historians have collected oral statements from the participants in the war, especially armed forces personnel, to preserve their memories of what it meant to be part of the war. The words of a man who at the time of the interview in the late 1980s was the head priest of a Zen temple, recall nostalgically his days in the naval academy in 1944–45, giving us a glimpse of one Buddhist's view of wartime: "'I was there only ten months, but the impression it made on me was very powerful. Were I young and able to live my life over again, I would still go. That kind of education—rigid discipline—is no longer available in the world.'" Koshu Itabashi, in Cook and Cook, *Japan at War: An Oral History,* p. 77. The larger issue of religious support for nationalism and militarism is taken up in Heisig and Maraldo, eds., *Rude Awakenings.*

7. See Union of New Religious Organizations in Japan, Research Office, ed., "Reminiscences of Religion in Postwar Japan," *Contemporary Religions in Japan,* vol. 6, no. 2 (June 1965), pp. 111–203. This work is serialized through five subsequent issues of this journal. Although focusing mainly on postwar Japan, it reflects back on the prewar situation. See also Murakami, *Japanese Religion in the Modern Century,* which discusses both governmental persecution of New Religions and the attempt of religions to interfere in government.

8. See Field, *In the Realm of a Dying Emperor,* pp. 33–104, for the account of Okinawans who objected to use of the "rising sun" flag and the national anthem as a revival of wartime militarism.

9. It is difficult for any religious tradition or government to face directly its own history: "People in all cultures and times have mythologized their own war dead, while soon forgetting their victims. . . ." (Dower, *Embracing Defeat,* p. 504). And although the focus in this book is on religious nationalism in Japan, we should keep in mind the fact that religions and governments in Europe and the United States, too, have had difficulty dealing with the

darker side of their pasts: recently the pope apologized for massacres during the medieval crusades, and the American Bureau of Indian Affairs apologized to Native American peoples for suppression of their cultures.

It is perhaps ironic for an American to point out the ambiguous relationship between religion and war in Japanese history; as this book goes to press the United States and Britain are engaged in war with Iraq, and religion has been invoked on both sides of this conflict. An alien from another planet would find both American and Iraqi governments seeing the other side as evil and as having God on their side, and might wonder how the human activity of religion could so neatly divide opposing sides into good/evil. The American Christian theologian Martin E. Marty has raised questions about the fact that "For decades, [American] chief executives have acted like priests of the national religion," and the fact that "Long having professed that 'our nation is chosen by God and commissioned by history to be a model to the world of justice,' President Bush boasts that we are the only remaining superpower left." Marty claims that "Christian theologians are wary when Bush uses the words of Jesus to draw neat lines and challenge the whole rest of the world: if you are not for us, or with us, you are against us." (Martin E. Marty, "The Sin of Pride," *Newsweek,* March 10, 2003, pp. 32–33.) The lessons we learn about the ambiguous relationship between religion and state, and religion and war, in our study of Japanese religion, should help us reconsider this ambiguous relationship in other times and places, past and future.

10. Many Westerners have alternately praised and criticized the Japanese educational system. Thomas P. Rohlen, in the conclusion of his *Japan's High Schools* (Berkeley: University of California, 1983), p. 320, cites "my own ultimate squabble with Japan's high schools. The well-intended teachers and well-behaved students put their efforts to purposes that are ultimately shallow and uninspired. The nation benefits economically. Society is well run. But it is a system without much heart."

11. Robert Kisala, "Aum Alone in Japan: Religious Responses to the Aum Affair," *Bulletin of the Nanzan Institute for Religion & Culture,* no. 19 (Spring 1995), pp. 6–34.

12. Okano Haruko, "A Feminist Critique of Japanese Religions," in *Women and Religion in Japan,* eds. Akiko Okuda and Haruko Okano, trans. Alison Watts (Wiesbaden: Harrassowitz, 1998), pp. 17–44. See other articles in this volume, especially Okano's "Afterword—The Future of Feminism and Religion" (pp. 197–202), where she suggests the possibility of recovering religion's original "power of liberation" (lost in its sectarian institutionalization). Whereas Okano gives a radical feminist view, Kyoko Nakamura provides a moderate view that "religion in both the Eastern and the Western worlds has repressed and discriminated against women . . ." but "it is also true that religion has served as a liberating force for women." Kyoko Nakamura, "The Religious Consciousness and Activities of Contemporary Women," *Japanese Journal of Religious Studies,* vol. 24, no. 1–2 (Spring 1997), pp. 87–120. See also Kyoko Nakamura, ed., *Women and Religion in Japan,* vol. 10, no. 2–3 *Japanese Journal of Religious Studies* (June–Sept. 1983).

13. Gordon Mathews, in his interviews of Japanese and Americans and how they "make sense of their worlds," reaches several conclusions: "religious belief as *ikigai* [making sense of the world] is apparently held only by a minority of Japanese and Americans," and the modern and secular character of Japanese and American society makes all religion ("the pursuit of transcendent significance") "peculiarly problematic." See Mathews, *What Makes Life Worth Living?,* pp. 201, 203.

14. Masaharu Anesaki was well aware of these issues even before World War II. See his views in his *History of Japanese Religion* pp. 375–409; and in his article, "An Oriental Evaluation of Modern Civilization," in *Recent Gains in American Civilization,* ed. Kirby Page (New York: Harcourt Brace Jovanovich, 1928), pp. 329–57.

15. See Robert N. Bellah, ed., *Religion and Progress in Modern Asia* (New York: Free Press, 1965), for a discussion of this problem and modernity in terms of the notion of progress.

Note especially the remarks of Clifford Geertz, pp. 166–67. For an extended treatment of the notions of "modern" and "modernity," and their significance for understanding Japan today, see Harry D. Harootunian, *Overcome by Modernity: History, Culture, and Community in Interwar Japan* (Princeton: Princeton University, 2000). This work focuses on such factors as "massive industrial transformation," mass consumption, heightened urbanization, and "ceaseless change" as marks of the condition called "modern life," which first flourished in Japan from the 1920s and 1930s. This work uses the term "modernism as an ideologization of the process of capitalist modernization and transformation Japanese were experiencing and trying to grasp" (pp. x, xviii–xx). Included are analyses of the intellectual and governmental strategies from Meiji times to the present to forge an identity for the Japanese "folk" and nation as a whole. While some of these developments are peculiar to Japan, the general situation of modern life and modernism as a strategy of ideology may be found in all "advanced" countries. In this sense, perhaps, Japanese and American and other "modern" people can learn from one another in the attempt to create their individual and collective identities in a meaningful fashion.

Study Questions

To use the study questions most efficiently, read them before beginning each assignment. Keeping the questions in mind, use them to identify the most important information. Then, after reading the material, test your general understanding by answering the questions. Any number of techniques may be used to answer the questions—making mental notes, underlining and writing in the book, keeping a journal. If you have trouble answering the questions, you may want to mention the troublesome points in class discussion. To check comprehension of basic facts, use the tutorial quiz on the book's companion website located at http://wadsworth.com/religion.

The study questions and multiple-choice tutorial enable readers to use together the present book and the companion volume, *Religion in the Japanese Experience: Sources and Interpretations*, 2d ed. Those reading only the present book may disregard the questions referring to the latter work.

Introduction to Japanese Religion
Japanese Religion, pp. 1–17

Identify all the religious traditions and aspects of religious life found in Japanese history. How can this plurality of traditions and aspects form a unity in the religious life of the individual? How can the diversity of religious expression result in unity at different levels of life? Identify the six persistent themes in Japanese religious history, and try to weave together these six themes into a total picture of Japanese religion. (These notions of plurality, diversity, unity, and persistent themes will be helpful to you in unifying the material from both books.)

Religion in the Japanese Experience, pp. 1–4

Note the major differences between religion in America and Japanese religion. Try to describe, in your own words, the major characteristics of Japanese religion and the major outlines of Japanese religious history.

Japanese Religion, pp. 21–29

How did religion in Japan begin? What are the earliest forms of Japanese religion, and how are they related to economic, social, and political developments in early Japan? Describe how the religious significance of the dead, of fertility, and of divine descent all define a general pattern of religion in early Japan. (Use the "Table of Japanese Religious History" to view at a glance the social and religious history of Japan.)

Early Shinto

Japanese Religion, pp. 31–39

Religion in the Japanese Experience, pp. 6–9

How is Shinto related to the earliest Japanese religious tradition, and how did it develop into a tradition in its own right? What are the main themes in Japanese mythology, and how are these important for Shinto? What is the general outline of Shinto as seen in priests, rituals, and shrines?

Religion in the Japanese Experience, pp. 9–13

Compare and contrast the Judeo-Christian notion of God with the Japanese notion of *kami.* Give at least three examples of *kami* to show how a wide variety of "things" can be divine beings or *kami.* What are the general features of such *kami?*

Religion in the Japanese Experience, pp. 13–19

Compare and contrast the Judeo-Christian story of creation with the Japanese story of creation. Analyze the Japanese creation story, noting the conditions at the beginning of creation, who the most important figures are, and the process by which creation occurred. One scholar has described Japanese religion in terms of "a sacred people in a sacred land." How does the creation story support such a description?

Religion in the Japanese Experience, pp. 19–22

Compare and contrast a Shinto shrine with a sacred place with which you are familiar, such as a church or a synagogue. What is it that makes a Shinto shrine "sacred"? What is the relationship between nature and shrines? How do the *kami,* shrines, and Shinto worshipers relate to one another?

Religion in the Japanese Experience, pp. 34–38

Compare and contrast the role of women in Shinto with what you know about the role of women in Western religions such as Judaism and Christianity. What are the various ways and roles in which women appear within Shinto?

Distinguish historically the roles of women within the three periods of "Primitive Shinto," "Organized Shinto," and "Shinto after the Meiji Restoration."

Early Japanese Buddhism

Japanese Religion, pp. 41–51

Religion in the Japanese Experience, pp. 45–47

How did the Indian religion of Buddhism happen to travel all the way to Japan, and how was it received in Japan? What was the role of the imperial court and the state in the acceptance of Buddhism in Japan?

Religion in the Japanese Experience, pp. 47–49

Note the particular circumstances surrounding Buddhism's arrival in Japan from Korea. How did the Korean envoys describe Buddhism, and how did the Japanese look upon this "foreign" religion?

Religion in the Japanese Experience, pp. 50–54

Describe the way in which Buddhist divinities and *kami* came to be very closely related—almost like two sides of the same coin. To what extent is this relationship the influence of Buddhist divinities on Shinto *kami*, and to what extent is it the influence of Shinto *kami* on Buddhist divinities?

Religion in the Japanese Experience, pp. 76–80

What has been the role of nuns in Buddhism from the time of the Buddha, and what was their role in Japanese Buddhism? Summarize the "life in a Zen nunnery" in contemporary times. How would you compare and contrast the role of nuns in Japanese Buddhism with the role of women in Shinto (pp. 34–38)?

Confucianism and Taoism

Japanese Religion, pp. 52–62

Religion in the Japanese Experience, p. 103

How did Confucianism come to Japan; what are the major components of Confucianism; and what impact did it have on Japanese culture and religion? How did elements of Taoism come to Japan; what are the major components of Taoism and Chinese customs in Japan; and what impact did they have on Japanese culture and religion?

Religion in the Japanese Experience, pp. 120–25

Analyze the Taoist-influenced Koshin cult, explaining the religious theory behind the cult and the practices the cult group (*ko*) engages in.

Folk Religion

Japanese Religion, pp. 66–73

Religion in the Japanese Experience, p. 126

How does folk religion differ from organized religion, and what are the major aspects of Japanese folk religion? How is folk religion delicately woven into family, village, occupational, and individual life?

Religion in the Japanese Experience, pp. 127–29

Identify each of the "rites of passage" mentioned and the religious obser-vances for each rite. What is the "discernible belief structure" expressed by all these rites of passage "as a homogeneous whole"? What similarities/differences do you see between rites of passage in Japan and in other cultures such as America?

Religion in the Japanese Experience, pp. 129–35

Trace carefully the steps by which a woman enters the sacred calling of a blind medium —list each of the requirements of this training. "Once a girl is fully initiated and possessed of her instruments of power," what tasks is she ex-pected to perform? Characterize each of these religious tasks.

Religion in the Japanese Experience, pp. 135–39

Sum up the story and message of each folk tale. How do folk tales consti-tute one aspect of folk religion?

Interaction in Japanese Religion

Japanese Religion, pp. 75–78

By about the ninth century how have all the five formative traditions in-teracted to constitute Japanese religion? Try to describe the general picture of Japanese religion in the ninth century.

Tendai and Shingon Buddhism

Religion in the Japanese Experience, pp. 81–83; *Japanese Religion,* pp. 81–82

Explain the different roles of Buddhism within Japanese religion by con-trasting "Buddhism *in Japan*" with "*Japanese* Buddhism."

Japanese Religion, pp. 83–96

Identify the major teachings and practices of Tendai and Shingon Bud-dhism. What changes were brought about by the founders of these two Bud-dhist sects? How did Shingon and Tendai provide a new basis for establishing Japanese Buddhism? Compare and contrast the earlier Nara Buddhism with Tendai and Shingon Buddhism.

Religion in the Japanese Experience, pp. 54–60

What are "expedient means" and "parable" in the *Lotus Sutra,* and how does the story of the rich man and his burning house illustrate these religious techniques? The phrase *anuttara-samyak-sambodhi* is the equivalent of "true en-lightenment" or "perfect understanding"; what does the *Lotus Sutra* say is nec-essary for attaining this state?

Religion in the Japanese Experience, pp. 83–85

What are the major features of Dengyo Daishi's regulations for ordinand students within monastic Buddhism? Dengyo Daishi says that these eight arti-cles, or regulations, "uphold the Buddha's Dharma, benefit the nation, draw sen-tient beings to the true teaching, and encourage future students to do good." How would you interpret the regulations as carrying out these intentions?

Religion in the Japanese Experience, pp. 85–88

What are the major features of Kobo Daishi's "list of newly imported sutras and other items"? Kobo Daishi says that the teaching of esoteric Buddhism (or Dharma) "is as useful to the nation as walls are to a city, and as fertile soil is to the people"; how would you interpret these items as having such value? (How does Kobo Daishi's notion of Dharma differ from Dengyo Daishi's view of Dharma, pp. 83–85?)

Pure Land Buddhism

Japanese Religion, pp. 98–113

Identify the major teachings and practices of Pure Land, Nichiren, and Zen Buddhism. How did each of these movements focus on faith (or devotion) and a single or "exclusive practice"? How did these movements help transform Japanese Buddhism into a more popular religion?

Religion in the Japanese Experience, pp. 88–91

What are the major features of Honen's "parting message"? How can "the method of final salvation" be "the mere repetition of the 'Namu Amida Butsu'"? How would you compare Honen's "advice on the repetition of the nembutsu" to the teachings of Dengyo Daishi and Kobo Daishi (pp. 83–85 and 85–88)?

Religion in the Japanese Experience, pp. 91–94

What are the major features of Shinran's recommendation of "'Just say the Name and be saved by Amida'"? Shinran contrasted Other Power and Self Power—which does he prefer and why? How does Shinran's ideal of Buddhism differ from that of Dengyo Daishi, Kobo Daishi, and Honen?

Religion in the Japanese Experience, pp. 65–73

The novel *The Buddha Tree* describes devotion to Amida. Interpret in your own words what devotion to Amida means. What problem do people have that needs help from Amida? What is the frame of mind in which people approach Amida? What religious power does Amida represent, such that Amida can grant this request?

Medieval Buddhism

Religion in the Japanese Experience, pp. 60–65

How does the author interpret medieval Japan as defined and determined by Buddhism? How did medieval Buddhism provide "not only salvation" but also a "map of reality"? What is the rokudo ("six courses"), and how does this "pervasive idea" determine the "depiction of the universe" in medieval Japan? Sum up in your own words this view of the world.

Nichiren and Zen Buddhism

Religion in the Japanese Experience, pp. 94–98

What are the major features of Nichiren's advocacy of the teaching of "Nam-myoho-renge-kyo"? Outline Nichiren's critique of Honen. How does

Nichiren's understanding of Buddhism differ from that of Dengyo Daishi, Kobo Daishi, Honen, and Shinran?

Religion in the Japanese Experience, pp. 99–102

What are the major features of Dogen's recommendation of sitting in meditation (*zazen*)? Contrast the practice of *zazen* and *koan* as found in Dogen's teaching. How does Dogen's understanding of Buddhism differ from that of Dengyo Daishi, Kobo Daishi, Honen, Shinran, and Nichiren?

Medieval Shinto
Japanese Religion, pp. 115–25

How does medieval Shinto differ from early Shinto? How does thorough interaction of Shinto with Buddhism alter the character of Shinto? To what extent, and in what way, does medieval Shinto tend to assume its own organizational style?

Religion in the Japanese Experience, pp. 23–25

Carefully notice the attitude and emotions in the medieval pilgrim to one of the most important Shinto shrines. Compare and contrast this pilgrim's frame of mind with the frame of mind of the priest practicing a devotion to Amida (pp. 65–73).

The Christian Century
Japanese Religion, pp. 128–35

How did the European religion of Christianity happen to travel all the way to Japan, and how was it received in Japan? Compare and contrast the earlier arrival of another "foreign" religion, Buddhism. (How did Buddhism become a permanent part of the Japanese tradition, whereas Christianity had much greater difficulties?) Analyze political and economic factors related to the acceptance of Christianity, and explain how Christianity was expelled from Japan.

Religion in the Japanese Experience, pp. 140–44

How does the author interpret the "Christian century" as "acceptance and rejection of Catholicism"? List the author's reasons for both the acceptance and the rejection of Catholicism.

Religion in the Japanese Experience, pp. 144–49

How does Fabian explain his conversion to Christianity, and later his departure from Christianity? Sum up Fabian's treatment of Christian teaching (given in the sections "The adherents of Deus claim"), and his refutation of that teaching (given in the sections "To counter, I reply").

Syncretism in Japanese Religion
Japanese Religion, pp. 137–40

By about the sixteenth century, how have all the formative traditions interacted and developed in such a way as to constitute Japanese religion? Try to describe the general picture of Japanese religion in the sixteenth century.

Religion in the Japanese Experience, pp. 157–61

Identify Buddhist, Taoist, Confucian, and Shinto elements in this medieval will, and show how they are interrelated in the personal code of conduct of a medieval man. Describe in your own words this man's philosophy of life.

Religion in the Japanese Experience, pp. 161–63

Identify Buddhist, Confucian, and Shinto elements in this formal government document, and show how they are interrelated in the policy of late medieval government. Describe in your own words this government's general philosophy of life.

Religion in the Japanese Experience, pp. 163–64

Identify Buddhist, Confucian, and Shinto elements in this late medieval teacher's statement. Describe in your own words this teacher's prescription for religious cooperation.

Closeness of Humans, Gods, and Nature
Religion in the Japanese Experience, pp. 166–69

Interpret in your own words the theme of "closeness of humans, gods, and nature." Within this theme, treat Matsudaira Sadanobu's "self-deification," or "blend of the profane and sacred." How does the author place Sadanobu's self-deification within the context of Japanese religious history?

Religion in the Japanese Experience, pp. 170–72

Analyze the attitude toward nature and gods in these poems. What do they tell us about ancient Japanese poetry and about the blending of religious and aesthetic themes?

Religion in the Japanese Experience, pp. 172–76

Analyze the understanding and expression of nature in Japanese theories of art, and try to locate the same in the painting of Sesshu. How do religious and aesthetic values concerning nature blend in these verbal and graphic expressions?

Religion in the Japanese Experience, pp. 176–80

In what way do *haiku* convey both an artistic and a religious message? Analyze the religious significance in each of the *haiku* in this selection.

The Family, Living and Dead
Religion in the Japanese Experience, pp. 181–84

In what way is the *dozoku* both a social and a religious institution? What is the religious significance of the calendar of festivals for the *dozoku*?

Religion in the Japanese Experience, pp. 185–88

Trace the process by which a corpse passes from a state of pollution to the purified state of an ancestor. Who must do what in order for this process to be successful? Note especially the roles of the household members and Buddhist priests.

Religion in the Japanese Experience, pp. 73–76

How does the author interpret the relationship between Buddhism, on the one hand, and families and ancestors, on the other hand? Identify and characterize the three connotations of Buddhist temple (*tera* or *jiin*) in Japan. What are the characteristics of "Buddhism as an Organized Religion," and how is the organization of Buddhism similar to the structure of the Japanese family?

Religion in the Japanese Experience, pp. 188–94

As the author describes Japanese religion and festivals, note her contrast between the roles of males and females. What is "androcentrism," and what does she mean by the statement "This androcentrism [of Shinto and Buddhism] is peculiarly lacking in nontraditional religions"? Describe the Japanese woman's "roles as a custodian of the *butsudan* and household religion . . . and as a liaison between the household and the temple."

Purification, Rituals, and Amulets

Religion in the Japanese Experience, pp. 195–200

What are the "sins" to be exorcised in the Great Exorcism, and what are the means of purification in this ritual? On the basis of this ritual, compare and contrast purification in Japanese religion with sin in Christianity.

Religion in the Japanese Experience, pp. 201–04

In this literary episode of evil spirits possessing Genji's wife (Aoi), what human and spiritual agents are thought to be responsible for this possession? What measures are taken to exorcise the malign spirits? How does the treatment of Aoi's corpse reflect the view that malign spirits were responsible for her death?

Religion in the Japanese Experience, pp. 205–12

Identify each of the ritual observances in the "annual round of observances" and the religious practices for each annual observance. Note how the author, after describing this annual round of observances, groups them into three categories: (1) ancestral festivals, (2) agricultural festivals, and (3) rituals of exorcism and purification. Characterize each of these three categories. Compare and contrast these Japanese observances with what you know of festivals (or holidays) in America and Europe.

Religion in the Japanese Experience, pp. 212–17

How does the author view the divergent or contrasting elements of festivals? Why does this author focus on the fact that in a festival "a person enters a state akin to religious ecstasy"? How does he contrast the notion of "structure" with "raw experience"? How does he relate *matsuri,* or festival, to the five senses (and bodily senses)?

Religion and Everyday Life

Religion in the Japanese Experience, pp. 218–21

What is the religious significance of archaeological remains, and how do they throw light on the penetration of religion in the daily life of prehistoric times?

Religion in the Japanese Experience, pp. 221–25

Use this selection to analyze the interrelationship between "social structure and folk religion." What is the difference between the "little tradition" and the "great tradition"?

Religion in the Japanese Experience, pp. 225–30

Follow the sequence of actions in the Shinto wedding ceremony. Compare the events in a Shinto marriage with the events in a Buddhist marriage and a home marriage. What similarities/differences do you notice in these Japanese ceremonies, compared with wedding ceremonies you have seen in your own culture?

Religion in the Japanese Experience, pp. 230–33

What is the religious significance of the "art of tea"? Relate this religious significance to the place, attitudes, and performance of the tea ceremony.

Religion and State

Religion in the Japanese Experience, pp. 234–36

What is the significance of Prince Shotoku's "constitution" as a precedent for the relationship between state and religion? Identify the religious traditions mentioned in the "constitution" and try to state the principle by which they are interrelated (in Shotoku's conception).

Religion in the Tokugawa Period: Buddhism, Neo-Confucianism, and Restoration Shinto

Japanese Religion, pp. 141–57

What does "formalism and renewal" mean? How does this set of terms describe the condition of Buddhism, Neo-Confucianism, and Shinto in the Tokugawa period? Identify the major teachings of Neo-Confucianism and Restoration Shinto.

Neo-Confucianism in Tokugawa Japan

Religion in the Japanese Experience, pp. 104–09

Explain how, in the author's words, Confucianism has "left its mark on Japanese society." Summarize the teaching of the Chinese Confucianist Chu Hsi. How did Neo-Confucianism blend with Shinto and Buddhist elements to help "legitimize" the Tokugawa government?

Religion in the Japanese Experience, pp. 109–13

How does the author contrast the previous view of early Tokugawa political thought as "simply a transplant of a monolithic body" of Chinese Neo-Confucianism, with his own view of Tokugawa ideology as "a conversion of thought constructs into a serviceable ideology"? Trace the career of Hayashi Razan and his role in establishing "the fiction of a Neo-Confucian . . . orthodoxy."

Religion in the Japanese Experience, pp. 113–15

How does Hayashi Razan use Neo-Confucianism to argue for "ruling and living in conformity with the order of heaven and earth"? How does Hayashi Razan argue for the unity of Shinto and Confucianism over against Buddhism?

Restoration Shinto

Religion in the Japanese Experience, pp. 25–28

How did Kitabatake, in medieval times, establish the argument for Japan's uniqueness and superiority? Trace Kitabatake's argument for Japan's uniqueness, especially in contrast to India and China.

Religion in the Japanese Experience, pp. 28–34

How does the author define and interpret *mono no aware* as "the key concept representing the essence of Norinaga's thought"? Trace the author's argument about *mono no aware*, and put in your own words the term's meaning as contained in the quotations from Norinaga.

The Meiji Restoration and State Shinto

Japanese Religion, pp. 161–76

What were the key political events of the Meiji Restoration, and how was religion interwoven with these political events? Trace the changes within Shinto during this period, showing how it emerged as "nationalistic Shinto" or State Shinto. How are nationalism and religion interrelated in Japan (and how would you compare/contrast the interrelationship of nationalism and religion in Western countries such as the United States)?

Religion in the Japanese Experience, pp. 236–37

Analyze the Imperial Rescript on Education in terms of its religious motivation, its political motivation, and its educational objectives. Compare this document with Shotoku's "Constitution" (p. 225) to show how it represents continuity with ancient themes. In what ways does it also constitute a remarkable change?

Religious Currents from 1868–1945

Japanese Religion, pp. 180–92

What was the condition of Buddhism and Christianity during this period, and how did the New Religions fare by comparison? What is "state orthodoxy"?

Religion in the Japanese Experience, pp. 150–52

What is the gist of Uchimura's criticism of Western missionary notions, and what does he mean when he proposes a "Japanese Christianity"?

Religion in the Japanese Experience, pp. 115–19

What does "the nationalisation of Confucianism in Japan" mean, and how did this kind of Confucianism happen to support Japanese nationalism and militarism?

Religion in the Japanese Experience, pp. 238–42

What religious principles are used as the basis for the *Kokutai no Hongi*, and how were these principles used to support the *Kokutai no Hongi*? What are the general objectives of this document?

New Religions

Japanese Religion, pp. 195–204

Trace the emergence, organization, and activities of Tenrikyo and Soka Gakkai. How do these two movements compare and contrast with one another, and how do they compare and contrast with traditional Shinto and Buddhism?

Religion in the Japanese Experience, pp. 268–74

Analyze the revelation experience of the founder of Tenrikyo. First identify in this revelation experience the religious elements from the earlier tradition. Then show how this revelation has new features that lead to a New Religion.

Religion in the Japanese Experience, pp. 275–78

Analyze the "message" of Soka Gakkai, first identifying the religious goal and then showing how people can reach this goal. What is the relationship between the individual's daily worship, missionary work (*shakubuku*), and the discussion meetings?

Religion in the Japanese Experience, pp. 152–56

Summarize the career of Teshima, the founder of the Makuya movement of Christianity. What are the institutional features of Makuya, and its major religious practices? How does the author compare Makuya to Japanese New Religions? What is the significance of his statement that "The Makuya is the only movement to indigenize Christianity . . . in the Japanese lower classes"?

Religion in the Japanese Experience, pp. 279–83

Restate the argument here that entry into a New Religion is a "process of reorientation of life set in motion by the cure or counseling." How does the author describe and interpret the experiences of the couple (the Abes) in joining Kurozumikyo? How did the Abes use their faith in Kurozumikyo to diagnose and resolve their problems?

Religion in the Japanese Experience, pp. 283–88

Restate the argument here that four kinds of Buddhist power can be found within the worldview of Japanese New Religions. How does the author describe and interpret a young man's work experience as a testimony to his faith in Gedatsu-kai? What problems did the young man face in work; how did his faith in Gedatsu-kai help him to diagnose and resolve those problems?

Religion in the Japanese Experience, pp. 288–90

How does the author describe and interpret Miss Nakata's entry into the New Religion Mahikari? How does Miss Nakata's previous religious experience and possession influence her to join Mahikari? How did Miss Nakata resolve her problems after joining Mahikari?

Religion in Postwar Japan

Japanese Religion, pp. 206–12

Religion in the Japanese Experience, pp. 244–45

What was the general condition of Shinto, Buddhism, Christianity, and the New Religions in the postwar period?

Religion in the Japanese Experience, pp. 38–44

What was the status of Shinto in 1945; why was the Allied Occupation opposed to the continuation of this status; and how did the Occupation eliminate this status without interfering with freedom of religion? How did this directive affect Shinto? In his Imperial Edict, how does the emperor appeal to the past; how does he change the religious-mythical heritage; and what does he see for the future?

Religion in the Japanese Experience, pp. 245–50

What is the religious ideal of Buddhism; how was this ideal compromised in the twentieth century; and how can the ideal be restored?

Religion in the Japanese Experience, pp. 251–55

What is the religious ideal of Shinto; how was this ideal compromised in the twentieth century; and how can the ideal be restored?

Religion in the Japanese Experience, pp. 255–63

In what way have changing conditions in Tokyo generally affected the people's religious life? How have these changed circumstances affected traditional Shinto and traditional Buddhism?

Religion in the Japanese Experience, pp. 263–67

The pornographers are secularists; nothing is sacred. Interpret this secularism in terms of the contrast between filming a pornographic movie at a shrine and the sincere piety of the old lady at the shrine. Why do these "secularist" pornographers still have to resort to their own kind of ritual at the wake? Interpret the religious significance of replacing a Buddhist sutra with a pornographic film.

Religious Life in Contemporary Japan

Japanese Religion, pp. 214–28

"Are the Japanese religious?" How would you compare and contrast "being religious" in Japan and in Western countries? Over the centuries, how has Japanese religion remained the same, and how has it changed in the past century or so? Recently, how has Japanese religion declined, and how has it "increased" or expanded?

The History and Future of Japanese Religion

Japanese Religion, pp. 230–34

Religion in the Japanese Experience, pp. 291–92

Now that you have studied twenty-five hundred years of the history of Japanese religion, how do you view its future? How do you see the chances for Japanese religion (1) dying out, (2) remaining the same, and (3) changing? How would you compare and contrast the future of religion in Japan with the future of religion in Western countries?

Religion in the Japanese Experience, pp. 292–95

How does the author of *Harp of Burma* compare and contrast compulsory military training in Japan and compulsory religious training in Burma in the discussion of what it means to be "advanced" and "modern"? What do the Japanese prisoners of war think about the notions of "civilized" and "uncivilized"?

Religion in the Japanese Experience, pp. 295–98

Why is the author critical of the relationship between religion and state seen in four events: (1) the ritual rebuilding of the Ise Shrine; (2) the proposed state administration of the Yasukuni Shrine; (3) the use of state funds for a Shinto ritual blessing a state building site; and (4) the enshrining of a Self-Defense Force official against his widow's wishes? Analyze each of these events and evaluate the author's criticism.

Religion in the Japanese Experience, pp. 298–304

How does the author approach the "ideology" of a Japanese business? Describe the main features of the "entering-bank-ceremony." Explain how this ceremony and the "major regularly scheduled ceremonies" of the bank are used to interpret the bank's "ideology." Summarize the author's view of this ideology.

Religion in the Japanese Experience, pp. 304–07

How does the author approach the relationship between men and machines as part of "traditional craftsmanship"? Describe the process of "humanizing the machine," especially the role of *kami* and Shinto in this process. How does the author interpret this "Solidarity . . . created between men and the world, and between men and men"?

Religion in the Japanese Experience, pp. 308–12

How is Christmas practiced in Japan; what does Christmas mean in Japan; and how is Japanese Christmas an attempt to "cope with modernity"?

Summary

At the end of this study of Japanese culture and religion, it may be useful to take stock of what you have learned and how your thinking has changed. Compare what you knew about Japan and Japanese religion before reading these materials with what you know now. What was the most interesting new information you learned about the Japanese tradition?

Compare your general attitudes or opinions toward Japanese culture you had before this course of study with those you have now. How has your thinking changed, and what persuaded you to change your thinking?

Most people outside Japan view the country in terms of its industrial achievements—cameras, electronics, and automobiles. How would you balance this industrial, technological, and commercial image of Japan with what you have learned about its distinctive culture?

How would you compare Japanese culture and religion with Western (or American) culture and religion? In the past, some Americans have thought that Japan should adopt Western customs, such as Christianity and democracy; some Americans have claimed recently that Americans should adopt Japanese customs, such as greater cooperation between labor and management, and better coordination of business and government. Do you think it is possible for one society to borrow from another society, and if so, how would you select the features to be borrowed? Are there ethical or humanitarian principles that transcend individual cultures and should guide all cultures? How would you like to see the Japanese tradition develop in the future?

Annotated Bibliography on Japanese Religion: Selected Works

The articles, chapters, books, and reference works included here are provided to help the reader find more material on Japan and Japanese religion. This bibliography is organized into the following sections:

Special Bibliographies on Japanese History and Religion

Special Reference Works on Japanese History and Religion

Periodicals for Japanese History and Religion

Histories and Works on Japanese Culture

Histories and General Works on Japanese Religion

Shinto

Buddhism

Confucianism

Taoism

Folk Religion

Christianity

New Religions

Those interested in more citations may find the bibliographies in the first section helpful. For looking up definitions of Japanese terms and brief articles on religious terminology, the dictionaries and encyclopedias in the reference works section will be useful. A list of periodicals will lead readers to recent scholarly articles. The person wanting to explore various aspects of Japan and Japanese culture can scan the selective titles in the Histories and Works on Japanese Culture section.

To find publications dealing broadly with Japanese history and religion, go to the Histories and General Works on Japanese Religion section. Subsequent sections feature material focusing more on one tradition. But because Japanese religions are closely interrelated, and the scholarship in the field often combines or crosses subjects, readers will profit from scanning several sections of the bibliography. For example, a student planning a term paper on Shinto will want to go through the Shinto section first, but will also find related material in the other sections such as bibliographies, reference works, and general works on Japanese religion, and even the Buddhism section. (Internet users will also find a great deal of information available on Web sites run by religious groups and by academic associations.)

This bibliography differs from the bibliographies in most books in two ways: first, in order to provide coverage in many areas (especially Japanese culture and history), books appear in the bibliography that are not cited in the text; second, due to space limitations, not every work cited in the text is listed in the bibliography.

SPECIAL BIBLIOGRAPHIES ON JAPANESE
HISTORY AND RELIGION

Algarin, Joanne P. *Japanese Folk Literature: A Core Collection and Reference Guide*. New York: R. R. Bowker, 1979. Features works on Japanese folklore, Japanese folktale anthologies, classic folktales; plus two appendixes: Japanese-language sources and a glossary of Japanese terms; and subject, article, and folktale indexes.

Allinson, Gary D. *The Columbia Guide to Modern Japanese History*. New York: Columbia University, 1999. A teaching aid providing chapters on historical periods, a "topical compendium," a "Resource Guide," and other useful features.

Association for Asian Studies. *Cumulative Bibliography of Asian Studies, 1941–1965*. Author Bibliography, 4 vols.; Subject Bibliography, 4 vols. Boston: G. K. Hall & Company, 1969–70. This work is continued in *Cumulative Bibliography of Asian Studies, 1966–70*. Author Bibliography, 3 vols.; Subject Bibliography, 3 vols. Boston: G. K. Hall & Company, 1972–73. The most convenient and comprehensive listing of materials on Asian subjects. For Japanese materials, see the heading "Japan" in the Subject Bibliography; for religion, see the subheading "Philosophy and Religion." Materials after 1970 will be found in the annual *Bibliography of Asian Studies* published by the Association for Asian Studies. (The Bibliography of Asian Studies is available at some libraries as a database.)

Clarke, Peter B. *Bibliography of Japanese New Religions with Annotations and an Introduction to Japanese New Religions at Home and Abroad*. "Plus an Appendix on Aum Shinrikyo." Richmond, Surrey: Japan Library, 1999. In addition to Japanese New Religions in Japan, covers these movements "abroad," especially in Europe and North America.

Collcutt, Martin. "Premodern Japan." In *The American Historical Association's Guide to Historical Literature*. 3d ed. Edited by Mary Beth Norton et al. New York: Oxford University, 1995, pp. 355–78. Brief introduction to premodern Japanese history (periodization, categorization, currents of research), followed by annotated items (by historical period, subdivided by subject). (See Notehelfer in this section for "Modern Japan.")

Dower, John W. "With Timothy S. George." *Japanese History and Culture from Ancient to Modern Times: Seven Basic Bibliographies.* 2d ed., rev. and updated. Princeton: Markus Wiener, 1995. Features five bibliographies by historical period, plus "bibliographies and research guides" and "journals and other serial publications."

Earhart, H. Byron. *The New Religions of Japan: A Bibliography of Western-Language Materials.* Tokyo: Sophia University, 1970. 2d ed., Ann Arbor: Center for Japanese Studies, University of Michigan, 1983. Provides a general introduction to the New Religions and a general bibliography, followed by listings for individual New Religions; includes author and topical indexes.

Fu, Charles Wei-hsun and Chan, Wing-tsit. *Guide to Chinese Philosophy.* Boston: G. K. Hall & Company, 1978. A comprehensive, annotated bibliography organized in terms of Chinese traditions, or "schools," and philosophical problems.

Gardner, James L. *Japan Access: A Bibliography of Bibliographies.* Salt Lake City: Wings of Fire, 1990. Includes general bibliographies and bibliographies arranged by subject; supplemented by an "author-title-institution-index."

Gardner, James L. *Zen Buddhism: A Classified Bibliography of Western-language Publications through 1990.* [Salt Lake City]: Wings of Fire, 1991. A comprehensive listing of 2,800 items in Western (mostly English) languages; includes author and subject indexes.

Ikado, Fujio and McGovern, James R., comps. *A Bibliography of Christianity in Japan: Protestantism in English Sources (1859–1959).* Tokyo: Committee on Asian Cultural Studies, International Christian University, 1966. Books, pamphlets, and articles arranged alphabetically by author, with separate indexes by title, author, and subject.

Makino, Yasuko and Miki, Mihoko, eds. *Japan and the Japanese: A Bibliographic Guide to Reference Sources.* Westport, CT: Greenwood, 1996. The first part is "General Reference Works on Japan"; the second part is "Subject Bibliographies and Reference Works Related to Japan"; 532 bibliographic items, followed by author, subject, and title indexes.

Notehelfer, F. G. "Modern Japan." In *The American Historical Association's Guide to Historical Literature.* 3d ed. Edited by Mary Beth Norton et al. New York: Oxford University, 1995, pp. 379–413. Brief introduction to modern Japanese history and major historical questions (Meiji Restoration, war, modernization), followed by annotated items (by historical period, subdivided by subject). (See Collcutt in this section for "Premodern Japan.")

Pas, Julian F. *A Select Bibliography on Taoism.* Stony Brook, NY: Institute for Advanced Studies of World Religions, 1988. 2d enlarged ed. Saskatoon: China Pavilion, 1997. See especially the opening section, "Bibliographies" (on Taoism).

Reynolds, Frank E., et al., eds. *Guide to Buddhist Religion.* Boston: G. K. Hall, 1981. A comprehensive bibliography on Buddhism arranged topically and geographically, and featuring author and subject indexes; includes references to Japanese Buddhism.

Schwade, Arcadio. *Shinto Bibliography in Western Languages, Bibliography on Shinto and Religious Sects, Intellectual Schools and Movements Influenced by Shintoism.* Leiden: E. J. Brill, 1986. Contains 2,006 items arranged alphabetically by author, with Topical Index.

Shulman, Frank Joseph. *Japan.* Oxford: Clio, 1989. Comprehensive bibliography on all aspects of Japan, with author, title, and subject indexes; see pp. 630–45 for "Bibliographies and Research Guides."

Thompson, Laurence G. *Studies of Chinese Religion: A Comprehensive and Classified Bibliography of Publications in English, French, and German through 1970.* Encino and Belmont, CA: Dickenson Publishing Company, 1976. Updates published as *Chinese Religion in Western Languages: A Comprehensive and Classified Bibliography of Publications in English, French, and German through 1980.* Tucson: Published for the Association for Asian Studies by the University of Arizona, 1985; *Publications on Religions in China, 1981–1989.* Compiled by Alvin P. Cohen, Occasional Papers Series University of Massachusetts at Amherst, Asian Studies Program, no. 15 (1991); *Chinese Religion: Publications in Western Languages, 1981 through 1990.* Compiled by Laurence G. Thompson, edited by Gary Seaman. The Association for Asian Studies Monographs, no. 47 (1993). *Chinese Religions: Publications in Western Language, vol. 3; 1991 through 1995.* Compiled by Laurence G. Thompson, edited by Gary Seaman. Association for Asian Studies, Monograph and

Occasional Paper Series, vol. 58 (1998). Divided between Buddhism and other religions, the many topical categories are useful for finding specific references.

SPECIAL REFERENCE WORKS ON
JAPANESE HISTORY AND RELIGION

Baroni, Helen Josephine. *The Illustrated Encyclopedia of Zen Buddhism*. New York: Rosen, 2002. Provides a brief overview of Zen, followed by short entries of Japanese and English terms; includes "Contents by Subject" lists for convenient location of terms (art, biography, Buddhas, monastic life, etc.), a bibliography, and index.

Basic Terms of Shinto. "Compiled by Shinto Committee for the IXth International Congress for the History of Religions." Tokyo: Jinja Honcho (Association of Shinto Shrines), Institute for Japanese Culture and Classics, Kokugakuin University, 1958. Rev. ed., 1985. A convenient vocabulary of some important Shinto terms.

Bocking, Brian. *A Popular Dictionary of Shinto*. Richmond, Surrey: Curzon, 1996. This work "lists in alphabetical order more than a thousand terms relating to Shinto," almost all in Japanese, plus a "Thematic *Index* of English and Japanese terms," cross-references, and index (in thirteen separate categories).

Buckley, Sandra. *Encyclopedia of Contemporary Japanese Culture*. London: Routledge, 2002. Contains 750 alphabetically arranged entries, supplemented by subject category lists and index.

Campbell, Alan, et al., eds. *Japan: An Illustrated Encyclopedia*. 2 vols. Tokyo: Kodansha, 1993. Profusely illustrated, and featuring numerous entries, it is a useful supplement to Itasaka, *Kodansha Encyclopedia of Japan*.

Collcutt, Martin, et al. *A Cultural Atlas of Japan*. New York: Facts on File, 1988. Combines historical atlas with narrative cultural history, prehistory to the present; includes geographical and historical maps, illustrations, chronology, glossary, table of Japanese rulers, bibliography.

Frederick, Louis. *Japan Encyclopedia*. Cambridge: Harvard University, 2002. A large (1,100-page) encyclopedia of brief entries using both English and Japanese terms; includes a brief bibliography and index.

Hall, John W., et al., eds. *The Cambridge History of Japan*. Cambridge: Cambridge University, 1988–99. Vol. 1, *Ancient Japan*. Edited by Delmer M. Brown. Vol. 2, *Heian Japan*. Edited by Donald H. Shively and William H. McCullough. Vol. 3, *Medieval Japan*. Edited by Kozo Yamamura. Vol. 4, *Early Modern Japan*. Edited by John Whitney Hall. Vol. 5, *The Nineteenth Century*. Edited by Marius B. Jansen. Vol. 6, *The Twentieth Century*. Edited by Peter Duus. Comprehensive, multivolume reference work with major articles by leading scholars, a standard reference.

Hunter, Janet E., comp. *Concise Dictionary of Modern Japanese History*. Berkeley: University of California, 1984. A convenient identification of "the individuals, events and organizations that have played a significant role in Japan's modern history," arranged alphabetically; also features maps and useful appendixes.

Inagaki, Hisao. *A Dictionary of Japanese Buddhist Terms Based on References in Japanese Literature.* "In collaboration with P. G. O'Neill." 3d ed., with supplement. Kyoto: Nagata Bunshodo, 1988. A convenient collection of 5,000 Buddhist terms with references to their appearance in literature; includes separate indexes for Chinese characters (by stroke order and by pronunciation), Japanese, Chinese, Sanskrit, and Pali terms.

Inagaki, Hisao. *A Glossary of Zen Terms*. Kyoto: Nagata Bunshodo, 1991. For serious students, includes 5,500 romanized Japanese terms, followed by Sino-Japanese characters, English definition, Chinese romanization, and Sanskrit equivalent; includes seven appendixes.

Itasaka, Gen and Dekker, Maurits, eds. *Kodansha Encyclopedia of Japan*. 6 vols. Tokyo: Kodansha International, 1977. The most convenient single reference work on all aspects of Japan.

Japanese-English Buddhist Dictionary. Tokyo: Daito Shuppansha, 1965. Rev. ed., 1991. Based on a standard Japanese dictionary, with the terms translated into Roman letters and alphabetized; includes separate indexes for Chinese characters, Sanskrit, Pali, and Romanized Chinese.

Kamei, Katsuichiro, et al. *The Heibonsha Survey of Japanese Art*. 31 vols. New York: Weatherhill/Heibonsha, 1972–79. English translation of a Japanese-language series of general introductions to the various media and periods of Japanese art; features readable texts and lavish illustrations; volume 31 is an index to the series. (For two volumes on religion, see Watanabe in the "Shinto" section of this bibliography and Sawa in the "Buddhism" section.)

Kokudo Chiriin (Geographical Survey Institute), ed. *The National Atlas of Japan*. Tokyo: Japan Map Center, 1977. A complete atlas of Japan in English; features hundreds of maps with extensive information in physical, social, economic, cultural, and administrative aspects.

Masuda, Koh, ed. *Kenkyusha's New Japanese-English Dictionary*. 4th ed. Tokyo: Kenkyusha, 1974. A standard work; because the Japanese words are transliterated into Roman letters and alphabetized, it can be used even by those who do not read Japanese.

Pas, Julian F. *Historical Dictionary of Taoism*. "In cooperation with Man Kam Leung." Lanham, MD: The Scarecrow Press, 1998. Provides a "Chronology of Taoist History," a lengthy "Introduction," and an extensive dictionary (of English and Chinese terms), and a Bibliography, pp. 377–412.

Yanagita, Kunio, comp. *Japanese Folklore Dictionary*. Translated by Masanori Takatsuka. Edited by George K. Brady. "Kentucky microcards, Series A, no. 18." Lexington: University of Kentucky, 1958. The microcards are awkward to use, but this standard reference work contains valuable material for anyone who does not read Japanese; arranged alphabetically by Japanese terms.

Yokoi, Yuho. *Japanese English Zen Buddhist Dictionary*. Kyoto: Sankibo Buddhist Bookstore, 1991. Features 856 pages of brief items, arranged by Japanese romanized terms and *kanji*; a 156-page index is subdivided into Sino-Japanese characters (by character stroke), Sanskrit, and Chinese.

PERIODICALS FOR JAPANESE
HISTORY AND RELIGION

Asian Folklore Studies. Tokyo, 1963–. (Formerly *Folklore Studies*, Peiking, 1942–52; Tokyo, 1953–62.) Covering Far Eastern folklore in general, it includes articles and monographs on Japanese subjects in German and English.

Bulletin de la Maison Franco-Japonaise. Tokyo, 1927–. In French; detailed monographs of a technical nature.

Bulletin of the Nanzan Institute for Religion and Culture. Nagoya, 1977–. Covers especially interreligious dialogue and religious issues and events in contemporary Japan.

The Eastern Buddhist. Kyoto, 1921–37; New Series, 1965–. Articles by Buddhists on popular and scholarly topics.

Japan Christian Quarterly. Tokyo, 1926–. Articles mainly on Protestantism and its missions in Japan.

Japan Quarterly. Tokyo, 1954–. A general journal dealing with all aspects of Japan.

Japanese Journal of Religious Studies. Tokyo, 1974–. (Formerly *Contemporary Religions in Japan*, 1960–74.) The earlier journal focused on postwar religious developments; its successor contains both theoretical and descriptive articles; the single most important journal for the study of Japanese religion; with a recent topical index.

Japanese Religions. Kyoto, 1959–. Popular articles on aspects of contemporary Japanese religions; frequently features dialogues between Christianity and Japanese religious groups.

The Journal of Asian Studies. Ann Arbor, MI: 1956–. (Formerly *Far Eastern Quarterly*, 1941–56.) The leading scholarly journal in English on Asian topics.

Journal of Japanese Studies. Seattle, 1974–. A periodical developed by scholars of Japanese studies, with specialized articles on Japanese history and culture.

Mitteilungen der Deutschen Gesellschaft für Natur- und Völkerkunde Ostasiens. Tokyo, 1873–. Includes monographs on specialized topics in German.

Monumenta Nipponica. Tokyo, 1938–. Scholarly articles, translations, and reviews in English on all aspects of Japanese history and culture.

Philosophy East and West. Honolulu, 1951–. Descriptive and comparative articles on Asian thought systems, especially Buddhism.

Tenri Journal of Religion. Tenri, 1955–. Articles on Tenrikyo history and doctrine, and also treatments of Japanese religion.

Transactions of the Asiatic Society of Japan. Tokyo, 1872–. The oldest general periodical of its kind; with a recent topical index.

HISTORIES AND WORKS ON
JAPANESE CULTURE

For additional references, see "Special Bibliographies on Japanese History and Religion."

Anderson, Joseph L. and Richie, Donald. *The Japanese Film: Art and Industry.* Expanded edition. Princeton: Princeton University, 1982. A complete history of the film industry from 1896 to 1980, with analysis of the distinctive characteristics of Japanese film such as content, technique, and directors; includes numerous film clips.

Asquith, Pamela J. and Kalland, Arne, eds. *Japanese Images of Nature: Cultural Perspectives.* Surrey: Curzon, 1997. Articles emphasizing the variety of views of nature in Japan across historical periods.

Association of Japanese Geographers, ed. *Geography of Japan.* Tokyo: Teikoku-Shoin, 1980. Eighteen articles by Japanese geographers, featuring both regional geography and the current "achievements of researchers in geographical studies"; the appendix provides a glossary of Japanese terms and both subject and place name indexes.

Bachnik, Jane M. and Quinn, Charles J., Jr., eds. *Situated Meaning: Inside and Outside in Japanese Self, Society, and Language.* Princeton: Princeton University, 1994. Essays on aspects of self and social context in Japan, especially the notions of *uchi/soto* ("inside/outside").

Beardsley, Richard K., et al. *Village Japan.* Chicago: University of Chicago, 1959. A pioneering postwar village study of a small rice-growing community through seven years of joint field work, with separate chapters on aspects of community life. See Chapter 14 for religion.

Befu, Harumi. *Japan: An Anthropological Introduction.* San Francisco: Chandler Publishing Company, 1971. A general introduction to aspects of Japanese culture, with suggested readings and many photographs.

Benedict, Ruth. *The Chrysanthemum and the Sword.* Boston: Houghton Mifflin, 1946 (and later editions). A wartime attempt to examine distinctively Japanese assumptions about life on the basis of written documents. (See Lebra and Lebra, *Japanese Culture and Behavior*, especially pp. 194–98, for a critique of Benedict and *on*.)

Bestor, Theodore C. *Neighborhood Tokyo.* Stanford: Stanford University, 1989. An anthropological record of life in one neighborhood of Tokyo; for treatment of a festival, see pp. 224–55.

Bix, Herbert P. *Hirohito and the Making of Modern Japan.* New York: HarperCollins, 2000. A massive (800-page) study of the life and activities of the Showa Emperor (Hirohito), including his involvement in World War II.

Brown, Delmer M. *Nationalism in Japan: An Introductory Historical Analysis*. Berkeley: University of California, 1955. Reprint ed., New York: Russell & Russell, 1971. A historical study of the complex development of nationalism in Japan.

Buruma, Ian. *Behind the Mask: On Sexual Demons, Sacred Mothers, Transvestites, Gangsters and other Japanese Cultural Heroes*. New York: New American Library, 1985. A bold description and interpretation of "the raunchy, violent, and often morbid side of Japanese culture."

Buruma, Ian. *The Wages of Guilt: Memories of War in Germany and Japan*. New York: Farrar, Straus, and Giroux, 1994. Compares the legacy of war guilt in Germany and Japan on the fiftieth anniversary of the end of World War II.

Chamberlain, Basil Hall. *Things Japanese: Being Notes on Various Subjects Connected with Japan for the Use of Travellers and Others*. 5th ed. rev. London: John Murray, 1905. A kind of handbook by one of the early Western authorities on Japan; the alphabetically arranged articles (rather dated) are still of interest.

Clark, Scott. *Japan, A View from the Bath*. Honolulu: University of Hawaii, 1994. Tracing the history of Japanese bathing as an emphasis both on cleanliness and purification, both field work and interviews yield the conclusion that "Bathing . . . is a metaphor of life renewal."

Cook, Haruko Taya and Cook, Theodore F. *Japan at War: An Oral History*. New York: The New Press, 1992. Stories about life in World War II as told by the civilians and military who lived through it.

Cooper, Michael. *They Came to Japan: An Anthology of European Reports on Japan, 1543–1640*. Berkeley: University of California, 1965. "This anthology is composed of selections from the writings of more than thirty Europeans who visited Japan sometime during the century of contact with the West and set down their impressions on paper."

Craig, Albert M. and Shively, Donald H., eds. *Personality in Japanese History*. Berkeley: University of California, 1970. A book of essays evaluating Japanese personality through case studies of major political and literary figures of the past few centuries.

Dale, Peter N. *The Myth of Japanese Uniqueness*. London: University of Oxford, 1986. An early critique of Nihonjinron, the notion of Japanese uniqueness.

de Bary, Wm. Theodore and Bloom, Irene, eds. *Sources of Chinese Tradition*. 2d ed. Vol. 1, New York: Columbia University, 1999. Vol. 2, de Bary, Wm. Theodore, and Lufrano, Richard, eds. New York: Columbia University, 2000. A companion volume to Tsunoda et al., *Sources of Japanese Tradition* (and de Bary et al., 2d ed.), this is a convenient resource for the Chinese background of Japanese culture and religion.

de Bary, Wm. Theodore, et al. *Sources of Japanese Tradition*. See Tsunoda in this section.

Denoon, Donald, et al., eds. *Multicultural Japan: Paleolithic to Postmodern*. "Paperback edition with new epilogue." Cambridge: Cambridge University, 1996. "This book challenges the conventional view of Japanese society as being monocultural and homogeneous."

Doi, Takeo. *The Anatomy of Dependence*. Translated by John Bester. Tokyo: Kodansha International, 1973. A book that interprets Japanese behavior in terms of distinctively Japanese psychological categories.

Dore, R. P. *City Life in Japan: A Study of a Tokyo Ward*. Berkeley: University of California, 1958. A detailed sociological analysis of life in one area of postwar Tokyo, valuable for its firsthand description of all facets of city life.

Dore, R. P. *Education in Tokugawa Japan*. Berkeley: University of California, 1965. A history of formal and informal educational institutions (including *terakoya*) in Tokugawa times.

Dore, R. P. *Shinohata: A Portrait of a Japanese Village*. London: Allen Lane, 1978. Reprint ed., New York: Pantheon Books, 1980. A firsthand account of all aspects of life in a village, noting changes between 1955 and 1975; includes photographs and many interviews with villagers.

Dower, John W. *Embracing Defeat: Japan in the Wake of World War II*. New York: W. W. Norton, 1999. A critical assessment of the complex interplay between conqueror and conquered, guilt and responsibility, in postwar Japan.

Dower, John W. *War Without Mercy: Race & Power in the Pacific War*. New York: Pantheon, 1986. Using wartime materials, deals directly with the explicit and implicit racism behind the United States's war with Japan.

Dunn, Charles J. *Everyday Life in Traditional Japan*. New York: Putnam, 1969; Rutland, VT: Charles E. Tuttle, 1972. Description of daily life before 1900, with separate chapters on various occupations; profusely illustrated with traditional drawings.

Duus, Peter. *Feudalism in Japan*. 2d ed. New York: Knopf, 1976. A general historical treatment of feudalism in Japan as compared with feudalism in Europe.

Earl, David Magarey. *Emperor and Nation in Japan: Political Thinkers of the Tokugawa Period*. Seattle: University of Washington, 1964. An analysis of the development of nationalism and the rise of the status of the emperor from Tokugawa times on.

Editorial Department of Teikoku-Shoin Co. *Teikoku's Complete Atlas of Japan*. 10th ed. Tokyo: Teikoku-Shoin, 1989. A handy set of national and regional maps with topographical and some economic and social information.

Ernst, Earle. *The Kabuki Theatre*. Oxford: Oxford University, 1956; reprinted, Honolulu: The University Press of Hawaii, 1974. A detailed treatment of *kabuki* theatre as an art form, and a perceptive appreciation of social and religious values expressed therein.

Field, Norma. *In the Realm of a Dying Emperor: Japan at Century's End*. New York: Random House, 1991. This book takes the death of the Showa Emperor (Hirohito) as the occasion for a critical look at contemporary Japanese society.

Fu, Charles Wei-hsun and Heine, Steven, eds. *Japan in Traditional and Postmodern Perspectives*. Albany, NY: State University of New York, 1995. "The central, underlying theme of this collection is to explore the implications of dubiousness by considering the question of the uniqueness and creativity of Japan as seen in terms of the interplay of traditional and postmodern perspectives."

Fujitani, T. *Splendid Monarchy: Power and Pageantry in Modern Japan*. Berkeley: University of California, 1996. Documents the "invention" of the Japanese monarchy as it is known and presented to the public today.

Golovnin, Vasilii Mikhailovich. *Memoirs of a Captivity in Japan, During the Years 1811, 1812, and 1813; with Observations on the Country and the People*. 2d ed., 3 vols. London: H. Colburn, 1824; reprinted, New York: Oxford University, 1973. A Russian observer of Japanese customs (including indifference to religion) during his "captivity" in Japan 1811–13.

Hall, Robert King. *Shushin: The Ethics of a Defeated Nation*. New York: Columbia University, 1949. A critical analysis of the nationalistic and ultranationalistic ethics textbooks of prewar and wartime Japan that were abolished by the Allied Occupation; contains lengthy translations from the textbooks concerning loyalty to emperor, ancestors, Shinto, and nation.

Hanayama, Shinsho. *The Way of Deliverance: Three Years with the Condemned Japanese War Criminals*. Translated by Hideo Suzuki, Eiichi Noda, and James K. Sasaki. London: Victor Gollancz, 1955. The religious faith of the Japanese convicted as war criminals shortly after World War II is recorded by their Buddhist chaplain for the three years they were being tried and awaiting execution.

Hane, Mikiso. *Peasants, Rebels, and Outcastes: The Underside of Japan*. New York: Pantheon Books, 1982. A history of the underside or other side of Japan, the common folk.

Harich-Schneider, Eta. *A History of Japanese Music*. London: Oxford University, 1973. A lengthy, technical survey of Japanese music from prehistoric times to the present century; includes three small long-play records of musical selections.

Harootunian, Harry D. *Overcome by Modernity: History, Culture, and Community in Interwar Japan*. Princeton: Princeton University, 2000. An extended treatment of the notions of "modern" and "modernity," and their significance for understanding Japan today.

Harris, Sheldon H. *Factories of Death: Japanese Biological Warfare, 1932–1945, and the American Cover-up*. London: Routledge, 1994. The history and activities of the infamous Unit 731 of the Imperial Japanese Army, which conducted bacterial warfare research in Manchuria.

Havens, Thomas R. H. *Valley of Darkness: The Japanese People and World War Two*. New York: Norton, 1978. An account of the effects of World War II on the Japanese people, including many translated wartime documents—letters, diaries, and newspapers.

Henderson, Harold G. *An Introduction to Haiku: An Anthology of Poems and Poets from Basho to Shiki*. Garden City, NY: Doubleday, 1958. A sensitive introduction to *haiku;* a first book for becoming acquainted with Japanese culture and art.

Hendry, Joy. *Beginning Japanese: The World of the Pre-School Child*. Manchester: Manchester University, 1986. An anthropological work treating "Japanese views of children," socialization, upbringing in home and preschool, and "the world view presented to the child."

Hendry, Joy. *Marriage in Changing Japan: Community and Society*. Rutland, VT and Tokyo: Charles E. Tuttle, 1981. An anthropological study discussing the historical background of family and community before treating married life, match-making, and ceremonies.

Hibbett, Howard S. "Akutagawa Ryunosuke and the Negative Ideal." In *Personality in Japanese History*. Edited by Albert M. Craig and Donald H. Shiveley. Berkeley: University of California, 1970, pp. 425–51. Analyzes the "negative ideal" of suicide, which has been the final statement of a number of modern Japanese writers.

Hibbett, Howard S. *The Floating World in Japanese Fiction*. London: Oxford University, 1959. An overview of the "floating world" *(ukiyo)* of Tokugawa times.

Hicks, George. *The Comfort Women: Japan's Brutal Regime of Enforced Prostitution in the Second World War*. New York: W. W. Norton, 1994. Includes graphic firsthand testimony of non-Japanese women forced to become prostitutes for the Japanese military (known euphemistically as "comfort women").

Hino, Ashino [Tamai, Katsunori]. *Wheat and Soldiers*. Translated by Baroness Shidzue Ishimoto. New York: Farrar & Rinehart, 1939. A firsthand account of the war in China from the viewpoint of the ordinary conscripted Japanese soldier.

Honda, Katsuichi. *The Impoverished Spirit in Contemporary Japan: Selected Essays of Honda Katsuichi*. Edited by John Lie. Translated by Eri Fujieda et al. New York: Monthly Review, 1993. Translated newspaper articles by a hard-hitting journalist for "the prestigious Japanese daily *Asahi Shinbun*."

Ienaga, Saburo. *Japan's Past, Japan's Future*. Translated and introduced by Richard H. Minear. Lanham, MD: Rowman & Littlefield, 2001. An autobiography tracing a famous historian's career before, during, and after World War II, especially his court battles with the government in the "textbook trials."

Ienaga, Saburo. *The Pacific War, 1931–1945: A Critical Perspective on Japan's Role in World War II*. Translated by Frank Baldwin. New York: Pantheon Books, 1978. A critical and controversial view of Japan's role as aggression; Ienaga's textbooks were not approved by the Ministry of Education in spite of court battles (see previous item by Ienaga).

Iga, Mamoru. *The Thorn in the Chrysanthemum: Suicide and Economic Success in Modern Japan*. Berkeley: University of California, 1986. Discusses the "pattern of Japanese suicide" for males and females, and also treats Japanese writers' suicides.

Imamura, Keiji. *Prehistoric Japan: New Perspectives on Insular East Asia*. Honolulu: University of Hawai'i, 1996. A detailed analysis of the archaeological evidence in Japan, discussing various notions of the periods, dating, and theories about prehistoric Japanese culture, arguing more for the "unique" character of Japanese prehistory.

Ishihara, Shintaro. *The Japan That Can Say No: Why Japan Will Be First Among Equals*. Translated by Frank Baldwin. New York: Simon & Schuster, 1991. A controversial politician's bold assertion of Japan's national pride and self-confidence over the United States.

Ishimoto, Shidzue. *The Story of My Life*. Stanford: Stanford University, 1984 (first published 1935). Provides a firsthand view of women's rights from the perspective of an upper-class woman in the early twentieth century.

Jansen, Marius B. *The Making of Modern Japan*. Cambridge: Harvard University, 2000. A comprehensive history of the development and features of modern Japan.

Japan National Tourist Organization, comp. *Japan: The New Official Guide*. Tokyo: Japan Travel Bureau, 1975. A useful guidebook to Japan, with detailed maps and historical information on every locale. The 1975 edition has much information on industry and commerce. Earlier editions, especially the ninth revision of *Japan: The Official Guide* (1962), usually available in used-book stores in Japan, contain more information on cultural and historical landmarks.

Johnson, Chalmers. *Japan: Who Governs?* New York: W. W. Norton, 1995. Essays on the development and working of the political economy of Japan; in contrast to scholars such as Bellah and Dore, who emphasize the importance of religious values in economic development, he supports "the likelihood that religion has nothing to do with economic development—in either the West or Asia."

Kaplan, David E. and Dubro, Alec. *Yakuza: Japan's Criminal Underworld.* Expanded edition. Berkeley: University of California, 2003. A study of the nature of criminal activity in Japan and its relationship to modern capitalism.

Katzenstein, Peter J. *Cultural Norms and National Security: Police and Military in Postwar Japan.* Ithaca, NY: Cornell University, 1996. A study of Japanese national security in comparison with that of Germany, from the perspective of political economy.

Keene, Donald, ed. *Anthology of Japanese Literature from the Earliest Era to the Mid-Nineteenth Century.* New York: Grove, 1955. Selected translations from all forms of literature, arranged by historical period.

Keene, Donald. *Japanese Literature: An Introduction for Western Readers.* New York: Grove, 1955. A concise survey of poetry, theater, and novels.

Kidder, J. Edward, Jr. *The Birth of Japanese Art.* New York: Praeger Publishers, 1965. A discussion of the art of prehistoric and early Japan, with some color plates and several hundred black and white illustrations.

Kiyota, Minoru. *Beyond Loyalty: The Story of a Kibei.* Translated by Linda Klepinger Keenan. Honolulu: University of Hawai'i, 1997. Autobiographical account of a *nisei* (second-generation) Japanese who went to Japan and returned to America *(kibei),* living through internment during World War II, and later becoming a professor of Buddhist studies.

Kondo, Dorinne K. *Crafting Selves: Power, Gender, and Discourses of Identity in a Japanese Workplace.* Chicago: University of Chicago, 1990. An anthropological study by a Japanese-American who worked in a family-owned factory as the basis for her description and analysis.

Lebra, Joyce, et al. *Women in Changing Japan.* Stanford: Stanford University, 1976. Separate chapters describe women in eleven occupational fields, providing valuable interviews of women engaged in these occupations; "women and suicide" is also treated.

Lebra, Takie Sugiyama. *Japanese Patterns of Behavior.* Honolulu: University Press of Hawaii, 1976. An analysis of both normal and deviant behavior, showing that "the Japanese are extremely sensitive to and concerned about social interaction and relationships."

Lebra, Takie Sugiyama. *Japanese Women: Constraint and Fulfillment.* Honolulu: University of Hawaii, 1984. Uses extensive interviews with Japanese women to construct a life cycle from "premarital constraints and options" to "later years."

Lebra, Takie Sugiyama and Lebra, William P., eds. *Japanese Culture and Behavior: Selected Readings.* Honolulu: University Press of Hawaii, 1974. Articles on various aspects of Japanese behavior by anthropologists, sociologists, and psychologists.

Malm, William P. *Japanese Music and Musical Instruments.* Rutland, VT: Charles E. Tuttle, 1959. A comprehensive overview of Japanese music and musical instruments, treating both history and performance; features many illustrations and some musical transcriptions.

Maraini, Fosco. *Japan: Patterns of Continuity.* Tokyo: Kodansha International, 1971. An appreciation of Japanese culture past and present, profusely illustrated with color photographs.

Maraini, Fosco. *Meeting with Japan.* Translated by Eric Mosbacher. New York: Viking, 1959. A kind of travel book, whose impressions are complemented by many photographs.

Miller, Roy Andrew. *The Japanese Language in Contemporary Japan: Some Socio-Linguistic Observations.* Washington, DC: American Enterprise Institute for Public Policy Research; Stanford: Hoover Institution on War, Revolution, and Peace, 1977. A general treatment of the nature of Japanese language and its relationship to Japanese social and cultural identity.

Minear, Richard H. *Japanese Tradition and Western Law: Emperor, State, and Law in the Thought of Hozumi Yatsuka.* Cambridge: Harvard University, 1970. Contains an extended discussion of the notion of *kokutai.*

Miner, Earl. *An Introduction to Japanese Court Poetry*. Stanford: Stanford University, 1968. Based on the longer work *Japanese Court Poetry* (by Miner and Robert H. Brower), this general treatment provides translations of major court poets from A.D. 550 to 1500 and an overview of themes such as nature and love as well as religious influence.

Mishima, Yukio. *The Sea of Fertility*. A tetralogy consisting of *Spring Snow* (1972), translated by Michael Gallagher; *Runaway Horses* (1973), translated by Michael Gallagher; *The Temple of Dawn* (1973), translated by E. Dale Saunders and Cecilia Segawa Seigle; and *The Decay of the Angel* (1975), translated by Edward G. Seidensticker. Publication dates are for the original English-language editions published in New York by Knopf; subsequently reprinted in a paperback edition in New York by Pocket Books. These four novels, in effect Mishima's last testament before his suicide in 1971, dramatize the plight of modern man; the extensive references to religion, especially Buddhist philosophy, occasionally temper Mishima's nihilism with a kind of existentialist quest.

Mitchell, Richard H. *Thought Control in Prewar Japan*. Ithaca, NY: Cornell University, 1976. A detailed analysis of the laws and actual prosecution for eliminating revolutionaries from 1868 to 1941; it documents measures used to develop a highly unified national consciousness in this period.

Mizoguchi, Koji. *An Archaeological History of Japan 30,000 B.C. to A.D. 700*. Philadelphia: University of Pennsylvania, 2002. A critical view of the way archaeology has been practiced and how archaeological evidence has been interpreted in Japan.

Morris, Ivan. *The Nobility of Failure: Tragic Heroes in the History of Japan*. New York: Holt, Rinehart and Winston, 1975; New York: New American Library, 1976. A historical and literary analysis of the "tragic hero," from mythological figures and medieval warriors to the *kamikaze* suicide feats of World War II.

Morris, Ivan. *The World of the Shining Prince: Court Life in Ancient Japan*. New York: Knopf, 1964; "with a new introduction by Barbara Ruch," New York: Kodansha, 1994. Provides insight into the values and aesthetics of court life.

Murasaki, Shikibu. *The Tale of Genji*. 2 vols. Translated by Edward G. Seidensticker. New York: Knopf, 1976. Reprint ed., Rutland, VT: Charles E. Tuttle, 1978. Translation of a Japanese classic, it reveals the court pageantry and religious life of medieval Japan.

Murasaki, Shikibu. *The Tale of Genji*. 2 vols. Translated by Royall Tyler. New York: Viking, 2001. The most recent translation of this medieval tale.

Najita, Tetsuo and Koschmann, J. Victor, eds., *Conflict in Modern Japanese History: The Neglected Tradition*. Princeton: Princeton University, 1982. Essays having as their common theme the questioning of the stereotype of a rather homogeneous and consensual Japanese society.

Nakamura, Hajime. *A History of the Development of Japanese Thought from 592 to 1868*. 2 vols. Tokyo: Kokusai Bunka Shinkokai (Society for International Cultural Relations), 1967. A historical survey, emphasizing the distinctiveness of Japanese thought.

Nakane, Chie. *Japanese Society*. Berkeley: University of California, 1970. Analysis of Japanese society emphasizing its "vertical structure."

Ohnuki-Tierney, Emiko. *Illness and Culture in Contemporary Japan: An Anthropological View*. Cambridge: Cambridge University, 1984. An anthropological treatment of the nature of illness and healing as an aspect of Japanese culture and religion.

Ohnuki-Tierney, Emiko. *Kamikaze, Cherry Blossoms, and Nationalisms: The Militarization of Aesthetics in Japanese History*. Chicago: University of Chicago, 2002. Using previously unpublished diaries of World War II *kamikaze* (suicide) pilots, she explores the complex motivations and symbolisms of these young men who came to see themselves as falling cherry blossoms.

Onoda, Hiroo. *No Surrender: My Thirty Year War*. Translated by Charles S. Terry. Tokyo: Kodansha International, 1974. The biography of a Japanese soldier who continued guerrilla warfare on a Philippine island from 1944 to 1974 provides insight into the psychology of wartime Japan.

Paine, Robert Treat and Soper, Alexander. *The Art and Architecture of Japan*. 3d ed. Baltimore: Penguin Books, 1981. A scholarly historical analysis divided into painting and sculpture, and architecture, with numerous plates.

Piggott, Joan R. *The Emergence of Japanese Kingship*. Stanford: Stanford University, 1997. "The purpose of this book is to illuminate processes that shaped early Japanese kingship. . . ."; it discusses the formation of the state and the role of religion in these processes.

Plath, David W. *Long Engagements: Maturity in Modern Japan*. Stanford: Stanford University, 1980. An account of aging or "maturity" told through the life histories of four contemporary Japanese, compared with characters in Japanese novels.

Raz, Aviad E. *Riding the Black Ship: Japan and Tokyo Disneyland*. Cambridge: Harvard University, 1999. A detailed study of the development of Tokyo Disneyland (including staff recruitment and training), with comparison to American Disneyland.

Reynolds, David K. *Morita Psychotherapy*. Berkeley: University of California, 1976. Introduction to the distinctively Japanese form of psychotherapy developed by Shoma Morita, which includes some Buddhist influence.

Reynolds, David K. *The Quiet Therapies: Japanese Pathways to Personal Growth*. Honolulu: The University Press of Hawaii, 1980. Afterword by George DeVos. Interpretation of Morita psychotherapy and four other forms of "quiet therapy," all of which "cause the client to spend time isolated, locked up in his own thoughts."

Rohlen, Thomas P. *For Harmony and Strength: Japanese White-Collar Organization in Anthropological Perspective*. Berkeley: University of California, 1974. An anthropological record of the organization and activities in a Japanese bank; shows some parallels to religious organization and practices.

Rohlen, Thomas P. *Japan's High Schools*. Berkeley: University of California, 1983. An anthropological record of Japanese high schools, with some comparisons to American high schools.

Rosenberger, Nancy R., ed. *Japanese Sense of Self*. Cambridge: Cambridge University, 1992. Essays on self and the social in Japan "as interactive rather than opposing forces."

Sansom, Sir George. *A History of Japan*. 3 vols. Stanford: Stanford University, 1958–63. A standard Western work, especially valuable for cultural history, covering the span from earliest times until 1867.

Schodt, Frederick L. *Dreamland Japan: Writings on Modern Manga*. Berkeley, CA: Stone Bridge, 1996. An overview of *manga* (Japanese comics).

Sheff, David. *Game Over: How Nintendo Zapped an American Industry, Captured Your Dollars, and Enslaved Your Children*. New York: Random House, 1993. Satirical title for a serious account of the success story of Nintendo.

Smith, Robert J. *Japanese Society: Tradition, Self, and the Social Order*. Cambridge: Cambridge University, 1983. A brief and readable overview of the nature of self and society in the Japanese tradition.

Smith, Robert J. *Kurusu: The Price of Progress in a Japanese Village, 1951–1975*. Stanford: Stanford University, 1978. A detailed anthropological description of life in the village of Kurusu, with an interpretation of social, economic, and religious life in villages.

Smith, Robert J. and Wiswell, Ella Lury. *The Women of Suye Mura*. Chicago: University of Chicago, 1982. A rare look at the life of prewar Japanese women, based on prewar ethnographic work.

Takeyama, Michio. *Harp of Burma*. Translated by Howard Hibbett. Rutland, VT: Charles E. Tuttle, 1966. A 1946 novel about Japanese prisoners of war in Burma at the end of World War II; originally written for high school students, it was widely read as a forceful dramatic rendering of the problems facing Japan after World War II.

Tanaka, Yuki. *Hidden Horrors: Japanese War Crimes in World War II*. Boulder, CO: Westview, 1996. Documents the dark side of the Japanese military during World War II; draws comparison with non-Japanese atrocities.

Thompson, Laurence G. *Chinese Religion: An Introduction*. 4th ed. Belmont, CA: Wadsworth, 1989. A brief introduction, helpful for understanding the Chinese background of Japanese religion; includes a bibliography.

Toby, Ronald P. "Why Leave Nara? Kammu and the Transfer of the Capital." *Monumenta Nipponica*, vol. 40, no. 3 (Autumn 1985), pp. 331–47. Interprets the move of the capital from Nara not only as an escape from overpowering Buddhist influence and avoidance of pollution, but also as part of the political process of the "gradual transition from 'court to capital.'"

Tsunoda, Ryusaku, et al. *Sources of Japanese Tradition*. New York: Columbia University, 1958. 2d ed. Vol. 1, compiled by Wm. Theodore de Bary et al. New York: Columbia University, 2001; vol. 2, forthcoming. A valuable collection of translated documents and comments on Japanese literature, thought, and religion. (See de Bary for the companion, *Sources of Chinese Tradition*.)

Tsunoda, Ryusaku and Goodrich, L. C., eds. *Japan in the Chinese Dynastic Histories*. South Pasadena, CA: P. D. & I. Perkins, 1951. Contains valuable Chinese perceptions of early Japan.

Ueda, Makoto. *Literary and Art Theories in Japan*. Cleveland, OH: Press of Western Reserve University, 1967. An overview of aesthetic theories in Japan, with translations of the writing of important Japanese writers on art theory.

Ueda, Makoto. *Modern Japanese Writers and the Nature of Literature*. Stanford: Stanford University, 1976. A study of eight major modern Japanese novelists, analyzing their writings especially in terms of their theory of literature; includes a useful bibliography of critical works and translated literature.

Varley, H. Paul. *Japanese Culture: A Short History*. 4th ed., updated and expanded. Honolulu: University of Hawai'i, 2000. This work "is intended as a survey for the general reader of Japanese culture," including the various aspects of culture "that have been uniquely cherished in Japan."

Varley, H. Paul and Kumakura, Isao, eds. *Tea in Japan: Essays on the History of* Chanoyu. Honolulu: University of Hawai'i, 1989. Articles by Japanese and Western scholars on the history, practice, and philosophy of *chanoyu* ("the way of tea").

Varley, H. Paul with Morris, Ivan and Nobuko. *Samurai*. New York: Bell, 1972. A general treatment of the origins of the *samurai* (warrior) class and its role in Japanese history.

Vogel, Ezra F. *Japan as Number One: Lessons for America*. Cambridge: Harvard University, 1979. Reprint ed., New York: Harper & Row, 1980. A provocative work interpreting the "success story" of modern Japanese business and society in terms of the lessons that America can learn from Japan.

Vogel, Ezra F. *Japan as Number One: Revisited*. Singapore: Institute of Southeast Asian Studies, 1986. A sequel to and reconsideration of the original work.

Vogel, Ezra F. *Japan's New Middle Class: The Salary Man and His Family in a Tokyo Suburb*. 2d ed. Berkeley: University of California, 1971. The result of extensive field work, it provides insight into contemporary family life.

Wheatley, Paul and See, Thomas. *From Court to Capital: A Tentative Interpretation of the Origins of the Japanese Tradition*. Chicago: University of Chicago, 1978. Treats the rise of the Japanese city as based on ceremonial-administrative centers.

Wilson, George M. *Patriots and Redeemers in Japan: Motives in the Meiji Restoration*. Chicago: University of Chicago, 1992. An analysis of the religious motives behind the Meiji Restoration.

Yoneyama, Lisa. *Hiroshima Traces: Time, Space, and the Dialectics of Memory*. Berkeley: University of California, 1999. Description and analysis of the symbolic ways Hiroshima has been memorialized.

HISTORIES AND GENERAL WORKS ON JAPANESE RELIGION

For additional references, see "Special Bibliographies on Japanese History and Religion."

Abe, Yoshiya. "Religious Freedom Under the Meiji Constitution." *Contemporary Religions in Japan*, vol. 9, no. 4 (Dec. 1968), pp. 268–338. This book-length work, continued in the four subsequent issues of this journal, is a balanced treatment of the extent of religious freedom under the Meiji Constitution, discussing the background issues and factions for and against actual religious freedom.

Ambros, Barbara and Williams, Duncan, eds. *Local Religion in Tokugawa History*, vol. 28, no. 3–4, of *Japanese Journal of Religious Studies* (Fall 2001). Counters the argument for "corruption" in Tokugawa religious institutions, and emphasizes that popular religion or "lived religion" was active and vital.

Anesaki, Masaharu. *History of Japanese Religion*. London: Kegan Paul, Trench, Trübner, 1930. Reprint ed., Rutland, VT: Charles E. Tuttle Company, 1963. An early one-volume history, whose coverage ends in 1930.

Anesaki, Masaharu. "An Oriental Evaluation of Modern Civilization." In *Recent Gains in American Civilization*. Edited by Kirby Page. New York: Harcourt Brace Jovanovich, 1928, pp. 329–57. Reprinted in Anesaki's *Katam Karaniyam: Lectures, Essays and Studies*. Boston: Marshall Jones Company, 1936, pp. 32–51. A provocative discussion of the role of religion in "modern" civilization.

Armstrong, Robert Cornell. *Just Before the Dawn: The Life and Work of Ninomiya Sontoku*. New York: Macmillan, 1912. An early popular presentation of the life and teachings of Ninomiya Sontoku (1787–1856), the farmer-philosopher, or "peasant sage of Japan."

Bellah, Robert N., ed. *Religion and Progress in Modern Asia*. New York: Free Press, 1965. A discussion of the problem of modernity in terms of the notion of progress.

Bellah, Robert N. *Tokugawa Religion: The Values of Pre-Industrial Japan*. Glencoe, IL: Free Press, 1957; reprinted as *Tokugawa Religion: The Cultural Roots of Modern Japan,* with a new introduction by the author, New York: Free Press, 1970. A sociological analysis of a highly eclectic Tokugawa movement; important for tracing popular values that helped shape modern Japan. See the continuation of this thesis in "Reflection on the Protestant Ethic Analogy in Asia," in Bellah's *Beyond Belief: Essays on Religion in a Post-Traditional World* (and other articles in this volume), New York: Harper & Row, 1970, pp. 53–63.

Bender, Ross. "The Hachiman Cult and the Dokyo Incident." *Monumenta Nipponica*, vol. 34, no. 2 (Summer 1979), pp. 125–53. Traces the origins and development of the divinity Hachiman, and Hachiman's oracular role in early Japan "as the ultimate arbiter of legitimacy," especially in the incident when Dokyo tried to become emperor.

Blacker, Carmen. "Religion in Japan." In *Historia Religionum: Handbook for the History of Religions*. Vol. 2, *Religions of the Present*. Edited by C. J. Bleeker and George Widengren. Leiden: E. J. Brill, 1971, pp. 516–49. A brief treatment of the history and nature of Japanese religion and a short treatment of the study of religion in Japan.

Bonet, Vincente M., ed. *Religion in the Japanese Textbooks*. 3 vols. Tokyo: Enderle Book Company, 1973–74. A critical review of the treatment of religion in all textbooks approved for junior and senior high schools by the Ministry of Education.

Crump, Thomas. *The Japanese Numbers Game: The Use and Understanding of Numbers in Modern Japan*. London: Routledge, 1992. An overview of Japanese fortune-telling, divination, and the horoscope.

Davis, Winston Bradley. *Toward Modernity: A Developmental Typology of Popular Religious Affiliation in Japan*. Ithaca, NY: Cornell China-Japan Program, 1977. A detailed sociological analysis of Japanese religion, focusing on "the religious affiliations of the so-called common man."

Deal, William E. "Hagiography and History: The Image of Prince Shotoku." In *Religions of Japan in Practice*. Edited by George J. Tanabe, Jr. Princeton: Princeton University, 1999, pp. 316–33. A brief treatment of the career and image of Shotoku, accompanying translated documents recording his life and achievements.

Earhart, H. Byron. "Mechanisms and Process in Japanese Amulets." In *Nihon shukyo e no shikaku*. Osaka: Toho Shuppan, 1994, pp. 611–20. An overview of amulets and how they function within Japanese religion.

Earhart, H. Byron. *Religion in the Japanese Experience: Sources and Interpretations*. Belmont, CA: Wadsworth, 1974. 2d ed., Belmont, CA: 1997. A convenient sourcebook of brief documents revealing the history and dynamics of Japanese religion.

Earhart, H. Byron. *A Religious Study of the Mount Haguro Sect of Shugendo: An Example of Japanese Mountain Religion.* Tokyo: Sophia University, 1970. A study of one Shugendo sect that incorporates influence from most Japanese religious traditions.

Earhart, H. Byron. *Religions of Japan: Many Traditions Within One Sacred Way.* San Francisco: Harper & Row, 1984. A brief introduction to Japanese religion.

Ebersole, Gary L. *Ritual Poetry and the Politics of Death in Early Japan.* Princeton: Princeton University, 1989. A study of death rituals and the practice of double burial in early Japan as a key to understanding the ideological and factional intentions of the court.

Erskine, William Hugh. *Japanese Festival and Calendar Lore.* Tokyo: Kyo Bun Kwan, 1933. A popular treatment of many religious aspects of the calendar, with brief descriptions of every national festival (listed by months); contains useful information on the various "cycles" governing astrological beliefs, such as lucky and unlucky days and directions, and features a complete index of Japanese calendar terms.

Garon, Sheldon M. *Molding Japanese Minds: The State in Everyday Life.* Princeton: Princeton University, 1997. In a discussion of the working of the state in prewar Japan, this study discusses the suppression of new religions and communism as heterodoxy, and defines the orthodoxy that opposed them (including "religious statism").

Gauntlett, John Owen, trans. *Kokutai no Hongi: Cardinal Principles of the National Entity of Japan.* Cambridge: Harvard University, 1949. A translation of the nationalistic textbook used in public schools after 1938.

Gluck, Carol. *Japan's Modern Myths: Ideology in the Late Meiji Period.* Princeton: Princeton University, 1985. A detailed study of the "common values" developed by state and society in Meiji Japan (1868–1912), which were crucial for the development of Japan as a nation-state and which continue to be significant for Japanese life today.

Graeburn, Nelson. *To Pray, Pay and Play: The Cultural Structure of Japanese Domestic Tourism.* Aix-en-Provence: Centre des Hautes Etudes Touristiques, 1983. A work showing how Japanese combine religion with play and pilgrimage with sightseeing.

Grapard, Allan. "Flying Mountains and Walkers of Emptiness: Toward a Definition of Sacred Space in Japanese Religions." *History of Religions,* vol. 20, no. 3 (Feb. 1982), pp. 195–221. Thesis is that "the definition of sacred space was gradually expanded from the sacred site to the sacred nation, and . . . ultimately resulted in a sacralization of the total human environment and all of human activity."

Grapard, Allan. "Institution, Ritual, and Ideology: The Twenty-two Shrine-temple Multiplexes of Heian Japan." *History of Religions,* vol. 27, no. 3 (Feb. 1988), pp. 246–69. Argues for not separating Shinto shrines and Buddhist temples, but seeing them as shrine-temple multiplexes.

Grapard, Allan. "Japan's Ignored Revolution: The Separation of Shinto and Buddhist Divinities in Meiji *(shimbutsu bunri)* and a Case Study: Tonomine." *History of Religions,* vol. 23, no. 3 (Feb. 1984), pp. 240–65. Uses a case study to demonstrate the revolutionary (but ignored) significance of the separation of Shinto and Buddhism.

Grapard, Allan. "Lotus in the Mountain, Mountain in the Lotus." *Monumenta Nipponica,* vol. 41, no. 1 (1986), pp. 21–50. Describes an example of a Shinto-Buddhist cult in the same religious center.

Grapard, Allan. *The Protocol of the Gods: A Study of the Kasuga Cult in Japanese History.* Berkeley: University of California, 1992. Develops the thesis that "the Kasuga belief system . . . is a combinative cult, which means that the elements of Shinto and Buddhist creeds and practices that compose it were conceived of as forming a single cohesive system."

Haga, Manabu and Kisala, Robert J., eds. *The New Age in Japan,* vol. 22, no. 3–4, of *Japanese Journal of Religious Studies* (Fall 1995). Includes the editors' introduction and eight articles on various aspects of new age beliefs and practices in Japan.

Haraguchi, Torao, et al. *The Status System and Social Organization of Satsuma: A Translation of the Shumon Tefuda Aratame Jomoku.* Honolulu: University Press of Hawaii, 1976. A translation and introduction to documents controlling the registration and investigation of religious groups in late Tokugawa times (and the use of personal identification tags).

Hardacre, Helen. *Marketing the Menacing Fetus in Japan.* Berkeley: University of California, 1997. "This study treats *mizuko kuyo* [rites for aborted fetuses] as a transsectarian practice that appears in the new religions, Shinto, Shugendo, and in the practice of contemporary religious entrepreneurs, as well as in Buddhism."

Hardacre, Helen. "The Postwar Development of Studies of Japanese Religions." In *The Postwar Development of Japanese Studies in the United States*. London: Brill, 1998, pp. 195–226. A survey of scholars, scholarship, and recent trends in the study of Japanese religion; a bibliography is appended.

Hori, Ichiro, ed. *Japanese Religion*. Translated by Yoshiya Abe and David Reid. Tokyo: Kodansha International, 1972. A convenient one-volume treatment of Japanese religion by Japanese scholars, with concise essays on the various Japanese religious traditions and organizations; also provides addresses and statistics.

Hunter, Jeffrey. *The Animal Court: A Political Fable from Old Japan*. New York: Weatherhill, 1992. See the larger study from which this work is taken, Toshinobu Yasunaga.

Inoue, Nobutaka, et al. "A Festival with Anonymous Kami." *Japanese Journal of Religious Studies*, vol. 6, no. 1–2 (Mar.–June 1979), pp. 163–85. Analysis and interpretation of the Kobe festival as a new kind of festival in urbanized society.

Ito, Kimio. "The Invention of *Wa* and the Transformation of the Image of Prince Shotoku in Modern Japan." In *Mirror of Modernity: Invented Traditions of Modern Japan*. Edited by Stephen Vlastos. Berkeley: University of California, 1998, pp. 37–47. An interpretation of the changing image of Shotoku, especially in association with the invented tradition of *wa* (harmony) and collectivism in changing historical circumstances.

Kanamori, Tokujiro, et al. *Religion and State in Japan: A Discussion of Religion and State in Relation to the Constitution*. Bulletin no. 7. Tokyo: International Institute for the Study of Religions, 1959. Contains four articles by leading Japanese scholars discussing the historical background, and continuing problems, in interpreting religious freedom in the postwar Constitution.

Kasahara, Kazuo, ed. *A History of Japanese Religion*. Translated by Paul McCarthy and Gaynor Sekimori. Tokyo: Kosei, 2001. A comprehensive history written by a team of leading Japanese scholars.

Kenney, Elizabeth and Gilday, Edmund T., eds. *Mortuary Rites in Japan*, vol. 27, no. 3–4, of *Japanese Journal of Religious Studies* (Fall 2000). Includes the editors' introduction and articles on aspects of funerals, cremation, and mortuary rites.

Kidder, J. E., Jr. *Japan Before Buddhism*. Rev. ed. London: Thames and Hudson, 1966. Focuses on prehistoric Japan, with discussion of the religious implications of the diverse archaeological evidence.

Kisala, Robert. *Prophets of Peace: Pacifism and Cultural Identity in Japan's New Religions*. Honolulu: University of Hawai'i, 1999. A comprehensive treatment of the relationship between Japanese religions (especially New Religions) and the ideal of peace.

Kishimoto, Hideo and Wakimoto, Tsuneya. "Introduction: Religion During Tokugawa." In *Japanese Religion in the Meiji Era*. Edited by Hideo Kishimoto. Translated by John F. Howes. Tokyo: Obunsha, 1956, pp. 3–33. This overview of religion in the Tokugawa period illustrates a critical approach to Japanese religion.

Kitagawa, Joseph M. *On Understanding Japanese Religion*. Princeton: Princeton University, 1987. Essays on various aspects of Japanese religion.

Kitagawa, Joseph M. *Religion in Japanese History*. New York: Columbia University, 1966. An account of Japanese religion by a scholar who trained many graduate students in Japanese religion.

Kitagawa, Joseph M. "Shinto" and "Mayahana Buddhism (Japan)." In *Historical Atlas of the Religions of the World*. Edited by Ismai'il Ragi al Faruqui and David E. Sopher. New York: Macmillan, 1974, pp. 127–32, 195–99. Contains maps showing distribution of population by religion and locations of important religious centers.

LaFleur, William R. *Liquid Life: Abortion and Buddhism in Japan*. Princeton: Princeton University, 1992. A detailed study of the interrelationship between abortion and Buddhism, especially the role of ritual "in the way Japanese Buddhists deal with abortion."

LaFleur, William R. "Saigyo and the Buddhist Value of Nature." *History of Religions*, vol. 13, no. 2 (Nov. 1973), pp. 93–128; vol. 13, no. 3 (Feb. 1974), pp. 227–48. A detailed analysis of the appreciation of nature in early Japanese Buddhism (and Shinto), especially as seen in the poetry of the twelfth-century poet Saigyo.

Law, Jane Marie. *Puppets of Nostalgia: The Life, Death, and Rebirth of the Japanese Awaji Ningyo Tradition*. Princeton: Princeton University, 1997. Focuses on itinerant performers of puppetry who use their arts to bring about appeasement of divine will and malevolent spirits, an important dynamic in Japanese popular religion.

Lebra, William P. *Okinawan Religion: Belief, Ritual, and Social Structure*. Honolulu: University Press of Hawaii, 1966. A convenient overview of indigenous religion in Okinawa, useful for comparison and contrast with indigenous religion in the Japanese tradition.

McMullin, Neil. "Historical and Historiographical Issues in the Study of Pre-Modern Japanese Religions." *Japanese Journal of Religious Studies*, vol. 16, no. 1 (Mar. 1989), pp. 3–40. A critical appraisal of the study of premodern Japanese religion, especially the relationship between Buddhism and Shinto.

Mathews, Gordon. *What Makes Life Worth Living? How Japanese and Americans Make Sense of Their Worlds*. Berkeley: University of California, 1996. A comparative study of life, values, and sense of worth based on field work in Japan and America.

Morioka, Kiyomi. *Religion in Changing Japanese Society*. Tokyo: University of Tokyo, 1975. A collection of short essays on the interaction of social factors and religion and the changing character of religion in the postwar period.

Morioka, Kiyomi and Newell, William H., eds. *The Sociology of Japanese Religion*. Leiden: E. J. Brill, 1968 (*Journal of Asian and African Studies*, vol. 3, no. 1–2 [Jan.–Apr. 1968], pp. 1–138). Short, scholarly articles featuring sociological analysis of folk religion and the changing character of religion in the postwar period.

Mullins, Mark, et al., eds. *Religion and Society in Modern Japan*. Berkeley, CA: Asian Humanities, 1993. Essays focusing on the issues of Japanese religiosity, religion and the state, traditional religious institutions, and new religious movements.

Munro, Neil Gordon. *Ainu Creed and Cult*. London: Routledge & Kegan Paul, 1962. A descriptive work based on field work earlier in this century, it includes numerous photographs.

Murakami, Shigeyoshi. *Japanese Religion in the Modern Century*. Translated by H. Byron Earhart. Tokyo: University of Tokyo, 1980. A critical analysis of government suppression of religion before 1945 and the conditions of freedom of religion since 1945; includes broad coverage of the New Religions.

Nakamura, Hajime. *Ways of Thinking of Eastern Peoples: India, China, Tibet, Japan*. Revised English translation edited by Philip P. Wiener. Honolulu: East-West Center, 1964. An attempt to describe the character of the Japanese people through the thought patterns that define their culture.

Nakamura, Kyoko. "The Religious Consciousness and Activities of Contemporary Japanese Women." *Japanese Journal of Religious Studies*, vol. 24, no. 1–2 (Spring 1997), pp. 87–120. "This paper examines the results of a survey of religious consciousness and practice among women in two Japanese religious groups, Rissho Koseikai and the Episcopal Church of Japan."

Nakamura, Kyoko, ed. *Women and Religion in Japan*, vol. 10, no. 2–3, of *Japanese Journal of Religious Studies* (June–Sept. 1983). Includes the editor's introductory remarks and six articles on aspects of women's religious lives.

Namihira, Emiko. "*Hare, Ke* and *Kegare*: The Structure of Japanese Folk Belief." Ph.D. dissertation, University of Texas, Austin, 1977. Sees the structure of Japanese folk belief through the three related categories of *kegare* (dissolution), *hare* (purity), and *ke* (profane).

Namihira, Emiko. "Pollution in the Folk Belief System." *Current Anthropology*, vol. 28, no. 4 (Aug.–Oct. 1987), pp. S65–S72 (with "Comment" by Emiko Ohnuki-Tierney, pp. S72–S73). A briefer treatment of the preceding item (especially *kegare*, dissolution or pollution).

Nishida, Kitaro. *Nishida Kitaro's Fundamental Problems of Philosophy: The World of Action and the Dialectical World*. Translated with an Introduction by David A. Dilworth. Tokyo:

Sophia University, 1970. Two of Nishida's late (1934–35) works, representing the mature "Nishida philosophy" of the pure experience understood in terms of his own Zen experience and in terms of Western philosophy.

Nishida, Kitaro. *A Study of Good.* Translated by V. H. Viglielmo. Tokyo: Ministry of Education, 1960. Nishida, considered the foremost Japanese philosopher of this century, in his first (1911) publication wrote what some consider to be the first original Japanese philosophical work to incorporate both Western and Japanese traditions.

Nishitani, Keiji. "The Religious Situation in Present-Day Japan." *Contemporary Religions in Japan*, vol. 1, no. 1 (Mar. 1960), pp. 7–24. A philosopher's analysis of recent Japanese religion, especially religious indifference and nihilism.

Nitobe, Inazo. *Bushido: The Soul of Japan.* Rev. and enlarged ed. Rutland, VT: C. E. Tuttle, 1969; reprint of the 1905 ed. An early modern advocate of Bushido, linking medieval ethics to national identity.

Norman, E. Herbert. *Ando Shoeki and the Anatomy of Japanese Feudalism*, vol. 2 of *Transactions of the Asiatic Society of Japan*, 3d ser., 1949; reprinted, Washington: University Publications of America, 1979. The first Western treatment of Ando Shoeki (as a critique of feudalism).

Nosco, Peter, ed. *The Emperor System and Religion in Japan*, vol. 17, no. 2–3, of *Japanese Journal of Religious Studies* (June–Sept. 1990). Essays examining the interrelationship of emperor and religion in Japan.

Nosco, Peter. "Keeping the Faith: *Bakuhan* Policy Towards Religions in Seventeenth-Century Japan." In *Religion in Japan: Arrows to Heaven and Earth.* Edited by P. F. Kornicki and I. J. McMullen. Cambridge: Cambridge University, 1996, pp. 135–55. Emphasizes that *bakuhan* policy was directed more at control of religions and religious institutions than personal faith, that such government control and public compliance were limited, and that eventually dissimulation (by both Buddhists and Christians) was practiced and tacitly accepted.

O'Brien, David M. *To Dream of Dreams: Religious Freedom and Constitutional Politics in Postwar Japan.* Honolulu: University of Hawai'i, 1996. Detailed descriptions and analyses of court cases about religious freedom.

Oguchi, Iichi and Takagi, Hiroo. "Religion and Social Development." In *Japanese Religion in the Meiji Era.* Edited by Hideo Kishimoto. Translated by John F. Howes. Tokyo: Obunsha, 1956, pp. 311–57. Interprets the background of Meiji religion, as determined by social and economic factors.

Ohnuki-Tierney, Emiko. *Rice as Self: Japanese Identities Through Time.* Princeton: Princeton University, 1993. A detailed treatment of the significance of rice in Japanese culture and religion.

Okuda, Akiko and Okano, Haruko, eds. *Women and Religion in Japan.* Translated by Alison Watts. Wiesbaden: Harrassowitz Verlag, 1998. Essays presenting a feminist critique of Japanese religions and society in general, and particular religious traditions, for oppression of women.

Ooms, Herman. "A Structural Analysis of Japanese Ancestral Rites and Beliefs." In *Ancestors.* Edited by William H. Newell. The Hague: Mouton Publishers, 1976, pp. 61–90. A systematic interpretation of the Japanese rites and beliefs related to ancestors; especially helpful for gaining a quick overview of the nature of such customs.

Ooms, Herman. *Tokugawa Ideology: Early Constructs, 1570–1680.* Princeton: Princeton University, 1985. A detailed analysis of the use of Shinto, Neo-Confucianism, and Buddhism in the formation of social and political values during Tokugawa times that also have been very influential down to the present day.

Otsuka, Yasuo. "Chinese Traditional Medicine in Japan." In *Asian Medical Systems: A Comparative Study.* Edited by Charles Leslie. Berkeley: University of California, 1976, pp. 322–40. A historical overview of Chinese traditional medicine (the use of acupuncture, moxibustion, and traditional substances) as accepted in Japan.

Piovesana, Gino K. *Recent Japanese Philosophical Thought 1862–1962: A Survey.* Tokyo: Enderle Bookstore, 1963. A survey of the broad range of Western philosophy among Japanese philosophers.

Plath, David W. "Where the Family of God Is the Family: The Role of the Dead in Japanese Households." *American Anthropologist,* vol. 66, no. 2 (Apr. 1964), pp. 300–17. Criticism of the older notion of ancestor worship and suggestion of its replacement with the three categories of the departed, ancestors, and outsiders.

Plutschow, Herbert E. *Chaos and Cosmos: Ritual in Early and Medieval Japanese Literature.* Leiden: E. J. Brill, 1990. A demonstration that not only in religion but also in literature, "ritual, by which I mean an activity with a religious purpose, pervades Japanese life . . . both ancient and modern—more so than does religious doctrine."

Proceedings of Tokyo Meeting of the International Conference on Sociology of Religion, 1978. Reprinted "as subsequently corrected and edited" in *Japanese Journal of Religious Studies,* vol. 6, no. 1–2 (Mar.–June 1979), pp. 1–386. A valuable collection of essays interpreting "secularization," modern religious activities, and New Religions.

Reader, Ian. *Religion in Contemporary Japan.* Honolulu: University of Hawaii, 1991. Essays on various activities and roles of religion in Japan today, covering Shinto, Buddhism, amulets, and new religions.

Reader, Ian and Swanson, Paul L., eds. *Pilgrimage in Japan*, vol. 24, no. 3–4, of *Japanese Journal of Religious Studies* (Fall 1997). Includes editors' general introduction to pilgrimage in the Japanese religious tradition, and six articles on specific pilgrimage locations and patterns.

Reader, Ian and Tanabe, George J., eds. *Conflict and Religion in Japan,* vol. 21, no. 2–3, of *Japanese Journal of Religious Studies* (June–Sept. 1994). Includes the editors' introduction and eight articles on conflict and disputes within aspects of Japanese religions.

Religious Studies in Japan. Edited by Japanese Association for Religious Studies. Tokyo: Maruzen, 1959. Short articles by Japanese scholars on various subjects.

Sansom, Sir George. "Early Japanese Law and Administration." *Transactions of the Asiatic Society of Japan,* Second Series, vol. 9 (1932), pp. 67–109; vol. 11 (1935), pp. 117–49. Includes a description of the governmental department of religion in ancient Japan.

Suzuki, Kentaro. "Divination in Contemporary Japan: A General Overview and an Analysis of Survey Results." *Japanese Journal of Religious Studies,* vol. 22, no. 3–4 (Fall 1995), pp. 249–66. Provides an overview of current divination techniques and the results of a survey of 300 clients at a "divination hall."

Tamaru, Noriyoshi, ed. *Religion in Modern Japan.* Special issue of *Acta Asiatica,* vol. 75 (1998). Essays by Japanese scholars intended to demonstrate "a major characteristic of Japanese religions since ancient times," "its rarely parallelled diversity."

Tanabe, George J., Jr., ed. *Religions of Japan in Practice.* Princeton: Princeton University, 1999. Translations of Japanese texts, and descriptions and interpretations of practices from all aspects of Japanese religion.

Tanabe, George J., Jr. and Reader, Ian. *Practically Religious: Worldly Benefits and the Common Religion of Japan.* Honolulu: University of Hawai'i, 1998. The first book-length study of this-worldly benefits, it sees them as part and parcel of the belief, practice, and action of religion in Japan (rather than as lowly superstition and magic).

ten Grotenhuis, Elizabeth. *Japanese Mandalas: Representations of Sacred Geography.* Honolulu: University of Hawai'i, 1999. An investigation of "certain paradigmatic mandalas from the Japanese Esoteric Buddhist, Pure Land Buddhist, and kami-worshiping traditions"; color illustrations.

Tyler, Royall. *The Miracles of the Kasuga Deity.* New York: Columbia University, 1990. Based on a study of the text *Kasuga Gongen genki,* it focuses on "the living pattern of *honji-suijaku* religion . . . as a distinct phase of Japanese religion."

Tyler, Susan C. *The Cult of Kasuga Seen through Its Art.* Ann Arbor: Center for Japanese Studies, University of Michigan, 1992. This study defines "the cult of Kasuga, as a model of a *honji suijaku* cult . . . , particularly in relation to Shinto."

Union of the New Religious Organizations in Japan, Research Office, ed. "Reminiscences of Religion in Postwar Japan." *Contemporary Religions in Japan,* vol. 6, no. 2 (June 1965), pp. 111–203. This book-length work, continued in five subsequent issues of this journal, provides a valuable inside view of the changed conditions and rapid developments among all religious organizations in postwar Japan.

Woodard, William P. *The Allied Occupation of Japan, 1945–1952, and Japanese Religions.* Leiden: E. J. Brill, 1972. A detailed analysis of religious developments and the Allied policy toward religion in the occupation period.

Woodard, William P. "Study on Religious Juridical Persons Law: Text of the Law no. 126 of 1951." *Contemporary Japan,* vol. 25, no. 3 (Sept. 1958), pp. 418–70; vol. 25, no. 4 (Mar. 1959), pp. 635–57; vol. 26, no. 1 (Aug. 1959), pp. 96–115; vol. 26, no. 2 (Dec. 1959), pp. 139–312. Text and discussion of the law governing religious bodies in postwar Japan.

Yasunaga, Toshinobu. *Social and Ecological Philosopher of Eighteenth-Century Japan.* New York: Weatherhill, 1992. The trenchant criticism of all religious groups in late Tokugawa Japan by a contemporary thinker.

SHINTO

For additional references, see "Special Bibliographies on Japanese History and Religion."

Aoki, Michiko Yamaguchi. *Ancient Myths and Early History of Japan: A Cultural Foundation.* New York: Exposition, 1974. A discussion of ancient Japanese myths in the light of archaeology and local traditions.

Aoki, Michiko Yamaguchi, trans. *Izumo Fudoki.* Tokyo: Sophia University, 1971. Translation and introduction to an eighth-century document recording local legends and religious practices.

Ashkenazi, Michael. *Matsuri: Festivals of a Japanese Town.* Honolulu: University of Hawaii, 1993. By focusing on a local festival in one town (not dominated by tourists), this work views *matsuri* as entertainment, as an economic transaction, and as a group activity.

Aston, W. G., trans. *Nihongi: Chronicles of Japan from the Earliest Times to A.D. 697.* Originally published in *Transactions of the Japan Society,* Supplement 1. London, 1896. Reprint ed., two volumes in one with original pagination, London: Allen & Unwin, 1956. Reprint ed., Tokyo: Charles E. Tuttle, 1978. Covers the same period as the *Kojiki* but adds other tales, adopts a Chinese style of writing, and continues the chronology to A.D. 697.

Bock, Felicia Gressitt, trans. *Engi-Shiki: Procedures of the Engi Era, Books I–V.* Tokyo: Sophia University, 1970. A translation of eighth-century government regulations concerning Shinto shrines, their administration, and rituals; includes introductory chapters on early Shinto.

Bock, Felicia Gressitt, trans. *Engi-Shiki: Procedures of the Engi Era, Books VI–X.* Tokyo: Sophia University, 1972. Continuation of the preceding work.

Borgen, Robert. *Sugawara no Michizane and the Early Heian Court.* Cambridge: Harvard University, 1986. See especially the last chapter, pp. 307–36, "Michizane as Tenjin," which includes "The Process of Deification" and "Evolution of Tenjin Worship."

Breen, John and Teeuwen, Mark, eds. *Shinto in History: Ways of the Kami.* Surrey: Curzon, 2000. Scholarly essays discussing the definition of Shinto, its history, and activities.

Buchanan, Daniel C. "Some Mikuji of Fushimi Inari Jinja." *Monumenta Nipponica,* vol. 2, no. 2 (July 1939), pp. 518–35. A general article on "fortunes" (*mikuji*) with an illustration of a *mikuji* and translation of ten fortunes.

Chamberlain, Basil Hall, trans. "*Ko-ji-ki,* or Records of Ancient Matters." *Transactions of the Asiatic Society of Japan,* vol. 10, supplement (1882). Reprinted as separate volume, New Edition (with "Additional notes by William George Aston"), Kobe: J. L. Thompson & Company, 1932. Reprint ed., Tokyo: Asiatic Society of Japan, 1973. The oldest written chronicle in Japan, combining mythology and court chronology to about the end of the fifth century C.E. (For a more recent translation, see Philippi in this section.)

Creemers, Wilhelmus H. M. *Shrine Shinto After World War II.* Leiden: E. J. Brill, 1968. A detailed study of the status and organization of Shinto, especially the impact of reorganization after World War II.

Ellwood, Robert S. *The Feast of Kingship: Accession Ceremonies in Ancient Japan.* Tokyo: Sophia University, 1973. A study of Shinto rituals for the emperor's accession; also includes the general Shinto background of the rituals.

Ellwood, Robert S. "The Saigu: Princess and Priestess." *History of Religions*, vol. 7, no. 1 (Aug. 1967), pp. 35–60. Describes the selection, purification, pilgrimage, and activities of "the Saigu, or office of virgin priestess, at the Grand Shrine of Ise."

Fridell, Wilbur M. *Japanese Shrine Mergers, 1906–12; State Shinto Moves to the Grassroots.* Tokyo: Sophia University, 1973. A detailed analysis of State Shinto in terms of shrine mergers—the general policies, their implementation, and overall results.

Gardner, Richard. "Nationalistic Shinto: A Child's Guide to Yasukuni Shrine." In *Religions of Japan in Practice.* Edited by George J. Tanabe, Jr. Princeton: Princeton University, 1999, pp. 334–39. Introduction to and translation of a guide to Yasukuni Shrine; a rationale for the shrine, a defense of Japan's modern wars, and praise for the war dead worshiped as gods.

Grapard, Allan. "The Shinto of Yoshida Kanetomo." *Monumenta Nipponica*, vol. 47 (1992), pp. 27–58. A description of "the Yoshida system [that] became an orthodoxy cum orthopraxy of sorts during the Tokugawa period."

Hardacre, Helen. *Shinto and the State 1868–1988.* Princeton: Princeton University, 1989. Historical analysis of the complex negotiations involved in the formation of State Shinto.

Hardacre, Helen. "The Shinto Priesthood in Early Meiji Japan: Preliminary Inquiries." *History of Religions*, vol. 27, no. 3 (Feb. 1988), pp. 294–320. This article aims "to identify major groups within the priesthood and to characterize their relation to contemporary debates on religion."

Harootunian, H. D. *Things Seen and Unseen: Discourse and Ideology in Tokugawa Nativism.* Chicago: University of Chicago, 1988. A description, analysis, and critique of Kokugaku as nativism.

Holtom, Daniel C. *The Japanese Enthronement Ceremonies.* 2d ed. Tokyo: Sophia University, 1972. A description of the three imperial regalia and the main ceremonies in the enthronement of Emperor Showa in the mid-1920s.

Holtom, Daniel C. "The Meaning of Kami." *Monumenta Nipponica,* vol. 3 (1940), pp. 1–27, 32–53; vol. 4 (1941), pp. 25–68. An attempt to interpret the Japanese term *kami* through the Melanesian term *mana*.

Holtom, Daniel C. *Modern Japan and Shinto Nationalism: A Study of Present-Day Trends in Japanese Religions.* Rev. ed., Chicago: University of Chicago, 1947. Reprint ed., New York: Paragon Book Reprint Corp., 1963. A historical treatment of nationalistic Shinto, including chapters on the accommodation of Christianity and Buddhism to Japanese nationalism.

Holtom, Daniel C. *The National Faith of Japan: A Study in Modern Shinto.* New York: Dutton, 1938. Reprint ed., New York: Paragon Book Reprint Corp., 1965. Important for its historical information on Shinto; the section on sect Shinto is a useful overview.

Hori, Ichiro and Toda, Yoshio. "Shinto." In *Japanese Religion in the Meiji Era.* Edited by Hideo Kishimoto. Translated by John F. Howes. Tokyo: Obunsha, 1956, pp. 35–98. A balanced treatment of Shinto in the Meiji period.

Hylkema-Vos, Naomi. "Kato Genchi: A Neglected Pioneer in Comparative Religion." *Japanese Journal of Religious Studies,* vol. 17, no. 4 (Dec. 1990), pp. 375–95. Depicts the career of one of the early Japanese scholars of comparative religion, who focused on Shinto.

Inoue, Nobutaka, ed. *Kami.* Translated by Norman Havens. Institute for Japanese Culture and Classics, Kokugakuin University, 1998. Translated articles by Japanese scholars on the nature of *kami*, and discussion of several *kami*.

Institute for Japanese Culture and Classics, Kokugakuin University. *Matsuri: Festival and Rite in Japanese Life.* Translated by Norman Havens. Tokyo: Institute for Japanese Culture and Classics, Kokugakuin University, 1988. Translated articles by Japanese scholars on individual festivals and the nature of festival.

Institute for Japanese Culture and Classics, Kokugakuin University. *Proceedings, The Second International Conference for Shinto Studies.* Tokyo: Kokugakuin University, 1968. Collected papers by Japanese and Western scholars from a conference dealing with continuity and change in Shinto.

Kageyama, Haruki. *The Arts of Shinto.* Translated by Christine Guth. New York: Weatherhill/Shibundo, 1973. Treats the arts of Shinto in terms of their religious context; includes more than one hundred excellent plates illustrating Shinto arts.

Kato, Genchi. "The Theological System of Urabe no Kanetomo." *Transactions of the Japan Society of London,* vol. 28 (1931), pp. 143–50. A treatment of the Shinto theologian Kanetomo, emphasizing his significance for later Shinto thinkers.

Kato, Genchi and Hoshino, Hikoshiro, trans. *Kogoshui: Gleanings from Ancient Stories.* 2d ed. rev., Tokyo: Meiji Japan Society, 1925. Written about C.E. 807, it records a rivalry between several Shinto priestly families.

Kuroda, Toshio. "Shinto in the History of Japanese Religion." Translated by Suzanne Gay and James C. Dobbins. *Journal of Japanese Studies,* vol. 7, no. 1 (1981), pp. 1–21. Reprinted in *Religion and Society in Modern Japan: Selected Readings,* edited by Mark R. Mullins et al. Berkeley: Asian Humanities, 1993, pp. 7–30. A provocative article emphasizing that Shinto as known today did not exist in earlier times, and in fact is a creation of modern times; the work of Kuroda has generated much discussion.

The Manyoshu. Translated by the Japan Society for the Promotion of Scientific Research. Tokyo: Iwanami Shoten, 1940. Reprint ed., New York: Columbia University, 1965. Compiled in the eighth century, it is a valuable source of ancient Japanese poetry and religion.

Matsumoto, Shigeru. *Motoori Norinaga, 1730–1801.* Cambridge: Harvard University, 1970. A detailed study of the life and writings of the foremost scholar and proponent of Restoration Shinto.

Miyazaki, Hiroshi. *Illustrated Festivals of Japan.* Translated by John Howard Loftus. Tokyo: Japan Travel Bureau, 1985. A popular work useful for its many illustrations of festivals and the actual paraphernalia of festivals.

Motoori, Norinaga. *Kojiki-den, Book 1.* "Introduced, translated, and annotated by Ann Wehmeyer." Ithaca, NY: Cornell University, 1997. A translation of part of Motoori's monumental study of the *Kojiki,* it includes Motoori's view of *kami* and the superiority of the way of the *kami* and things Japanese over Confucian, Chinese, and Buddhist ideas.

Muraoka, Tsunetsugu. *Studies in Shinto Thought.* Translated by Delmer M. Brown and James T. Araki. Tokyo: Ministry of Education, 1964. Scholarly articles on the nature of Shinto, with close attention to major proponents of the Shinto thought system.

Nelson, John K. *Enduring Identities: The Guise of Shinto in Contemporary Japan.* Honolulu: University of Hawai'i, 2000. Describes the contemporary yearly cycle of rites and festivals of an ancient Kyoto shrine while assessing the significance of Shinto for cultural identity.

Nelson, John K. *A Year in the Life of a Shinto Shrine.* Seattle: University of Washington, 1996. Based on a year of field work, gives details of the dynamics of a contemporary shrine.

Nosco, Peter. "Masuho Zanko (1655–1742): A Shinto Popularizer Between Nativism and National Learning." In *Confucianism and Tokugawa Culture.* Edited by Peter Nosco. Princeton: Princeton University, 1984, pp. 166–87. Focuses on Zanko's life and a summary of the major features of his thought as a transitional figure between syncretic Shinto (nativism) and National Learning.

Nosco, Peter. *Remembering Paradise: Nativism and Nostalgia in Eighteenth Century Japan.* Cambridge: Harvard University, 1990. A description and interpretation of Kokugaku as nativism and nostalgia.

Okano, Haruko. *Die Stellung der Frau im Shinto.* Wiesbaden: Otto Harrassowitz, 1976. Text in German, but see the English "Summary: Woman and the Shinto Religion," pp. 206–13, which provides an overview of the different roles of women through the history of Shinto.

Ono, Sokyo. *Shinto: The Kami Way*. Tokyo: Bridgeway, 1962. A systematic or "theological" interpretation of Shinto by a modern Shinto scholar.

Philippi, Donald L., trans. *Kojiki*. Tokyo: University of Tokyo, 1968. A recent translation emphasizing linguistic accuracy.

Philippi, Donald L., trans. *Norito: A New Translation of the Ancient Japanese Ritual Prayers*. Tokyo: Institute for Japanese Culture and Classics, Kokugakuin University, 1959. The most recent scholarly translation of the *norito*, with brief notes.

Plutschow, Herbert E. *Matsuri: The Festivals of Japan*. Surrey: Japan Library, 1996. Views *matsuri* as distinctive local practices, as a group of events having common features, and in comparison with rituals in other countries.

Ponsonby-Fane, R. A. B. *Studies in Shinto and Shrines*. Rev. ed. Kamikamo, Kyoto: Ponsonby Memorial Society, 1953. Collected articles of a technical nature by a lifelong student of Shinto. This is the first volume of the six-volume series of Ponsonby-Fane's works, all of which contain valuable detailed articles.

Robertson, Jennifer. *Native and Newcomer: Making and Remaking a Japanese City*. Berkeley: University of California, 1991. An anthropological view of the citizens and activities of a Tokyo suburb; see "New Festivals for Old," pp. 38–71.

Sadler, A. L., trans. *The Ise Daijingu or Diary of a Pilgrim to Ise*. Introduction by Genchi Kato. Tokyo: Meiji Japan Society, 1940. This fourteenth-century pilgrim's diary provides an inside view of sincerity and piety in a Shinto context.

Sakurai, Haruo. "Tradition and Change in Local Community Shrines." *Acta Asiatica*, vol. 51 (1987), pp. 62–76. Discusses the forced merging of local Shinto shrines by the government in late Meiji times, and the postwar response of local people to that policy.

Satow, Sir Ernest and Florenz, Karl. "Ancient Japanese Rituals." *Transactions of the Asiatic Society: Reprints*, vol. 2 (1927), pp. 5–164. An older translation of *norito* (ritual prayers) with illustrations and commentary on their religious significance.

Saunders, E. Dale. "Japanese Mythology." In *Mythologies of the Ancient World*. Edited by S. N. Kramer. New York: Doubleday Anchor Books, 1961, pp. 409–40. A brief overview of the central myth and regional tales in Japanese mythology.

Schnell, Scott. *The Rousing Drum: Ritual Practice in a Japanese Community*. Honolulu: University of Hawai'i, 1999. Combines historical and ethnographic perspective to study the significance of ritual in a local Shinto festival.

Schwartz, M. L. "The Great Shrines of Idzumo: Some Notes on Shinto, Ancient and Modern." *Transactions of the Asiatic Society of Japan*, vol. 61, pt. 4 (1913), pp. 493–681. An early Western description of a major Shinto shrine, with translations of shrine documents.

Smeyers, Karen. *The Fox and the Jewel: Shared and Private Meanings in Contemporary Japanese Inari Worship*. Honolulu: University of Hawai'i, 1999. A detailed study of beliefs and customs related to Inari, emphasizing individualized forms of practice.

Sonoda, Minoru, ed. *Studies on Shinto*. *Acta Asiatica*, vol. 51 (1987). "This special issue of *Acta Asiatica* features five essays which approach the basic character of Shinto or important changes within Shinto primarily from the standpoints of comparative religion or the history of Japanese religions."

Starr, Frederick. "Ema." *Transactions of the Asiatic Society of Japan*, vol. 48 (1920), pp. 1–22. A general description (with many illustrations) of the *ema*, literally "horse-pictures," or votive offerings traditionally hung at Shinto shrines.

Sugahara, Shinkai. "The Distinctive Features of Sanno Ichijitsu Shinto." *Japanese Journal of Religious Studies*, vol. 23, no. 1–2 (Spring 1996), pp. 61–84. Distinguishes Sanno Shinto from Sanno Ichijitsu Shinto, which "centers on religious ritual for Tosho Daigongen, the deified soul of Tokugawa Ieyasu."

Tange, Kenzo and Kawazoe, Noboru. *Ise: Prototype of Japanese Architecture*. Cambridge: M.I.T., 1965. A large photo study of Ise, the most important Shinto shrine complex, with an introduction to its architecture and a closing essay on the religious and cultural features of the shrine.

Tsuda, Sokichi. "The Idea of Kami in Ancient Japanese Classics." *T'oung Pao*, vol. 52 (1966), pp. 293–304. A philological study of the term *kami*, distinguishing the generic root as a thing or spirit possessing divine potency and intrinsic magic power, from the mistaken notion of *kami* (a homophone) as high rank or position.

Ueda, Kenji. "Shinto." In *Japanese Religion.* Edited by Ichiro Hori. Translated by Yoshiya Abe and David Reid. Tokyo: Kodansha International, 1972, pp. 29–45. A concise overview of the aspects and dynamics of Shinto.

Watanabe, Yasutada. *Shinto Art: Ise and Izumo Shrines.* Translated by Robert Picketts. Heibon-sha Survey of Japanese Art, vol. 3. New York: Weatherhill/Heibonsha, 1974. A lavish presentation (180 plates) and general introduction to the architectural form of the most important Shinto shrines, with brief comments on other shrine types.

Yanagawa, Keiichi. "The Sensation of *Matsuri.*" In *Matsuri: Festival and Rite in Japanese Life.* Translated by Norman Havens. Tokyo: Institute for Japanese Culture and Classics, Kokugakuin University, 1988, pp. 3–19. A provocative argument for *matsuri* (festival) as a key feature of Japanese life, focusing on the "sensations" (sounds, smells, and tastes) that make up the actual experience of *matsuri.*

BUDDHISM

For additional references, see "Special Bibliographies on Japanese History and Religion."

Abe, Ryuichi. *The Weaving of Mantra: Kukai and the Construction of Esoteric Buddhist Discourse.* New York: Columbia University, 1999. A detailed study of Kukai and Shingon Buddhism, emphasizing the significance of esoteric Buddhism for the development of Japanese Buddhism.

Adolphson, Mikael S. *The Gates of Power: Monks, Courtiers, and Warriors in Premodern Japan.* Honolulu: University of Hawai'i, 2000. An examination of three Buddhist-Shinto monastic centers as "important providers of rituals and support for the state," focusing on "an integrated treatment of religion and politics," especially warrior monks and the role of religious violence.

Arai, Paula Kane Robinson. *Women Living Zen: Japanese Soto Buddhist Nuns.* New York: Oxford, 1999. A critique of androcentric views of the role of nuns in Japanese Buddhism, this work focuses on the contributions of nuns from ancient times to the present.

Baroni, Helen Josephine. *Obaku Zen: The Emergence of the Third Sect of Zen in Tokugawa Japan.* Honolulu: University of Hawai'i, 2000. Views Obaku Zen as an instance of innovation (a new religious movement) in Tokugawa Buddhism.

Ch'en, Kenneth. *Buddhism in China: A Historical Survey.* Princeton: Princeton University, 1964. A detailed survey of Chinese Buddhism, including descriptions of major Buddhist schools; useful as a background to the study of Japanese Buddhism.

Collcutt, Martin. "Buddhism: The Threat of Eradication." In *Japan in Transition: From Tokugawa to Meiji.* Edited by Marius B. Jansen and Gilbert Rozman. Princeton: Princeton University, 1986, pp. 143–67. Views the Shinto policies of the new Meiji government as Buddhism's most severe crisis in its long history in Japan; gives detailed examples of the persecution of Buddhist institutions and clergy.

Collcutt, Martin. *Five Mountains: The Rinzai Monastic Institution in Medieval Japan.* Cambridge: Harvard University, 1981. A detailed historical study of Rinzai Zen temples as social and economic institutions.

Conze, Edward. *Buddhism: Its Essence and Development.* New York: Philosophical Library, 1951. Reprint ed., New York: Harper & Row, 1959. A general and concise introduction to Buddhism, and various schools and philosophies within Buddhism.

Cooke, Gerald. "Traditional Buddhist Sects and Modernization in Japan." *Japanese Journal of Religious Studies,* vol. 1, no. 4 (Dec. 1974), pp. 267–330. Discusses attempts to reform the organization of Buddhist institutions, including those within Pure Land Buddhism.

de Bary, Wm. Theodore, et al. *The Buddhist Tradition in India, China, & Japan*. New York: Modern Library, 1969. A convenient anthology of translated texts (the materials on Japanese Buddhism are taken from Tsunoda's *Sources of Japanese Tradition*, 1st ed.).

Demieville, Paul. *Buddhism and Healing. Demieville's Article "Byo" from Hobogirin*. Translated by Mark Tatz. New York: University Press of America, 1985. A scholarly treatment of the textual references relating Buddhism to medicine and healing, it examines the nature of life as "illness" and the character of the Buddha as the "king of physicians."

de Visser, Marinus Willem. *Ancient Buddhism in Japan: Sutras and Ceremonies in Use in the Seventh and Eighth Centuries A.D. and Their History in Later Times*. 2 vols. Leiden: E. J. Brill, 1935. Difficult reading, but contains useful information.

de Visser, Marinus Willem. *The Bodhisattva Ti-tsang (Jizo) in China and Japan*. Berlin: Oesterheld, 1914. A literary study of Jizo, one of the most important *bodhisattvas* in Japanese Buddhism.

Dobbins, James C. *Jodo Shinshu. Shin Buddhism in Medieval Japan*. Bloomington, IN: Indiana University, 1989. Includes accounts of Honen and Shinran, as well as the formation of Shin Buddhism (the True Pure Land Sect).

Dobbins, James C., ed. *The Legacy of Kuroda Toshio*, vol. 23, no. 3–4, of *Japanese Journal of Religious Studies* (Fall 1996). Includes the editor's introduction, translations of Kuroda's articles, and articles discussing Kuroda's theories about Shinto and Buddhism.

Eliot, Sir Charles. *Japanese Buddhism*. London: Edward Arnold, 1935. Reprint ed., London: Routledge & Kegan Paul, 1959. An early handbook, it emphasizes continuity with Indian and Chinese Buddhism.

Faure, Bernard. *The Rhetoric of Immediacy: A Cultural Critique of Chan/Zen Buddhism*. Princeton: Princeton University, 1991. A critical treatment attempting to balance Zen Buddhism's rejection and acceptance of various practices.

Foard, James. "In Search of a Lost Reformation: A Reconsideration of Kamakura Buddhism." *Japanese Journal of Religious Studies*, vol. 7, no. 4 (Dec. 1980), pp. 274–81. A critique of the notion of Kamakura Buddhism as an example of "reformation."

Goodwin, Janet R. *Alms and Vagabonds: Buddhist Temples and Popular Patronage in Medieval Japan*. Honolulu: University of Hawaii, 1994. "The central theme of this book is the interaction between Buddhist institutions and lay society, as demonstrated by kanjin [donation] campaigns"; provides a grassroots view of "the Kamakura Buddhist transformation."

Groner, Paul. *Saicho: The Establishment of the Japanese Tendai School*. Berkeley, CA: Berkeley Buddhist Studies Series, 1984. Provides a "biography of Saicho" as well as a study of Saicho's view of Buddhist precepts.

Hakeda, Yoshito S., trans. *Kukai: Major Works*. New York: Columbia University, 1972. An introduction to the life and thought of the founder of Shingon Buddhism with translations of his works.

Heisig, James W. and Maraldo, John C., eds. *Rude Awakenings: Zen, the Kyoto School, & the Question of Nationalism*. Honolulu: University of Hawai'i, 1995. A critical study of the way some philosophers and some Buddhists, especially Zen Buddhists, supported nationalism and militarism during World War II.

Hirota, Dennis, trans. *The Collected Works of Shinran*. 2 vols. Kyoto: Jodo Shinshu Hongwan-ji-ha, 1997. The major works of Shinran, published by the True Pure Land Sect.

Hirota, Dennis, trans. *No Abode: The Record of Ippen*. Kyoto: Ryukoku University, 1986. An account of the itinerant *nembutsu* practitioner Ippen.

Hur, Nam-lin. *Prayer and Play in Late Tokugawa Japan*. Cambridge: Harvard University, 2000. A study of one of the leading Buddhist temples and tourist attractions in Japan, showing that "Edo commoners found within the popular culture of prayer and play an expression of cultural vitality and new spiritual authority."

Ishida, Hisatoyo. *Esoteric Buddhist Painting*. Translated and adapted by E. Dale Saunders. Tokyo: Kodansha, 1989. Includes a general introduction by the translator, and treatment of mandala and esoteric painting and iconography.

Jaffe, Richard and Mohr, Michel, eds. *Meiji Zen*, vol. 25, no. 1–2, of *Japanese Journal of Religious Studies* (Spring 1998). Includes editors' introduction to Meiji Zen and six articles on specific aspects of Zen.

Kamens, Edward. *The Buddhist Poetry of the Great Kamo Priestess Daisaiin Senshi and* Hosshin Wakashu. Ann Arbor: Center for Japanese Studies, University of Michigan, 1990. Analyzes the "'Buddhist poems'" of Senshi which "expressed something of her Buddhist faith, while she was at the same time High Priestess of the Kamo Shrines (*Saiin*)—that is, an imperially appointed official of the indigenous religious tradition called 'Shinto.'"

Kashiwahara, Yusen and Sonoda, Koyu, eds. *Shapers of Japanese Buddhism*. Translated by Gaynor Sekimori. Tokyo: Kosei, 1994. A convenient reference work for "twenty major biographies" of Buddhist leaders and "brief biographies" of many Buddhist figures.

Ketelaar, James Edward. *Of Heretics and Martyrs in Meiji Japan: Buddhism and Its Persecution*. Princeton: Princeton University, 1989. Historical analysis of the complex factors and strategies behind the persecution of Buddhism in early Meiji Japan.

Kidder, J. Edward. *Early Buddhist Japan*. New York: Praeger Publishers, 1975. An archeological study of the earliest traces of Buddhism in Japan (with a brief chapter on Shinto ritual sites).

Kiyota, Minoru. "Buddhism in Postwar Japan: A Critical Survey." *Monumenta Nipponica*, vol. 24, no. 1–2 (1969), pp. 113–36. Analyzes the shortcomings of postwar Buddhism by reference to the success of New Religions such as Soka Gakkai.

Kiyota, Minoru. "Presuppositions to the Understanding of Japanese Buddhist Thought." *Monumenta Nipponica*, vol. 22, no. 3–4 (1967), pp. 251–59. A technical treatment of Japanese Buddhist thought in relation to Mahayana philosophy.

Kiyota, Minoru. *Shingon Buddhism: Theory and Practice*. Los Angeles: Buddhist Books International, 1978. This technical analysis focuses on the basic sutras, *mandala*, and practice that lead to the Shingon goal of "instant Buddhahood"; features a helpful glossary of Buddhist terms.

LaFleur, William R. *The Karma of Words: Buddhism and the Literary Arts in Medieval Japan*. Berkeley: University of California, 1983. Treats at length the notion of *hongaku* (original enlightenment) and Buddhist themes as providing the rationale of medieval Japanese religious life.

McCallum, Donald. *Zenkoji and Its Icon: A Study in Medieval Japanese Religious Arts*. Princeton: Princeton University, 1994. Study of the Zenkoji cult, which unlike other Pure Land phenomena, had no charismatic founder and developed in a provincial area, but was influential through its object of worship and itinerant religious practitioners.

McFarland, H. Neill. *Daruma: The Founder of Japanese Art and Popular Culture*. Tokyo: Kodansha, 1987. An overview of the art and folklore related to the monk Bodhidharma of Ch'an (Zen) Buddhism, known in Japan as Daruma; numerous illustrations.

McMullin, Neil. *Buddhism and the State in Sixteenth-Century Japan*. Princeton: Princeton University, 1984. "The purpose of the present work is to examine, through the lens of Oda Nobunaga's policies toward the temples, the changes that took place in the power of the Buddhist institutions and the place of Buddhism in Japanese society at the end of the medieval period."

Marcure, Kenneth A. "The *Danka* System." *Monumenta Nipponica*, vol. 40, no. 1 (Spring 1985), pp. 39–67. A study of the Buddhist temple-household relationship, based on historical research and five years' residence in a rural temple.

Marra, Michele. "The Development of Mappo Thought in Japan (I)." *Japanese Journal of Religious Studies*, vol. 15, no. 1 (Mar. 1988), pp. 25–54; "The Development of Mappo Thought in Japan (II)." *Japanese Journal of Religious Studies*, vol. 15, no. 4 (Dec. 1988), pp. 287–305. A detailed history of the notion of *mappo* in Japanese Buddhism.

Masutani, Fumio and Undo, Yoshimichi. "Buddhism." In *Japanese Religion in the Meiji Era*. Edited by Hideo Kishimoto. Translated by John F. Howes. Tokyo: Obunsha, 1956, pp. 99–169. A balanced treatment of Buddhism in the Meiji period.

Matsunaga, Alicia. *The Buddhist Philosophy of Assimilation: The Historical Development of the Honji-Suijaku Theory*. Tokyo and Rutland, VT: Sophia University and Charles E. Tuttle,

1969. Interprets the interaction between aspects of Buddhism and aspects of Japanese culture.

Matsunaga, Daigan and Matsunaga, Alicia. *Foundation of Japanese Buddhism.* 2 vols. Los Angeles: Buddhist Books International, 1974. A survey of Buddhist sects in English, from the appearance of Buddhism in Japan through the medieval period.

Morrell, Robert E. *Early Kamakura Buddhism: A Minority Report.* Berkeley: Asian Humanities, 1987. This study argues for the significance of four leaders of the older, established Buddhist orders in Kamakura times, against the view of Kamakura Buddhism as dominated by Zen, Nichiren, and Pure Land movements and leaders.

Nakamura, Kyoko Motomochi, trans. *Miraculous Stories from the Japanese Buddhist Tradition: The Nihon Ryoiki of the Monk Kyokai.* Cambridge: Harvard University, 1973. Translation of a ninth-century document, "the earliest collection of Buddhist legends in Japan," which was important for the spread of Buddhism; a valuable overview of the ninth-century worldview is also provided.

Niwa, Fumio. *The Buddha Tree.* Translated by Kenneth Strong. London: Peter Owen, 1966; Rutland, VT: Charles E. Tuttle, 1971. A novel that spins a complicated web of human emotions within the settings of a Pure Land Buddhist temple; valuable for one Buddhist interpretation of the problem of desire and human failing.

Orzech, Charles D. *Politics and Transcendent Wisdom:* The Scripture for Humane Kings *in the Creation of Chinese Buddhism.* University Park, PA: Pennsylvania State University, 1998. Useful for the Chinese background of Shingon (Chen-yen) Buddhism.

Payne, Richard K., ed. *Re-Visioning "Kamakura" Buddhism.* Honolulu: University of Hawai'i, 1998. This re-visioning views the Buddhism of Kamakura times not from the retrospective viewpoint of the few sects that eventually were successful, but in terms of the movements and figures competing with one another at that time.

Reischauer, Edwin O., trans. *Ennin's Diary: The Record of a Pilgrimage to China in Search of the Law.* New York: Ronald, 1953. The Japanese monk Ennin (792–862), who spent the years 838 to 847 in China studying Buddhism, has recorded in his diary a rare Japanese perception of Chinese Buddhism.

Reischauer, Edwin O. *Ennin's Travels in T'ang China.* New York: Ronald, 1955. Commentary and interpretation based on the translation of Ennin's diary.

Robinson, Richard H. and Johnson, Willard L., et al. *The Buddhist Religion: A Historical Introduction.* 4th ed. Belmont, CA: Wadsworth, 1997. A brief survey of Buddhism, its philosophical and religious developments, and geographical expansion; includes a bibliography.

Rogers, Minor and Ann. *Rennyo: The Second Founder of Shin Buddhism: With a Translation of His Letters.* Berkeley, CA: Asian Humanities, 1991. Emphasizes the significance of the medieval Buddhist priest Rennyo as "the second founder of Shin Buddhism."

Saso, Michael. *Tantric Art and Meditation.* Honolulu: University of Hawai'i, 1990. A comparison/contrast of Shingon and Tendai meditation on mandalas.

Saunders, E. Dale. *Mudra: A Study of Symbolic Gestures in Japanese Buddhist Sculpture.* New York: Pantheon Books, 1960. A detailed study of the artistic expression of esoteric Buddhism (and Buddhist sculpture in general), with profuse illustrations.

Sawa, Takaaki (or Ryuken). *Art in Japanese Esoteric Buddhism.* Translated by Richard L. Gage. Heibonsha Survey of Japanese Art, vol. 8. New York: Weatherhill/Heibonsha, 1972. A survey of esoteric Buddhist temples, *mandala,* and deities, with lavish illustrations.

Senchakushu English Translation Project ("Translated and Edited with an Introduction by"). *Honen's Senchakushu: Passages on the Selection of the Nembutsu in the Original Vow (Senchaku Hongan Nembutsu Shu).* Honolulu: University of Hawai'i; Tokyo: Sogo Bukkyo Kenkyujo, Taisho University, 1998. An introduction to Honen and his work, and a translation of Honen's key work outlining faith in Amida and salvation through the *nembutsu.*

Sharf, Robert H. "The Zen of Japanese Nationalism." In *Curators of the Buddha: The Study of Buddhism under Colonialism.* Edited by Donald S. Lopez. Chicago: University of Chicago, 1995, pp. 107–60. A critical appraisal of D. T. Suzuki's and others' views of "a pure, and quintessentially Japanese, Zen," and the relationship of these views to colonialism and nationalism.

Stevens, John. *The Marathon Monks of Mount Hiei.* Boston: Shambhala, 1988. An overview of Tendai Buddhism, followed by a description of "marathon monks" who run thousands of miles as Buddhist training.

Stone, Jacqueline Ilyse. *Original Enlightenment and the Transformation of Medieval Japanese Buddhism.* Honolulu: University of Hawai'i, 1999. A study focusing on *hongaku* ("original enlightenment") as a key concept informing and transforming medieval Japanese Buddhism.

Stone, Jacqueline. "A Vast and Grave Task: Interwar Buddhist Studies as an Expression of Japan's Envisioned Global Role." In *Culture and Identity: Japanese Intellectuals During the Interwar Years.* Edited by Thomas J. Rimer. Princeton: Princeton University, 1990, pp. 217–33. A critical study of the way Buddhist studies were involved in nationalism and imperialism leading up to World War II.

Suzuki, D. T. *Zen and Japanese Culture.* New York: Pantheon Books, 1959. Essays on the Zen penetration of Japanese culture by the foremost spokesman and popularizer of Zen in the West. (Many of Suzuki's works are in paperback editions.)

Swanson, Paul L. *Foundations of T'ien-T'ai Philosophy: The Flowering of the Two Truths Theory in Chinese Buddhism.* Berkeley, CA: Asian Humanities, 1989. A comprehensive treatment of T'ien-t'ai (Tendai) teachings.

Swanson, Paul L., ed. *Tendai Buddhism in Japan,* vol. 14, no. 2–3, of *Japanese Journal of Religious Studies,* vol. 14, no. 2–3 (Sept. 1987). Includes editor's introduction and bibliography, with ten articles on Tendai Buddhism.

Tamaru, Noriyoshi. "Buddhism." In *Japanese Religion.* Edited by Ichiro Hori. Translated by Yoshiya Abe and David Reid. Tokyo: Kodansha International, 1972, pp. 47–69. An overview of the origin and historical development of Japanese Buddhism.

Tamura, Yoshiro. *Japanese Buddhism: A Cultural History.* Tokyo: Kosei, 2000. A comprehensive history of Japanese Buddhism by a leading Japanese scholar.

Tanabe, George J., Jr. *Myoe the Dreamkeeper: Fantasy and Knowledge in Early Kamakura Buddhism.* Cambridge: Harvard University, 1992. A detailed study of a leader of Nara Buddhism who sought to revitalize traditional Buddhism during Kamakura times.

Thornton, S. A. *Charisma and Community Formation in Medieval Japan: The Case of the Yugyo-ha (1300–1700).* Ithaca, NY: Cornell, 1999. Uses Weber's notion of charisma to evaluate the development of the Pure Land Buddhist order Yugyo-ha, a "leading representative of *nembutsu* propagation," "not in a pattern of decline, but rather of adaptation and survival."

Tominaga, Nakamoto. *Emerging from Meditation.* Translated with an introduction by Michael Pye. Honolulu: University of Hawaii, 1990. A rare instance of a contemporary critique of Tokugawa Buddhism.

Tsukamoto, Zenryu. "Japanese and Chinese Buddhism." In *Religions and the Promise of the Twentieth Century.* Edited by Guy S. Metraux and Francois Crouzet. New York: New American Library, 1965, pp. 229–44. A Buddhist scholar's critical analysis of the stagnation of "formalized Buddhism" in Tokugawa times and the resulting dilemma for contemporary Buddhism.

Victoria, Brian (Daizen) A. *Zen at War.* New York: Weatherhill, 1997. A detailed description and critical analysis of the way Buddhist sects in general, and Zen sects in particular, supported colonialism and militarism in the Pacific War; surveys their postwar responses.

Watanabe, Shoko. *Japanese Buddhism: A Critical Appraisal.* Translated by Alfred Bloom. Tokyo: Kokusai Bunka Shinkokai, 1964. A frank analysis of "the strong and weak points of Japanese Buddhism" by a Buddhist priest.

Watson, Burton, trans. *The Lotus Sutra.* New York: Columbia University, 1993. A translation of one of the most important Buddhist texts in East Asia; it is central to some Japanese sects such as Tendai and Nichiren.

Watson, Burton, et al., trans. *Selected Writings of Nichiren.* Edited with an introduction by Philip B. Yampolsky. New York: Columbia University, 1990. "The purpose of the present work is to introduce to readers of English a sampling of the most important and influential of Nichiren's writings."

Yamasaki, Taiko. *Shingon: Japanese Esoteric Buddhism.* Translated by Richard and Cynthia Peterson. Boston: Shambhala, 1988. A general overview of Shingon, from its origins in India to its thought and practice in Japan.

Yampolsky, Philip B., trans. *The Zen Master Hakuin: Selected Writings.* New York: Columbia University, 1971. Translation of excerpts from works of an important Zen (Rinzai) master, preceded by a helpful introduction to Hakuin and Rinzai Zen.

CONFUCIANISM

For additional references, see "Special Bibliographies on Japanese History and Religion."

Bito, Masahide. "Ogyu Sorai and the Distinguishing Features of Japanese Confucianism." In *Japanese Thought in the Tokugawa Period, 1600–1868: Methods and Metaphors.* Edited by Tetsuo Najita and Irwin Scheiner. Chicago: University of Chicago, 1978, pp. 153–60. A brief but technical article concluding that this particular Japanese thinker (Ogyu Sorai) did not simply ape Chinese Confucian thought but "reflects Japanese consciousness."

de Bary, Wm. Theodore. *The Trouble with Confucianism.* Cambridge: Harvard University, 1991. A brief and provocative work that takes up the question "What significance has Confucianism for the world today?"

Hall, John Whitney. "The Confucian Teacher in Tokugawa Japan." In *Confucianism in Action.* Edited by David S. Nivison and Arthur F. Wright. Stanford: Stanford University, 1959, pp. 268–301. Describes the Confucian contribution to Tokugawa Japan and its relationship to Shinto and Buddhism.

Ishida, Ichiro. "Tokugawa Feudal Society and Neo-Confucian Thought." In *Philosophical Studies of Japan,* vol. 5. Edited by Japanese National Commission for UNESCO. Tokyo, 1964, pp. 1–37. A technical article analyzing Neo-Confucian thought and its significance in terms of a "secularized religion."

Jensen, Lionel M. *Manufacturing Confucianism: Chinese Traditions & Universal Culture.* Durham, NC: Duke University, 1997. A critical treatment of the way Westerners have perceived Confucius and interpreted Confucianism.

McMullen, I. J. "The Worship of Confucius in Ancient Japan." In *Religion in Japan: Arrows to Heaven and Earth.* Edited by P. F. Kornicki and I. J. McMullen. Cambridge: Cambridge University, 1996, pp. 39–77. Surveys the development of "state Confucianism" and the state rites for Confucius in China, and the adoption and the adaptation of these rites in early Japan.

Shively, Donald H. "Motoda Eifu: Confucian Lecturer to the Meiji Emperor." In *Confucianism in Action.* Edited by David S. Nivison and Arthur F. Wright. Stanford: Stanford University, 1959, pp. 302–33. An interpretation of the life and thought of Motoda Eifu (1818–91), who after the Meiji Restoration was "the man who more than any other was responsible for this resurgence of Confucianism."

Smethurst, Mae J. *Dramatic Representations of Filial Piety: Five Noh in Translation.* Ithaca, NY: Cornell University, 1998. Translations of and commentaries on five noh plays, whose plots depict "people bound up with each other in a close relationship of loyalty, or fraternal, conjugal, or filial piety."

Smith, Warren W., Jr. *Confucianism in Modern Japan: A Study of Conservatism in Japanese Intellectual History.* 2d ed. Tokyo: Hokuseido, 1973. A treatment of Confucianism's (Neo-Confucianism's) cultural impact in Japan from 1600 through postwar times.

Taylor, Rodney. *The Religious Dimensions of Confucianism.* Albany: State University of New York, 1990. A general treatment of Confucianism as a religious tradition.

Tomikura, Mitsuo. "Confucianism." In *Japanese Religion*. Edited by Ichiro Hori. Translated by Yoshiya Abe and David Reid. Tokyo: Kodansha, 1972, pp. 105–22. A concise overview of the role of Confucianism in Japanese thought and society.

Tucker, Mary Evelyn. *Moral and Spiritual Cultivation in Japanese Self-Cultivation: The Life and Thought of Kaibara Ekken, 1630–1740 [1714]*. Albany, NY: State University of New York, 1989. A study of the Neo-Confucian writer Kaibara Ekken, with treatment of the significance of Neo-Confucianism as a way of life.

Waley, Arthur, trans. *The Analects of Confucius*. London: Allen & Unwin, 1938. Reprint ed., New York: Random House, 1966. A standard translation of the collected teachings of Confucius.

TAOISM

For additional references, see "Special Bibliographies on Japanese History and Religion."

Bock, Felicia G., translator and annotator. *Classical Learning and Taoist Practices in Early Japan: With a Translation of Books XVI and XX of the Engi-Shiki*. Tucson: Center for Asian Studies, Arizona State, 1985. Occasional Paper no. 17, pp. 49–76. A treatment of Taoism in early Japan based on ancient writings.

Bokenkamp, Stephen R. *Early Daoist Scriptures*. Berkeley: University of California, 1997. Provides a general introduction to Taoism (Daoism, including "The Worldview of the Daoist Religion"), and translations of six major texts.

Clarke, John James. *The Tao of the West: Western Transformations of Taoist Thought*. London: Routledge, 2000. An overview of the Western acceptance and adaptation of Taoism.

Frank, Bernard. "Kata-imi et Kata-tagae: Etude sur les Interdits de direction a l'epoque Heian." *Bulletin de la Maison Franco-Japonaise*, Nouvelle Serie, tome 5, no. 2–4 (1958), pp. 1–246. The only lengthy treatment of the problem, but concerned mainly with the influence of religious Taoism upon medieval literature.

Kirkland, Russell. "Person and Culture in the Taoist Tradition." *Journal of Chinese Religion*, no. 20 (Fall 1992), pp. 77–90. A reevaluation of Taoism as philosophy and as religion.

Kohn, Livia. "Taoism in Japan: Positions and Evaluations." *Cahiers d'Extreme-Asie*, vol. 8 (1995), pp. 389–412. The most comprehensive treatment of Taoism in Japan.

Kubo, Noritada. "Introduction of Taoism to Japan." In *Religious Studies in Japan*. Tokyo: Maruzen, 1959, pp. 457–65. A summary of an important Taoistic cult.

Miller, Alan L. "Ritsuryo Japan: The State as Liturgical Community." *History of Religions*, vol. 11, no. 1 (Aug. 1971), pp. 98–124. Includes descriptions of the bureau of *yin* and *yang* (Onmyoryo) in early Japan.

Saunders, E. Dale. "Koshin: An Example of Taoist Ideas in Japan." In *Proceedings of the IXth International Congress for the History of Religions*. Tokyo: Maruzen, 1960, pp. 423–32. Analyzes the history of Koshin and its dynamics as a Taoist cult.

Seidel, Anna K. "Chronicle of Taoist Studies in the West 1950–1990." *Cahiers d'Extreme-Asie*, vol. 5 (1989–90), pp. 223–47. A critical and comprehensive treatment of Taoist studies, useful as a bibliographical tool and for a conceptual approach to Taoism.

Seidel, Anna K. "Taoism." In *Encyclopaedia Britannica*, 15th ed., vol. 17. Chicago: Encyclopaedia Britannica, 1978, pp. 1034–44. A succinct summary and interpretation of the various aspects of Taoism and its interaction with Confucianism.

Sivin, Nathan. "On the Word 'Taoist' as a Source of Perplexity: With Special Reference to the Relations of Science and Religion in Traditional China." *History of Religions*, vol. 17 (1978), pp. 303–31. A reconsideration of terms such as "Taoist" and "Confucian."

Waley, Arthur, trans. *The Way and Its Power: A Study of the Tao Te Ching and Its Place in Chinese Thought*. London: Allen & Unwin, 1934. Reprint ed., New York: Grove, 1958. A standard translation and helpful interpretation of a basic philosophical text of Taoism.

Waterhouse, David. "Notes on the *Kuji*." In *Religion in Japan: Arrows to Heaven and Earth.* Edited by P. F. Kornicki and I. J. McMullen. Cambridge: Cambridge University, 1996, pp. 1–35. Discusses *kuji* as an example of Taoist beliefs and practices in Japan.

FOLK RELIGION

For additional references, see "Special Bibliographies on Japanese History and Religion."

Blacker, Carmen. *The Catalpa Bow: A Study of Shamanistic Practices in Japan.* London: Allen & Unwin, 1975. The first comprehensive interpretation of shamanistic practices in Japan; includes accounts of shamanism and observations of contemporary "shamans."

Bownas, Geoffrey. *Japanese Rainmaking and Other Folk Practices.* London: Allen & Unwin, 1963. Popular descriptions of folk religion and customs.

Casal, U. A. *The Five Sacred Festivals of Ancient Japan: Their Symbolism & Historical Development.* Tokyo and Rutland, VT: Sophia University and Charles E. Tuttle, 1967. A description of the major annual Japanese festivals showing the interpenetration of Buddhism and Shinto in folk religion.

Czaja, Michael. *Gods of Myth and Stone; Phallicism in Japanese Folk Religion.* New York: Weatherhill, 1974. A popular treatment, valuable especially for the hundred plates of the traditional stone statues of Dosojin.

Dorson, Richard M. *Folk Legends of Japan.* Rutland, VT: Charles E. Tuttle, 1962. A topical collection with brief introductions for each tale.

Dorson, Richard M., ed. *Studies in Japanese Folklore.* Chief translator, Yasuyo Ishiwara. Bloomington, IN: Indiana University, 1963. Translated articles by leading Japanese folklorists, with a helpful introductory chapter on Japanese folklore by the editor.

Earhart, H. Byron. "Four Ritual Periods of Haguro Shugendo in Northeastern Japan." *History of Religions,* vol. 5, no. 1 (Summer 1965), pp. 93–113. Description of the ritual year in an eclectic religious movement.

Embree, John F. *Suye Mura.* Chicago: University of Chicago, 1939. Reprinted, with a new introduction by Richard Beardsley, 1964. Reprinted, Michigan Classics in Japanese Studies, 1995. The pioneer Western "village study" in Japan; Chapter 7, "Religions," demonstrates the interrelationships among the several religious traditions.

Harootunian, H. D. "Disciplinizing Native Knowledge and Producing Place: Yanagita Kunio, Origuchi Shinobu, Takata Yasuma." In *Culture and Identity: Japanese Intellectuals During the Interwar Years.* Edited by J. Thomas Rimer. Princeton: Princeton University, 1990, pp. 99–127. A critique of folklorists such as Yanagita for using folk materials to construct or invent a unified or "unique" Japanese identity.

Holtom, Daniel C. "Some Notes on Japanese Tree Worship." *Transactions of the Asiatic Society of Japan,* Second Series, vol. 8 (Dec. 1931), pp. 1–19. An article on traditional folk (and Shinto) beliefs and practices associated with trees.

Hori, Ichiro. *Folk Religion in Japan: Continuity and Change.* Edited by Joseph M. Kitagawa and Alan L. Miller. Chicago: University of Chicago, 1968. Essays showing the complex makeup of folk religion and its importance for understanding Japanese religion.

Ikeda, Hiroko. *A Type and Motif Index of Japanese Folk-Literature.* FF Communications, no. 209. Helsinki: Soumalainen Tiedeakatemia, Academia Scientarum Fennica, 1971. The most complete index of Japanese folk tales, with brief summaries of tales; sources and distribution of the tales are given, with cross-references to standard Western and other Japanese motif-indexes.

Jeremy, Michael and Robinson, M. E. *Ceremony and Symbolism in the Japanese Home.* Manchester: Manchester University, 1989. A detailed account of "traditional" religious practices in family and village based on lengthy field work; includes many photos.

Koschmann, J. Victor, et al., eds. *International Perspectives on Yanagita Kunio and Japanese Folklore Studies*. Ithaca, NY: China-Japan Program, 1985. Essays providing a variety of viewpoints on Yanagita and the use of the category "folk."

Miyake, Hitoshi. "Folk Religion." In *Japanese Religion*. Edited by Ichiro Hori. Translated by Yoshiya Abe and David Reid. Tokyo: Kodansha International, 1972, pp. 121–43. A brief analysis of folk religion, describing its annual festivals, rites of passage, and social organization.

Miyake, Hitoshi. *Shugendo: Essays on the Structure of Japanese Folk Religion*. Edited by H. Byron Earhart. Ann Arbor: University of Michigan, 2001. Treatments of the history and practices of Shugendo, descriptions of folk religious practices, and theoretical approaches to the study of folk religion.

Ouwehand, C. *Hateruma: Socio-religious Aspects of a South-Ryukyuan Island Culture*. Leiden: E. J. Brill, 1985. Detailed results from extensive field work in a Ryukyu (Okinawan) island.

Ouwehand, C. *Namazu-e and Their Themes: An Interpretative Approach to Some Aspects of Japanese Folk Religion*. Leiden: E. J. Brill, 1964. The most thorough and systematic treatment of Japanese folk religion in English, important for its holistic interpretation.

Seki, Keigo, ed. *Folktales of Japan*. Translated by Robert J. Adams. Chicago: University of Chicago, 1963. A representative collection, featuring a scholarly foreword and comparative remarks on each tale.

Smith, Robert J. *Ancestor Worship in Contemporary Japan*. Stanford: Stanford University, 1974. The only full-length study of Japanese ancestor worship in English; it provides historical background and extensive reporting of actual practices and attitudes toward ancestor worship.

Yamamoto, Yoshiko. *The Namahage: A Festival in the Northeast of Japan*. Foreword by Robert J. Smith. Philadelphia: Institute for the Study of Human Issues, 1978. A field study of a New Year's festival of "masked visitors," with a survey of Japanese theories interpreting the religious significance of the festival.

CHRISTIANITY

For additional references, see "Special Bibliographies on Japanese History and Religion."

Boxer, C. R. *The Christian Century in Japan, 1549–1650*. Rev. ed. Berkeley: University of California, 1967. A detailed survey of early Roman Catholicism in Japan, with translations of English documents.

Caldarola, Carlo. *Christianity: The Japanese Way*. Leiden: E. J. Brill, 1979. An interpretation of Mukyokai (the non-church movement) and an offshoot Makuya as examples of an indigeneous Japanese Christianity.

Cary, Otis. *A History of Christianity in Japan*. 2 vols. New York: Fleming H. Revell, 1909. Republished, St. Clair Shores, MI: Scholarly, 1970. Valuable especially for the detailed treatment of Protestantism up to 1909 in Volume 2.

Drummond, Richard H. *A History of Christianity in Japan*. Grand Rapids, MI: William B. Eerdmans, 1971. A convenient, one-volume history covering the entire span of Catholic, Protestant, and Orthodox developments.

Durfee, Richard E., Jr. "Portrait of an Unknowingly Ordinary Man: Endo Shusaku, Christianity, and Japanese Historical Consciousness." *Japanese Journal of Religious Studies*, vol. 16, no. 1 (Mar. 1989), pp. 41–62. An evaluation of the life and writing of Endo, and "the conflicts implicit in being both Japanese and Christian."

Elison, George. *Deus Destroyed: The Image of Christianity in Early Modern Japan*. Cambridge: Harvard University, 1973. A detailed analysis of the "acceptance" and "rejection" of Christianity during the Christian century, with extensive translations of anti-Christian documents from this period.

Endo, Shusaku. *The Samurai: A Novel*. Translated by Van C. Gessel. New York: Harper & Row, 1982. A historical novel by a contemporary Japanese Roman Catholic chronicling both the spiritual journey, and actual journey, of sixteenth-century Japanese Christians across the Pacific Ocean to Mexico, and by land across Mexico to continue their sea voyage to Europe and on to Rome—and back to Japan.

Endo, Shusaku. *Silence*. Translated by William Johnston Tokyo: Sophia University, 1969. A historical novel by a contemporary Japanese Roman Catholic about the trials of faith for both Japanese converts and European missionaries during the persecution of Christianity in the 1600s.

Furuya, Yasuo, ed. and trans. *A History of Japanese Theology*. Grand Rapids, MI: Eerdmans, 1997. Traces the development of Christian theology in Japan, especially as a distinctively "Japanese theology."

Germany, Charles H. *Protestant Theologies in Modern Japan*. Tokyo: HSR Press, 1965. A survey of the broad range of Protestant theology among Japanese theologians.

Higashibaba, Ikuo. *Christianity in Early Modern Japan: Kirishitan Belief and Practice*. Leiden: E. J. Brill, 2001. "This study examines [the] various aspects of Kirishitan faith and practice by following their historical development," especially the interaction between "the syncretic religious world of Japan" and sixteenth-century Catholicism.

Iglehart, Charles W. *A Century of Protestant Christianity in Japan*. Rutland, VT: Charles E. Tuttle, 1959. A historical treatment of Protestantism in Japan.

Jennes, Joseph. *A History of the Catholic Church in Japan from Its Beginnings to the Early Meiji Era (1549–1873)*. Rev., enlarged ed. Tokyo: Oriens Institute for Religious Research, 1973. Intended as a handbook for missionaries, it surveys the Catholic mission to Japan and its interaction with political and cultural forces.

Kagawa, Toyohiko. *Christ and Japan*. Translated by William Axling. New York: Friendship, 1934. A famous Japanese (Protestant) Christian's praise and criticism of Japan, as viewed through his Christian faith.

Kitamori, Kazoh. *Theology of the Pain of God*. Richmond, VA: John Knox, 1965. Kitamori, hailed as the first original theological writer in Japan, has here attempted a genuinely Japanese theology.

Laures, Johannes. *The Catholic Church in Japan: A Short History*. Rutland, VT: Charles E. Tuttle, 1954; Notre Dame, IN: University of Notre Dame, 1962. A popular work by a church historian.

Mullins, Mark. *Christianity Made in Japan: A Study of Indigenous Movements*. Honolulu: University of Hawai'i, 1998. Treats some Christian groups in Japan as indigenous movements or as new religious movements, or as forms of a Japanese Christianity.

Notehelfer, F. G. *American Samurai: Captain L. L. Janes and Japan*. Princeton: Princeton University, 1985. Traces the life and career of Janes, an American teacher who was a pioneer of Protestant Christianity in early Meiji Japan.

Ohata, Kiyoshi and Ikado, Fujio. "Christianity." In *Japanese Religion in the Meiji Era*. Edited by Hideo Kishimoto. Translated by John F. Howes. Tokyo: Obunsha, 1956, pp. 171–309. A historical treatment by two Japanese Christians, emphasizing the ideals of Christianity and the social realities of Japan.

Phillips, James M. *From the Rising of the Sun: Christians and Society in Contemporary Japan*. Mary Knoll, NY: Orbis Books, 1981. A detailed treatment of Christianity in Japan since 1945, covering its relation to social, political, and educational issues as well as biblical and theological studies.

Plath, David W. "The Japanese Popular Christmas: Coping with Modernity." *Journal of American Folklore*, vol. 76 (1963), pp. 309–17. A description of the widespread celebration of Christmas in Japan.

Reid, David. *New Wine: The Cultural Shaping of Japanese Christianity*. Berkeley: Asian Humanities, 1991. Emphasizes the interaction between Christianity and Japanese culture and religion.

Scheiner, Irwin. *Christian Converts and Social Protest in Meiji Japan*. Berkeley, CA: University of California, 1970. Examines the relationship between *samurai* ideals and Christian ethics in the lives of *samurai* converts to Christianity.

Suzuki, Norihisa. "Christianity." In *Japanese Religion*. Edited by Ichiro Hori. Translated by Yoshiya Abe and David Reid. Tokyo: Kodansha International, 1972, pp. 71–87. An overview of the "foreignness" of Christianity in Japan and its major developments.

Takeda, Kiyoko. "Japanese Christianity: Between Orthodoxy and Heterodoxy." In *Authority and the Individual in Japan: Citizen Protest in Historical Perspective*. Edited by J. Victor Koschmann. Tokyo: University of Tokyo, 1978, pp. 82–107. A critical interpretation of the role of Christianity in modern Japan.

Thelle, Notto R. *Buddhism and Christianity in Japan: From Conflict to Dialogue, 1854–1899*. Honolulu: University of Hawaii, 1987. Thesis is that in "Buddhist-Christian relations in Japan . . . the radical transformation—from conflict to dialogue—took place primarily in the 1890s"; places this dialogue in social and historical perspective.

Turnbull, Stephen R. *The Kakure Kirishitan of Japan: A Study of Their Development, Beliefs, and Rituals to the Present Day*. Richmond, Surrey: Japan Library, 1998. A study of Kakure Kirishitan as "the modern, separated communities . . . and not their secret Christian predecessors," aiming to "identify the influences which have led to the creation, preservation, development and expression of the Kakure Kirishitan faith."

Uchimura, Kanzo. *How I Became a Christian: Out of My Diary*. Tokyo: Keiseisha, 1895. An account of the spiritual biography of a first-generation Japanese Christian, including his tribulations as a Christian in a "heathen" land as well as his disappointments while in "Christian" America.

Whelan, Christal, trans. *The Beginning of Heaven and Earth: The Sacred Book of Japan's Hidden Christians*. Honolulu: University of Hawai'i, 1996. A translation of "the only text the Kakure Kirishitan [Hidden Christians] produced"; it is preceded by a convenient introduction to the subject.

Yamaji, Aizan. *Essays on the Modern Japanese Church*. "Translated by Graham Squires, with Introductory Essays by Graham Squires and A. Hamish Ion." Ann Arbor: Center for Japanese Studies, University of Michigan, 1999. Translated essays from "the first Japanese-language history of Christianity in Meiji Japan," tracing the reintroduction of Christianity into Japan.

NEW RELIGIONS

For additional references, see "Special Bibliographies on Japanese History and Religion."

Arai, Ken. "New Religious Movements." In *Japanese Religion*. Edited by Ichiro Hori. Translated by Yoshiya Abe and David Reid. Tokyo: Kodansha International, 1972, pp. 89–104. An overview of the definition and major features of the New Religions.

Caldarola, Carlo. "The Makuya Movement in Japan." *Japanese Religions*, vol. 7, no. 4 (Dec. 1972), pp. 18–34. (Also included in Caldarola, *Christianity: The Japanese Way*, listed in the "Christianity" section.) Originally derived from the Japanese Christian movement known as Mukyokai ("Non-Church" movement), Makuya or Genshi Fukuin Undo is perhaps the most successful Christian movement among the lower classes and has incorporated so many Japanese features that it may be considered a Japanese New Religion.

Clarke, Peter B., ed. *Japanese New Religions in Global Perspective*. Surrey: Curzon, 2000. Ten articles on the activities of Japanese new religions outside Japan.

Clarke, Peter B. and Somers, Jeffrey, eds. *Japanese New Religions in the West*. Sandgate: Japan Library, 1994. Includes eleven articles on Japanese new and "new, new" religions in Japan and outside Japan.

Davis, Winston Bradley. *Dojo: Exorcism and Miracles in Modern Japan*. Stanford: Stanford University, 1980. A detailed sociological analysis of the beliefs and practices of members of the New Religion Sukyo Mahikari.

Earhart, H. Byron. *Gedatsu-kai and Religion in Contemporary Japan: Returning to the Center.* Bloomington, IN: Indiana University, 1989. Study of a new religion based on life histories of members and a nationwide survey.

Fujiwara, Hirotatsu. *I Denounce Soka Gakkai.* Translated by Worth C. Grant. Tokyo: Nishin Hodo, 1970. A polemical work; alleged suppression of the Japanese edition of this book was the cause of a public scandal investigated by the National Diet.

Guthrie, Stewart Elliott. *A Japanese "New Religion": Rissho Kosei-kai in a Mountain Hamlet.* Ann Arbor: Center for Japanese Studies, University of Michigan, 1988. An anthropological study of a new religion featuring extensive use of life histories of members.

Hardacre, Helen. *Aum Shinrikyo and the Japanese Media: The Pied Piper Meets the Lamb of God.* New York: East Asian Institute, Columbia University, 1995. "New issues for scholars of religion highlighted by this incident are largely summed up in the necessity to become as fully informed as possible about the media on whom we inevitably depend."

Hardacre, Helen. *Kurozumikyo and the New Religions of Japan.* Princeton: Princeton University, 1986. Based on field work and life histories, this study shows that counseling in this new religion is not a quick-fix such as provided by occultists, but actually helps members "restructure their way of life."

Hardacre, Helen. *Lay Buddhism in Contemporary Japan: Reiyukai Kyodan.* Princeton: Princeton University, 1984. Rejecting earlier notions of new religions as reactions to social crisis, develops the argument that Reiyukai (and by extension other movements) has a coherent set of beliefs and practices.

Ikado, Fujio. "Trend and Problems of New Religions: Religion in Urban Society." In *The Sociology of Japanese Religion.* Edited by Kiyomi Morioka and William H. Newell. Leiden: E. J. Brill, 1968, pp. 101–17. Analysis of statistical and sociological information about the membership of the New Religions in the postwar urban setting.

Inoue, Nobutaka, ed. *New Religions.* Translated by Norman Havens. Tokyo: Institute for Japanese Culture and Classics, Kokugakuin University, 1991. Includes a number of articles on new religions, including the editor's "Recent Trends in the Study of Japanese New Religions."

Kisala, Robert J. and Mullins, Mark R., eds. *Religion and Social Crisis in Japan: Understanding Japanese Society through the Aum Affair.* Houndmills: Palgrave, 2001. Essays focusing on the development of the New Religion Aum Shinrikyo, its responsibility for the use of poison gas, and the general response.

Kiyota, Minoru. *Gedatsu-kai: Its Theory and Practice. A Study of Shinto-Buddhist Syncretic School in Contemporary Japan.* Los Angeles: Buddhist Books International, 1982. A treatment of the teachings of Gedatsu-kai.

Machacek, David and Wilson, Bryan, eds. *Global Citizens: The Soka Gakkai Buddhist Movement in the World.* Oxford: Oxford University, 2000. Includes essays on the background and activities of Soka Gakkai in Japan, and on its "international appearances."

Metraux, Daniel A. "The Dispute between the Soka Gakkai and the Nichiren Shoshu Priesthood: A Lay Revolution against a Conservative Clergy." *Japanese Journal of Religious Studies,* vol. 19, no. 4 (Dec. 1992), pp. 325–36. Outlines the arguments on each side of the dispute between (and split of) Soka Gakkai and Nichiren Shoshu.

Murakami, Haruki. *Underground: The Tokyo Gas Attack and the Japanese Psyche.* Translated by Alfred Birnbaum and Phillip Gabriel. London: The Harvill Press, 2000. A contemporary novelist's assessment of Aum and the gas attack through many personal interviews.

The Nichiren Shoshu Sokagakkai. Tokyo: Seikyo, 1966. An introduction to this New Religion by its staff, covering the history, doctrine, and distinctive features.

Niwano, Nikkyo. *Lifetime Beginner.* Translated by Richard L. Gage. Tokyo: Kosei, 1978. The autobiography of one of the co-founders of Rissho Kosei-kai.

Plath, David W. "The Fate of Utopia: Adaptive Tactics in Four Japanese Groups." *American Anthropologist,* vol. 68, no. 4 (Aug. 1966), pp. 1152–62. Analyzes the attempt of four communal groups to achieve utopian alternatives to the dilemmas of modernization.

Reader, Ian. *Religious Violence in Contemporary Japan: The Case of Aum Shinrikyo.* Honolulu: University of Hawai'i, 2000. Places this controversial movement within the context of contemporary Japanese religious patterns, examining the life of the founder and the character of its teachings that led it to violence.

Rissho Kosei-kai. Tokyo: Kosei, 1966. An introduction to this New Religion by its staff, covering such topics as the history, doctrine, and activities of the group.

Shimazono, Susumu. "In the Wake of Aum: The Formation and Transformation of a Universe of Belief." *Japanese Journal of Religious Studies,* vol. 22, no. 3–4 (Fall 1995), pp. 381–415. Reprinted as "The Evolution of Aum Shinrikyo as a Religious Movement" in *Religion and Social Crisis in Japan: Understanding Japanese Society Through the Aum Affair.* Edited by Robert J. Kisala and Mark R. Mullins. Houndmills: Palgrave, 2001, pp. 19–52. Treats the development of Aum and its activities as a religious movement.

Shimazono, Susumu. "The Living Kami Idea in the New Religions of Japan." *Japanese Journal of Religious Studies,* vol. 6, no. 3 (Sept. 1979), pp. 389–412. A synthetic interpretation of the nature of founders as living *kami* in the rise and institutionalization of New Religions.

A Short History of Tenrikyo. Tenri, Japan: Tenrikyo Kyokai Honbu, 1956. Published by Tenrikyo headquarters, it includes chapters on the life of the founder, the history of the movement, and its activities.

Sugihara, Yoshie and Plath, David W. *Sensei and His People: The Building of a Japanese Commune.* Berkeley: University of California, 1969. A firsthand account of the development of a communal group, partly an offshoot of Tenrikyo, by the second wife of the founder.

Tsushimsa, Michihito, et al. "The Vitalistic Conception of Salvation in Japanese New Religions: An Aspect of Modern Religious Consciousness." In *Proceedings of Tokyo Meeting of the International Conference on Sociology of Religion, 1978.* Reprinted in *Japanese Journal of Religious Studies,* vol. 6, no. 1–2 (Mar.–June 1979), pp. 139–61. A synthetic overview of "the common underlying structure to the teachings of the various New Religions."

White, James W. *The Sokagakkai and Mass Society.* Stanford: Stanford University, 1970. The first comprehensive study of a Japanese New Religion using the social sciences, evaluating it as a mass movement.

Index

To simplify use of the index, English equivalents are given for most Japanese and other foreign-language terms. Many religious terms have been grouped under the religion of which they are a part, such as Buddhism, Shinto, Confucianism, or Christianity. Dates or approximate century are provided for historical figures and historical periods. An entry illustrated in the text has "(illus.)" following the page number; terms found in a caption are identified by page number and "(caption)."